European Observatory on Health Systems and Policies Series

The European Observatory on Health Systems and Policies is an international project that builds on the commitment of all its partners to improving healthcare systems:

- World Health Organization Regional Office for Europe
- Government of Belgium
- Government of Finland
- Government of Greece
- Government of Norway
- Government of Spain
- Government of Sweden
- European Investment Bank
- Open Society Institute
- World Bank
- London School of Economics and Political Science
- London School of Hygiene & Tropical Medicine

Series Editors

Josep Figueras is Head of the Secretariat and Research Director of the European Observatory on Health Systems and Policies and Head of the European Centre for Health Policy, World Health Organization Regional Office for Europe.

Martin McKee is Research Director of the European Observatory on Health Systems and Policies and Professor of European Public Health at the London School of Hygiene & Tropical Medicine as well as a co-director of the School's European Centre on Health of Societies in Transition.

Elias Mossialos is Research Director of the European Observatory on Health Systems and Policies, Brian Abel-Smith Professor of Health Policy, Department of Social Policy, London School of Economics and Political Science and Co-Director of LSE Health and Social Care.

Richard B. Saltman is Research Director of the European Observatory on Health Systems and Policies and Professor of Health Policy and Management at the Rollins School of Public Health, Emory University in Atlanta, Georgia.

The series

The volumes in this series focus on key issues for health policy-making in Europe. Each study explores the conceptual background, outcomes and lessons learned about the development of more equitable, more efficient and more effective health systems in Europe. With this focus, the series seeks to contribute to the evolution of a more evidence-based approach to policy formulation in the health sector.

These studies will be important to all those involved in formulating or evaluating national healthcare policies and, in particular, will be of use to health policy-makers and advisers, who are under increasing pressure to rationalize the structure and funding of their health systems. Academics and students in the field of health policy will also find this series valuable in seeking to understand better the complex choices that confront the health systems of Europe.

The Observatory supports and promotes evidence-based health policy-making through comprehensive and rigorous analysis of the dynamics of healthcare systems in Europe.

European Observatory on Health Systems and Policies Series

Series Editors: Josep Figueras, Martin McKee, Elias Mossialos and Richard B. Saltman

Published titles

Funding health care: options for Europe
Elias Mossialos, Anna Dixon, Joseph Figueras, Joe Kutzin (eds)

Health care in central Asia
Martin McKee, Judith Healy and Jane Falkingham (eds)

Health policy and European Union enlargement
Martin McKee, Laura MacLehose and Ellen Nolte (eds)

Hospitals in a changing Europe
Martin McKee and Judith Healy (eds)

Regulating entrepreneurial behaviour in European health care systems
Richard B. Saltman, Reinhard Busse and Elias Mossialos (eds)

Regulating pharmaceuticals in Europe: striving for efficiency, equity and quality
Elias Mossialos, Monique Mrazek and Tom Walley (eds)

Social health insurance systems in western Europe
Richard B. Saltman, Reinhard Busse and Josep Figueras

Forthcoming titles

Effective purchasing for health gain
Josep Figueras, Ray Robinson and Elke Jakubowski (eds)

Mental Health Policy and Practice across Europe
Martin Knapp, David McDaid, Elias Mossialos and Graham Thornicroft (eds)

European Observatory on Health Systems and Policies Series

Edited by Josep Figueras, Martin McKee, Elias Mossialos and Richard B. Saltman

Social health insurance systems in western Europe

Edited by
**Richard B. Saltman,
Reinhard Busse and
Josep Figueras**

Open University Press

Open University Press
McGraw-Hill Education
McGraw-Hill House
Shoppenhangers Road
Maidenhead
Berkshire
England
SL6 2QL

email: enquiries@openup.co.uk
world wide web: www.openup.co.uk

and Two Penn Plaza, New York, NY 10121-2289, USA

First published 2004

A catalogue record of this book is available from the British Library

ISBN 0 335 21363 4 (pb)   0 335 21364 2 (hb)

Library of Congress Cataloging-in-Publication Data
CIP data applied for

Typeset by RefineCatch Limited, Bungay, Suffolk
Printed in Great Britain by Bell and Bain Ltd, Glasgow

Contents

List of contributors

Helmut Brand is Director of the Institute of Public Health NRW in Bielefeld, Germany.

Jan Bultman is Lead Health Specialist at the World Bank in Washington DC, USA.

Reinhard Busse is Professor and Department Head of Health Care Management at the Technical University in Berlin, Germany, and Associate Research Director of the European Observatory on Health Systems and Policies.

Laurent Chambaud is President of the French Society of Public Health and Director of the Regional Department of Health and Social Affairs (DRASS) of Franche-Comté in Besançon, France.

David Chinitz is Senior Lecturer at the Hebrew University-Hadassah School of Public Health in Jerusalem, Israel.

Diana M.J. Delnoij is Senior Research Coordinator at the Netherlands Institute of Health Services Research (NIVEL) in Utrecht, the Netherlands.

Aad A. de Roo is Professor of Strategic Health Care Management at the Faculty of Social and Behavioural Sciences, Tilburg University, the Netherlands.

André P. den Exter is Assistant Professor of Health Law at the Department of Health Policy and Management, Erasmus University in Rotterdam, the Netherlands.

Anna Dixon is Lecturer in European Health Policy at the Department of Social Policy, London School of Economics and Political Science in London, UK.

Hans F.W. Dubois is Research Officer of the European Observatory on Health Systems and Policies in Madrid, Spain.

Isabelle Durand-Zaleski is Assistant Professor at the Department of Public Health of the Henri Mondor Hospital in Paris, France.

Josep Figueras is Head of the Secretariat and Research Director of the European Observatory on Health Systems and Policies and Head of the European Centre for Health Policy, Brussels, WHO Regional Office for Europe.

Bernhard Gibis is Director of the Department of Quality Assurance at the National Association of Statutory Health Insurance Physicians (KBV) in Berlin, Germany.

Stefan Greß is Assistant Professor at the Institute of Health Care Management, University of Duisburg-Essen in Essen, Germany.

Bernhard J. Güntert is Professor for Management of Health Services and Health Economics at the University for Health Information and Technology Tyrol in Innsbruck, Austria.

Jean Hermesse is National Secretary at the National Federation of the Christian Sickness Funds in Brussels, Belgium.

Maria M. Hofmarcher is Senior Researcher at the Institute for Advanced Studies (IHS) in Vienna, Austria.

Pedro W. Koch-Wulkan is Head of the Medical Technology Unit at the Swiss Federal Office of Health in Bern, Switzerland.

Claude Le Pen is Professor of Economic Sciences at the Paris-Dauphine University in Paris, France.

Martin McKee is Professor of European Public Health at the London School of Hygiene and Tropical Medicine in London, UK, and Research Director of the European Observatory on Health Systems and Policies.

Kieke G.H. Okma is Senior Adviser with the Ministry of Health, Welfare and Sport in The Hague, the Netherlands.

Martin Pfaff is Professor of Economics at the University of Augsburg and Director of the International Institute for Empirical Social Economics (INIFES) in Stadtbergen, Germany.

Richard B. Saltman is Professor of Health Policy and Management at the Rollins School of Public Health, Emory University in Atlanta, USA and Research Director of the European Observatory on Health Systems and Policies.

Wendy G.M. van der Kraan is a doctoral student at the Institute of Health Management and Policy at the Erasmus University in Rotterdam, the Netherlands.

Jürgen Wasem is Professor and Director of the Institute of Health Care Management, University of Duisburg-Essen in Essen, Germany.

Manfred Wildner is Unit Head GE 4 (Health Reporting, Health Promotion, Disease Prevention, Social Medicine) at the Bavarian Health and Food Safety

Authority and Lecturer at the Ludwig-Maximilians-University in Munich, Germany.

Matthias Wismar is Health Policy Analyst at the European Centre for Health Policy in Brussels, WHO Regional Office for Europe.

Series editors' introduction

European national policy makers broadly agree on the core objectives that their health care systems should pursue. The list is strikingly straightforward: universal access for all citizens, effective care for better health outcomes, efficient use of resources, high-quality services and responsiveness to patient concerns. It is a formula that resonates across the political spectrum and which, in various, sometimes inventive configurations, has played a role in most recent European national election campaigns.

Yet this clear consensus can only be observed at the abstract policy level. Once decision makers seek to translate their objectives into the nuts and bolts of health system organization, common principles rapidly devolve into divergent, occasionally contradictory, approaches. This is, of course, not a new phenomenon in the health sector. Different nations, with different histories, cultures and political experiences, have long since constructed quite different institutional arrangements for funding and delivering health care services.

The diversity of health system configurations that has developed in response to broadly common objectives leads quite naturally to questions about the advantages and disadvantages inherent in different arrangements, and which approach is 'better' or even 'best' given a particular context and set of policy priorities.

These concerns have intensified over the last decade as policy makers have sought to improve health system performance through what has become a European- wide wave of health system reforms. The search for comparative advantage has triggered – in health policy as in clinical medicine – increased attention to its knowledge base, and to the possibility of overcoming at least part of existing institutional divergence through more evidence- based health policy making.

The volumes published in the European Observatory series are intended to provide precisely this kind of cross- national health policy analysis. Drawing on an extensive network of experts and policy makers working in a variety of academic and administrative capacities, these studies seek to synthesize the available evidence on key health sector topics using a systematic methodology. Each volume explores the conceptual background, outcomes and lessons learned about the development of more equitable, more efficient and more effective health care systems in Europe. With this focus, the series seeks to contribute to the evolution of a more evidence- based approach to policy formulation in the health sector. While remaining sensitive to cultural, social and normative differences among countries, the studies explore a range of policy alternatives available for future decision making. By examining closely both the advantages and disadvantages of different policy approaches, these volumes fulfil a central mandates of the Observatory: to serve as a bridge between pure academic research and the needs of policy makers, and to stimulate the development of strategic responses suited to the real political world in which health sector reform must be implemented.

The European Observatory on Health Systems and Policies is a partnership that brings together three international agencies, six national governments, two research institutions and an international non- governmental organization. The partners are as follows: the World Health Organization Regional Office for Europe, which provides the Observatory secretariat; the governments of Belgium, Finland, Greece, Norway, Spain and Sweden; the European Investment Bank; the Open Society Institute; the World Bank; the London School of Hygiene & Tropical Medicine and the London School of Economics and Political Science.

In addition to the analytical and cross- national comparative studies published in this Open University Press series, the Observatory produces Health Care Systems in Transition (HiTs) profiles for the countries of Europe, the journal *Eurohealth* and the newsletter *Euro Observer*. Further information about Observatory publications and activities can be found on its website *www.observatory.dk*.

Josep Figueras, Martin McKee, Elias Mossialos and Richard B. Saltman

Foreword

Countries that rely upon social health insurance (SHI) for the preponderant portion of their health system funding present many paradoxes. SHI systems are constructed upon privately owned and operated funding arrangements, yet these arrangements – and the bodies that administer them – are tightly confined by statutory requirements. They are based on institutions rooted in civil society, yet most important decisions are subject to review by the state. They call themselves SHI systems, yet some rely for up to 50 per cent of total funding upon public taxes and/or out-of-pocket payments. They announce the centrality of solidarity in their operation, yet not all citizens are covered by these SHI institutions. They are highly popular with their citizenry, yet they require higher funding levels and larger total payments than do their predominantly tax-funded counterparts.

A further paradox has been the long-term stability of SHI systems in countries that have undergone numerous changes of political regime. From their beginnings in the late medieval period, the sickness funds that form the core of SHI developed into mandatory statutory structures, starting with Bismarck's Germany in 1883. After World War II they were reconfigured to form a key component of the modern European welfare state. In the post-1989 transformation of central and eastern Europe (CEE), SHI has often been a preferred policy objective or, failing that, remains a desirable objective still to be pursued. Whether historically or in the present-day, whether in western or eastern Europe, SHI remains a core building block of what a large majority of citizens perceive to be the good society.

This volume seeks to unravel these and other paradoxes that sit at the heart of what proponents of the SHI model view as not just a healthcare system but rather 'a way of life'. Drawing on a wide variety of expert as well as statistical resources, the book systematically examines the logic, history, structure and performance of seven SHI systems in western Europe – Austria, Belgium, France, Germany, Luxembourg, the Netherlands and Switzerland – as well as the similarly configured SHI system in Israel. In doing so, it presents SHI systems in a new light, exploring commonalities and disparities between and among these systems. The book also probes a number of key policy issues that can be expected to influence decision-making in SHI countries over the next period of years. Its contribution will be gauged by the degree to which the policy debate about the future of SHI systems in Europe moves beyond individual country arrangements to focus on the long-term prospects for this model in Europe as a whole.

Marc Danzon
WHO Regional Director for Europe

Acknowledgements

The editors are indebted to numerous people who generously gave of their time and knowledge to this project. Major contributions were made by our chapter authors, in their own chapters and also with their comments and suggestions at the authors' workshop in Storkow, Germany on 6–7 October 2001. Additional policy experts at that workshop included Philip Berman, Geert Jan Hamilton, Michael Hübel, Manfred Huber, Nick Jennett, Ralf Kocher, Xenia Scheil-Adlung, Michel Yahiel and Herbert Zöllner. We especially thank the German Federation of Company-based Sickness Funds (BKK-Bundesverband) and the Federation of General Regional Sickness Funds (AOK-Bundesverband) for their generous support by funding the workshop.

We are indebted for generous assistance with data and fact-checking to a substantial number of staff in national ministries of health and in OECD and WHO. Special thanks are owed to: Valérie Meftah (French Social Security representative in Brussels), Carmel Shalev (Gertner Institute for Health Policy, Israel), Willy Storm-Gravesteyn, Lia Vermeulen, Saskia van Eck (Dutch Ministry of Public Health, Welfare and Sport), Gabriel Sottas (Swiss Federal Office of Social Insurance), Jean-Marie Feider, Jean-Marie Rossler (Union of Sickness Funds, Luxembourg), Manfred Pöltl (Austrian Federal Ministry of Social Security, Generations and Consumer protection), Louis Van Damme (National Institute for Sickness and Invalidity Insurance, Belgium) and Anne-Kathrin Haas (AOK-Bundesverband). We are also grateful to representatives of several associations, including Delice Gan (International Diabetes Federation). Valuable comments on an early draft of Part One were provided by five external reviewers: Gabi Ben Nun, Geert Jan Hamilton, Aad de Roo, Michel Yahiel and Herbert Zöllner. Project coordination was expertly provided by Wendy Wisbaum, and Charlotte Brandigi cheerfully transformed multiple drafts into final text. We would also like to thank Jeffrey V. Lazarus, who was responsible for the book's delivery process and production.

Richard B. Saltman, Reinhard Busse and Josep Figueras

part one

chapter one

Social health insurance in perspective: the challenge of sustaining stability

Richard B. Saltman

Introduction

The concept of social health insurance (SHI) is deeply ingrained in the fabric of health care systems in western Europe. It provides the organizing principle and a preponderance of the funding in seven countries – Austria, Belgium, France, Germany, Luxembourg, the Netherlands and Switzerland. Since 1995, it has also become the legal basis for organizing health services in Israel. Previously, SHI models played an important role in a number of other countries that subsequently changed to predominantly tax-funded arrangements in the second half of the twentieth century – Denmark (1973), Italy (1978), Portugal (1979), Greece (1983) and Spain (1986). Moreover, there are segments of SHI-based health care funding arrangements still operating in predominantly tax-funded countries like Finland, Sweden and the United Kingdom, as well as in Greece and Portugal. In addition, a substantial number of central and eastern European (CEE) countries have introduced adapted SHI models since they regained control over national policy-making – among them Hungary (1989), Lithuania (1991), Czech Republic (1992), Estonia (1992), Latvia (1994), Slovakia (1994) and Poland (1999).

Despite this pivotal role in European health care, the organization and operation of SHI systems has received notably less attention from academics and researchers than have tax-funded systems. Neither the core system characteristics that define the SHI model, nor the performance of various SHI models in comparison with that of various tax-funded systems, have received the type of systematic assessment they deserve. This is the case not only in the English language literature. Those comparative studies available in Dutch, French or

German language (the seven western European SHI countries) tend to be limited to neighbouring (border) countries, and often focus on narrow technical rather than broader conceptual issues. Wide structural and organizational differences between western European SHI countries (as well as with Israel) further complicate efforts to delineate common patterns and problems.

The availability of widely accessible, comparative knowledge about SHI systems could be helpful for health policy-making both outside and inside Western European SHI systems. Outside, policy-makers in central and eastern Europe (CEE), but also in other potentially interested areas such as south-east Asia, South America and the United States, would benefit from being able to obtain a clear picture of how western European SHI systems are organized and how well they perform. Among other advantages, this might reduce political tendencies within some former Soviet Bloc countries to focus on only the official form of SHI systems without considering the equally important societal characteristics necessary to make those systems work successfully. Inside SHI systems, a clearer comparative picture could assist policy-makers as they grapple with increasing challenges to the economic, political and social sustainability of the traditional SHI framework (see below).

One of the most striking observations about contemporary SHI systems is the contrast between this knowledge gap about what they are and how well they function, on the one hand, and the strength of the emotional attachment of the citizens within these countries to their particular SHI system, on the other hand. How can one account for such a powerful popular attachment to a health care arrangement that is so hard to describe and about the performance of which information is so limited? This observation suggests that, before detailing the dilemmas that contemporary SHI systems confront, it may be useful to consider how SHI systems look in the eyes of those who support them.

An insider's perspective

The attraction of the SHI approach for both citizens and policy-makers appears, on initial viewing, to be based on three structural characteristics. First, SHI systems are seemingly private in both the funding and delivery of health services.[1] Second, as seemingly private, SHI systems appear to be self-regulating, managed by the participants themselves (e.g. sickness funds, physicians and, to a lesser degree, patients). Third, as perhaps the most important consequence of being seemingly private and self-regulatory, SHI systems are perceived as stable in organizational and especially financial terms. This stability often appears to be the most highly prized of all the outcomes associated with SHI systems. Indeed, when one considers the political turmoil that the twentieth century brought to western Europe, and the number of new governmental systems adopted or imposed on France (four), and Germany (three), as well as on Austria, Belgium, Luxembourg and the Netherlands, one cannot help but being impressed with the extraordinary stability and longevity of SHI within these countries.

Beyond these three perceived characteristics of private, self-regulating, and stable, however, lies a deeper, less discussed essence that is implicitly understood by both citizens and policy-makers alike as separating off SHI systems sharply from other arrangements for funding and providing health care services. This perspective can be summarized by the observation – made persistently by policy-makers from SHI countries – that SHI is not simply an insurance arrangement but rather a 'way of life'. In this view, SHI is a key part of a broader structure of social security and income support that sits at the heart of civil society. As such, SHI helps define how 'social order is established in society' (De Roo 2003). It is part of the 'fabric of society' (Zöllner 2001), supported by a 'social consensus' that is deeply rooted in the 'balance of society as a whole' (Le Pen 2001). A central (if not entirely correct) presumption is that both funders (sick funds) and providers (hospitals and physicians) are in the private sector. Thus, crucially, the state is not seen to be the owner of these social security structures, but rather their guardian and administrator – their steward (Saltman and Ferroussier-Davis 2000). In consequence, there is a firm belief that these health care systems are not artificial bureaucratic structures but rather 'living entities'. To operate successfully, they require major commitments of energy and time by many parties involved, often on a voluntary basis. They also require a high level of trust among many actors (see Chapter 6), leading to a conclusion that 'certain non-written rules are essential' (Pfaff 2001). In Germany, for example, 'traditions and unwritten rules' play a critical part in managing its SHI system (Normand and Busse 2002).

A central dimension of this deeper understanding of SHI systems is that, in structure, they are intentionally very different from standard commercial insurance. Instead, SHI systems are constructed first and foremost as part of a social incomes policy, to be redistributive in nature (Glaser 1991). They are thus consciously designed to achieve a series of societal objectives through a set of financial cross-subsidies – not just from healthy to ill but also from well-off to less well-off, from young to old and from individuals to families. It is this redistributive focus that distinguishes SHI from what is normally understood as 'insurance' – the latter being an actuarially precise device by which each individual seeks to protect his or her own interests (Glaser 1991; Stone 1993). Thus SHI is understood inside SHI countries as not being 'insurance' at all, but rather exactly the opposite. Instead of enabling each individual to focus on his or her own perceived personal interests, SHI requires individuals to contribute toward the best interest of the population generally through its structure of financial redistribution. It is this understanding of SHI that leads the citizenry in SHI countries to link it to the notion of solidarity (see Chapter 2).

The deeply-rooted popular view of SHI systems as a 'way of life', grounded in the core of civil society in an organic manner, and structured on solidarity rather than on actuarial principles, highlights an additional core characteristic of how these social health systems are viewed. It is that they are not, in the mind of either citizens or policy-makers, intended to be primarily *economic* arrangements. They are, rather, *sociological* and *psychological* structures, in which the economic dimension is distinctly secondary (De Roo 2003). Indeed, taking an exclusively economic and/or financial view of SHI systems is typically viewed by policy-makers in these countries to be inappropriately reductionist. In practice, one can readily see the imprint of SHI's sociological or civil society role in the pattern of health system reforms over the 1990s in SHI countries, as policy-makers sought to accommodate growing financial pressures while still maintaining the core social arrangements and purpose of the SHI project (see Chapter 3).

Looked at in this way, SHI systems can be understood as more than just a set of institutions, and the decisions made about the reform of those institutions to be based on considerably more than the currently pre-eminent political science notion of 'path dependency' (Wilsford 1994; Peters 1999; Saltman and Bergman 2004 forthcoming). These institutions themselves serve rather as intermediaries, as the administrative embodiment of a set of values deeply rooted in the society as a whole, which underscore and reinforce this particular set of institutional arrangements. In the case of western European countries with health systems based on social insurance, these values are tied to national culture and grounded in the historically generated principles of collective responsibility and social solidarity. As the literature on cultural anthropology suggests, if new institutions were to be introduced, the strength of this national culture and its associated social values is such that 'the persistent influence of a majority value system patiently smoothes the new institutions until their structure and functioning is again adapted to the societal norms' (Hofstede 1980: 26).

In short, the historical experience of SHI systems supports the thesis that it is the national culture and its associated social values that are broadly stable, and that the stability of particular SHI institutions is a consequence of that social continuity, rather than an independent event (Saltman and Bergman 2004 forthcoming).

From this cultural anthropological perspective, it is unsurprising that SHI institutions are perceived inside SHI countries as being as much sociological as economic in character (e.g. as a 'way of life'). Much like the broader configuration of social security arrangements within which SHI systems sit, SHI reflects core values that are 'socially embedded' in the very heart of how these societies understand themselves (Granovetter 1985; Saltman 1997). This organic view of SHI is an important part of the explanation for why policy-making in SHI systems appears to be cautious and incremental, why institutions – once established – are rarely uprooted, and, consequently, why the overall pattern in SHI systems continues to be one of stability and resilience.

A structural description

When one moves from this inside view to a more detached, outsider's perspective, SHI systems can be described in more structural terms. This structural understanding incorporates seven core components that exist across all eight studied countries, and that can be considered to comprise the organizational kernel of an SHI system.[2]

Risk-independent and transparent contributions

The raising of funds is tied to the income of members, typically in the form of a percentage of the member's wages (sometimes up to a designated ceiling). This has two equally important characteristics. First, contributions or premiums are not linked to the health status of the member. If a member has a spouse and/or children, they are automatically covered for the same income-related premium and under the same risk-independent conditions. Second, contributions or premiums are collected separately from state general revenues. Health sector funding is transparent and thus insulated from the political battles inherent in public budgeting.

Sickness funds as payers/purchasers

Premiums are either collected directly by sickness funds (Austria, France, Germany, Switzerland) or distributed from a central state-run fund (Israel, Luxembourg, the Netherlands) to a number of sickness funds (Belgium employs both methods). These funds are private not-for-profit organizations, steered by a board at least partly elected by the membership (except France and Switzerland), and usually with statutory recognition and responsibilities (Israel is an exception). The rules under which these sickness funds operate typically are either directly established by national legislation (Austria, France, Germany, Luxembourg, the Netherlands, Switzerland) and/or tightly controlled through a state regulatory process (Israel) (Belgium is an exception). The sickness funds use the revenues from members' premiums (health tax in Israel) to fund collective contracts with providers (private not-for-profit, private for-profit, and publicly operated) for health services to members.

Solidarity in population coverage, funding, and benefits package

Depending on the country, 63 per cent (the Netherlands) to 100 per cent (France, Israel, Switzerland) of the population are covered by the statutory sickness fund system. In countries with less than 100 per cent mandatory participation, typically it is the highest-income individuals who are allowed (Germany) or required (the Netherlands) to leave the statutory system to seek commercial health insurance on their own (small exceptions exist for illegal immigrants, for people with objections by principle and for civil servants). Funding for all members is equalized either within national state-run pools (Israel, the Netherlands); within regional government (Austria) or foundation-based (Switzerland) pools; through mandatory risk-adjustment mechanisms (Belgium, Germany, Israel, the Netherlands); or through state subsidies (Belgium, France). In all eight SHI systems, the state requires the same comprehensive benefits package for all subscribers.

Pluralism in actors/organizational structure

SHI systems incorporate a broad range of organizational structures. Both within as well as between SHI countries, the number and provenance of sickness funds may vary widely, based on professional, geographic, religious/political and/or non-partisan criteria. Nearly all hospitals, regardless of ownership, and nearly all physicians, regardless of how they are organized (solo practice, group practice etc.) have contracts with the sickness funds and are part of the SHI system. Professional medical associations, municipal, regional and national governments, and also suppliers such as pharmaceutical companies are all seen as part of the SHI system framework.

Corporatist model of negotiations

Negotiations typically occur at regional and/or national level among 'peak organizations' representing each health sub-sector involved. This corporatist framework enables the self-regulation and contract processes to proceed more smoothly, with substantially more uniformity of outcome and substantially lower transaction costs. A corporatist approach among a group of 'social partners' (sick funds, health professionals, provider groupings and supplier groupings) is also consistent with policy-making arrangements in other parts of the social sector in the seven studied European countries (less so in Israel).

Participation in shared governance arrangements

As befits the pluralist configuration described just above, SHI systems typically incorporate participation in governance decisions by a wide range of different actors. The most visible manifestation is the traditional process of self-regulation by which sickness funds and providers negotiate directly with each other over payment schedules, quality of care, patient volumes and other contract matters. Medical associations, hospital associations and other professional groups frequently have some decision-making responsibilities as well.

Individual choice of providers and (partly) sickness funds

Members of sickness funds can usually seek care from nearly all physicians and hospitals. In six of the eight studied systems, a referral to see a specialist is not required (Israel and the Netherlands are exceptions). Increasingly, members can also choose to change their sickness fund (Austria, France and Luxembourg are exceptions).

These seven characteristics – risk-independent contributions, sickness funds as payers, solidarity, pluralism, corporatism, participation and choice – comprise what is described in many writings about SHI systems as the 'core structural arrangements' (Glaser 1991; Hoffmeyer and McCarthy 1994; Normand and Busse 2002). Combined, they can be taken as the institutional mechanics of how an SHI system is organized.

Policy questions and challenges

The picture of SHI systems presented thus far describes the beliefs that drive the SHI model and its core structural elements. The complex character of these systems, however, leads to several questions about their overall behaviour and performance. It also suggests a series of important concerns about the policy challenges that SHI policy-makers currently confront.

Turning first to the analytic questions, the seeming stability and resilience of SHI systems – the ability to tie health insurance and delivery structures into civil society so tightly that they consistently survive major changes in the configuration of political power in society – raises a host of practical comparative issues. One question is why the SHI systems in these six countries (Israel and Switzerland only introduced SHI models during the 1990s) have grown and prospered, particularly through the efforts of left-of-centre parties when they held national power, whereas similar, if incomplete, SHI systems in Greece, Italy, Portugal and Spain (INSALUD) became associated with rightist regimes and, when left-of-centre parties took power, were largely dismantled (in practice if not name), respectively in 1983, 1978, 1979 and 1986 in favour of predominantly tax-funded arrangements. A second question is whether SHI systems are in actual fact more stable than tax-funded systems – for example, the NHS in the UK (established in 1948) or Swedish tax-funded services (publicly-funded hospital services began in 1864) – or whether 'stability' is being assessed in terms of some other baseline, such as not-for-profit foundations or for-profit commercial companies, or perhaps in terms of other, less stable public institutions within SHI countries. Similarly, are SHI systems in fact more solidaristic than tax-funded systems? Despite extensive discussion about solidarity in the Dutch or the German SHI systems, is social solidarity in fact actually greater than in, say, Denmark or Sweden?

A further question concerns the apparent contradiction between the overall technical performance of SHI systems as against the strong defence of SHI arrangements from national policy-makers in SHI countries. Among other dilemmas, SHI countries tend to expend relatively high levels of GDP on their health sector (OECD 2003); yet in aggregate SHI countries have populations which have at best similar and, on some indices, poorer outcomes than do their tax-funded brethren (see Chapter 12). SHI systems have particular difficulty in marshalling resources for prevention and public health purposes, which suggests difficulties in restraining future costs in an ageing society. Several SHI systems (Belgium, Germany) have also been criticized for a lack of coordination between office-based and hospital-based care, for consequently high levels of duplication in expensive diagnostic testing (Schwartz and Busse 1996) and for an absence of systematic supervision and enforcement of quality of care (Berwick 1990). More recently, private corporations and also health economists have criticized the SHI system in Germany as inefficient and an obstacle to higher rates of economic growth (Henke 2002; Simonian 2002). How is it, then, one might ask, that a health care system which apparently performs at best at only an average level on such critical variables as cost, prevention, and continuity of care, continues to maintain such high levels of commitment from stakeholders as well as from experienced national policy-makers?

Beyond these specific analytic questions, there are major policy challenges regarding the future of western European SHI systems which need to be addressed. Many commentators have noted that, in contrast to these systems' track record of evolution and stability, the current economic, political and social period is one characterized by rapid economic, technological and political change, accompanied by substantial social dislocation. How well, and for how long, can a stable system survive in such a dynamic environment? How sustainable – economically, politically, socially – will these SHI systems be over the next period of 10 to 20 years?

Economically sustainable?

Although their proponents may not see SHI systems as first and foremost economic systems, economic challenges to existing SHI arrangements appear at each level of institutional abstraction: at national, at supra-national/EU and at global levels (Figure 1.1). In each case, the uncertainty is relatively well-managed at present, however, it increases the further one peers out into the future. The central question is how to reduce the seemingly inherent structural tension between the socially embedded character of SHI systems, on the one hand, and the specific practical requirements of efficient economics, on the other.

National level

At the national level, several major challenges exist. Financial sustainability is at or near the top of most lists of future concerns. This financial pressure is seen to be compounded by the rapid ageing of the population and the consequent reduction in the ratio of the number of active workers to the number of elderly retired in these countries (Israel is an exception). Germany, for example, has

Figure 1.1 Challenges to economic sustainability of SHI systems

National level
- sufficient financial resources
- sufficient operational efficiency
- impact of competition
  - between not-for-profit sickness funds
  - between not-for-profit sickness funds and for-profit companies

EU (supra-national) level
- competition between different SHI benefit packages inside EU
- pressure from EU single market
  - undermining mixed public-private character of SHI
  - dismantling pharmaceutical regulation
  - aggressive for-profit commercial insurers

Global level
- pressure from globalized companies and markets on wage levels and benefits

responded by linking the growth in overall SHI revenues to the rate of increase in salaries on which contributions must be paid. The Netherlands, pursuing the same policy objectives, has sought to restrain the rate of increase in national premiums by creating an additional, out-of-pocket payment for subscribers, subsumed under the notion of a 'nominal premium' (Hermans *et al.* 1996; Fluit 1999). France has sought to restrain health care spending by removing expensive non-essential drugs from the publicly reimbursed package (*Le Journal Permanent de Nouvel Observateur* 2002), while Belgium increased co-payments and co-insurance rates in 1993 and in 1995 sought to give the mutualities more direct financial responsibility (Kerr 2000). Belgium also added an index that limited expenditure growth which was subsequently reviewed and increased.

In this concern with sustainable funding, western European countries with SHI systems appear to differ little in terms of core causes (ageing, new technology, patient pressures) from tax-funded systems. Hospitals in SHI systems, as in their tax-funded counterparts, will need to invest sufficient funds in new clinical and electronic data-handling technologies to stay close to the international standard (De Roo 1995). The implications of increased SHI premiums also have an impact on the competitiveness of national businesses, in that premium increases directly raise hourly wage costs and thus the cost of finished goods in the international marketplace. The central drivers, however, are similar across both types of funding system, and – as will be considered below in the section on political sustainability – the importance of the state in intervening to provide a remedy for these funding problems does not vary greatly either.

A second national-level economic challenge for the future of SHI systems concerns the ability to operate more efficiently. It appears inevitable that the same spotlight highlighting what Herbert Simon (1947) famously termed 'organizational slack' which fell on tax-funded health systems in the 1990s will be trained on SHI systems in the first decade of the twenty-first century. The early 2003 furore over proposals to improve operating efficiency within the German health care system (Steinmeier Proposals) is likely to be the opening round of this broad debate.

The third national-level challenge concerns the degree of competitive forces to be incorporated within SHI systems, and, specifically, on the funding side between different insurers. This has become a major issue in all eight SHI systems, with differing perspectives steeped as much in disciplinary and ideological belief systems as in hard facts (see Chapter 7). To what extent can market-style funding mechanisms be incorporated into SHI before they begin to jeopardize the basic self-governing principles of a solidaristic system (see Altenstetter 1999)? Can specific competitive incentives be utilized to produce greater operating efficiency without shifting greater risks to vulnerable groups? What types of enhanced regulatory and risk adjustment arrangements will be required to prevent the type of 'de-solidarization' that has begun to creep in around the edges of the German SHI system, where savvy entrepreneurs within some sickness funds have exploited the time lag in the risk adjustment process to target younger and healthier subscribers (Pfaff 2001), and that has begun to damage the ability of not-for-profit sickness funds to operate normally in Belgium (Hermesse 2001)? Is it possible to ever have equal ground rules between statutory and commercial competitors in a solidaristic health insurance system? How much stability, transparency and democracy should be traded off for increases in (narrowly defined) economic efficiency? In short, what is required to make competition and solidarity compatible rather than antithetical operating models for funding health care?

EU (supra-national) level

Economic challenges to the future of SHI systems also arise at the cross-national and/or supra-national level, reflecting in particular conflicts created by the continued evolution of the EU's single market initiative. Perhaps the most difficult dilemma concerns the EU's apparent insistence on categorizing all economic activity as either wholly public (e.g. command and control) or wholly private (subject to all open market requirements). This 'black-white' approach has created serious difficulties for both tax-funded and SHI health systems alike (Hermans *et al.* 1996). In the early days of this EU initiative, policy-makers in tax-funded systems worried that they could be interpreted as unfairly excluding private for-profit bidders (EHMA 2000), and there was speculation that rigorous enforcement of existing EU regulations would force these systems to abandon their internal contracting programmes as the only way to preserve public control over the delivery of health services. In SHI systems, similarly, there are growing fears of an EU legal squeeze in which the complex privately-managed-but-statutory-public character of SHI systems would have to be designated either fully private or fully public for legal purposes. In Belgium, for example, three for-profit commercial insurers sued to abolish legal advantages that mutualities have in selling complimentary policies to their subscribers (Hermesse 2001). While the case was dismissed by the Belgian court in September 2002, the commercial insurers are expected to file a European-level appeal. A parallel issue concerns whether the regulation of for-profit commercial insurers should be an EU regional level or a national level member state responsibility. Legal pressures regarding this and similar issues (e.g. pharmaceutical regulations) can be expected to grow under current interpretations of single market requirements.

A second, interrelated supra-national issue concerns the intervention of the European Court in Luxembourg (Court of Justice of the European Communities) on the permeability of national SHI boundaries. Through its judgements in the Kohll/Decker (1998), Smits/Peerbooms (2001), and other related cases, the Court has built up a body of single market decisions that on balance appear to favour the rights of individual subscribers to pursue (appropriate) medical care in adjoining countries (Mossialos and McKee 2002). This case law can be expected to expand over the coming years (Wismar 2001), widening these rights for patients in both SHI and tax-funded systems alike. It thus becomes possible in the foreseeable future that western European SHI systems may find themselves to some degree in competition with each other to induce their own subscribers to receive treatment at home, as well as to attract patients from adjacent countries (Hermans *et al.* 1996). This type of cross-country competition could generate strong pressure on national policy-makers to harmonize benefit packages so as not to find patient flows running against them. This, in turn, could reinforce nascent political efforts to develop a common substantive EU health policy (Wismar and Busse 2002).

Global level

Economic pressures on SHI systems at the global level reflect the need for exports from these countries to remain competitive in international markets. This leads to concerns that wage and benefit levels need to be tightly constrained, with limits on employers' (typically) 50 per cent contribution to SHI premiums (only two of eight countries deviate dramatically from this split: 96 per cent in France but 0 per cent in Israel) and also on additional social taxes paid by employers to support state subsidies in some SHI countries. National policy-makers in countries like Germany and Austria have worried since the early 1990s about the potential impact of high health care premiums on the competitiveness of domestic industry *vis-à-vis* lower wage rates in the transition countries of central Europe (Collier 1995; Hinrichs 1995; Guger 1996).

Politically sustainable?

The long-term political stability of SHI systems can be attributed to their being anchored in civil society not the state, to their calculated public-private mix and to the preference of most stakeholders for continuing these relatively successful arrangements. The central dilemma for SHI systems concerns their ability to sustain this strong political legacy over the next generation of policy-making.

As alluded to earlier, the role of the state in governance and decision-making for SHI systems appears to be changing. Traditionally, that role, while powerful, was relatively indirect (see Chapter 3). Statutory legislation typically empowered sickness funds and providers to work out the necessary budgeting and service delivery arrangements themselves – an arrangement which can be described as 'enforced self-regulation' (Saltman and Busse 2002). The responsibility of the state resembled that of a referee in a football match: the state would only step in if agreed ground rules were broken, or in the case of a deadlock that threatened public access to services.

A key change in SHI systems over the past ten years has been an increasing willingness of the state to breach these traditional relationships, intervening on a wide variety of new issues, and as a result seeming to render important aspects of traditional self-regulatory arrangements obsolete. Examples of this new state role include Belgium (sick fund/provider payment negotiations in 2001), France (Plan Juppé in 1995), Germany (1998), Israel (1995) and the Netherlands (1995). Increasing state pre-emption of traditional self-regulating mechanisms can carry major implications for the social legitimacy of SHI institutions, and for the willingness of SHI stakeholders to continue to commit substantial resources and credibility to self-regulatory negotiations and other regular SHI processes. In Belgium in 2001, as one example, the Physicians' Association pulled out for a time from the traditional negotiation with sickness funds, arguing that the state planned to intervene to set the payment rates anyway (Hermesse 2001).

This shift toward a more state-based, decree-oriented governance structure raises questions about the survivability of the unique model of 'democratic representation' that SHI systems are considered to embody (Altenstetter 1999). As the state takes a growing role, the self-regulatory channels of representation and communication may be short-circuited, as key actors seek to influence state decision-makers directly and, often, off the record.

A second set of political challenges to traditional SHI models concerns the fraying around the edges of the EU practice of subsidiarity in the health sector, as outlined in Article 152 of the Amsterdam Treaty. The dilemmas created by the EU single market project for the formulation of health policy generally led to a commitment in the December 2001 Laeken Declaration of EU Heads of State and Government to begin consideration of developing an explicit EU health policy. Subsequently, a so-called 'high level process of reflection' was undertaken to consider the various policy options. This or some other similar approach could potentially result in a changed balance between national governments and the EU; however, it remains unclear when this might occur.

A further aspect of the political challenge to existing SHI systems concerns the role of the European Court. Here the range of corrective or protective options appears to be decidedly more circumscribed. Key aspects of recent case law made by the Court have been based not on single-market related regulations, but rather on more fundamental principles concerning the freedoms of individual citizens (Mossialos and McKee 2002). These rulings, therefore, will likely reduce the ability of national SHI systems to define the allowable package of covered services and to steer patients to their own national providers and institutions. While the impact of this erosion of control may initially affect only contiguous border areas and certain disputed conditions and treatments, over time there may well be a more general effect on the overall authority of national SHI systems.

Socially sustainable?

As discussed above, SHI systems are premised first and foremost on a set of strongly held social values and beliefs, and the 'non-economic benefits' of an SHI approach are understood by both citizens and policy-makers as equally if not more important than the strictly economic benefits of such systems. To date, this relationship between social as against economic advantages has survived in more or less reasonable balance (see De Roo 1995; Altenstetter 1999). A central question for the future, however, concerns the degree to which the economic challenges detailed above threaten to erode the strength and scope of these core social values, and in turn substantially reduce the 'non-economic benefits' of the SHI model. One can speculate that such an imbalance could put the long-term survival of the entire model at risk.

Sustaining the historical and social base

This review of the economic, political, and social challenges facing SHI systems underscores the critical character of the present period for the future of SHI systems. The fundamental dilemma for national policy-makers involves more than devising an appropriate new mechanism to restrain expenditure growth in some new surgical procedure or on some newly patented pharmaceutical compound. It involves more than finding mechanisms to improve coordination between outpatient and inpatient care, or to increase preventive approaches to long-term population-based threats, or even to deal more cohesively with the delivery of health care services to immigrants and refugees. Rather, the pre-eminent issue is one of shoring up the conceptual 'pillars' – a word with important historical connotations in some of these countries (Lijphart 1969) – upon which the entire SHI edifice has been built. The core of SHI policy-making should be focused on reinventing these systems, on transforming a socially successful but historically based model for a new, volatile and uncertain economic era.

A conceptual framework

Efforts to assess the performance of funding and delivery systems in the eight studied SHI countries confront a series of analytic complications. As earlier sections indicate, SHI systems comprise not just the 'nuts and bolts' of administrative institutions, but also extend to important aspects of the broader social security and private sector/civil society contexts that staff and sustain them. Precisely because these systems have social as well as economic dimensions, their activities cannot be evaluated solely with the tools of micro- and macro-economics. A second dilemma, noted above, is the broad diversity of institutions and arrangements incorporated within the eight studied systems. Reflecting a national set of culturally tied, historically developed institutions, this diversity poses difficulties for efforts to describe and evaluate commonalities across the eight countries.

Efforts to evaluate the SHI approach also run up against an ongoing dialogue within the health policy community about the appropriateness of relying solely upon the preponderant source of funding as a suitable discriminator between different types of health care system. Some commentators believe that the impact of the reform process over the last 15 years has now reduced – even in some cases eliminated – certain traditional financial distinctions between SHI and tax-funded health care systems.

For example, in France, the broad CSR tax implemented in 2002 helps supplement funds for its SHI system with a mandatory state-imposed wealth tax. In Israel, premiums paid to the four sick funds were replaced in 1995 with a mandatory health tax levied on all but very low income taxpayers. There is also, at the extreme of this debate, the observation that both Greece (since 1983 a predominantly tax-funded system) and Belgium (a long-standing SHI system) each generate nearly the same amount of revenue from taxes as from SHI premiums (Mossialos *et al.* 2002).

Despite these and similar concerns about traditional, funding-based analytic categories, and despite the importance of additional non-economic factors in assessing the character and logic of SHI systems, no consensus has formed on a new nomenclature that could replace SHI versus tax-funded as an appropriate framework through which to classify health care systems. A nascent effort by some UK-influenced academics to categorize all tax-funded systems as 'NHS systems', with NHS standing for National Health Service, compounds the problem they seek to resolve, not only by conflating a funding-based (SHI) with a production-based (NHS) label, but by selecting a concept to describe tax-funded systems which does not fit Nordic countries like Finland, Sweden and Denmark, where the production side of the system (as well as most of the funding side) is the responsibility not of national but of regional (Denmark, Sweden) or municipal (Finland) governments. There are also increasing questions about the appropriateness of applying the NHS label to southern European countries like Spain and Italy, which in 2003 were in the process of decentralizing operating responsibility for health services to elected regional bodies (the 17 Autonomous Communities in Spain and the twenty Regional Governments[3] in Italy). Given these analytic dilemmas, this study has opted to retain the standard 'SHI versus tax-funded' framework of health system analysis.

One additional question concerns the conceptual framework that should be appropriately employed both to assess the behaviour and performance of SHI health systems, and to contrast them with equivalent outcomes observed in tax-funded health systems. In the *World Health Report 2000*, WHO put forward a three-part framework primarily designed for evaluating all health care systems in the world regardless of income level or stage of development. This framework took a high-concept approach by assessing health systems in terms of fairness, responsiveness and stewardship. While these three normative characteristics can also certainly be applied to western European SHI systems, the limitations of this framework in capturing the complexities of specifically SHI systems suggests that this WHO framework ought to be supplemented with a simultaneously broader as well as a more nuanced approach.

The rough outline of an appropriate conceptual framework for both describing and assessing the complexities of SHI systems needs to incorporate the various central elements already discussed. The framework should reflect the main structure of the formal financing and delivery institutions, capturing their character as – simultaneously – mandatory, self-regulatory, pluralist, participatory and corporatist. In addition, the framework should also capture the core nature of SHI as, respectively, a central element in the broader social security system of income protection (what in tax-funded systems is directly termed 'welfare state responsibilities'); as grounded in civil society although administered under the auspices of the state; as based on collective solidarity rather than actuarial insurance principles; and as a culturally and historically defined set of social values – a 'way of life'.

These multiple imperatives are captured in the SHI pyramid presented in Figure 1.2. In this conceptual approach, the lowest level serves as the essential foundation from which higher levels draw their character and legitimacy, and upon which these higher levels are thus integrally dependent. As Figure 1.2 suggests, the base of the four-part SHI pyramid incorporates the national culture and historically-tied values found in the broad society. The second level – dependent on society but functioning independently – is the nation state, which constructs the legislative, regulatory and judicial arrangements for SHI systems. Built on these two lower levels are, at the third level of the pyramid, the actual

Figure 1.2 Pyramid model of SHI systems

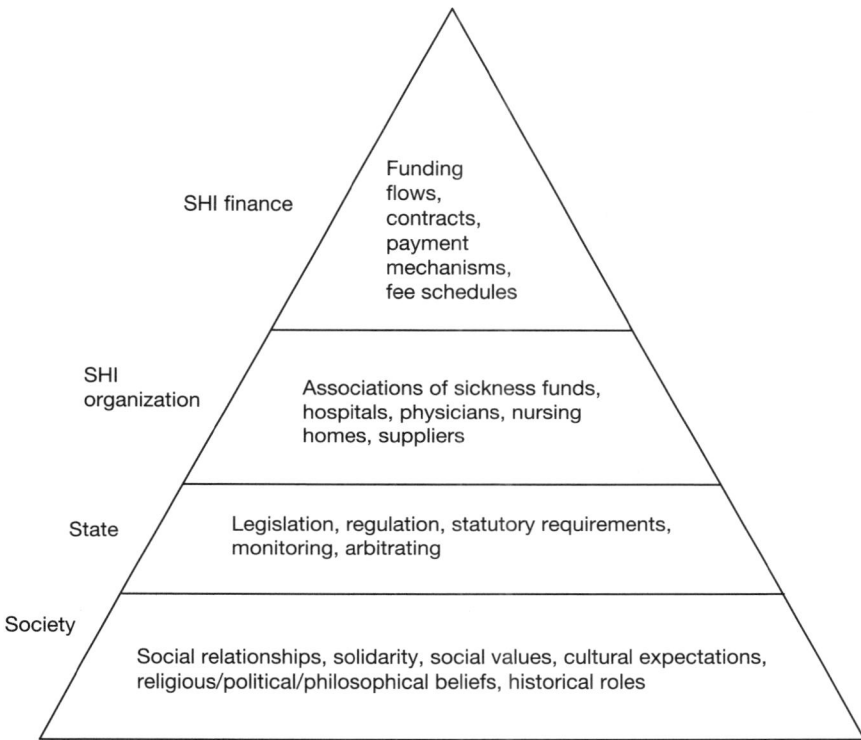

organizational and administrative arrangements of each studied country's SHI system. Lastly – and therefore most contingent upon and least independent of the lower three levels of the pyramid – one finds issues of funding. Thus, discussions and analyses that focus exclusively on the funding level alone implicitly assume the existing configuration and activities of the three lower levels.

The next two chapters are constructed upon this pyramid framework. Chapter 2 explores key components of the national culture and social values that help compose the base level, 'society'. It begins with a brief review of the history of SHI in western Europe, followed by a critical assessment of the central value that underpins both popular support and the policy-making process in the eight studied SHI countries, namely solidarity. Chapter 3 examines the three upper levels of the pyramid. It describes the core organizational characteristics of SHI systems along with the financial mechanisms that are built upon them. It then briefly reviews the regulatory and stewardship roles of the national government in setting the rules and serving as the referee for decisions made within these two upper levels of the SHI pyramid. Recent patterns of health sector reform in all three upper levels of the pyramid are also briefly considered.

With Chapter 4, the study draws together the available quantitative evidence about how well SHI systems have performed in comparison with tax-funded systems in northern Europe (which have similar levels of income to the eight SHI countries) and also with all tax-funded systems in western Europe. This assessment focuses on health status, satisfaction/responsiveness, equity, and efficiency, exploring different methodological approaches within each of these general categories. This exercise is necessarily limited by the type of statistical data available and the inevitable inadequacies of the statistical methods used to collect that data. Despite these limitations, however, this chapter provides a useful overview of how well the eight studied SHI systems actually meet a number of their key policy objectives, and the degree to which these systems do or do not perform – on these limited statistical criteria – 'better' or 'worse' than do western European tax-funded health systems.

Chapter 5 concludes Part One by seeking to draw policy lessons for future consideration within the eight studies SHI countries and, where appropriate, more widely. These observations incorporate material from the previous chapters in Part One, but also reflect Part Two. This second part of the volume, comprising Chapters Six through Thirteen, provides in-depth source material for the broader strategic assessments conducted in Chapters One through Five. Broken out into three subsections – the challenge to solidarity, key organizational issues, and beyond acute care – the Part Two chapters enable readers to probe further into core components of SHI structure and behavior. These deeper perspectives, coupled with the historical, organizational and empirical reviews in Part One, then serve as the background to Chapter Five's consideration of potential responses to future issues raised earlier in this chapter, as well as highlighting potential policy options that decision-makers in these studied and other countries might want to take into consideration.

Notes

1 This characteristic – and the two that follow – are in reality only partly correct. For example, as noted in Chapter 3, partial exceptions here are Israel, which in 1995 switched all health funding to a nationally collected health tax; France, which in 2000 shifted a portion of its health funding to a broadly-based wealth tax; and Germany, where *Länder* funds pay for capital improvements in the hospital sector.
2 Aspects of these components are developed in considerably more detail in Chapter 3.
3 One of Italy's twenty regions is divided into two highly autonomous provinces.

References

Altenstetter, C. (1999) From solidarity to market competition? Values, structure and strategy in German health policy, 1883–1997, in F.D. Powell and A.F. Wesson (eds) *Health Care Systems in Transition: An International Perspective*, pp. 47–88. London: Sage.
Berwick, D.M. (1990) *Curing Health Care: New Strategies for Quality Improvement*. San Francisco: Jossey-Bass.
Collier, I.W. (1995) Rebuilding the German welfare state, in D.P. Conradt, G.R. Kleinfeld, G.K. Romoser and C. Soe (eds) *Germany's New Politics: Parties and Issues in the 1990s*. Oxford: Berghahn Books.
De Roo, A.A. (1995) Contracting and solidarity: market-oriented changes in Dutch health

insurance schemes, in R.B. Saltman and C. von Otter (eds) *Implementing Planned Markets in Health Care: Balancing Social and Economic Responsibility*, pp. 45–64. Buckingham: Open University Press.

De Roo, A.A. (2003) Written communication, 18 April.

EHMA (2000) *The Impact of Market Forces on Health Systems: A Review of Evidence in the 15 European Union Member States*. Dublin: European Healthcare Management Association.

Fluit, P.S. (1999) Verzekeringsplicht en solidariteit: de argumenten voor een wettelijk verplichte sociale verzekering [Mandatory insurance and solidarity: the arguments for a mandatory social insurance], *Beleidswetenschap*, 13: 333–51.

Glaser, W.A. (1991) *Health Insurance in Practice*. San Francisco: Jossey-Bass.

Granovetter, M. (1985) Economic action and social structure: the problem of embeddedness, *American Journal of Sociology*, 91(3): 481–510.

Guger, A. (1996) Internationale Lohnstückkostenposition 1995 deutlich verslechtert [1995 International labour cost competitiveness clearly worsened], *WIFO Monatsberichte no. 8*. Vienna: Austrian Institute of Economic Research.

Henke, K-D. (2002) The permanent crisis in German healthcare, *Eurohealth*, 8(2) (Spring): 26–8.

Hermans, H.E.G.M., Tiems, I. and Schut, F.T. (1996) Zorgverzekeraars en uitvoeringsorganen sociale zekerheid: ondernemingen in het licht van het E-recht? [Health insurers and executory institutions of social security: companies in the light of E-law], *Sociaal maandblad arbeid*, 51: 227–38.

Hermesse, J. (2001) Comment at author's workshop, Storkow, Germany, 6 October.

Hinrichs, K. (1995) The impact of German health insurance reforms on redistribution and the culture of solidarity, *Journal of Health Politics Policy and Law*, 20(3): 653–88.

Hoffmeyer, U.K. and McCarthy, T.R. (1994) *Financing Health Care*. Dordrecht: Kluwer.

Hofstede, G. (1980) *Culture's Consequences: International Differences in Work-Related Values*. London: Sage.

Kerr, E. (2000) *Health Care Systems in Transition: Belgium*. Copenhagen: European Observatory on Health Care Systems.

Le Journal Permanent de Nouvel Observateur (2002) Jean-François Mattéi donne un coup d'arrêt au remboursement des médicaments de confort [Jean-François Mattéi gives a halt to reimbursement of comfort drugs], *Le Journal Permanent de Nouvel Observateur*, 25 September.

Le Pen, C. (2001) Comment at author's workshop, 5 October.

Lijphart, A. (1969) Consociational democracy, *World Politics*, 21(2): 207–25.

Mossialos, E.A. and McKee, M. (2002) *EU Law and the Social Character of Health Care*. Brussels: PIE – Peter Lang.

Mossialos, E.A., Dixon, A., Figueras, J. and Kutzin, J. (eds) (2002) *Funding Health Care: Options for Europe*. Buckingham: Open University Press.

Normand, C. and Busse, R. (2002) Social health insurance (SHI) financing, in E. Mossialos, A. Dixon, J. Figueras and J. Kutzin (eds) *Funding Health Care: Options for Europe*, pp. 59–79. Buckingham: Open University Press.

OECD (2003) *OECD Health Data 2003: A Comparative Analysis of 30 Countries*, 2nd edn. Paris: OECD.

Peters, B.G. (1999) *Institutional Theory in Political Science: The New Institutionalism*. London: Continuum Press.

Pfaff, M. (2001) Comment at author's workshop, Storkow, Germany, 6 October.

Saltman, R.B. (1997) Convergence vs. social embeddedness: debating the future direction of healthcare systems, *European Journal of Public Health*, 7(4): 449–53.

Saltman, R.B. and Bergman, S.E. (2005 forthcoming), Renovating the commons: Swedish healthcare reforms in perspective, *Journal of Health Politics Policy and Law*.

Saltman, R.B. and Busse, R. (2002) Balancing regulation and entrepreneurialism in Europe's health sector: theory and practice, in R.B. Saltman, R. Busse and E. Mossialos (eds) *Regulating Entrepreneurial Behavior in European Health Care Systems*, pp. 3–52. Buckingham: Open University Press.

Saltman, R.B. and Ferroussier-Davis, O. (2000) The concept of stewardship in health policy, *Bulletin of the World Health Organization*, 78(6): 732–9.

Schwartz, F.W. and Busse, R. (1996) Fixed budgets in the ambulatory care sector: the German experience, in F.W. Schwartz, H. Glennerster and R.B. Saltman (eds) *Fixing Health Budgets: Experience from Europe and North America*, pp. 93–108. London: Wiley.

Simon, H. (1947) *Administrative Behavior*. New York: The Free Press.

Simonian, H. (2002) Berlin ponders radical change in welfare state, *Financial Times*, 21 December: 2.

Stone, D.A. (1993) The struggle for the soul of health insurance, *Journal of Health Politics Policy and Law*, 18(2): 287–318.

WHO (2000) *World Health Report 2000*. Geneva: World Health Organization.

Wilsford, D. (1994) Path dependency, or why history makes it difficult but not impossible to reform healthcare in a big way, *Journal of Public Policy*, 14(3): 251–63.

Wismar, M. (2001) ECJ in the driving seat on health policy. But what's the destination? *Eurohealth*, 7(4): 5–6.

Wismar, M. and Busse, R. (2002) Scenarios on the future of healthcare in Europe, in R. Busse, M. Wismar and P. Berman (eds) *The European Union and Health Services – The Impact of the Single European Market on Member States*, pp. 261–72. Amsterdam: IOS Press.

Zöllner, H. (2001) Comment at author's workshop, 5 October.

chapter two

The historical and social base of social health insurance systems

Richard B. Saltman and Hans F.W. Dubois

Introduction

The cultural core of social health insurance (SHI) is deeply rooted in the societies which first spawned it. Germany is often considered to be the source of this approach to health insurance, as it was the first western European country to codify existing voluntary structures into mandatory state-supervised legislation in 1883. The history of SHI in Europe, however, as well as its animating principle of social solidarity, extends considerably earlier than 1883 and more widely than Germany. In many respects, the history of SHI and of its particular concept of solidarity is the history of the evolving social development of western Europe, starting with medieval guilds in the late Middle Ages through to the structuring of the modern European welfare state in the aftermath of World War II. Precisely the fact that the current configuration of institutions and the social values that undergird them are the result of such a long historical process can help explain the degree of stability of existing SHI institutions as well as the difficulty policy-makers confront in seeking to modify those institutions. As both historians and sociologists recognize, it takes generations to build up a 'way of life', and wise political actors rarely seek to disrupt those long-standing patterns.

This chapter examines two key elements in the base or 'society' level of the four-part pyramid framework presented in Chapter 1. First, it briefly reviews the history of SHI across western Europe, highlighting the central structural lineants that led to present-day arrangements in the eight studied countries. Subsequently, the chapter probes more closely into what many commentators consider to be the core cultural value that both generates and is generated by

SHI, namely social solidarity, examining in particular its different historical and cultural roots in the eight countries. The chapter concludes with a brief consideration of the implications of this historical and social base for policy-makers as they seek to address current challenges.

A brief history of SHI in western Europe

The present system of nearly universal SHI in Western Europe is the culmination of a 700-year historical process. Over that period, the number of individuals covered has grown from a small number of workers in particular trades to (depending on the national variant) all residents or at least all residents whose earnings are below a rather high threshold. Equally as important, the central concept of this form of social insurance also has changed, evolving from wage replacement and a death benefit into payment for and/or the provision of outpatient physician services, inpatient hospital care and pharmaceuticals. Lastly, the administrative character of SHI has shifted over time, having begun as voluntary worker cooperatives but from 1883 in Germany and subsequently throughout the twentieth century (from 1941 in the Netherlands to 1996 in Switzerland) taking on a state-mandated legislative character. All three types of change demonstrate that the present configuration reflects an extended developmental process and the deep roots of the current institutional structure in the social fabric of these countries.

The initial phase of this historical process involved small groups of workers in the late medieval period, who created mutual assistance associations under the auspices of their craft guild. The first recorded guild funds date back to the 1300s (Veraghtert and Widdershoven 2002). These funds generally covered only guild members, with overall coverage restricted to less than 5 per cent of the total population. All others were dependent on charitable and/or religious organizations for care. This precedent of basing health coverage on occupation became a core tenet of the social insurance model in German-speaking countries and Sweden (Abel-Smith 1988).

It was not until the late eighteenth century that the state began to take on an active role in the provision of health services. Two important trends helped shape the European health sector's future. One was in the Nordic Region, where district physicians in Sweden were given royal commissions contingent on their willingness to see indigent patients without payment (Serner 1980; Hjortsberg and Ghatnekar 2001). Similar policies were followed in the then Swedish colony of Finland, as well as in Norway (Furuholmen and Magnussen 2000; Järvelin 2002). This is the first known effort by a state to provide health services to the poor. The second, parallel trend was more indirect but, in retrospect, nearly as important. This was the continual effort by various newly consolidating states to break the economic power of the guilds (Abel-Smith 1988). This culminated in one of the first acts of the French Revolution when on 4 August 1789 guilds were abolished with the objective of creating a more liberal labour market, as well as increasing social equality (Veraghtert and Widdershoven 2002). Guilds were similarly prohibited in the Netherlands in 1798 (Veraghtert and Widdershoven 2002) and in Denmark in 1861 (Abel-Smith

1988). With the banning of the guilds, their health insurance function continued as independent (and politically unprotected) mutual assistance societies, thus setting the stage for the process of consolidating state legislative control that commenced in 1883.

Once the guilds disappeared, there was an extended period in which various collective not-for-profit as well as private for-profit attempts were made to organize the provision of health insurance. These civil society efforts produced mixed results, varying by country and by historical and/or cultural situation. In the Netherlands, for example, private commercial insurers tried to establish a market for health insurance, with unsatisfactory results (Hogarth 1963). In the late 1800s, voluntary health insurance societies grew up administered by the insured themselves or occasionally by industrial firms or by charitable foundations (Abel-Smith 1988). Similarly, voluntary health insurance emerged during this period in the Nordic countries (Hogarth 1963) and, for more middle-class individuals, in France (Saint-Jours 1983). In Switzerland, voluntary insurance appeared in response to the 'bad reputation' that private commercial insurers acquired, linked in part to their high-pressure door-to-door salesmen (Maurer 1983). In Israel, the first voluntary sickness fund was established by a small group of agricultural workers in 1911. Later on, in 1920, this fund was taken over by the National Labor Union. (Carrin and James 2004). The diversity of organizational format, members covered and services provided among voluntary health insurance systems is captured in a description of the United Kingdom during the early twentieth century:

> The largest category of health insurers involved 'friendly societies' which provided cash benefits for the sick, treatment by contracted general practitioners, and drugs. Later, some dental and ophthalmic benefits were added by some societies. Other insurers included trade union clubs, slate clubs or tontines (clubs which distributed any annual surplus among the members), works clubs (based on the factory), and provident dispensaries which were subsidized by charitable funds. There were also some medical aid societies run on similar lines by commercial life insurance companies (Green 1985), but they were in the minority. Membership grew to include not only the mass of wage earners but small shopkeepers and a substantial proportion of the middle classes.
>
> (Abel-Smith 1988:689)

There were, of course, exceptions to this new pattern. In Germany, for example, the guilds and their health insurance funds were largely maintained (Veraghtert and Widdershoven 2002). Moreover, the emerging state supervisory role was presaged in Austria in its 1859 Industrial Code (Hofmarcher and Rack 2001), and by state replacement of private philanthropy in substantial parts of the Netherlands and Belgium (Veraghtert and Widdershoven 2002).

The modern era in SHI was ushered in by Bismarck in 1883. Worried about rising political pressure from Marxist-influenced labour unions and consumed by his desire to build a powerful German state, Bismarck seized upon the idea of retaining independent occupation-based sick funds but placing their activities under state tutelage. The resulting legislation established both the legal and social foundation for sickness funds not just for Germany but for much of western Europe as well. Indeed, Austria followed suit in 1887/8 (Hofmarcher and Rack 2001), and in 1892, the Danish government adopted a variant plan that gave subsidies to existing voluntary funds so that those who were already ill would be admitted (Abel-Smith 1988; Vallgarda *et al.* 2001). Belgium adopted similar legislation, establishing state subsidies for sickness funds in 1894 (Veraghtert and Widdershoven 2002). In Switzerland, although an 1899 referendum to adopt a German-style model was rejected, a 1911 law required voluntary funds that accepted federal subsidies to register and abide by state-imposed regulations (Minder *et al.* 2000). In the United Kingdom, Lloyd George successfully passed a health insurance act in the same year.

This process continued after the conclusion of World War I, when France – confronted by existing health insurance in the re-acquired region of Alsace-Lorraine – passed a compulsory health insurance law in 1920 which was not implemented until ten years later (Saint-Jours 1983; Sandier *et al.* 2004). One of the last northern European countries to adopt compulsory health insurance legislation was the Netherlands which, in 1941 under German occupation (Den Exter *et al.* 2002) passed legislation that was retained after the end of World War II in 1945.

This period of growing state activity was characterized by rising rates of population coverage. The legislation passed during this period not only established the principle of state supervision and regulation of sick funds, but also required certain segments of the population (typically various groups of workers) to obtain coverage – hence the application of the term 'compulsory'. However, rates of coverage still fell substantially short of universal. Depending upon the country, a number of steps were required after 1945 to complete the process of covering all regular workers below a fixed income threshold, their dependants, and also the unemployed and pensioners. This process extended through 1996 in Switzerland.

In the largely agricultural southern European countries, where the industrial revolution began much later than in northern Europe, the first major sickness funds were created by enterprises in the new industrial sector. Levels of coverage in southern European countries like Spain and Portugal lagged behind during the period of dictatorship, in part due to sluggish economic growth, but in the late twentieth century, these rates were parallel with the rest of Europe (see Figure 2.1). In Portugal, for example, in the first half of the twentieth century, coverage was limited to industrial workers, with other sectors of the workforce added through extensions of coverage in 1959, 1965, 1971 and 1978 (Benges and Dias 2003). In Spain, coverage was extended substantially by the 1967 Basic Social Security Act (Rico 2000).

In western Europe, in the post-World War II period, a substantial number of countries moved from an SHI system to a fully tax-based system. The first wave, from 1948 to 1973, included the United Kingdom, Denmark and Finland, while from 1978 to 1986 a second, post-dictatorship (except for Italy) wave followed in southern Europe from 1978 to 1986 in Italy, Portugal, Greece and Spain (see Table 2.1). Moreover, during the latter half of the post-WW II period, the French system increased the proportion of tax-based funding, in 1992 Luxembourg's government proposed the abolition of sickness funds

Figure 2.1 Key extension public coverage 1960–2002

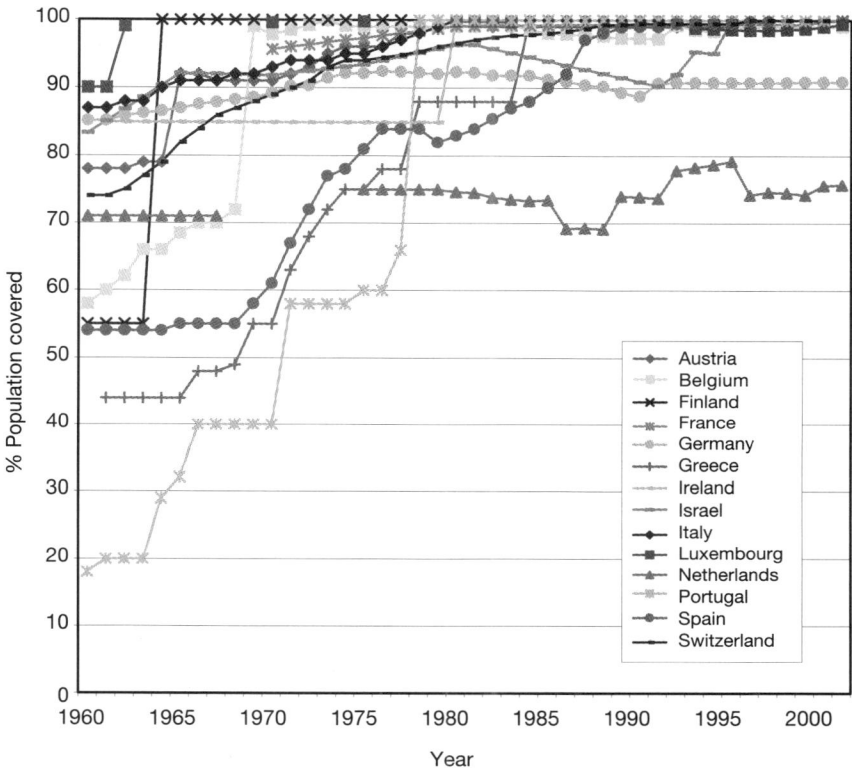

Note: countries with more than 90 per cent coverage since 1960 are excluded (Denmark, Norway, Sweden and the UK). For the Netherlands the population coverage ratios are weighted averages of share of the population covered by the health insurance funds (public) and the whole population covered by AWBZ. The weights are the shares in total costs of the costs covered by health insurance funds and AWBZ. For the social protection ratio, the shares of public finance (government, social security payments and AWBZ) in total expenditure are presented. For Israel the data for 1961–4, 1966–9, 1976–80 and 1982–90 were extrapolated from the available data.

Sources: OECD (2003) and, for Israel, Ben Nun (1999).

(unsuccessfully) (Kerr 1999), and in Israel 1995 legislation replaced premiums paid directly to the sick fund with a progressive national health tax (Rosen 2003).

This process of increasing state power over health insurance, however, is less apparent in the traditionally SHI heart of western Europe. In Austria, Belgium, Germany and the Netherlands, there is still strong attachment to the SHI model, and, as reviewed in Chapter 3, state power is typically exercised with considerable caution. Indeed, as noted in the political challenges discussed in Chapter 1, there is substantial concern in these countries over what is seen as the growing encroachment of state authority in the traditionally self-regulatory

Table 2.1 Funding of health care systems

	Predominantly SHI-based	Predominantly tax-based	Year of major legislative change from a role for SHI to a predominantly tax-based system
Austria	X		
Belgium	X		
Denmark		X	1973
Finland		X	1972*
France	X		
Germany (Federal Republic until 1990)	X		
Greece		X	1983
Ireland		X	1970*
Israel	X		
Italy		X	1978
Luxembourg	X		
Netherlands	X		
Norway		X	1967
Portugal		X	1979
Spain		X	1986
Sweden		X	1970*
Switzerland	X		
United Kingdom		X	1946

* SHI never played a significant role and/or the date indicated marks a break-point where the central state took increased financial responsibility to provide more extended coverage and the role of the tax-based system was substantially increased.

Sources: European Observatory on Health Care Systems' Health Care Systems in Transition reports; Pinto and Oliveira (2001); Guillén (2002); Department of Health and Children of Ireland (2003).

aspects of the SHI system. These concerns are magnified by the degree to which SHI systems have, since World War II, become enmeshed in a wider, bureaucratized welfare state structure. While there is keen awareness that a new approach to the broad structure of social welfare has become essential (Esping-Andersen 2002; Vandenbroucke 2002), there are strong reservations about applying these reforms to SHI. One key concern, as befits SHI's long history, is that state-instituted changes could damage the well-articulated role of civil society, replacing pluralism and participation with a rigid state bureaucracy that is in need of reform when it comes to other welfare state services. This same concern also was raised, conversely, about state efforts during the 1990s in countries like Germany and the Netherlands to introduce seemingly opposite, liberalizing, measures to create more market-like relationships inside SHI systems, particularly between the sickness funds. As the second section of this chapter suggests, concerns about the growing role of both market and/or state reflect worries that these changes may damage the existing configuration of social solidarity built up over centuries on the civil side of society.

The resilience of solidarity

The concept of solidarity provides the core animating principle of SHI systems. Its long historical evolution in Europe parallels that of social insurance generally, running from late-medieval guilds through nineteenth-century mutual aid societies up to the late twentieth-century welfare state. Moreover, despite the political upheavals in western Europe in the first half of the twentieth century – some argue because of those upheavals and in particular World War II – solidarity remains the dominant political principle that defines key elements of national and now European Union social policy (Hinrichs 1995; Stone 1995; Altenstetter 1999; Bayertz 1999; Gevers *et al.* 2000; Gilbert 2000; Houtepen and Ter Meulen 2000b). Even in Germany, where fascism during the 1930s played a role in the evolution of corporatist and self-regulatory relationships (Moran 1999; Veraghtert and Widdershoven 2002), the resulting pattern was both stable across subsequent governmental regimes and strongly resembled arrangements that emerged in other western European SHI systems. As a normative value, the principle of solidarity has been and remains a core tenet of the dominant Christian religion (both Catholic and Protestant); of Marxian socialism; of the modern trade union movement; and of both ancient and renascent nationalist sentiment. In the eyes of western European commentators and policy-makers, it is simultaneously inconceivable and incomprehensible to discuss the concept of SHI without basing it in broad societal support for the concept of solidarity.

Solidarity has been defined as 'a sense of non-calculating co-operation based on identification with a common cause' (Houtepen and Ter Meulen 2000a: 334). The individual is viewed as 'embedded in social contexts' rather than as an independent agent, and thus solidarity is not a characteristic of particular individuals but instead reflects 'a specific type of association among people'. This understanding is consistent with a predominantly German idealist philosophical understanding of the relationship between the individual and the society: that individuals obtain their freedom in and through the social group, making mutual relationships a 'precondition' for individual development and freedom. Similarly, as Chinitz *et al.* point out in Chapter 6, the degree of solidarity that inheres within a particular population can be viewed as an important component of 'civil society', of collective resources that serve as a mediating structure between state and market, and which build social cohesion. More concretely, solidarity in the health sector is sometimes presented as 'operationalizing social justice'; that is, as putting physical flesh on the abstract philosophical belief that all individuals should be treated equally. Solidarity in this view grows organically out of the natural needs and behaviours of communities – it is not an artificial construction that is externally imposed by decree upon an individual or a community. It sits at the centre of the 'way of life', of the social understanding of SHI systems discussed in Chapter 1.

The 'communities of mutual recognition' (Houtepen and Ter Meulen 2000b) that embody solidarity typically follow a pattern that starts with an individual's immediate surroundings and then grows slowly outward, moving from personal to communal to occupational and finally to national in character. Initially, solidarity extended from the family to small local groups built around face-to-face relationships and close interaction: guilds, churches, and, later on, union locals and political movements. By the late nineteenth century, the need for sustainable funding instigated a fundamental shift from voluntary and local to mandatory and national participation, under the aegis of the state. Although this represented a major change in the organizing agent, it was understood by most citizens as simply a way to achieve the same objectives but by a different means (Houtepen and Ter Meulen 2000a). This was evidenced by the degree to which, regarding health insurance, the new welfare state entities retained both the institutions and procedures of the former voluntary model. In practice, however, this change involved a fundamental shift in how the need for care was conceptualized in these western European countries. It was 'lifted out of the context of mutual recognition' among local groupings and relocated as a 'general right' to be guaranteed and financed by the coercive power of government (Houtepen and Ter Meulen 2000b). This evolution explains the key structural shift by which solidarity came to be absorbed by and represented in the institutions of the welfare state. Of course, as noted in Chapter 1, solidarity in this welfare state form also exists in countries where health care is directly funded from publicly collected taxes (e.g. United Kingdom and Nordic countries). Indeed, many of the peculiarities that restrict achieving full solidarity in SHI countries are not present in tax-funded systems, such that, while solidarity is widely discussed within SHI systems, it is in practice more completely achieved – at least in a formal financial sense – within the universal tax-funded systems.

Exactly who comprises a solidaristic 'community of mutual recognition' can vary quite considerably across historical periods and within countries. Bayertz (1999) developed a set of four somewhat conflicting types of groups to which, at various times, the attribute of solidarity has been ascribed:

- reciprocity (brotherhood) as well as asymmetry (help needy)
- individuals (assist the weak) as well as communities (social cohesion)
- individual relationships (altruism, fellowship) as well as institutional relationships (citizenship duties)
- outsiders (universal brotherhood) as well as one's own ethnic or political sub-group (rallying together).

Solidarity can thus take on a variety of different permutations in society. In this respect, it can be conceived of as having a considerably wider range, central to the broad process not just of health insurance but also of social organization in these countries.

When one explores how the concept of solidarity has been applied specifically within the health sectors of the eight studied countries, one finds substantial variation in both the predominant cultural/philosophical/political source and in who are the most influential groups. In broad terms, solidarity in the Netherlands stems from a cultural predisposition toward pragmatic rationality, which is itself composed of three related elements: self-interest, political concerns and true altruism (Dubois 2002). Quite differently, the sources of solidaristic values in France are the philosophical notions of *fraternité* and *egalité* consecrated by the French Revolution and adopted by all subsequent French republics. Different again, Belgian notions of solidarity strongly reflect Catholic principles of obligation while the concept of solidarity as it has emerged in Switzerland reflects small-scale interpersonal relations tied to local geography (the canton).

Not surprisingly, the central agent that carries and sustains solidarity within the health sector also differs between countries. In France, Germany and Luxembourg, sickness funds are predominantly defined by professional (labour) characteristics. In Belgium, the sickness funds are defined by religious and ideological affiliations. In the Netherlands, sickness funds have lost their prior pillar-based religious and ideological affiliations to become regional (now national) non-partisan bodies. In Austria, they are organized by occupational groups and/or by region. In Switzerland, sickness funds are organized on a wide-ranging mix of religious and geographical (local and national) foundations. Lastly, in Israel, the four sickness funds reflect a mix of ideology (the largest fund) and non-partisanship.

One can further consider the varying impact of religious and ideological convictions on the internal administration of the sickness funds. In several countries, some funds retain the strongly religious (e.g. Catholic in Belgium) or ideological (e.g. Bernsteinian socialist in Germany) beliefs upon which they were founded. These carry through to the policies of the funds, and even to the self-effacing, non-self-interested approach of fund administrators (Glaser 1991).

Given this diversity among country arrangements, it also is not surprising to find – as explored more fully in Chapter 3 – that the practical organizations and structural frameworks that have been adopted vary considerably as well. In Germany, the self-regulatory range of the sickness funds and providers is tightly constrained by a published code book of federal regulations – *Social Code Book V* (Busse 2000). In the Netherlands, quite differently, rather than a published social code book, there exists a wide range of 'collegium' – or *'colleges'* – that incorporate most key actors in any particular health-related sub-sector and that – within broadly defined limits – take many relevant decisions for the health sector (Den Exter *et al.* 2002). In France, administration and decision-making for the sickness funds (and also for the largest hospitals) is handled by state-run agencies (sometimes acting through regional sick fund offices).

The complexity of solidarity underscores its organic character. Its roots are embedded in the social fabric of at least six of the studied countries (Israel and Switzerland are recent additions to SHI arrangements). Solidarity frames how citizens view health and social security concerns, and it sits at the core of national policy-makers' thinking and of the policy judgements they make. It would not be inappropriate to consider solidarity as the engine that animates the pluralistic administrative structure of SHI systems. Solidarity, understood as it is constructed within Belgium, France, Germany, Luxembourg and the Netherlands, is not just a set of financial cross-subsidies but is a central element in transforming the technical administration of SHI systems from just health insurance into 'a way of life'. It seems fair to conclude that the resilience of solidarity is a major explanatory factor in the overall long-term stability that SHI systems have achieved.

Future implications

Looking forward, a critical aspect of SHI's future will be the degree to which traditional notions of solidarity – the 'beating heart' of an SHI approach – can be sustained in a period of growing economic volatility. The combined pressures of cultural atomization in a mass consumer society, along with economic individualization as highlighted by the slow erosion of wage solidarity, collective (state) pensions and the power of labor unions, challenge the survival of solidarity – and thus SHI – at its very core. Pressures to emphasize the separate individual rather than the collective social dimension of citizenship threaten to erode key values that underpin social solidarity in all its forms, and especially SHI with its central focus on socially generated cross-subsidies and social justice.

To be certain, the unpleasant social impact of economic recessions may remind the broad population of the potential dangers of reducing their commitment to the collective institutions that operationalize solidarity – such as an SHI system. Moreover, some commentators suggest that the traditional concept of solidarity can be reconfigured so as to maintain its position in a post-Rawlsian, post-individuated world (Houtepin and Ter Meulen 2000b). This philosophical work seeks to respond to the criticism that solidarity – and thus ultimately SHI systems as well – were designed for countries in a previous stage of history and an earlier stage of economic development. Such concepts as 'dialogic democratization' (Giddens 1994) and 'reflexive solidarity' (Habermas 1992; Dean 1995) seek to focus on the 'social interchange' and 'relational' characteristics of social solidarity, reinvigorating it to play a central organizing role in future as well as past institutional arrangements (Houtepin and Ter Meulen 2000b). Whether the prior balance between social and economic pressures can be sustained in an era of economic regionalization and globalization represents one of the greatest challenges that policy-makers in SHI countries will confront.

References

Abel-Smith, B. (1988) The rise and decline of the early HMOs: some international experiences, *Milbank Memorial Fund Quarterly*, 66(4): 694–719.

Altenstetter, C. (1999) From solidarity to market competition? Values, structure and strategy in German health policy 1883–1997, in F.D. Powell and A.F. Wesson (eds) *Health Care Systems in Transition: An International Perspective*, pp. 47–88. London: Sage.

Bayertz, K. (ed.) (1999) *Solidarity*. Dordrecht: Kluwer.

Ben Nun, G. (1999) *Distribution of Members Between Health Plans Before and After National Health Insurance, 1950–1998*. Jerusalem: Ministry of Health.

Benges, M. and Dias, M. (2003) *Health Care Systems in Transition: Portugal*. Copenhagen: European Observatory on Health Care Systems (to be published).

Busse, R. (2000) *Health Care Systems in Transition: Germany*. Copenhagen: European Observatory on Health Care Systems.

Carrin, G. and James, C. (2004) Reaching universal coverage via social health insurance: key design features in the transition period. Health financing policy issue paper. Geneva: WHO.

Dean, J. (1995) Reflexive solidarity, *Constellations*, 2: 114–40.

Den Exter, A., Hermans, H., Dosljak, M. and Busse, R. (2002) *Health Care Systems in Transition: The Netherlands*. Copenhagen: European Observatory on Health Care Systems (to be published).

Department of Health and Children of Ireland (2003) Personal communication with Fiona Prendergast, 22 May.

Dubois, H.F.W. (2002) *The Rationality of Dutch Solidarity*. Mimeo, European Observatory on Health Care Systems, Madrid office.

Esping-Andersen, G. (2002) Towards the good society, once again? in G. Esping-Andersen, A. Hemerijck, D. Gallie and J. Myles (eds) *Why We Need a New Welfare State*, pp. 1–25. Oxford: Oxford University Press.

Furuholmen, C. and Magnussen, J. (2000) *Health Care Systems in Transition: Norway*. Copenhagen: European Observatory on Health Care Systems.

Gevers, J., Gelissen, J., Arts, W. and Muffels, R. (2000) Public healthcare in the balance: exploring popular support for healthcare system in the European Union, *International Journal of Social Welfare*, 9(4): 301–21.

Giddens, A. (1994) *Beyond Left and Right: The Future of Radical Politics*. Cambridge: Polity Press.

Gilbert, N. (ed.) (2000) *Targeting Social Benefits: International Perspectives and Trends*. Geneva: International Social Security Association.

Glaser, W.A. (1991) *Health Insurance in Practice*. San Francisco: Jossey-Bass.

Green, D.G. (1985) *Working Class Patients and the Medical Establishment*. Oxford: Pergamon.

Guillén, A.M. (2002) The politics of universalisation: establishing national health services, *Southern Europe West European Politics*, 25(4): 49–68.

Habermas, J. (1992) *Faktizität und Geltung. Beiträge zur Diskurstheorie des Rechts und des demokratischen Reichsstaats [Between Facts and Norms: Contributions to a Discourse Theory of Law and Democracy]*. Frankfurt am Main: Suhrkamp.

Hinrichs, K. (1995) The impact of German health insurance reforms on redistribution and the culture of solidarity, *Journal of Health Politics Policy and Law*, 20(3): 653–88.

Hjortsberg, C. and Ghatnekar, O. (2001) *Health Care Systems in Transition: Sweden*. Copenhagen: European Observatory on Health Care Systems.

Hofmarcher, M.M. and Rack, H. (2001) *Health Care Systems in Transition: Austria*. Copenhagen: European Observatory on Health Care Systems.

Hogarth, J. (1963) *The Payment of the General Practitioner*. Oxford: Pergamon.

Houtepen, R. and Ter Meulen, R. (2000a) New types of solidarity in the European welfare state, in R. Houtepen and R. ter Meulen (eds) Special issue: Solidarity in Health Care, *Health Care Analysis*, 8(4): 329–40.

Houtepen, R. and Ter Meulen, R. (2000b) The expectation(s) of solidarity: matters of justice, responsibility and identity in the reconstruction of the healthcare system, in R. Houtepen and R. ter Meulen (eds) Special issue: Solidarity in Health Care, *Health Care Analysis*, 8(4): 355–76.

Järvelin, J. (2002) *Health Care Systems in Transition: Finland*. Copenhagen: European Observatory on Health Care Systems.

Kerr, E. (1999) *Health Care Systems in Transition: Luxembourg*. Copenhagen: European Observatory on Health Care Systems.

Maurer, A. (1983) Switzerland, in P.A. Kohler and H.F. Zacher (eds) *The Evolution of Social Insurance, 1881–1981*, pp. 384–442. London: Frances Pinter.

Minder, A., Schoenholzer, H. and Amiet, M. (2000) *Health Care Systems in Transition: Switzerland*. Copenhagen: European Observatory on Health Care Systems.

Moran, M. (1999) *Governing the Health Care State*. Manchester: Manchester University Press.

OECD (2003) *OECD Health Data 2003: A Comparative Analysis of 30 Countries*, 2nd edn. Paris: OECD.

Pinto, M. and Oliveira, C.G. (2001) *The Portuguese Health Care System: Current Organisation and Perspectives for Reform*. Paper presented at European Health Care Systems Discussion Group London, 19–20 March.

Rico, A. (2000) *Health Care Systems in Transition: Spain*. Copenhagen: European Observatory on Health Care Systems.

Rosen, B. (2003) *Health Care Systems in Transition: Israel.* Copenhagen: European Observatory on Health Care Systems (to be published).

Saint-Jours, Y. (1983) France, in P.A. Kohler and H.F. Zacher (eds) *The Evolution of Social Insurance 1881–1981*, pp. 105, 119–20. London: Frances Pinter.

Sandier, S., Polton, D. and Paris, V. (2004) *Health Care Systems in Transition: France.* Copenhagen: European Observatory on Health Care Systems.

Serner, U. (1980) Swedish health legislation: milestones in re-organization since 1945, in A.J. Heidenheimer and N.J. Elvarder (eds) *The Shaping of the Swedish Health Care System*, pp. 99–116. New York: St. Martin's Press.

Stone, D.A. (1995) Commentary: the durability of social capital, *Journal of Health Politics Policy and Law*, 20(3): 689–94.

Vallgarda, S., Krasnik, A. and Vrangbaek, K. (2001) *Health Care Systems in Transition: Denmark.* Copenhagen: European Observatory on Health Care Systems.

Vandenbroucke, F. (2002) Forward, in G. Esping-Andersen, A. Hemerijck, D. Gallie and J. Myles (eds) *Why We Need a New Welfare State*, pp. vii–xxiv. Oxford: Oxford University Press.

Veraghtert, K. and Widdershoven, B. (2002) *Twee eeuwen solidariteit: De Nederlanse, Belgische en Duitse ziekenfondsen tijdens de negentiende en twintigste eeuw [Two centuries of solidarity: the Dutch, Belgian and German sickness funds during the nineteeth and twentieth century]*. Amsterdam: Aksant.

three

Organization and financing of social health insurance systems: current status and recent policy developments

Reinhard Busse, Richard B. Saltman and Hans F. W. Dubois

Introduction

This chapter probes more deeply into the complex technical commonalities and variations among the seven social health insurance (SHI) countries in western Europe, and Israel. Reflecting the four-level pyramid model introduced in Chapter 1 (Figure 1.2), this chapter details the structural characteristics, respectively from its top, of the funding, organization and (to a lesser degree) state levels of SHI systems as well as recent developments. Since the funding flows are inextricably linked to the institutions that organize SHI systems, these top two tiers will be reviewed simultaneously, followed by the role of the state. As the four-level pyramid model highlights, these financial and organizational relationships are embedded within, and heavily steered by, the two lower levels of the pyramid (e.g. the state and, below that, the broader society in which the state sits).

The chapter is organized into three main sections. In the first, the eight SHI systems, as they are currently configured, are described in relation to ten key structural dimensions. This is followed by a brief review of the role of the state in these systems. In the third section, the main trends of recent policy developments in the eight studied SHI systems are categorized and assessed.

The current organizational make-up

One useful way to explore the key organizational and financial components in the eight studied SHI health care systems is a modified version of the classic triangle composed of 'insured/patients', 'third-party payers' and 'providers' (Figure 3.1). These three main actors – or rather four as the collector of the revenue is considered separately since it is not the same as the actual payer in many countries – are linked by a correlating set of relationships. Using this triangle as a basis, this first section of the chapter explores the following dimensions of these eight SHI systems (the numbers are used to place each dimension in the figure):

- number, governance and accountability of sickness funds
- the extent to which the population is insured
- relationship between insurees and sickness funds, especially degree of choice for the insurees
- by whom the contributions are collected
- how contributions/premiums are calculated or based
- mechanisms and extent of pooling and (re-)allocation of contributions to/ among sickness funds
- benefits available under SHI, especially regarding the non-acute sectors of public health/health promotion and long-term care
- forms and organizational set-up of providers
- contractual relationships between sickness funds and providers about types of services, reimbursement and quality; and
- patient access to, as well as gatekeeping by, providers.

Issues 1 to 6 concern the sickness funds as well as organizational and financial aspects of the relationships between funds and the insured. Important information and data regarding the issues 1 to 6 are summarized for the eight countries in Table 3.1. Issues 7 to 10, presented subsequently, concern the covered benefits, the providers and the structure of relationships between providers, the sickness funds and patients.

The sickness funds

The number of funds, their size and their structure vary widely. Austria, France and Luxembourg have a comparatively small and stable number of funds (Table 3.2) defined on the basis of occupational status or, in the case of Austria, by occupational group and/or by region of residence, with no insuree choice among them. In the French system, sickness funds have to be differentiated from the various 'regimes'. Most notably, the largest sickness fund (*Caisse Nationale de l'Assurance Maladie des Travailleurs Salariés*, CNAMTS, or: *Régime Générale*), operates the General Regime of Social Security covering employees, industrial workers, pensioners, unemployed and their dependants. Eighty-four per cent of the population are covered by this fund (2000 data) which has a pyramidal structure, with a national office, 16 regional coordinating funds (*Caisses Régionales d'Assurance-Maladie*) and 129 local *'caisses'* (*Caisses Primaires*

Figure 3.1 Actors and relationships in SHI countries with issues explored in this chapter numbered 1 to 10

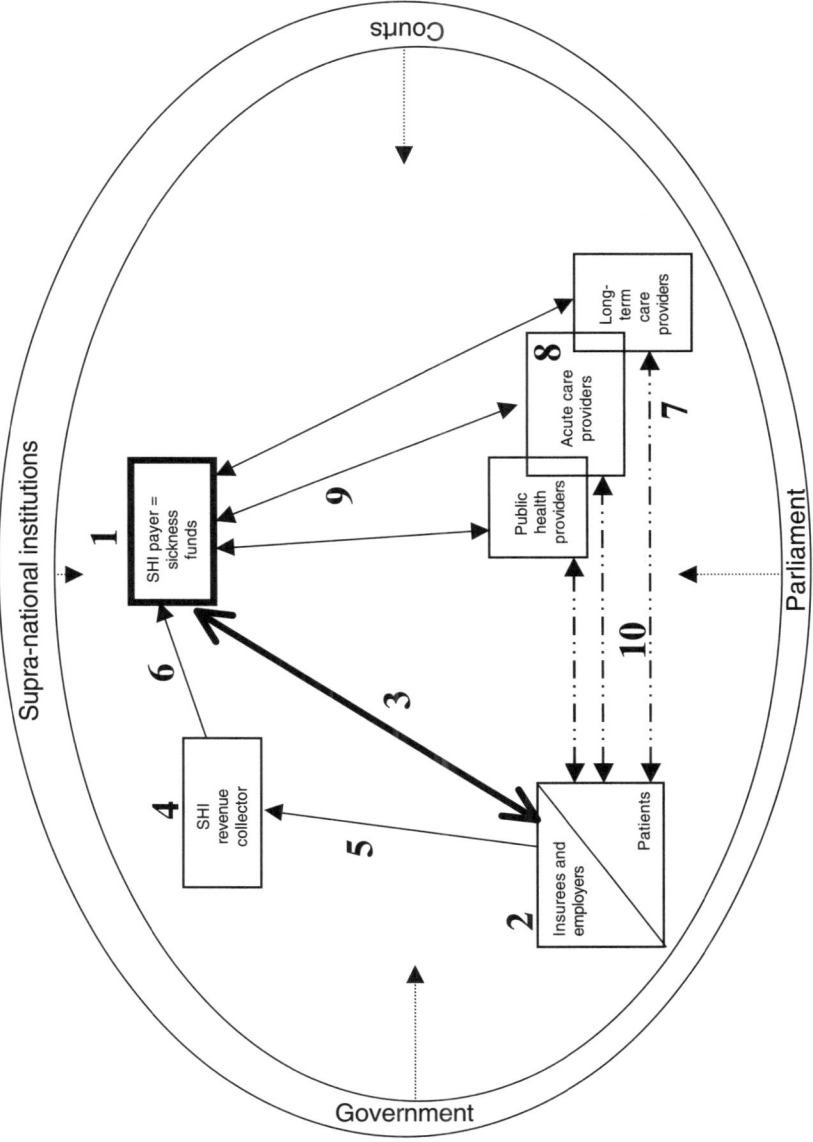

Table 3.1 Important characteristics of SHI systems relating to organization and financing (unless noted, all data for 2002/3) (amended and updated from Normand and Busse 2002)

Issue (with number)	Austria	Belgium	France	Germany	Israel	Luxembourg	Netherlands	Switzerland
1) Number of sickness funds (2002)	24	94 (organized in 7 associations)	17	355	4	9	22[1]	93
Size of largest fund (% of all insured)	18	5	84	12	55	38	15	15
2) SHI coverage (% of pop.)	98	99–100	100	88	100	97–99	AWBZ: 100; ZFW: 63	100
3) % of insured with choice of fund; interval for change	0	Ca. 99, 3 months	0	96, 18 months	100, 12 months	0	100, 12 months	100, 6 months
4a) General contribution rate: uniform or varying, % of wage	Varying by profession: 6.4–9.1[4]	Uniform: 7.4	Uniform: 13.6	Varying by fund: mean 14.1	Uniform: 3.1 of income up to the minimum wage and 4.8 above that level	Uniform: 5.1 (+ 0.3–5.0% sick pay)	Uniform: AWBZ 10.25, ZFW 8.45; 4.6% for sailors	No
4b) Distribution employer/employee	Variable[4]	52/48	94/6	50/50	0/100	50/50	AWBZ 0/100, ZFW 80/20; 50/50 for sailors	0/100

4c) Ceiling on contributory income (in €1,000/year)	Yes (46)	Generally no (for self-employed 73)	Generally no (for self-employed 146)	Yes (normally 41, higher for miners' fund)	Yes (5 × average wage)	Yes (82)	Yes (AWBZ: 29; ZFW: 29/20 [self-employed])	Not applicable
4d) Other personal contributions to funds (i.e. excluding co-payments to providers)	No	+ nominal premium per capita (varying by fund)[5]	Social security tax (CSG) 7.5% + social debt tax (CRDS) 0.5%	No	No	No	+ premium per capita (varying by fund), mean €345/year[2]	Only premium per capita
4e) Contributions for non-wage earners[3]	Pensioners 11% (7.25% of which pension fund)	Pensioners 3.55%	Pensioners 3.95%	Pensioners: same as for employees	Pensioners/unemployed: flat premium of €32, if on welfare €17/month	Pensioners: same as for employees but higher lower threshold	ZFW: Pensioners on pension 8.45%, on other income 6.45%	Might qualify for tax subsidy

Notes:
1 January 2003.
2 Ranging between €239.4 and €390 in 2003 (Ministerie van Volksgezondheid, Welzijn en Sport 2003b): almost double the amount of 2002.
3 See Table 3.5 for more complete information on this issue.
4 Manual workers 7.9% (50/50) + 2.1% sick pay (100/0), white-collar workers 6.9% (51/49), civil servants 7.1% (44/56), self-employed 9.1%, farmers 6.4%.
5 Small yearly contribution to build up reserves, small monthly sickness fund membership contribution, and a substantial monthly premium for self-employed who opt to have equal coverage as wage-earners (including large risks).

Table 3.2 Number of sickness funds, 1990–2002

	1990	1991	1992	1993	1994	1995	1996	1997	1998	1999	2000	2001	2002	Change 1990–2002[2]
Austria	26	26	26	26	26	26	26	26	26	26	26	25	24	−7.7%
Belgium[1]	119	127	127	121	121	114	116	111	109	107	103	95	94	−21.0%
France	18	17	17	17	17	17	17	17	17	17	17	17	17	−5.6%
Germany[2]		1209	1223	1221	1152	960	642	554	482	455	420	396	355	−70.6%
Israel	4	4	4	4	4	4	4	4	4	4	4	4	4	0%
Luxembourg	9	9	9	9	9	9	9	9	9	9	9	9	9	0%
Netherlands[3]	37	31	27	26	26	27	29	30	28	28	27	25	24	−35.1%
Switzerland	220	203	191	207	178	166	145	129	118	109	101	99	93	−57.7%

Notes:

1 Forming part of seven national associations which are financially responsible for the compulsory health insurance system.

2 For Germany: 1991–2002. 1990 is difficult to compare being from before German reunification; data from 1 January of the corresponding year. 2002 data take into account the 1 January 2002 merger of Groene Land and PWZ (even though they still had a separate nominal premium during that year).

3 Only counted as one sickness fund if merged; 2002 data take into account the 1 January 2002 merger of Groene Land and PWZ (even though they still had a separate nominal premium during that year).

Sources: Austria: Bundesministerium für Soziale Sicherheit und Generationen und Konsumentenschutz (2003b); Belgium: RIZIV (2003a) and Schokkaert and Van de Voorde (2003); France: Meftah (2003); Germany: Bundesministerium für Gesundheit und Soziale Sicherung (2003a); Israel: Gross and Harrison (2001); Luxembourg: Union des caisses de maladie (2003); Netherlands: Vektis (1996, 1998, 2000, 2002) and CVZ/CTZ (2003); Switzerland: BSV/OFAS/UFAS (2003a).

d'Assurance-Maladie). Luxembourg has nine sickness funds – one each for manual workers (CMO, the largest), white-collar workers in the private sector, self-employed, the agricultural sector, civil servants of the state, civil servants of local authorities, manual workers at ARBED, white-collar workers at ARBED, and the Luxembourg railways (Kerr 1999).

The other five countries have competing funds with greatly varying numbers. Israel has, with four, the smallest number of competing funds. The Netherlands has 22 funds (January 2003) with several of them forming part of the same holding company. Just after World War II there were about 250 sickness funds in the Netherlands (Veraghtert and Widdershoven 2002), thus in the Netherlands as well as in Germany and Switzerland, there has been a substantial decrease in the number of separate funds. Each Dutch fund still has a regional stronghold, although these links are weakening (see Chapter 4, Table 4.12). The introduction of limited competition in the mid-1990s led to both mergers and new funds. Another Dutch phenomenon is the fact that many sickness funds have merged with private health insurers to form holding companies with both a statutory and a private arm (Den Exter *et al.* 2002).

In Belgium, there are some 100 funds, organized according to religious and/or political affiliation. All are governed by public law, and all but two groups (the Auxiliary Association and the Railway Association) are members of one of the five sickness fund associations (i.e. Christian, Neutral, Socialist, Liberal, Free and Professional). The association of Auxiliary funds is not organized as a mutual society but is rather state-organized. In addition to those individuals who choose this fund, persons who fail to affiliate themselves with any fund are by law insured by it (Kerr 2000).

In Germany, as a result of competition and the professionalization of fund management (the latter was made mandatory by law from 1993 onwards), the number of funds has been radically reduced from more than 1000 in the early 1990s to 355 in 2002. These have been historically organized on the basis of geographical areas, occupation or employer and are legally classified into seven groups which reflect their origin: 17 general regional funds; 12 substitute funds; 287 company-based funds; 24 guild funds; 13 farmers' funds; 1 miners' fund; and 1 sailors' fund.

In Germany (as in Austria, Belgium, France and Luxembourg), all sickness funds are not-for-profit entities under public law. Besides that legal status, they share a management structure with, as a general rule, equal representation of employers and employees – with differences both between countries (e.g. in France, the ratio between employers and employees in boards is 1:2) and within countries (e.g. in the case of the German substitute funds which are managed by the employees only). Both the composition of the management and supervision boards as well as the decision-making powers of those boards are defined by law; for example, whether they include the right/obligation to determine the contribution rate (see 'The role of the state', p. 58). They are also subject to control either directly by the government or by an agency charged with that responsibility; i.e. the relationship between the state and the sickness funds in these countries is a classic example of 'enforced self-regulation' (cf. Saltman and Busse 2002).

Since the 1990s, the decision-making powers of these SHI decision-making bodies have, as a general rule, decreased. In France, the national parliament now passes a budget for all sickness funds, which is subdivided into 'envelopes' (i.e. sectoral sub-budgets). In Germany, the governmental aim to exercise more control over the types of services included in the benefit catalogue as well as the way they are delivered has paradoxically led to the creation of new self-governmental committees charged with the implementation and actual running of those legal stipulations. Whether the current government's proposal to create a National Institute for Quality in Medicine marks the end of that development in favour of more direct governmental control, remains to be seen.

In Switzerland, the number of insurers offering compulsory health insurance has declined from almost 1000 in 1965 (Beck *et al.* 2003) to less than 100 in 2001. Compulsory health insurance is offered both by sickness funds and by private insurance companies (which may only make profits from the provision of supplementary insurance). Sickness funds can be incorporated under public or private law in various legal forms (e.g. association, foundation, mutuality or not-for-profit stock company).

In all countries except Germany, the sickness funds are supplemented by a national umbrella organization. In the Netherlands, there is a difference between the voluntary association which also includes the private insurers (*Zorgverzekeraars Nederland*) and the statutory Health Care Insurance Board (*College voor zorgverzekeringen*) charged, among others, with the management of the collective resources (Den Exter *et al.* 2002).

Insured persons

The eight countries use different frameworks to define the group of persons insured. France, Israel, the Netherlands (for their long-term care insurance [AWBZ]) and Switzerland have by law universal coverage for their SHI system. Belgium also has universal coverage but as a two-tier system for the 88 per cent in the 'general regime' (with a comprehensive benefits package) and the 12 per cent in the 'regime for self-employed' (for whom the benefits package covers 'major' risks only) (Nonneman and Van Doorslaer 1994).[1] Austria and Luxembourg have *de facto* universal coverage though some persons remain uninsured. In Germany, a large proportion of the population (c. 74 per cent) has mandatory insurance and a small portion is legally excluded (6 per cent)[2] – leaving a third group (mainly employed people with income above a relatively high threshold)[3] with a choice between statutory and private health insurance (PHI). Of the approximately 18 per cent eligible for voluntary SHI membership, about 14 per cent are insured with the sickness funds and 4 per cent privately (Busse and Riesberg 2003). The percentage of voluntary members differs between 2.3 per cent and 37.9 per cent among the 35 largest sickness funds (MedWell Gesundheits-AG 2002).

In the Netherlands, there is a strict legal separation based on an income limit between the mandatory ZFW (statutory health insurance) system and private health insurance (PHI), allowing insured persons no choice between the two systems (Den Exter *et al.* 2002). As the income limit is lower than in Germany, the share of the population insured under ZFW is smaller than in Germany.

Table 3.3 Total sickness fund insured (thousands), 1990–2002

	1990	1991	1992	1993	1994	1995	1996	1997	1998	1999	2000	2001	2002
Austria	7652	7735	7835	7912	7949	7966	7979	7991	7998	8011	8029	8051	8073
Belgium	9690	9724	9960	9930	9945	10040	10055	10084	10030	10070	10100	10130	10166
France	56369	56634	56896	57122	57313	57497	57678	57858	58047	58564	58835	59129	59422
Germany		71281	71975	72165	71710	71886	72132	71601	71373	71283	71257	70948	70815[3]
Israel[4]	4300	4460	4710	4950	5077	5202	5492	5664	5820	5986	6158	6328	6460
Luxembourg	419	429	434	444	455	465	474	486	500	516	535	554	566
Netherlands	9190	9250	9334	9428	9574	9706	9769	9907	9909	9940	10311	10287	10267[1]
Switzerland	6874	6967	7017	7057	7132	7166	7195[2]	7215[2]	7249[2]	7267[2]	7268[2]	7321[2]	7350

Data include nationals living abroad who are insured with a sickness fund.

Notes:

1 Data for January 2002, while rest of the Dutch data are for July.
2 End year values in contrast with the mean values used for 1990–5.
3 Data for 1 January 2002, while other German data are for 1 October.
4 Data do not include insured living abroad for more than one year.

Sources: Austria: OECD (2003); Belgium: RIZIV (2003a) and OECD (2003); France: Eco-Santé France (2003); Germany: Bundesministerium für Gesundheit und Soziale Sicherung (2003b); Israel: Ben Nun (1999, 2003) and National Insurance Institute of Israel (1996; 1997; 1998; 1999; 2000; 2001; 2002; 2003); Luxembourg: Union des caisses de maladie (2003) and OECD (2003); Netherlands: Vektis (1996, 1998, 2000, 2002); Switzerland: BSV/OFAS/UFAS (2003a); estimation for 2002.

Since 1994 the (even lower) income limit for pensioners for inclusion into ZFW was increased considerably, and since 2000 a similar limit applies to the self-employed who previously were excluded altogether.

Relationship between insured persons and sickness funds, including degree of choice

A mandatory relationship between insured individuals and third-party payers that administer payments separately from governmental funds is one of the backbones of SHI systems. The requirement for a relationship may include a fixed assignment to a certain sickness fund or there may be choice. The presence of more funds in a country does not necessarily mean more choice, as demonstrated in the case of Germany where membership of most funds was legally assigned until 1995. In Germany[4] as well as in the Netherlands, almost all insurees now have the right to choose a sickness fund (only farmers, miners and sailors are assigned membership to the corresponding funds in Germany and sailors in the Netherlands), with these countries thus joining Belgium, Israel and Switzerland (see Table 4.11 in Chapter 4). Four of these five countries (all except Belgium) offer choice as part of a policy to increase efficiency through limited competition for insurees. Choice for insurees (and competition among funds for insurees) does not exist in Austria, France and Luxembourg. In these three countries, the assignment is based on two criteria: (1) professional status or employer; and (2) place of residence. If a person belongs to a profession or works for an employer which has its own fund or scheme, he or she will be mandatorily insured with that fund. Otherwise, one belongs to a regionally-based fund (or a local branch of a fund in the case of France).

Where insured persons are entitled to switch between funds, there are differences in how often this is possible. When the Netherlands opened their funds to competition for insurees in 1995, they opted for two-year intervals but subsequently changed to an annual option from 1997. In Belgium, a change is possible every 3 months, in Switzerland every 6 months and in Israel every 12 months. When competition started in Germany, the interval for changing was annual, with a fixed date (30 September) to decide to revoke existing membership which took effect towards the end of the year. As this fixed date opportunity was felt to encourage too many insurees to switch, the opportunity to do so in 2001 (for 2002) was cancelled. Since 2002, change is possible at any time but the interval to remain insured with a particular fund must be 18 months. However, voluntary members, i.e. those earning above the threshold, could always – and still can – move from one fund to another at any time with two months' notice. A decision to leave the SHI system in favour of obtaining private insurance cannot be revoked, however. In the Netherlands – which also has an income threshold for eligibility for statutory membership – high-earning individuals whose income subsequently falls below the threshold are again eligible for statutory coverage. Change is also allowed in the Netherlands and elsewhere (except Belgium) within 1 to 2 months after an increase in premiums, and, if in a regional fund, upon moving out of that region (Austria).

Insurees who are unhappy about the treatment they receive from their SHI system must take their case through a special legal process. The structure and organization of these social, labour, or administrative courts vary considerably among the eight studied countries (Table 3.4). This separate system for legal redress reflects both the unique legal standing of SHI institutions as well as the strong link between SHI and the broader national systems of social insurance within which they sit.

Collecting contributions and other revenue

In the eight studied countries, there is great variety in the relationship between the collection of revenues for health care and the actual payer. The sickness funds are the actual collectors of the contributions only in Austria, Germany and Switzerland. Associations of funds (Luxembourg), or special agencies under government control (Belgium and Israel), or the tax authorities directly (the Netherlands) are other collectors.

In Belgium, most contributions are paid directly to the National Social Security Department (RSZ/ONSS) which in turn redistributes the money to the respective agencies responsible for the administration of different sectors of social security, (e.g. unemployment, health, pensions). The agency responsible for health benefits is the National Institute for Sickness and Invalidity Insurance (RIZIV/INAMI). This institution also collects the contributions of self-employed persons.

Table 3.4 Legal arrangements for SHI, 2003[1]

	Potential path through national courts/tribunals for administrative (health insurance) claims[2]	Potential path through national courts/tribunals for social health insurance (SHI) claims[3]
Austria	(Verwaltungsbehörde) ↓ Verwaltungsgerichtshof	Landes Arbeits- und Sozialgericht ↓ Oberlandesgericht ↓ Oberster Gerichtshof
Belgium	Raad van State/Conseil d'Etat	Arbeidsgerecht/Tribunal du Travail ↓ Arbeidshof/Cour du Travail ↓ Hof van Cassatie/Cour de Cassation
France	Tribunal Administratif ↓ Court Administrive d'Appele ↓ Conseil d'Etat	Tribunal des Affaires de Sécurité Sociale ↓ Cour de Cassation (Chambre Sociale)
Germany	Sozialgericht ↓ Landessozialgericht ↓ Bundessozialgericht	Sozialgericht ↓ Landessozialgericht ↓ Bundessozialgericht

Table 3.4 *Cont.*

	Potential path through national courts/tribunals for administrative (health insurance) claims[2]	Potential path through national courts/tribunals for social health insurance (SHI) claims[3]
Israel	Health funds ombuds/National ombud/State Comptroller/Regional Labour Court ↓ National Labour Court ↓ Supreme Court as High Court of Justice	Health funds ombuds/National ombud/State Comptroller/Regional Labour Court ↓ National Labour Court ↓ Supreme Court as High Court of Justice
Luxembourg	Tribunal administratif ↓ Cour administrative	Conseil Arbitral des Assurances Sociales ↓ Conseil Supérieur des Assurances Sociales
Netherlands	Rechtbank (department: bestuursrecht) ↓ Raad van State (department: bestuursrechtspraak)	Rechtbank (department: bestuursrecht) ↓ Centrale Raad van Beroep/Social-economical: College van Beroep voor het bedrijfsleven
Switzerland	Decision by a cantonal authority ↓ Kantonales Verwaltungsgericht or Besondere Gerichte (e.g. Rekurs-kommissionen, Versicherungs-gericht)/Tribunaux spécialisés (e.g. commissions de recours, tribunal des assurances) ↓ Bundesgericht/Tribunal fédéral or Eidgenössisches Versicherungsgericht/Tribunal fédéral des assurances	Decision by a federal authority ↓ Eidgenössische Rekurskommissionen ↓ Bundesgericht/Tribunal fédéral or Eidgenössisches Versicherungsgericht/Tribunal fédéral des assurances

Notes:
1 In general the countries have different courts if the case's argument is based on constitutional law.
2 The distinction is not perfectly comparable in every country (e.g. the Belgian Raad van State/Conseil d'Etat is very different from the Israeli District Courts) and several of the courts mentioned deal with many more issues than administrative issues.
3 The distinction is not perfectly comparable in every country (e.g. the German Sozialgericht is not exactly the same as the French Tribunal des Affaires de Sécurité Sociale) and several of the courts mentioned deal with many more issues than social issues.

Sources: Association of the Councils of State and Supreme Administrative Jurisdictions of the European Union i.n.p.a. (2003); Bundesgericht (2003); Bundesministerium der Justice (2003); Der Österreichische Verfassungsgerichtshof (2003); Gertner Institute for Health Policy (2003); Raad voor de Rechtspraak (2003); Service central de legislation (2003).

In France, revenues are also collected for several branches of social security, namely by the *Unions de Recouvrement des Cotisations de Sécurité Sociale et d'Allocations Familiales* at the local level which are managed by the social partners, i.e. employers and employees. The money is passed to a national agency, the *Agence Centrale des Organismes de Sécurité Sociale*, which is in charge of managing and allocating the money to the different social security organizations and their branches. In Israel, the contributions are collected by the National Insurance Institute which also receives the national tax allocation before distributing the money to the sickness funds according to an age-adjusted capitation formula.

SHI contributions and other revenue

The financial relationship between the individual and the sickness fund varies and has changed in several countries. The main part of the health care revenue is, in all countries except Switzerland,[5] mainly raised through wage-related contributions which are shared between employers and employees. Nonetheless, there are important differences relating to: a) the uniformity of the rate; b) the ratio of contributions from employer and employee; c) the existence of an upper contribution ceiling; d) the existence of additional non-wage-related revenues; e) the calculation of contributions for non-waged persons; and f) the role of general taxes in funding. These issues are presented in turn.

a) **Uniformity** of the rate. The contribution rate is uniform for all insurees regardless of the sickness fund and membership status in five of the eight countries: Belgium, France, Israel, Luxembourg and the Netherlands. In Austria, rates vary between 6.4 per cent and 9.1 per cent according to employment status but within a given employment status, not between funds. In Germany, on the other hand, the contribution rates differ among funds but not by employment status.[6]

b) *Ratio of* **contributions from employer and employee**. An almost equal distribution of 50:50 between employer and employee exists in Austria, Belgium, Germany and Luxembourg. In France, the split had been 80:20 in the early 1970s, with adjustments to around 70:30 by the late 1980s/early 1990s. With the virtual abolition of the employees' contribution in 1999 in favour of a health tax (see below) it is now nominally 94:6. In Israel, contributions were divided almost evenly between the insured and the employers until 1997. The insured continue to pay contributions (termed a 'health tax'), however, employers no longer contribute directly to health care (as their share has been replaced by increased funding from general taxation since 1998).[7] Thus in Israel the ratio of the direct contribution is now 0:100 – constituting the opposite development in comparison to France. In the Netherlands, employers cover the majority of the ZFW but nothing of the AWBZ – taken together, this amounts to 35:65.

c) *Existence of an* **upper contribution ceiling**. There is a ceiling on contributions in Austria, Germany,[8] Israel, Luxembourg and the Netherlands (different between the two insurance schemes) but generally not in Belgium or France (where it was phased out between 1968 and 1983), where it is limited to the regimes for the self-employed. Ceiling definitions vary, with multiples of social security, minimum wage or average wage limits being the most common forms (in France, Luxembourg and Israel respectively). In other countries it is determined independently of such figures – for example, in Germany or the Netherlands. In these countries, the contribution limit has to be conceptionally differentiated from the threshold for mandatory membership, even though the latter was the same as the former in Germany until the end of 2002 and is very similar in the Netherlands.

d) *Existence of **additional non-wage-related revenues***. There are revenue components in addition to the wage-based contribution in Belgium, France and the Netherlands. In Belgium and the Netherlands, the insured pay a non-income related per capita premium (which varies among funds but is currently only nominal in Belgium) on top of their contributions. These differ in the Netherlands, but have mostly remained uniform in Belgium: only one fund lowered its rate from the usual yearly BEF 90 (€2.23) to BEF 50 (€1.24) in 1998 but reverted in 1999 (Schut and Van Doorslaer 1999). In 2003 it amounted to 12€/year (for further non-income related per capita costs in Belgium see footnote Table 3.1). Through this mechanism, overall contributions vary between funds even though the baseline contribution rate is uniform. France has effectively substituted the employee's part of the contributions with a General Social Levy Tax that is based also on non-wage income; in addition a Social Debt Tax is charged. For both taxes, a uniform rate is applied to everybody making it a proportional source of financing (Sandier *et al.* 2002a).

The reasons for these complementary financing components differ. While increasing the financial base of the funds was the driving force in France (and rhetorically also in Belgium),[9] in the Netherlands it was the introduction of competition among funds which was thought to require some price competition (Normand and Busse 2002).

The opposite of supplementary contributions is also possible. Germany experimented with 'no claim' bonuses – i.e. a partial refund of contributions if no services are used – after 1989 and opened up this option for all funds in 1997, in spite of equity concerns. This was accompanied by the introduction of other market-derived instruments. All sickness fund members were given the right to choose care delivered under the 'reimbursement' rather than the 'benefit-in-kind' principle, thereby enabling them to be treated as 'private' patients. Sickness funds were also given the option to introduce deductibles. These instruments were eliminated by the Social Democratic government that came into power in 1998 on the basis that they were not compatible with the basic solidaristic values of Germany's SHI system. In Switzerland, voluntary no-claim bonuses exist since the early 1990s, but currently apply to only 0.12% (2002) of the population (Bundesamt für Gesundheit 2004).

e) *Calculation of contributions for non-waged and low-waged persons*. Since contributions rely on wages as a basis, the calculation for non-waged persons causes difficulties. For the largest such group – pensioners – contributions vary between countries, both in terms of how much they pay as well as who actually pays the contribution. In most cases pensioners pay the same percentage rate on their pension as employees pay on their income (or, in the case of Switzerland, the same per capita premium). This amount may be split between the pensioner and the statutory pension fund (substituting for the employer) as in Germany and Luxembourg, or it may be placed entirely on the pensioner as in the Netherlands. The contribution rate may also be lower or higher. The former is the case in Belgium where pensioners pay only the employees' part of 3.55 per cent; the latter is the case in Austria with a contribution rate of more than 11 per cent for pensioners. Since Austrian pensioners themselves pay only the average for working members (3.75 per cent), two thirds of their contributions fall on the statutory pension funds (Table 3.5).

For persons with low wages, regulations lead to contributions which are often lower but sometimes also higher than for other employees. In the former category, France and Luxembourg exempt persons below a certain threshold income from any contributions and Israel charges a reduced contribution rate. Germany, however, while exempting the employee from any contributions for monthly wages up to €400 and reducing the contribution rate for wages up to €800, does not provide health insurance to these workers (assuming they either have a second job, that they are covered via other family-related arrangements or are insured via communal arrangements). Employers pay an increased share for wages up to €400. Austria, Belgium and the Netherlands all charge a certain minimum contribution, which in effect raises the actual percentage for persons with low incomes (Table 3.5).

f) *Role of **general taxes in funding***. The common assumption is that SHI countries rely predominantly on wage-related contributions to fund their health systems. In international statistics on sources of health care funding, however, it is often unclear whether expenditure through taxation includes tax subsidies to sickness funds or whether these are included as SHI expenditure. Austria and Switzerland finance a substantial part of hospital care directly through taxation (and therefore have relatively low figures for the expenditure share covered by SHI) while in other countries (e.g. the Netherlands), hospital care is financed exclusively by the sickness funds which in turn receive substantial subsidies from general taxation (see Chapter 9). In Austria, on the other hand, as in Germany, sickness funds receive no tax subsidies (with the exception of the farmers' funds in both countries) although in Germany the 16 *Länder* governments pay for all major capital investments. Besides the Netherlands, tax subsidies – which are paid to the joint sickness funds' institutions – are substantial in Belgium, Israel and Luxembourg. The high Belgian tax component is the result of a deliberate policy change in 1981 when social security contributions were lowered by 6.17 percentage points and VAT was increased in an attempt to become internationally more competitive. Similarly, as mentioned, Israel has replaced employers' contributions by general tax-funding since 1997.

France has a mixed approach in this respect. While its subsidies from general taxes are rather low (and limited to funds with low income/high need members such as the farmers' fund), it has allowed the funds to accumulate sizeable deficits which were covered by the state and are now being paid off through a

Table 3.5 Sickness fund contributions for unemployed, pensioners and persons with low wages (2002/2003)

	Unemployed	Pensioners	Persons with low wages
Austria	6.8% of unemployment benefit. For unemployed without social benefits (including asylum seekers who are recognized as such by the federal state) the government pays.	Contribution of 3.75%. The rest is paid by the social insurance fund that pays the pension.	Below €309.38/month: no compulsory contribution (only accident insurance is compulsory). Voluntary assurance is possible at about €14/month for their illness insurance.
Belgium	Unemployed with and without benefits do not pay, but are covered by the sickness fund of choice. The sickness fund pays.	If worked for more than 15 years: no premiums; if less than 15 years: fixed amount of premiums €17.02 (with dependants: €25.57)/3 months, supplemented by a government subsidy.	Minimum contribution to be insured is based on an income of €4,652.08/year for employees of 21 years[1] and older.[2]
France	General social contribution (CSG) 3.95% of benefits.[3] For those without benefits, expenditure will be pooled and shared among funds.	General social contribution (CSG) 3.95% of benefits.[3]	No contribution if taxable income lower than €6,600/year. Lower contribution rate for low wages (for self-employed: 0.6% until social security limit of €29,184/year; after that 5.9%).
Germany	Unemployment funds pays fully; contribution is based on 80% of pre-unemployment salary.	Retirement funds pays in place of employer, i.e. pensioner pays half out of pension.	Wages below €400/month[4] employers pay 11% and employees 0% for 0–€400/month.[5] (No health insurance provided.) For €400.01–800/month reduced fee.
Israel	Unemployed with welfare pay 3.1% on wages up to half the average national wage, and 4.8% on income beyond that level. Unemployed without welfare pay the minimum health tax of NIS84/month.	Pensioners who are on welfare pay the minimum health tax of NIS84/month. Pensioners not on welfare pay NIS157/month (NIS227 for pensioner couples).	Individuals pay 3.1% on wages up to half the average national wage, and 4.8% on income beyond that level.

Luxembourg	No state benefits: no compulsory coverage. Voluntary assurance is possible at same contribution level as minimum guaranteed income (€1,369/ month).	Same rate as employed, but minimum cut-off point is 30% higher than social minimum wage (€1,779/month).	Below minimum guaranteed income (€1,369/month): no compulsory contribution. Voluntary assurance is possible at same contribution level as minimum guaranteed income.
Netherlands	Nominal contribution independent of income. Social benefit treated as wage (1.7% for employee, 6.75% for employer). No premium discount for unemployed. Unemployed without any benefits have to buy private insurance.	8.45% (same as the sum of regular employer and employee contribution) of general old-age pension (additional funds, when older than 65: 6.45%).	Nominal contribution independent of income and no premium discount for low wages.
Switzerland	Premium payment independent on income, but subsidies are available in case of inability to pay.[6]	Premium payment independent on income, but subsidies are available in case of inability to pay.[6]	Premium payment independent on income, but subsidies are available in case of inability to pay.[6]

Notes:
1 €3,489.06/year for persons under 21.
2 Contributions for widows, some pensioners, some students, and persons registered in the *rijksregister* (government register): €542.88/3 months when income > €26,832.59/year, €271.44/3 months when income between €26,832.59 and €12,482.92/year, €46.02/3 months when income lies between €12,482.92 and €9,338.52/year and no contribution if income < €9,338.52/year.
3 While 5.25 per cent on earned income, capital gains and winnings from gambling.
4 Since April 2003.
5 Most already have a sickness insurance through a second job or through their family. Otherwise the same applies as to the unemployed.
6 A person who is not able to pay his or her premium has to ask the social administration for help. The amount of financial help and the threshold under which one is entitled to be helped varies from one canton to another (no range is available currently, but as a general, not always valid, rule subsidies target to limit sickness fund contributions for a family to 6 per cent of income). Half of the funding comes from the state and the other half from the canton.

Sources: Health Care Systems in Transition profiles. Additional sources: Austria: Bundesministerium für Soziale Sicherheit und Generationen und Konsumentenschutz (2003a, 2003c, 2003d); Belgium: Belgian Federal Ministry of Social Affairs, Public Health and Environment (2003), RIZIV (2003b); France: Sandier *et al.* (2002a, 2002b); Germany: Bundesknappschaft (2003), Minijobzentrale (2003); Israel: Bassan (2003), Chinitz (2003), Rosen (2003); Luxembourg: Ministère de la Securité Sociale du Grand-Duche de Luxembourg (2003); Netherlands: Ministerie van Volksgezondheid, Welzijn en Sport (2003d); Switzerland: Santé Suisse (2003).

special social debt tax – a mechanism through which SHI financing is retrospectively changed into tax financing. To estimate the degree to which countries rely on SHI contributions *per se*, based on wages, two factors have to be combined: the percentage of SHI income generated through wage-based contributions and the percentage of overall health expenditure covered through SHI. Based on such a calculation, Germany and the Netherlands are the only countries that cover more than 60 per cent of total health care expenditure through wage-related contributions. Until 1997, France was the country that relied most heavily on such contributions but, since its shift to a wider base for contributions, the share is now below 60 per cent. Austria and Luxembourg finance a little less than 50 per cent and Belgium even less than 40 per cent of total health care expenditure through wage-related contributions (Normand and Busse 2002). Among the eight countries, the percentage is lowest in Israel (25 per cent).

Pooling and (re)allocating revenue to/among sickness funds

The (re)allocation of resources for health care between the collector and the payer does not occur at all in Austria, since individual sickness funds are both collector and payer (although funds in financial difficulties may apply to the Association of Social Insurance Funds for financial aid). The situation is similar in France, even though there is a compensation scheme among the local branches of the National Sickness Fund and the smaller funds (with lower-paid insured persons) get support from the National Sickness Fund as well as through taxes.

In Belgium, Luxembourg and the Netherlands, the complete national pooling of contributions and a *de facto* joint expenditure (i.e. *ex-post* allocation of contributions according to actual expenditure) was the customary approach before reforms in the mid-1990s. Reforms in Belgium and the Netherlands have led to the gradual introduction of per capita risk-adjusted allocations to the sickness funds. Currently, however, the funds are financially responsible for only a fraction of total expenditure.[10] In Luxembourg, the Union of Sickness Funds directly covers the expenses for services delivered on a contract basis (e.g. hospital care), therefore the *ex-post* approach is used only for services requiring patient reimbursement such as physicians' services.

From 1989 to 1994/5, Germany had a mixed system whereby expenditure for pensioners was covered jointly by all funds while for all other insurees there was no reallocation at all. The introduction of competition between funds in 1996 was preceded by the introduction of a risk adjustment mechanism equalizing both income of insurees and (average) expenditure by age, sex and disability (Busse and Riesberg 2003). With this mechanism, sickness funds have to cover all (actual) expenditures with the redistributed money. Switzerland employs a similar mechanism, with the main difference that the equalization mechanism is limited to each canton, i.e. the high per capita expenditure in Geneva is not shared with the inhabitants of Appenzell with a low per capita expenditure. In both countries, all expenditure needed to cover the uniform benefits basket – i.e. more than 90 per cent of all income – is in theory liable to redistribution.

The risk structure compensation is carried out by the Federal Insurance Office in Germany and the joint organization of insurers offering compulsory health insurance (known as Foundation 18 after the relevant paragraph in the health insurance law) in Switzerland. In Israel, sickness funds receive a capitated amount for each covered individual from the national pool that has been adjusted only for age but there are also special payments for each member with one of five major illnesses (Table 3.6). Age is the only risk adjuster used in all five countries, with the number of age sub-groups ranging from less than 10 (Belgium and Israel) to 92 (Germany) (Van de Ven *et al.* 2003).

Germany, Israel and Switzerland have made the most systematic moves in this realm, as sickness funds have to cover actual expenditure with the risk-adjusted resources that they receive or alternatively increase their contribution rate (Germany) or per capita premium (Switzerland) – or run into deficit as in the case of Israel.

Table 3.6 Risk adjusters in the capitation formulas for (re-)distribution of funds among sickness funds

Country	Year of implementation	Risk adjusters[4]
Austria	None	
Belgium	1995	Age, sex, social insurance status, employment status, mortality, income
France	None	
Germany	1994/5[1]	Age, sex, disability pension status
	2002	Age, sex, disability pension status, inscription into a disease management programme
Israel	1995	Age[2]
Luxembourg	None	
Netherlands[3]	1993	Age, sex
	1996	Age, sex, region, disability status
	1999	Age, sex, social security/employment status, region of residence
	2002	Age, sex, social security/employment status, region of residence, pharmaceutical cost groups
Switzerland (within canton)	1994	Age, sex

Notes:
1 Risk adjustment was implemented in 1994 for the non-retired sickness fund members and in 1995 for the retired members too. In the first five years, the risk adjustment system was separate for East and West Germany.
2 And supplements if insured has one of five major illnesses.
3 90 per cent of the cost of outpatient and production-dependent hospital care of an individual enrollee in excess of €7500 (2003; up from €2042.01 when introduced in 1997) is reimbursed afterwards from an outlier pool.
4 The precise design of the formulas varies largely among the five countries.

Sources: Hermesse and Beeckmans (1998); Schut and Van Doorslaer (1999); Beck (2000); Busse (2001); Buchner and Wasem (2003); Chinitz (2003); Ministerie van Volksgezondheid, Welzijn en Sport (2003c).

Ensuring an equitable financial basis in countries where individual funds are the contribution collectors is difficult. Money needs not only to be allocated according to some criteria but, actually, needs to be reallocated, i.e. the money necessary for compensating one sickness fund has to be taken from another fund. However the better-off funds tend to regard their contributions as 'theirs', so that the issue becomes politically contentious. A second reason is of a more technical nature: the reallocation has not only to take 'need' factors (or other factors determining utilization and expenditure) into account but also the different contribution bases of the funds. Not surprisingly, the topic of 'risk-structure compensation' is discussed fiercely in Germany and Switzerland (though there is more scientific literature on the Netherlands, e.g. Van Barneveld *et al.* 1998; Van de Ven 2001).

Benefit catalogue

One of the central characteristics of SHI systems is the existence of defined benefits to which the insurees are entitled (see Chapter 8). This characteristic was recently reinforced in 2001 in the Netherlands when a court ruled that entitlements (in this case, in AWBZ) had to be guaranteed independent of the costs associated to them. The actual contents of the benefit baskets as well as the processes applied to define them vary between the countries, however, ranging from a list of benefits by law (as in Israel) via decrees (as in the Netherlands) to negotiations between sickness funds and providers (as in Germany). Among the notable difference in the contents is the inclusion of benefits outside acute curative care, especially regarding health promotive measures and long-term care. Germany and the Netherlands have separate social insurance schemes to cover the latter.

Providers

In all eight countries, providers are a mix of public, private not-for-profit and private commercial in status – but almost all are separated from the payers (with the notable exception of Israel). This cannot be considered a necessary characteristic of SHI, however, since many funds originally started as institutions which combined the role of payers and providers. Visible reminders of this are the sickness fund-owned policlinics and hospitals in Austria as well as hospitals in Belgium and Germany (due to its special status, by the miners' fund only) – in addition to the provider network owned and operated by Israel's largest fund, *Kupat Holim Chalit*. In the late 1990s, this integrated approach was sometimes readvocated as 'managed care'. Accordingly, so-called HMOs were established in Switzerland. Somewhat similarly, Dutch sickness funds have been allowed to operate their own pharmacies since 1999 (Van de Ven *et al.* 2003).

Hospitals in Austria, Belgium and Germany are mainly public (with c. 70 per cent, 60 per cent and 55 per cent of beds respectively) with private not-for-profits in second place (c. 25 per cent, 40 per cent and 40 per cent)[11] and a small, but growing private for-profit sector (c. 5 per cent) in Austria and Germany.

France also has mainly public hospital beds (65 per cent) but private for-profits are in second place (20 per cent) with private not-for-profits only in third (15 per cent). Hospitals in Luxembourg are equally divided between public and private not-for-profit. Israel has the most pronounced public-private mix: while 33 per cent of beds are government-owned, 16 per cent are owned by the four sickness funds, 26 per cent by (other) not-for-profit organizations and 26 per cent are private for-profit. In the Netherlands, all hospitals are legally private not-for-profit entities; vertical mergers (e.g. hospitals with nursing homes) happen increasingly. These percentages of different types of hospitals have been determined in all countries by historical developments and have not changed recently as a result of deliberate reform attempts – with the exception of the Netherlands where in 1998 the last public hospitals were transformed into independent not-for-profit entities under private law. (Note: due to a new data collection system, no data are currently available on this issue for Switzerland.)

In all countries except Israel and the Netherlands, both primary and secondary ambulatory care is provided by physicians in private practice – with Belgian physicians directly competing with the outpatient departments of hospitals. In the Netherlands, only GPs are in private practice while specialists are mainly hospital-based (but not hospital-employed). In Switzerland, a limited number of physicians (c. 1 per cent of all ambulatory care physicians) are directly employed by the new HMO-like companies. Physicians are often employees of sickness funds in Israel. Ambulatory care physicians work either on a salary or a contract basis for (one of) the sickness funds, while a minority are employed by hospitals. Many otherwise hospital-employed specialists (for inpatient care) also have private practices, or are employed by private hospitals or other private institutes to provide ambulatory care services.

Relationships between payers and providers

Due to the customary payer-provider split that is a key structural characteristic of all SHI systems – with the partial exception of Israel – contracts have been a standard feature of SHI systems. Traditionally, however, contracting established a fixed and static relationship between sickness funds and providers – it was not intended to be a means of instilling competition.

The changing nature of contracting over the 1990s in some SHI systems thus becomes of particular interest. Such changes build on a varied inheritance both regarding the contract partners and the contract contents (see Chapter 9). In Belgium, France, Israel and Luxembourg, specific benefits are defined by the government, leaving volume and prices to the contract partners (who often do not fix numbers, however). In Germany, a detailed benefits package is negotiated and put into the form of a contract (on the federal level) as well as reimbursement levels or the size of total reimbursement in a given region (except from 1993 to 1995 when total reimbursement levels were set by the government). In 1997 there was a move towards pro-market policies which abolished total reimbursement levels and returned to a pattern of fee for service with negotiated prices. However, this was in turn stopped in 1998 by the then new Social Democratic government (Busse and Riesberg 2003).

In all countries except in Israel and the Netherlands, collective contracts are the prevailing model for non-hospital-services (see Chapter 9). However, collective contracting in one country does not equal collective contracting in another country. First, the term is used ambiguously – both for bilaterally collective contracts between all funds and provider associations as well as for unilaterally collective contracts (as usually in ambulatory care), and between all funds and individual providers (as usually for hospitals). Second, collective contracts may be final and binding (as those between funds and physicians associations in Germany where individual physicians have no contractual relationship with funds), or may require additional unilaterally collective contracts (as between all funds and individual physicians in Austria), or may require the approval of individual providers to be binding (as in Belgium where physicians may reject a bilaterally collective contract). In Israel, since 2001 the four funds must legally negotiate collectively with health care providers; similarly, in the Netherlands, sickness funds still retain collective contracts with GPs.

Collective contracting between all funds and all providers has been the norm in SHI countries, often as a result of governmental efforts to standardize conditions of health care benefits and delivery. In most countries selective contracts are therefore illegal, although Germany has allowed selective contracting under certain conditions since 1997. In the Netherlands, on the other hand, selective contracting has been encouraged since 1992. According to the Anti-Cartel Act of 22 May 1997, collective contracting in health care will – after a period of five years – be *per se* illegal (Den Exter *et al.* 2002). While hospitals were exempted from this regulation during that period, the Anti-Cartel Authority announced after the five years were over that it would in future sue sickness funds that did not contract acute care providers selectively (De Roo 2003).

Regarding the contents of contracts, payment issues receive the most attention. These are, however, the result of a combination of legal or governmental regulations and decision-making by funds and providers through negotiations. Recent changes have included limitations on growth rates of overall expenditure, the introduction of budgets or spending caps for all types of physician, the integration of service definitions for the purposes of reimbursement (to replace individual item reimbursement), and the inclusion of physician services in hospital budgets. In the hospital arena, new measures have included the introduction of explicit budgets and/or the introduction of Diagnosis-Related Groups (DRG) like forms of payment.[12] The principal area of contracting between funds and providers (both physicians and hospitals) in all countries has, therefore, been less on the structure of payments but rather on the details of the structure and, more importantly, the amount of the reimbursement, be they in the form of fee-for-service payments or budgets. Especially in the case of hospitals, the (financing) relationship between sickness funds may be supplemented through direct payments for services from taxes – most visibly in Switzerland where cantons cover 50 per cent of ordinary hospitalization bills (Minder *et al.* 2000).

Capital funding (especially of hospitals) is usually separated from payments for operating costs. Separate payments do not necessarily mean separate payers, however (as capital costs may still be provided by the sickness funds as in the Netherlands). Other countries have mixed systems – such as Belgium where 60 per cent is provided by the regions directly and 40 per cent by the federal government via per diem fees (Kerr 2000) – or place the requirement for capital funding entirely on the public purse (the 16 *Länder* in Germany). There are – not always successful – tendencies in most SHI countries to include at least part of capital investments in operating payments.

In the field of pharmaceuticals, government-led reforms (and not contracts) have primarily included the introduction of reference prices and overall spending caps, as well as the tendency to lower drug prices to the international average (Mossialos 1998; Mossialos *et al.* 2004 forthcoming).

Patient access to providers

There is no 'gatekeeping system' in these SHI countries except in the Netherlands. As a result, patients are free to go to the provider of their choice (Table 3.7). This choice is, however, often restricted by the fact that it is limited to contracted providers. This arrangement ensures that the patient receives a service in kind (as the provider is directly reimbursed by the sickness fund, or through the respective physicians' association in the case of ambulatory care in Germany). While this is the usual situation for inpatient care, only Austria, Germany, Israel and the Netherlands operate this type of system for ambulatory care. Belgium, France, Luxembourg and Switzerland have a patient reimbursement system for ambulatory care, i.e. the patient is invoiced by the physician and reclaims the amount from the sickness fund. Two factors limit the reimbursable amount. First, the physician may have charged above the fees set by the sickness fund in its fee schedule or those agreed upon with representatives of physicians' organizations. Second, from the set fee a certain percentage might be a co-insurance (see below). Austria has a system of contracted ambulatory care providers but allows free access to other providers as well.

In Belgium, France and Luxembourg the system of reimbursement generally leaves patients with a co-insurance of 30 per cent for ambulatory care. Swiss insurees generally have a co-insurance of 10 per cent and a deductible of €157 (and up to €1026 on a voluntary basis). One fifth of the population in Austria generally pays a co-insurance of 20 per cent for ambulatory care. Additionally, if an Austrian patient chooses a non-contracted provider, the reimbursement is limited to 80 per cent of that paid to contracted ones for the same service. In Germany, the patient reimbursement system was an option for voluntary members until 1997 when it became an option for all members. Since 1999, the option has again been restricted to voluntary members. If they choose this option, patients pay both the difference between the reimbursement of patients (at the level of agreed contract payments) and their actual costs as 'private' patients *and* a percentage between 1.5 and 7.5 per cent (differs from fund to fund) of the contract payment which the sickness funds deduct to cover their higher administrative costs. Cost-sharing for ambulatory medical care was introduced on 2004. The Netherlands is the only other country without cost-sharing in ambulatory care, as the charges introduced from 1997 were abandoned after only two years.

In the Netherlands, insurees register with a GP who is partly freely chosen but

Table 3.7 Choice of provider and insurer in eight SHI countries in 2003

	Austria	Belgium	France	Germany	Israel	Luxembourg	Netherlands	Switzerland
GP	YES[1]	YES	YES	YES	PARTLY YES[2]	YES	PARTLY YES[2]	PARTLY YES[3,4]
Ambulatory specialist care	YES[1]	YES	YES	YES	PARTLY YES[2,5]	YES	PARTLY YES[2,6]	PARTLY YES[3,4]
Hospital (inpatient care)[6]	YES	YES	YES	YES	YES	YES	PARTLY YES[2]	PARTLY YES[3,7]
Nursing home[6]	YES	YES	YES	YES	YES	YES	PARTLY YES[2]	PARTLY YES[3,7]
Sickness fund	NO (geographical/ occupational)	YES[8] 1×/3 months	NO (occupational)	YES[9] 18 month interval	YES 1×/12 months	NO (occupational)	YES 1 year interval	YES[7] 1×/6 months

Notes:
Referring physicians (especially in the Netherlands) have an important say in which specialist/hospital a patient goes to. Also there is a small number of private hospitals/clinics/departments that are limited to usage by people with a private (co-)insurance (in e.g. the Netherlands and Switzerland). In addition (e.g. in Austria and Germany) there may be minimum periods of time during which you can't change GP (sometimes consent of the sickness fund is needed as in Austria and of the GPs in the Netherlands).

1 By choosing a physician who is not under contract to the scheme, reimbursement is 80 per cent of the fee of a contracted physician.

2 If the physicians/hospitals have a contract with the sickness fund (in the Netherlands only privately insured and civil servants with public sickness fund arrangements have real free choice).

3 35 per cent of the insured can choose for a HMO or PPO (preferred provider organization) that restricts the patient's choice of physician/hospital (HMOs and PPOs are not offered in every canton). About 8 per cent of the Swiss formed part of a HMO or PPO (2000 data).

4 People do not have free access to physicians outside their canton of residence (exceptions: people working outside a canton have access to physicians at the place where they work, and in case of urgency, have free access to all physicians also outside their canton).

5 The largest sickness fund limits access to specialists to five specialities, while the other three Israeli sickness funds guarantee free access.

6 Referral necessary if no emergency.

7 Only within the canton; there is a limited cantonal list of hospitals and nursing homes for which cost are reimbursed; only in emergency cases and when permission is obtained before treatment can patients get care in hospitals not on the cantonal list of their home canton.

8 Except for railway employees.

9 Except for farmers, miners and sailors.

Sources: European Observatory's Health Care in Transition reports, Weber (2000); Österreichische Sozialversicherung (2002); Beck (2003); Belgian Federal Ministry of Social Affairs, Public Health and Environment (2003); Bundesministerium für Soziale Sicherheit und Generationen und Konsumentenschutz (2003a); Chinitz (2003); Lamers *et al.* (2003); Ministère de la Sécurité Sociale du Gran-Duche de Luxembourg (2003); Ministerie van Volksgezondheid, Welzijn en Sport (2003a; 2003d) BSV/OFAS/UFAS (2003b).

who then acts as a gatekeeper to specialists and to inpatient care. Upon referral, the patient has free choice for the respective type of provider. Of particular interest is the tension between the traditional free access and the recent trends towards managed-care type arrangements, most explicitly in Switzerland, or instruments such as clinical pathways and guidelines or the option for insurees to register on a voluntary basis for GP gatekeeping in Germany since 2000. In Israel, the power to introduce gatekeeping lies with the sickness fund; currently the largest fund limits direct access to specialists to some specialties while the other three funds allow free access.

Inpatient hospital care in all countries is covered through contract payments by either the individual funds or – in Austria and Luxembourg – joint institutions. Patient cost-sharing in the form of co-payments exists in all countries (between c. €4 and 10/day except in Belgium for the first day [€35]). These payments have been introduced or raised during the last ten years (Mossialos and Le Grand 1999). The same is true for pharmaceuticals; in addition, the removal of certain drugs from the benefits package has led to 100 per cent patient cost 'sharing' for a growing number of drugs.

The role of the state

The role of the state in SHI systems is often misunderstood. Commentators outside these countries often consider it to be weak while inside these countries the state influence is seen as a dominating factor. Utilizing the ten-dimension list (see p. 34), one can see that decision-making on many key points lies with the state: the make-up of the decision-making boards as well as their competencies (no. 1); the decision to introduce universal compulsory health insurance or to define groups of the population with mandatory membership (no. 2); whether sickness funds have defined membership or operate in a competitive environment (though the state may leave the decision to define their actual clientele to the funds) (no. 3); how contributions are calculated (no. 4); who collects the contributions (no. 5); whether resources will be pooled and (re-)allocated to the individual funds using a particular formula – or whether expenditure will effectively be done jointly (no. 6); how extensive the benefit catalogue is, whether it's uniform for all funds and who has the actual power to decide on the inclusion of particular services (no. 7); which providers have to be or may be included in the contracts by the sickness funds (no. 8); whether contracting of the providers by the sickness funds will be done collectively or selectively and which rules apply for contracting (e.g. observing global or sectoral budgets or maximum/ reference process) (no. 9); and the conditions for accessing providers in terms of gatekeeping and co-payments/co-insurance rates/deductibles etc. (no. 10).

This is not to say that sickness funds have no decision-making powers – but their degrees of discretion depend on the central framework established by the state. When it comes to setting the contribution rate(s), for example, the national government and/or parliament have a decisive influence in most countries. In France, contribution rates are negotiated between the government, representatives of employees and employers and the social security organizations themselves, but ultimately it is the government that decides. In the Netherlands, the Supervising Board for Health Care Insurance, which runs the Central Funds of ZFW and AWBZ, recommends contribution rates for the following year to the Ministry of Health which has the authority to set the rates. In Austria and Israel, changes in contribution rates must be approved by parliament. Only Germany and Luxembourg have (still) delegated the power to decide upon contribution rates to self-governing bodies[13] – in Germany to the individual funds and in Luxembourg to the Union of Sickness Funds. Their decision is, however, subject to governmental approval. Similarly, Swiss insurers are, under supervision of the Federal Office for Social Insurance, allowed to set their own community-based premiums. The contribution ceilings are amended annually by the government in all countries, taking into account changes in wages. The Belgian and Dutch sickness funds can only set their own per capita premiums.

The executive or legislative branches have good but often competing reasons for their regulations of the SHI organization and financing. Most notably, governments in their stewardship role pursue objectives such as ensuring access, making funding sustainable, ensuring high quality and maintaining social cohesion or solidarity. These four objectives lead to a set of regulated requirements (Table 3.8, left column). Depending on the assessment of the various

Table 3.8 Objectives and instruments to regulate sickness funds (modified/amended from Saltman and Busse 2002)

Regulation to ensure achieving social objectives of access (A), sustainable funding (F), quality (Q) or social cohesion/solidarity (S)	Regulation to facilitate sustainable competitive markets for sickness funds	Regulation that stimulates entrepreneurial opportunities of sickness funds
A: Require contracts between sickness funds and all willing providers	Pool contributions of all sickness funds or install risk-related adjustments of contributions between sickness funds (to lessen market distortion due to risk selection)	Allow the insured choice of sickness fund
A, F & S: Require collective contracts (to ensure equal access and to lower transaction costs)	Require payers to accept all applicants (to lower chance of market distortion due to risk selection)	Allow additional services to be included in benefit catalogue
F: Regulate maximum expenditure for administrative/overhead costs	Mandate annual open enrolment period	Allow differing levels of contributions, per capita premiums, co-payments, co-insurance or deductibles
F: Impose actuarial controls, i.e. regulate minimum and/or maximum reserves and types of acceptable investments	Restrict or define conditions for (horizontal) mergers between sickness funds	Require financial responsibility of sickness fund (i.e. no retrospective cost cover by government or association of funds)

Table 3.8 *Cont.*

Regulation to ensure achieving social objectives of access (A), sustainable funding (F), quality (Q) or social cohesion/solidarity (S)	*Regulation to facilitate sustainable competitive markets for sickness funds*	*Regulation that stimulates entrepreneurial opportunities of sickness funds*
Q: Mandate the evaluation of (new) services before inclusion in the benefit catalogue (health technology assessment)	Restrict (vertical) mergers, acquisitions and running of other health care institutions	Allow/mandate selective contracting
Q & S: Set uniform benefit catalogue/mandate the setting of a uniform benefit catalogue through self-regulatory bodies	Install supervisory agency(ies) to approve contracts/supervise financial behaviour and stability	
S: Require sickness funds to accept all applicants (to enforce right to health insurance)		
S: Mandate community rating or income-related contributions (i.e. not risk-related)		
S: Mandate lower, not cost-covering contributions for poor		

options, governments may, however, choose contradictory instruments to pursue the same objectives: to make funding sustainable, collective contracting may be mandated to avoid high transaction costs in one country, while selective contracting to improve efficiency may be chosen in another so as to stimulate sickness funds to behave entrepreneurially. Consequently, various governments – most notably in the Netherlands and Switzerland, and more recently, but so far less consequently in Germany – have chosen to base part of their regulatory instrumentarium on market-derived instruments (Table 3.8, middle and right columns) as a vehicle to improve quality and efficiency, even though this often clashes with ensuring objectives such as maintaining solidarity (see Chapter 13).

Recent policy developments

As discussed in the first section of this chapter, the eight countries changed various dimensions of their organizational and financial arrangements during the 1990s. Table 3.9 summarizes the most prominent reforms by issue, while Table 3.10 lists the main reforms, their contents and the issue concerned, by country over time. This section does not review developments issue by issue or country by country but rather seeks to identify underlying patterns and trends.

Much of the political and scientific attention has focused on 'financial' aspects, driven by the concern for cost containment and, though often to a lesser degree, increased efficiency. At the same time, these systems were also

Table 3.9 Main changes regarding the ten issues in the eight countries since 1990

	Issue	Main changes
1	Sickness funds	D: requirement for professional management NL: supervision mechanisms restructured
2	Insured population	B, F, ISR, CH: establishment of universal coverage NL: low-income self-employed included in SHI
3	Choice of fund	D, NL: choice of fund newly introduced ISR, CH: choice of fund component of new population-wide insurance
4	Contribution collection	ISR: centralization of contribution collection
5	Calculation/base for contributions and other revenue	F, ISR: revenue base widened (tax instead of wage-based contribution) B, D, F etc.: limitations in contribution/expenditure growth rates B, NL: sickness funds received right to determine per capita premium (on top of wage-based contribution) F: additional forms of revenue introduced
6	Pooling of and allocating to funds	B, NL: less pooling (from full pooling) through introduction of (partial) prospective payments to funds D, CH, ISR: more pooling (from no/little pooling) through introduction of risk structure compensation mechanism
7	Benefits	A, D, L: introduction of long-term care benefits/insurance A, D: introduction of health promotion (partly re-abolished) CH, D, NL: benefits made dependent on evaluation (HTA) ISR: legal fixing of benefits
8	Providers	F: accreditation of hospitals introduced NL: transformation of public hospitals into foundations completed Otherwise little deliberate change (except that long-term care benefits/insurance led to incorporation of new provider types)
9	Payers-providers	Budgets for all sectors or certain important sectors D, NL etc.: quality assurance mechanisms made mandatory NL: replacement of collective by selective contracts (not in inpatient care) L: individal contracts by funds replaced by common contracts
10	Patient access	A, B, D, NL, CH: introduction or increase of co-payments, especially for inpatient care and pharmaceuticals (re-abolished in NL)

Table 3.10 Major health insurance reforms that came into force between 1990 and 2002

Country	Year	Law/Act/Measure	Content	Issue no.
Austria	1990	Co-payment for inpatient stays	The first 28 days – about €6 per day	10
	1992	Price Act	Federal Ministry for Social Security and Generations has been entitled to fix an 'economically justified maximum price' for medicines	9
	1993	Reorganization of funding for long-term care	A new and comprehensive system of long-term care benefits. Entitlement is independent of income, personal wealth or the cause of disability (in 1995 and 1996 a stepwise long-term care insurance was introduced)	7
	1997	Co-payment for primary care doctor visits	€3.6 per voucher	10
	1997	Overall budgeting on states' level	Introduction of a dynamic budget for the health insurance expenses (i.e. inpatient care expenses increase only with the same rate as health insurance revenues)	9
	1997	Reform of health care system and hospital financing	Development of hospital plans into health plan including high-technology and eventually ambulatory care	8, 9
			Introduction of a performance-based, DRG-like reimbursement system for hospitals	
	1998	Expanding the number of insured persons	Part-time workers (with a monthly income of up to €278.40) may make voluntary social insurance contributions in order to establish their entitlements to health insurance and retirement benefits. In addition, insurance coverage is provided for self-employed business people who do not have a licence issued by a professional body (called *Gewerbeschein*) and whose annual income is above a defined level.	2
	1998	Health Promotion Act	€7 million per year will be allocated to health promotion	7, 9

	2001	Flat co-payment for outpatient treatment in hospitals	A flat co-payment of €18.17 per visit in an outpatient department is charged €10.90 if referred by GP or specialist, with an upper limit of €72.67 per person per year	10
Belgium	1990	Law with social provisions	Fixed budget within the health insurance system for each sub-sector of health care, as well as a global budget for the health insurance, activated correction mechanisms if these budget limits were surpassed, increased central government powers of supervision to oversee the new system	9
	1992	Reduction reimbursement	The level of reimbursement for several categories of pharmaceuticals was reduced	9
	1993, 1994	Health financing	Increased fees-for-service	7, 9, 10
			Strict maximum limit of 1.5% on the real growth of health care spending from year to year	
			Reductions in coverage of health care services by statutory insurance	
			Increased co-payments and co-insurance	
	1993– 1997	Co-payment increase	16 increases in out-of-pocket amounts	10
	1994	Bar code introduction	Bar codes on prescriptions, which automatically identify each doctor's prescribing behaviour to detect and control pharmaceutical over-use	9
	1994	System of social and fiscal deductibles	Payment exemptions which established a limit (varying according to patient income) above which health care services were fully reimbursed to redress the inequitable effects of the 1993–4 reductions in health care service reimbursement	10
	1995	Financial responsibility of sickness funds by risk-based capitation formula	Mutualities receive a prospective budget to finance the health care costs of their members, and they would be responsible for an (increasing) proportion of any discrepancy between this budget and their actual spending	6

Table 3.10 *Cont.*

Country	Year	Law/Act/Measure	Content	Issue no.
	1997	Restructuring health promotion	Decentralization and target-setting	7
	1998	Extension coverage	Residence in Belgium is sufficient basis to have the right to reimbursement for health care within the insurance system	2
France	1993	Mandatory medical references	Physicians and health funds agreed on a list of practical mandatory guidelines that doctors have to fulfil in ordinary practice. They are not systematically checked by sickness funds. Nevertheless, they had a great impact as it was the first time physicians and health funds had discussion about medical practice and quality of care and not only about prices	9
	1996	Plan Juppé	A comprehensive attempt to grasp all the aspects of health care (ambulatory care, hospital care and sickness funds' organization) at a time when health insurance experiences a huge financial deficit: <ul><li>a global budget for reimbursed health care is voted annually by the parliament; the government divides this in separate budgets for the different actors</li><li>regional hospitalization agencies are created in order to better organize the supply of hospital beds at the local level</li><li>an accreditation policy for hospitals is set up under the auspices of the ANAES (quality of care national agency)</li><li>some experiments of doctors' networks are launched (cooperative structure between GPs and specialists in order to coordinate health care in some chronic pathologies)</li></ul>	8, 9

		• the respective role of the state and of sickness funds is clarified (at the expense of the latter); the government directly manages contracts re: hospitals (private as well as public), pharmaceuticals and medical devices; only negotiations with health care professionals (about their fees) remain in the competency of sickness funds	
1998	Law on health care financing	Part of the financing of public health insurance is shifted from salary-based social contribution to generalized income tax, the base of which is constituted of all income sources (salary, financial income, real estate income). This tax, named Generalized Social Contribution (CSG), was created in 1990. The rate is a flat rate which was consequently raised from 2.4% to 7.5%. This raise was compensated (for salaried people) by the suppression of social contribution	3
2000	Universal health care coverage	Health insurance is no longer obtained through the professional status but through residence in France. Therefore about 250,000 people who were still not protected or badly protected (for instance non-working divorced women) benefited from health insurance	2, 3
		A free complementary health insurance is provided to the poorest part of the population (about 4.5 million people). Consequently presently covered are: 100% of the residential population for public mandatory health insurance; 92% of the residential population for the optional private complementary insurance	

Table 3.10   *Cont.*

Country	Year	Law/Act/Measure	Content	Issue no.
	2000	Law on the financing of social security	General health insurance scheme is entrusted with the management of ambulatory care expenditure. The pricing negotiation for fee-for-service lists for GPs, specialists, dentists, physiotherapists etc. will no longer be the responsibility of the ministry. To meet cost containment objectives, the general health insurance scheme will be entitled to lower if necessary the price of health care services	9
			Health insurance medical staff may call in patients whose medical consumption is particularly high and suggest a more suitable health care plan to the patient and practitioner	
Germany[1]	1991	Unification treaty	(West) German SHI system with system of sickness funds, corporatist provider organizations, monopoly of ambulatory care for physicians' associations, collective contracting etc. extended to East Germany	1, 2, 5, 7, 8, 9
	1993	Health Care Structure Act	Freedom to choose sickness fund for most of the insured population (from 1996)	3, 6, 7, 9
			Risk compensation scheme to redistribute contributions among sickness funds (from 1996)	
			Abolition of the full cost cover principle for hospitals	
			Increased co-payments	
			Introduction of a positive list of pharmaceuticals (from 1996; but regulation abolished in 1995)	
			Introduction of reimbursement claims auditing of ambulatory care physicians at random	
			New health promotion benefits	
	1996	Statutory Long-term Care Insurance (SLTCI)	SLTCI established as fifth pillar of social insurance, separate from SHI but managed by the sickness funds	7

1997	Health Insurance Contribution Rate Exoneration Act	Exclusion of operative dental treatment and dentures from the benefits catalogue for persons born after 1978 (subsequently abolished from 1999)	3, 7, 10
		Reduction of all contribution rates by 0.4 percentage points on 1 January 1997	
		Reduction of benefits for rehabilitative care	
		Increased co-payments for pharmaceuticals and rehabilitative care	
		Reduction of health promotion benefits	
1997/ 98	1st and 2nd Statutory Health Insurance Restructuring Act	Establishment of a link between an increase in the contribution rate of a sickness fund to an increase in the co-payments for the insured of that fund*	5, 7, 9, 10
		Option for sickness funds to introduce 'no claim' bonus, deductibles and higher co-payments*	
		The option of all insured to choose 'private' treatment with reimbursement by sickness fund at contract rate*	
		Increased co-payments for inpatient care, pharmaceuticals, medical aids, ambulance transportation and dentures (for those still covered)*(partly)	
		Increased possibilities for non-collective contracts between sickness funds and providers	
		Transfer of the responsibility for maintaining and further developing the catalogue of prospective payments from the Ministry of Health to self-government (sickness funds and hospital organizations)	
		Abolition of public committees for expensive medical technology	
		New requirements for HTA in ambulatory care	

Table 3.10   *Cont.*

Country	Year	Law/Act/Measure	Content	Issue no.
			New hospice care benefit	
			Annual amount of €10.23 per insured (not shared with employers) for restoration and repair of hospitals*	
			For operative dental treatment/dentures a privatization of relationship between patient and dentist, i.e. patients have to negotiate services and ultimate prices with the dentist and receive only a flat rate from their sickness fund (from 1998)*	
			Cancellation of the budgets in ambulatory care and the spending caps for pharmaceuticals (from 1998)*	
	1999	Act to Strengthen Solidarity in Statutory Health Insurance	Several reforms (ones with*) of the 1st and 2nd statutory health insurance restructuring act were reversed by the new government in power	5, 9, 10
			Co-payment rates for pharmaceuticals and dentures were lowered	
			Budgets or spending caps were reintroduced for the relevant sectors of health care and in the case of dental care more strictly than ever before	
	1999	Health insurance contribution on low incomes	Introduction of 10% employers' contribution for incomes below €322 per month (employees continued to be exempted)	5
	2000	Reform Act of Statutory Health Insurance	Removal of ineffective or disputed technologies and pharmaceuticals from the sickness funds benefits catalogue	7, 9
			Improvements to the cooperation of GPs, ambulatory specialists and hospitals	
			New corporatist structures created to decide on benefits in hospitals, guidelines etc.	
			DRG payment in hospitals (from 2003)	

Israel	1991	Diagnosis-related payment	Government instituted a prospective diagnosis-related group (DRG)-type payment for 15 major procedures	9
	1995	National Health Insurance Law	Compulsory universal coverage for all Israeli residents in four sickness funds of their choice (rejection of applicants and risk selection became illegal)	2, 4, 6, 7, 9
			Other key components of the law includes: central collection of contributions; institution of risk-adjusted formula for per capita allocations to funds; legal entitlement to a defined benefit package	
			Budgetary ceilings on sickness funds (growth additional to increases in the index of health costs limited to 2% per year; from 1998 an additional increase of 1% per year was allowed for a new technology) and state hospitals	
	1997	Health insurance tax restructured	The employers' tax for health insurance of their employees was abolished	5
	1997	Restriction means of competition	Restriction registration for sickness fund membership to post offices and a ban on advertising	3
Luxembourg	1992	Reform of the sickness insurance system	Sickness funds are tax-subsidized at a far higher rate for pensioners than for the currently employed	5, 9
			Tasks of sickness funds limited to direct contact with insured All other responsibilities (e.g. direct reimbursement to providers) were transferred to the Union of Sickness Funds	
			Definition nomenclature of all medical and nursing acts, and hospital budgeting (abolishment of per diem payment system	
	1998	Insurance to cover the cost of long-term care	Insurance was introduced covering home and institutional nursing care, rehabilitation, home aid, nursing appliances, counselling and other support	7

Table 3.10 *Cont.*

Country	Year	Law/Act/Measure	Content	Issue no.
			for the elderly and the mentally and physically handicapped	
Netherlands	1991	Health Insurance System First Phase Amendment Act (passed 1989)	Sickness funds free to set per capita premium	5
	1991	Price system	Reference price system for pharmaceuticals	9
	1992	Health Insurance System First Phase Amendment Act	Free choice of sickness fund for insured	3, 7, 9
			End of mandatory contracting of self-employed health professionals by sickness funds	
			Shifting of benefits (e.g. pharmaceuticals) from Sickness Fund Act to Exceptional Medical Expenses Act (AWBZ)	
	1994	Van Otterloo Act	Extending access to the Sickness Fund Act scheme for low-income elderly	2
	1996	Pharmaceuticals Pricing Act	Government employs a reimbursement system for pharmaceuticals, which is included in the public sickness fund insurance package and which sets maximum prices	9
	1996	Directive on Sickness Fund Insurance Provisions	Shifting of benefits (e.g. pharmaceuticals, medical aids, rehabilitation) from AWBZ to Sickness Fund Act	5, 7
			Abolition of flat-rate contribution for AWBZ	
	1997	AWBZ	Retirement homes funded under AWBZ	7
	1997	General Co-Insurance Scheme	Sickness fund insured had to pay 20% of the cost of services received (except for costs related to GP care, dentistry and obstetrics). For each day in hospital €4 had to be paid, but an out-of-pocket maximum was set for this new cost-sharing (abolished after two years)	10
	1998	Restructuring Sickness Fund Act	After reaching the age of 65 years, people who were privately insured could opt for a sickness fund, while those with a	2

			sickness fund insurance could continue to be insured under the sickness fund act	
	2000	27 March 1999 Act	Self-employed people up to the age of 65 years who were insured under the Incapacity Insurance (Self-employed Persons) Act and whose gross income is less than €19,650 are insured mandatorily under the Sickness Fund Act	2
	2001	Act amending the 27 March Act	Amended the role, composition and procedures of the administrative bodies governed by the sickness fund act; supervisory board for health care insurance established	1
Switzerland	1996	Revised Federal Law on Health Insurance	Legal obligation on permanent residents to purchase compulsory health insurance	2, 5, 6, 7, 10
			Premiums have to be uniform in one region within one sickness fund/insurer (children and trainees pay lower premiums)	
			Risk structure compensation among funds/insurers in each region	
			Binding catalogue of services which have to be offered within the basic insurance scheme; addition of new services dependent on evaluation	
			Mandatory deductible with an annual maximum	
	2001	First partial revision Federal Law on Health Insurance	Modifications aiming for more uniform implementation of premium reductions for the less well-off. Pharmacists should opt for non-brand name drug, if not explicitly demanded by the prescription	5, 9

Note:
1 If parts of the law are implemented later, this is explicitly mentioned.

quite substantially reformed in pursuit of other, non-financial and/or solidarity-related objectives such as widening coverage and comprehensiveness in order to increase both access and equity.

Most notably, Israel, in 1995, and Switzerland, in 1996, introduced mandatory 100 per cent population coverage by their SHI systems, thereby surpassing countries with a long and established SHI tradition. Belgium (1998) and France (2000) followed by extending their SHI systems to those parts of the population which were still uninsured due to the prevailing principle of actual or past professional status as the basis for sickness fund enrolment. The Netherlands did not expand their ZFW scheme to the whole population but included low-income elderly (1994) and low-income self-employed (2000).

The most important expansion of coverage occurred with regard to long-term care. At least three of the eight studied SHI countries either established separate insurance programmes to fund long-term care or included such benefits in the sickness funds' benefit catalogue: Austria in 1993; Germany in 1996, and Luxembourg in 1998. Two other SHI countries, the Netherlands[14] and France, expanded funding for their previously established elderly care programmes. Thus, with regard to long-term care, the issue of financial sustainability was subordinated to the clearly perceived need to expand publicly financed services to a growing segment of the population – i.e. the elderly. This was true (as de Roo *et al.* note in Chapter 13) despite the difficulty SHI systems are having in identifying and implementing a consistent, integrated approach to the production and delivery of long-term care services.

Typically for SHI systems, the concern about costs is not primarily about health care costs *per se* (e.g. measured as a percentage of GDP or in absolute terms per capita), but the percentage of the funding base needed to fund health care. As the major component of funding health care in the eight countries at the beginning of the 1990s was wages, the contribution rate became a politically sensitive indicator. To prevent this rate from increasing, policy-makers employed various options (beyond allowing the SHI system to run into deficit as in France), such as widening the base for SHI revenue, limiting SHI expenditure and increasing patient cost-sharing.

The widening of the SHI revenue base was most notably pursued in France and Israel. In France contributions are, since 1999, based not only on wages but on all income, i.e. including earnings from rent and capital investments, which in effect changed contributions into a tax. A similar development had taken place two years earlier in Israel where the employers' part of contributions was substituted by funding from general taxation. France also introduced specific taxes on other products and services (e.g. pharmaceutical advertisements and tobacco).

Limiting SHI expenditure was on the agenda in almost all of the studied countries. Global, sectoral and/or institutional fixed budgets or spending caps were introduced or conditions on their application strengthened (i.e. 'soft' budgets were transformed into 'hard' ones). While these instruments varied in structure as well as their intended focus, they serve as eloquent testimony to the desire of national SHI policy-makers to contain aggregate health expenditures. Moreover, as noted in Chapter 1, they also indicate the growing willingness of the state to override the formally self-regulatory character of traditional SHI systems when major national priorities are placed at financial risk. This increasing intervention of the state in the operation of SHI systems raises fundamental questions about the sustainability of these self-managing arrangements in the current period of economic volatility. In addition to the introduction of budgets, the collectivization of contracts between sickness funds and providers was extended, partly to make budgeting more effective, partly to save transaction costs. Luxembourg in 1992 removed all reimbursement of providers from its sickness funds and centralized this responsibility in the Union of Sickness Funds. Similarly, Austria introduced regional pooled funds for hospital care in 1997. Also in Switzerland, there was serious discussion about giving up competition and replacing all sickness funds with only one state-owned and centralized sickness fund (Beck *et al.* 2003).

In contrast – some would say contradiction – to the above-described state regulatory measures, national governments also introduced a number of market-derived changes that were intended to increase competition among sickness funds in the belief that this would increase both efficiency and quality. Choice of sickness fund for the insured (in Germany, Israel, the Netherlands and Switzerland) was introduced and the degree of 'risk-bearing' for the individual sickness funds increased. In the Netherlands, for example, funds have been made responsible for an increasing (from 3 per cent in 1993–5 to 35 per cent since 1999) if still relatively small proportion of their total operating revenues (Schut and Van Doorslaer 1999; Okma and Poelert 2001). This is intended to increase internal pressures on sickness funds to use existing revenues more efficiently. Both Israel and Switzerland also incorporated risk-related pressures on their sickness funds when they established their national SHI structures respectively in 1995 and 1996. However, in order to avoid the danger of cream-skimming potential members under such circumstances, complex mechanisms of adjusting revenues available to each sickness fund were needed. In Germany, for example, a complex risk-adjustment formula with over 700 categories is used to reallocate a portion of revenues retrospectively at the end of the budget year from those sickness funds with low illness rates to those with higher rates (Busse 2001). These risk-adjustment efforts (see Table 3.5), increasingly prevalent in the SHI countries examined, are designed to mitigate some of the inequalities, caused by cream-skimming, that potentially might emerge along with the introduction of sick fund based risk-bearing responsibility.

A particular common concern about financial sustainability concerned pharmaceuticals. Here, policy was complicated and occasionally tentative due to the presence of large pharmaceutical firms in several of these countries (particularly Germany and Switzerland) and the consequent need for national policy-makers to balance health-related financial concerns with industrial policy objectives to retain and expand pharmaceutical research and production facilities within their national borders. Nonetheless, rapidly growing pharmaceutical expenses have led most SHI countries to adopt a variety of restrictive measures such as reference pricing, positive lists (Mossialos *et al.* 2004 forthcoming) and promoting generic drug prescription.

The final financial pattern concerns increased reliance on out-of-pocket co-payments by patients at the point of service. Although such payments are highly regressive as revenue-raising mechanisms (Barer *et al.* 1998; Evans 2002) and are not considered to be clinically appropriate tools of demand moderation (Kutzin 1998; Robinson 2002), they continue to grow as national policy-makers search for short-term financial solutions. Germany increased co-payments in 1993 and 1997 (although several were subsequently lowered in 1998). Switzerland, in 1996, introduced mandatory co-payments with a legal maximum. Belgium increased out-of-pocket amounts 16 times between October

1993 and April 1997 (Peers 1999 as in Louckx 2002) (although subsequently reduced them for certain groups in 1994). Austria, in 2001, required outpatient hospital co-payments with an annual maximum. In the Netherlands, in 1997, out-of-pocket payment (co-payments for hospital stay and specialist care; with a maximum) was increased – but abolished only two years later (Louckx 2002). Also in Israel, the 1998 legislation allowed co-payments to be introduced and to increase at a controlled rate.

Looking at these varying instruments, two opposing trends become visible: on the one hand, SHI systems pursued greater financial stability through an increased role for the state, typically via increased intervention in the heretofore relatively separate corporatist process of SHI self-regulation. An extreme example of this intervention, in operating matters, could be seen in Belgium, where, in response, the employers in 2002 stopped participating in the annual budget negotiations, believing that such traditional corporatist activity had been superseded by the state. Other forms of strong intervention could be seen in France and, to a lesser degree, in Germany and the Netherlands. In Israel and Switzerland, the state stepped in to fundamentally restructure the funding system through new national legislation.

On the other hand, a number of the studied countries sought to introduce or strengthen more explicitly market-oriented forms of incentives and, in some instances, market-oriented structures. This appeared to be influenced by a school of economic thought which argued that traditional administrative arrangements generated a more expensive system and/or patient behaviour than would a more market-oriented approach. Examples here include the adoption of 'no use rebates' on premiums in Switzerland and (although subsequently dropped) in Germany, as well as continued efforts in the Netherlands to increase the percentage of total funding for which sickness funds were 'at risk'. These were accompanied by expansions of choice among sickness funds in the Netherlands (1992) and Germany (1996), as well as efforts to introduce limited forms of selective (rather than comprehensive) contracting of providers such as hospitals. In the Netherlands, market-driven efforts to open funds to competition led to the introduction of a per capita premium – which differs between funds – on top of the income-related contribution, which created the potential for contribution differences between sick funds. In Germany, on the other hand, the introduction of a 'risk structure compensation mechanism' to ensure equal market conditions for all funds before opening them to competition – and not competition between funds *per se* – has narrowed traditional differences in contributions by individuals to funds.

The overall picture that emerges from the multiple measures examined in this chapter is both multi-faceted and complex. The eight studied SHI countries vary considerably along specific dimensions, reflecting diverse histories and quite different national norms and values that serve to underpin the organization of their health funding and delivery arrangements. As Chapter 2 suggests, this is not surprising given the range of countries reviewed, and speaks to the broadly diverse character of SHI as a conceptual model. Perhaps even more so than with tax-funded systems, there are numerous ways to construct an SHI system, and, as a result, observations about the 'average' or 'typical' SHI configuration often require substantial oversimplification.

Underneath these different national configurations, however, there are nonetheless certain clear patterns. One such pattern, as discussed in Chapter 2, is a common commitment (even if variously interpreted) to the concept of solidarity, and, more fundamentally, a grounding of these different health systems in its resilience and long-term survival. One visible symbol of this commitment was the 'export' of the West German SHI organizational and financial arrangements into East Germany upon reunification (Busse and Nolte 2003).

In this chapter, beyond all the particularities, there are specific patterns that emerge from assessing the policy experience for these eight systems over the 1990s. However, the application of both stronger state and stronger market measures suggests an overall policy ambivalence about how best to proceed. Much as in tax-funded systems (Saltman and Figueras 1997; Le Grand *et al.* 1998), one can see an effort by national policy-makers to step carefully as they moved forward in what they perceived to be uncharted territory.

Notes

1   Since historically the SHI system is a work-related insurance programme, population-wide coverage was not the original intention. While coverage has been gradually expanded to non-working parts of the population in all countries, the achievement of population-wide coverage is only a very recent phenomenon, being introduced in Israel in 1995 (Gross and Harrison 2001), in Switzerland in 1996, in Belgium in 1998 and in France in 2000. As a partial exception here, the Netherlands introduced their AWBZ insurance on a population-wide basis already in 1968.

2   Self-employed people are excluded from SHI unless they have been a member previously (except those who fall under mandatory SHI cover like farmers), and active and retired permanent public employees such as teachers, university professors, employees in ministries etc. are excluded *de facto* as they are reimbursed by the government for most of their private health care bills (they receive private insurance to cover only the remainder). The Reform Act of SHI 2000 widened the group of excluded persons by excluding privately insured persons above 55 years who would, through a falling income (e.g. through reduced working hours), fall in the mandatory membership group. This was done to stop these persons from a deliberate return to SHI (Busse and Riesberg 2003).

3   €41,400 (2003) to be raised to €46,350 in 2004.

4   Not all sickness funds are open to new applicants, however: company-based sickness funds may choose to remain closed, thus creating a form of risk selection (Buchner and Wasem 2003).

5   Since the introduction of compulsory health insurance from 1996, Switzerland has a system of both income- and risk-unrelated per capita health insurance premiums. These differ between insurers but are community-rated for all insured of a particular insurer in a certain region (usually the canton) (Minder *et al.* 2000).

6   There are certain exceptions to this rule: the largest group treated differently were pensioners until July 1997 since their contributions were based uniformly on the average contribution rate of all funds. For that purpose, the average rate on each 1 January was used for half a year both retro- and prospectively (i.e. from 1 July of the previous year until 30 June). Since 1999, there is a legal uniform rate of 10 per cent for all workers below a threshold of Euro 325 – a group which was not mandatorily insured before. Students are another exception to the rule as they pay a uniform per capita premium (Busse and Riesberg 2003).

7 In 1999, 48 per cent of the national health expenditure came from general taxation, 25 per cent from the 'health tax' and 27 per cent from direct payments for services and medicines by patients (Gross and Harrison 2001).

8 The only exemption being the ceiling for miners (mandatorily insured in the miners' fund) which is one third higher than that which applies normally.

9 To ease the financial burden on employers (and not for the sake of competition among funds), Germany also introduced a flat per capita premium on top of the income-related contributions in 1997. This was abolished after the change of the parliamentary majority in 1998, however.

10 In Belgium, the prospective allocation amounted to 10 per cent of the total health care budget for 1995–7 and was raised to 20 per cent for 1998–2000 and 30 per cent since 2001. Since the funds are, however, only financially responsible for 15 per cent, 20 per cent and 25 per cent of that allocation in the respective years, the actual percentages 'at risk' amounted to only 1.5 per cent, 4 per cent and 7.5 per cent. In the end, however, sickness funds are responsible for only 25 per cent of, maximally, the first 2 per cent of over-spending (Hermesse and Beckmans 1998; Breda 2003). The Netherlands went ahead more rapidly, from 3 per cent in 1993–5 to 15 per cent in 1996, 27 per cent in 1997, 29 per cent in 1998 and 35 per cent in 2000 – but a special provision that expenses for extremely expensive patients are shared provides a 'safety net' for the funds (Den Exter *et al.* 2002).

11 These numbers include the hospitals which are owned and managed by the sickness funds (c. 8 per cent in Austria and 5 per cent in Belgium).

12 These policy requirements may still leave some room for negotiations and contracts between funds and providers, though. For example, in December 1999, German legislators decided in the new law of SHI 2000 that hospital reimbursement has to be DRG-based from 2003. The only requirement the law made was that the DRG system chosen should already be established somewhere, while the decision on the actual system was left to the contracting partners (hospital organization and sickness fund associations). On 30 June 2000, they decided to adopt the Australian Refined DRGs. This contrasts with the Austrian and the French experience where DRG-type systems were developed inside the countries.

13 In Belgium, decision-making by the sickness funds on the contribution rates was replaced by governmental decision-making in 1963.

14 This reflects a 2001 court judgment that care within the AWBZ had to be guaranteed, no matter the costs. Since then human resources has been the main restriction rather than finances.

References

Association of the Councils of State and Supreme Administrative Jurisdictions of the European Union i.n.p.a. (2003) Personal communication with C. Morel, 3 June.

Barer, M., Evans, R.G., Hertzman, C. and Johri, M. (1998) *Lies, Damned Lies and Health Care Zombies: Discredited Ideas that will not die.* HPI Discussion Paper #10 (March). Texas: Health Policy Institute, University of Texas – Houston Health Science Center.

Bassan, S. (2003) Personal communication, 8 September.

Beck, K. (2000) Growing importance of capitation in Switzerland, *Health Care Management Science*, 3(2): 111–19.

Beck, K. (2003) Personal communication, 16 September.

Beck, K., Spycher, S., Holly, A. and Gardiol, L. (2003) Risk adjustment in Switzerland, *Health Policy*, 65: 63–74.

Belgian Federal Ministry of Social Affairs, Public Health and Environment (2003) *Beknopt overzicht van de sociale zekerheid in België*, http://socialsecurity.fgov.be/overzicht/2003/ (accessed 17 September 2003).

Ben Nun, G. (1999) *Distribution of Members Between Health Plans Before and After National Health Insurance, 1950–1998*. Jerusalem: Ministry of Health.

Ben Nun, G. (2003) Personal communication, 21 September.

Breda, M. (2003) Personal communication with spokesperson RIZIV, April and June.

BSV/OFAS/UFAS (2003a) *Assurance Obligatoire des Soins: Assurés et Assureurs de 1990 à 2001*, http://www.bsv.admin.ch/statistik/details/f/svs/am_5_1.pdf (accessed 18 September 2003).

BSV/OFAS/UFAS (2003b) *Die obligatorische Krankenversicherung kurz erklärt*, http://www.bsv.admin.ch/kv/beratung/d/wegweiser_01.htm (accessed 25 August 2003).

Buchner, F. and Wasem, J. (2003) Needs for further improvement: risk adjustment in the German health insurance system, *Health Policy*, 65: 21–35.

Bundesamt für Gesundheit (2004) Statistiek der obligatorische Krankenversicherung 2002. Table 1.05. Bern: Bundesamt für Gesundheit. http://www.bag.admin.ch/kv/statistik/d/2004/KV_2002.pdf (accessed 23 April 2004).

Bundesgericht (2003) Personal communication with J. Vocanson, 19 June.

Bundesknappschaft (2003) Personal communication with S. Schröder, spokesperson of bundesknappschaft, September.

Bundesministerium der Justice (2003) Personal communication with U. Gerder, 27 May.

Bundesministerium für Gesundheit und Soziale Sicherung (2003a) *Zahl der Gesetzliche Krankenkassen*, http://www.bmgs.bund.de/download/statistiken/stattb2002/09/9.04.pdf (accessed 18 September 2003).

Bundesministerium für Gesundheit und Soziale Sicherung (2003b) *Zahl der Versicherte einschließlich Rentner nach Kassenarte*, http://www.bmgs.bund.de/download/statistiken/stattb2002/09/9.14.pdf (accessed 18 September 2003).

Bundesministerium für Soziale Sicherheit und Generationen und Konsumentenschutz (2003a) Personal communication with H. Rack, January, 29 August and 9 September.

Bundesministerium für Soziale Sicherheit und Generationen und Konsumentenschutz (2003b) Personal communication with J. Stefanits, 20 February and 22 May.

Bundesministerium für Soziale Sicherheit und Generationen und Konsumentenschutz (2003c) Personal communication with M. Pöltl, 29 September.

Bundesministerium für Soziale Sicherheit und Generationen und Konsumentenschutz (2003d) Personal communication with L. Recnik on behalf of Mag. Bettelheim, 17 March.

Busse, R. (2001) Risk adjustment compensation in Germany's statutory health insurance, *European Journal of Public Health*, 11(2): 174–77.

Busse, R. and Nolte, E. (2003) New citizens: East Germans in a united Germany, in J. Healy and M. McKee (eds) *Health Care and Minority Populations*. Oxford: Oxford University Press.

Busse, R. and Riesberg, A. (2003) *Health Care Systems in Transition – Germany*. Copenhagen: European Observatory on Health Care Systems.

Chinitz, D. (2003) Personal communication, February.

CVZ/CTZ (2003) Personal communication with M. Hagen on behalf of C. Oranje, 27 February 2003.

De Roo, A.A. (2003) Personal communication, 24 April and August.

Den Exter, A., Hermans, H., Dosjlak, M. and Busse, R. (2002) *Health Care Systems in Transition – The Netherlands*. Copenhagen: European Observatory on Health Care Systems.

Der Österreichische Verfassungsgerichtshof (2003) Personal communication with R. Müller, 3 June.

Eco-Santé France (2003) *Les données de la base*, http://www.credes.fr/ecosante/francedata.htm (accessed 16 September 2003).

Evans, R.G. (2002) Financing healthcare: taxation and the alternatives, in E.A. Mossialos, A. Dixon, J. Figueras and J. Kutzin (eds) *Funding Health Care: Options for Europe*, pp. 31–58. Buckingham: Open University Press.

Gertner Institute for Health Policy (2003) Personal communication with S. Bassan (unit for Health Rights and Ethics), July.

Gross, R. and Harrison, M. (2001) Implementing managed competition in Israel, *Social Science and Medicine*, 52: 1219–31.

Hermesse, J. and Beeckmans, J. (1998) L'assurance soins de santé: organisation financement et remboursement, *Journal d'economie medicale*, 16: 5–20.

Hofmarcher, M. (2001) *Health Care Systems in Transition – Austria*. Copenhagen: European Observatory on Health Care Systems.

Kerr, E. (1999) *Health Care Systems in Transition – Luxembourg*. Copenhagen: European Observatory on Health Care Systems.

Kerr, E. (2000) *Health Care Systems in Transition – Belgium*. Copenhagen: European Observatory on Health Care Systems.

Kutzin, J. (1998) The appropriate role for patient cost-sharing, in R.B. Saltman, J. Figueras and C. Sakellarides (eds) *Critical Challenges for Health Care Reform in Europe*, pp. 78–112. Buckingham: Open University Press.

Lamers, L.M., Van Vliet, R.C.J.A. and Van de Ven, W.P.M.M. (2003) Risk adjustment premium subsidies and risk sharing: key elements of the competitive sickness fund market in the Netherlands, *Health Policy*, 65: 49–62.

Le Grand, J., Mays, N. and Mulligan, J. (1998) *Learning from the NHS Internal Market*. London: King's Fund.

Louckx, F. (2002) Patient cost sharing and access to healthcare, in J. Mackenbach and M. Bakker (eds) *Reducing Inequalities in Health – a European Perspective*. London: Routledge.

MedWell Gesundheits-AG (2002) *Vergleichende Untersuchung der Satzungsregelungen der 35 größten Krankenkassen zum Wahlrecht auf Kostenerstattung*, http://www.medwell.de/download/kassenvergleich_uebersicht.pdf (accessed 3 June 2003).

Meftah, V. (2003) Personal communication with French social security representative, May 2003.

Minder, A., Schoenholzer, H. and Amiet, M. (2000) *Health Care Systems in Transition – Switzerland*. Copenhagen: European Observatory on Health Care Systems.

Minijobzentrale (2003) *Was sich 2003 ändert*, http://www.minijobzentrale.de/4_Service/Download-Center/Arbeitnehmerflyer.pdf (accessed 30 August 2003).

Ministère de la Securité Sociale du Grand-Duche de Luxembourg (2003) *Parametres Sociaux*, http://www.etat.lu/MSS/paramsoc.htm (accessed 25 August 2003).

Ministerie van Volksgezondheid, Welzijn en Sport (2003a) Personal communication with M. Van Uchelen, August.

Ministerie van Volksgezondheid, Welzijn en Sport (2003b) *Ziektekostenverzekeringen in Nederland: Stand van zaken per 1 Januari 2003 [Sickness fund insurances in the Netherlands: current state per 1 January 2003]*. Den Haag: Ministerie van Volksgezondheid, Welzijn en Sport.

Ministerie van Volksgezondheid, Welzijn en Sport (2003c) Personal communication with W. de Haart, August and 22 September.

Ministerie van Volksgezondheid, Welzijn en Sport (2003d) Personal communication with E. van den Berg, 24 and 25 September 2003.

Mossialos, E. (1998) Regulating expenditure on medicines in European Union countries, in R.B. Saltman, J. Figueras and C. Sakellarides (eds) *Critical Challenges for Health Care Reform in Europe*, pp. 261–86. Buckingham: Open University Press.

Mossialos, E. and Le Grand, J. (1999) Cost containment in the EU: an overview, in E. Mossialos and J. Le Grand (eds) *Health Care and Cost Containment in the European Union*, pp. 1–154. Aldershot: Ashgate.

Mossialos, E., Mrazek, M. and Walley, T. (eds) (2004 forthcoming) *Regulating the Cost and use of Pharmaceuticals in Europe*. Buckingham: Open University Press.

National Insurance Institute of Israel (1996, 1997, 1998, 1999, 2000, 2001, 2002, 2003) *Annual Survey*. Jerusalem: National Insurance Institute of Israel.

Nonneman, W. and Van Doorslaer, E. (1994) The role of the sickness funds in the Belgian healthcare market, *Social Science and Medicine*, 39(19): 1483–95.

Normand, C. and Busse, R. (2002) Social health insurance financing, in E. Mossialos, A. Dixon, J. Figueras and J. Kutzin (eds) *Funding Health Care – Options for Europe*, pp. 59–79. Buckingham: Open University Press.

OECD (2003) *OECD Health Data 2003: A Comparative Analysis of 30 Countries*, 2nd edn. Paris: OECD.

Okma, K. and Poelert, R. (2001) Implementing prospective budgeting for Dutch sickness funds, *European Journal of Public Health*, 11(2): 178–81.

Österreichische Sozialversicherung (2002) *Soziale Sicherheit: 2002 Special Issue*, http://www.sozialversicherung.at/media/12458.PDF (accessed 27 August 2003).

Peers, J. (1999) *Gezondheid in België: uitdagingen en opportuniteiten* (*The Belgian Healthcare System: Challenges and Potentialities*). Brussels: Ministerie van Sociale Zaken.

Raad voor de Rechtspraak (2003) Personal communication with M. Boer, 18 June.

RIZIV (2003a) Personal communication with L. Van Damme, RIZIV (Rijksinstituut voor Ziekte- en invaliditeitsverzekering), Dienst bijdragebescheiden, Administratieve cel en Ledentallen, February.

RIZIV (2003b) Personal communication with E. Teunkens, RIZIV (Rijksinstituut voor Ziekte- en invaliditeitsverzekering), 14 and 15 October.

Robinson, R. (2002) User charges in healthcare, in E.A. Mossialos, A. Dixon, J. Figueras and J. Kutzin (eds) *Funding Health Care: Options for Europe*, pp. 161–83. Buckingham: Open University Press.

Rosen, B. (2003) Personal communication, March 2003.

Saltman, R.B. and Busse, R. (2002) Balancing regulation and entrepreneurialism in Europe's health sector: theory and practice, in R.B. Saltman, R. Busse and E. Mossialos (eds) *Regulating Entrepreneurial Behaviour in European Health Care Systems*, pp. 3–52. Buckingham: Open University Press.

Saltman, R.B. and Figueras, J. (eds) (1997) *European Health Care Reform: Analysis of Current Strategies*. Copenhagen: WHO.

Sandier, S., Polton, D. and Paris, V. (2002a) *Health Care Systems in Transition: France*. Copenhagen: European Observatory on Health Care Systems.

Sandier, S., Polton, D., Paris, V. and Thomson, S. (2002b) France, in A. Dixon and E. Mossialos (eds) *Health Care Systems in Eight Countries: Trends and Challenges*. Copenhagen: European Observatory on Health Care Systems.

Santé Suisse (2003) Personal communication with U. Müller, 24 September.

Schokkaert, E. and Van de Voorde, C. (2003) Belgium: risk adjustment and financial responsibility in a centralised system, *Health Policy*, 65: 5–19.

Schut, F.T. and Van Doorslaer, E.K.A. (1999) Towards a reinforced agency role of health insurers in Belgium and the Netherlands, *Health Policy*, 48(1): 47–67.

Service central de legislation (2003) Personal communication with J-L. Schleich, 11 June.

Union des caisses de maladie (2003) Personal communication with Jean-Marie Rossler on behalf of Robert Kieffer, February and June.

Van Barneveld, E.M., Lamers, L.M., Van Vliet, R.C.J.A. and Van de Ven, W.P.M.M (1998) Mandatory pooling as a supplement to risk adjusted capitation payments in a competitive health insurance market, *Social Science and Medicine*, 47(2): 223–32.

Van de Ven, W.P.M.M. (2001) Risk selection on the sickness fund market, *Health Economics in Prevention and Care*, 2: 91–5.

Van de Ven, W.P.M.M., Beck, K., Buchner, F. *et al.* (2003) Risk adjustment and risk selection on the sickness fund market in five European countries, *Health Policy*, 65(1): 75–98.

Vektis (1996) *Zorgmonitor 1996*. Zeist: Vektis.

Vektis (1998) *Zorgmonitor 1998*. Zeist: Vektis.

Vektis (2000) *Zorgmonitor 2000*. Zeist: Vektis.

Vektis (2002) *Zorgmonitor 2002*, http://www.vektis.nl/busa/busa.htm. Zeist: Vektis.

Veraghtert, K. and Widdershoven, B. (2002) *Twee eeuwen solidariteit: De Nederlandse, Belgische en Duitse ziekenfondsen tijdens de negentiende en twintigste eeuw* [*Two centuries of solidarity: the Dutch, Belgian and German sickness funds during the nineteenth and twentieth century*] Amsterdam: Aksant.

Weber, A. (2000) HMOs und Hausartzmodelle [HMOs and GP models], *Lehrgang Gesundheitswesen Schweiz*, Chapter 4.4, http://www.medpoint.ch/other/LehrgangGW/lehrg_permanent_content.html (Accessed 17 June 2003).

four

Patterns and performance in social health insurance systems

Josep Figueras, Richard B. Saltman,
Reinhard Busse and Hans F. W. Dubois

Introduction

The complex, often divergent organizational arrangements within social health insurance (SHI) systems make them difficult to assess and evaluate. While this dilemma affects other health care systems as well, precisely the core characteristics that define SHI systems – e.g. pluralist, corporatist, self-regulatory – tend in practice to further complicate the assessment process. This chapter collects and reviews available quantitative data about SHI systems, looking for patterns of activity that make it possible to assess the performance of these systems along four key parameters: health status, satisfaction/responsiveness, equity and efficiency. As noted in Chapter 1 above, this conceptual framework is better tailored to examining key elements of the eight studied SHI systems than is the more globally focused tri-partite framework put forward by WHO in the World Health Report 2000 (WHO 2000). The parameters used here were selected as measures generally agreed by experts to be important to the functioning of a good health system, as well as for their political importance to national decision-makers in the formulation of health policy. The logic of their presentation is designed to look first at three parameters of outcomes achieved (health status, satisfaction/responsiveness, equity), and then to consider data regarding expenditures made to achieve these reported outcomes (efficiency). The objective of the chapter is to examine the degree to which it is possible to measure the performance of SHI systems along these four parameters, and the extent to which the available data allows us to draw useful observations about SHI systems generally.

Data about the eight SHI countries are presented in a comparative format, contrasting available information about these health systems with that from a group of peer counterpart systems in western Europe. The selection of this counterpart group of countries was guided by several structural considerations. Since six of the eight SHI countries are member states of the European Union (EU), with seven of the eight being in western Europe, the comparison group has been composed of the nine remaining western European member states of the EU, plus Norway, for a total of ten. All ten countries in this comparison group have predominantly tax-funded health care systems. Further, these ten countries have been divided, where useful, into two groups – northern European tax-based (six countries) and southern European tax-based (four countries). This two-part approach allows readers to consider the impact of per capita GDP on the observed results (the eight SHI countries and the six northern European tax-funded countries all have relatively high levels). It also, in most cases (Denmark is an exception), reflects the longer experience of the northern European group with tax-funded structures: the southern European countries shifted to predominantly tax-funded systems in the late 1970s and the 1980s.

The approach taken by this chapter on four technical issues may be helpful in interpreting the data it presents. The first technical matter concerns the general labels used to identify the compared systems. As discussed in Chapter 1, there has been some (to date inconclusive) debate within the comparative health systems research community about the appropriateness of labelling health systems according to their funding source (e.g. SHI vs. tax-funded systems). Moreover, Chapters 1 and 2 both demonstrate that the overall role of SHI in the eight studied countries is substantially greater than just as a funding mechanism, referring to a complex set of social relationships and activities, supported with strong but sympathetic regulatory supervision by the state. Therefore, given the absence of an agreed alternative nomenclature, this chapter continues the pattern adopted throughout this volume of referring to SHI and tax-funded health systems with the understanding that these terms refer to the entire system, not just their funding mechanisms.

A second technical concern revolves around numerous difficulties with the quality of the available quantitative data. The OECD data presented below, for example, reflect four different levels of compliance by western European countries with its May 2000 health accounts reporting system (OECD 2003). In some instances, the last 2003 OECD data is from 1995 – e.g. eight years earlier. Further, since Israel is not a member of either OECD or the EU, some data is not collected by the same methodology or is not available. In the area of satisfaction/responsiveness, available data suffers from systematic flaws due to the subjective character of the data itself as well as the inherent limitations of survey research methodologies. Lastly, health system activity is typically responsible for only a small segment of observed changes in overall health status – although recent clinical developments may have increased the contribution of curative health care (McKee 2001). All these concerns necessarily limit the results presented below.

A third technical matter is the use of what is termed 'relative order' in the tables. These numerical sequences are presented as a way to make differences between countries easier to see, especially in tables that present more than one data series. They are not intended to rank individual countries, or to make any normative judgements with regard to health system performance.

The fourth, last, technical concern reflects the limitations of exclusively quantitative data in supporting assessments about the reasons that explain the observed results. Health systems are highly complex organizations, and useful statements about observed behaviour also require an understanding of key qualitative factors and how they interact. Consequently, this chapter, since it is based exclusively on quantitative data, seeks only to explore observed patterns and, where appropriate, performance – it alone cannot provide a suitable explanation of *why* these patterns and/or performance take place.

One additional point should be made about how the data is presented. For all groups (i.e. SHI countries, all western European tax-funded countries as well as northern and southern countries separately) unweighted averages have been calculated[1] and the ratios between the SHI average vs. tax-funded averages are given, using SHI as the numerator and tax-funded countries as the denominator, thereby creating a consistent comparative format. To reduce methodological problems in comparisons across health care systems, this chapter utilizes longitudinal data when available. This makes it possible to compare developments over time between the groups of countries.

Health status

The concept of health status reflects the baseline health of the population. It plays a prominent role in benchmarking the comparative relationship of countries in the health sector, with indicators of health status providing a key marker from which to evaluate the impact of organizational change.

Epidemiological studies typically conclude that health care systems play only a minor role in achieving the health status levels attained. Other factors such as clean water, proper sanitation and good nutrition, along with additional environmental, economic and lifestyle dimensions, are considerably more important in determining the outcomes a country experiences (McKeown 1976). The actual contribution of medical and clinical services is usually considered to be in the range of 10 up to 25 per cent of observed outcome (McKeown 1976; Bunker *et al.* 1995; Or 1997).

A central component of health status is life expectancy. Table 4.1, in its left half, gives these data for five-year-intervals in time between 1980 and 2000. In 1980, the Netherlands, Sweden, Norway and Switzerland had the highest life expectancies, while Austria, Luxembourg, Ireland and lastly Portugal were at the low end of the spectrum. On average, SHI countries' life expectancy (74.1 years) was slightly lower than in the southern (74.2) and northern European (74.3) tax-funded health systems. Twenty years later, Switzerland and Sweden continued to have the highest life expectancy while Denmark had joined Portugal in having the lowest. SHI countries, on average, had a life expectancy which was 0.6 years higher than in all western European tax-based countries, 0.4 years higher than the southern and 0.7 years higher than the northern tax-based countries. Being averages, these statistics combine countries at both ends of the spectrum (e.g. Switzerland and Belgium in the case of SHI [difference of 2.4

Table 4.1 Life expectancy (LE) at birth 1980–2000: development and change; disability adjusted life expectancy (DALE) 2000 (in years)

	Cross-sectional								Longitudinal	
	LE 1980	LE 1985	LE 1990	LE 1995	LE 2000	DALE 2000 (% of LE)	Relative order: LE 2000	Relative order: DALE 2000	LE change 1980–2000	Relative order: LE change
Switzerland	75.8	77.1	77.6	78.8	80.0[1]	72.5 (91%)	1	1	4.2	9
Sweden	75.9	76.8	77.8	79.1	79.9	71.6 (90%)	2	2	4.0	13
Italy	74.4	75.7	77.2	78.4	79.5[1]	70.9 (89%)	3	4	5.1	3
France	74.9	76.0	77.6	78.7	79.0[1]	71.1 (90%)	4	3	4.1	11
Spain	75.6	76.5	77.0	78.1	78.8[1]	70.7 (90%)	5	5	3.2	14
Norway	75.8	76.1	76.7	77.9	78.8	70.7 (90%)	5	5	3.0	16
Austria	72.8	74.1	76.0	77.1	78.7	70.7 (90%)	7	5	5.9	1
Luxembourg	72.7	73.8	75.5	77.4	78.6	70.3 (89%)	8	9	5.9	1
Israel	74.0	75.4	76.8	77.5	78.5[2]	69.4 (88%)	9	15	4.5	7
Greece	75.4	76.0	77.2	77.8	78.4[1]	70.4 (90%)	10	8	3.0	16
Germany	73.6	75.2	75.5	76.8	78.4	70.1 (89%)	10	10	4.8	5
Netherlands	76.0	76.6	77.2	77.7	78.3	69.7 (89%)	12	13	2.3	17
UK	73.6	74.7	76.0	76.9	78.2	69.2 (88%)	13	16	4.6	6
Finland	73.7	74.5	75.1	76.8	77.9	69.9 (90%)	14	11	4.2	9
Belgium	73.2	74.7	76.3	77.1	77.6[3]	69.6 (90%)	15	14	4.4	8
Ireland	72.5	73.5	74.8	75.5	76.6	68.9 (90%)	16	17	4.1	11
Denmark	74.2	74.7	75.1	75.5	76.5[1]	69.8 (91%)	17	12	2.3	17
Portugal	71.2	72.9	74.0	75.0	76.2	66.8 (88%)	18	18	5.0	4

SHI average	74.1	75.4	76.6	77.6	78.6	70.4 (90%)	–	4.5	–
Tax-funded average	74.2	75.1	76.1	77.1	78.1	69.9 (90%)	–	3.8	–
– northern	74.3	75.1	75.9	77.0	78.0	70.0 (90%)	–	3.7	–
– southern	74.2	75.3	76.4	77.3	78.2	69.7 (89%)	–	4.1	–
Ratio SHI/tax	0.9986	1.0030	1.0062	1.0070	1.0071	1.0077	–	–	–
Ratio SHI/northern tax	0.9979	1.0042	1.0085	1.0089	1.0084	1.0058	–	–	–
Ratio SHI/southern tax	0.9997	1.0012	1.0028	1.0040	1.0053	1.0104	–	–	–
Difference SHI – tax	-0.1	0.2	0.5	0.5	0.6	0.5	–	0.7	–
Difference SHI – northern tax	-0.2	0.3	0.6	0.7	0.7	0.4	–	0.8	–
Difference SHI – southern tax	0.0	0.1	0.2	0.3	0.4	0.7	–	0.4	–

Notes:
1 1999
2 1998
3 1997
Ordering is only to facilitate easy interpretation of the data. It does not reflect overall national rankings – see caveat page 82/83. Countries are sorted according to life expectancy in 2000.

Sources: WHO (2003), for Germany 1980 and 1985: WHO (2000a).

years], Sweden and Denmark for northern tax-based systems [difference of 3.4 years] and Italy and Portugal for southern tax-based countries [difference of 3.3 years]).

Longitudinally viewed, SHI countries had started in 1980 at a level lower than tax-based countries. Over the 20-year period, however, their rate of increase (4.5 years) was marginally better (by 0.7 years) than all tax-funded countries with somewhat less improvement over the southern (0.4 years) than northern (0.8 years) country groupings. Encouraging and also discouraging experiences are spread among all three groups: Austria and Luxembourg, with +5.9 years, saw the steepest increases, followed by Italy and Portugal. At the other end of the spectrum, Denmark and the Netherlands, both with +2.3 years, have seen the smallest increase, followed by Greece and Norway.

An important concern regarding the use of life expectancy as a proxy for population health is that it does not differentiate between years lived in good health from those lived in ill health. One statistical effort to estimate the difference is the concept of Disability-Adjusted Life Expectancy (DALE), utilized in the *World Health Report 2000* (WHO 2000). It measures years lived minus an estimated percentage for each year lived in incomplete health, using the Sullivan method based on age-specific information on the prevalence of non-fatal health outcomes. For this approach, no longitudinal data are currently available. The cross-sectional data for 2000 show, as a percentage of life expectancy, minimal variation extending from 91 per cent of the full life expectancy figure in Denmark and Switzerland to 88 per cent in Portugal and the United Kingdom (Table 4.1).

Over the last decades, several approaches have been developed in attempts to quantify the contribution of health care to population health in methodologically more adequate ways. The most widely used is based on the concept of deaths from certain causes that should not occur in the presence of timely and effective health care, termed 'avoidable mortality' or 'mortality amenable to medical/health care', which was first proposed by Rutstein and colleagues in 1976. Such conditions include, for example, perinatal and maternal deaths, tuberculosis, malignant neoplasms of the breast, diabetes mellitus, pneumonia and appendicitis.

Based on recent calculations using 1998 data by Nolte and McKee (2003) for a selection of European countries (using an updated list of conditions and extending the age limit until when deaths from most causes considered are deemed 'amenable' to the age of 75), Sweden, France, Spain and Norway showed the lowest levels of such mortality, i.e. the highest level of such mortality actually 'avoided' (Table 4.2). Thus, three of the four countries with the lowest levels were tax funded. However, four other tax-funded countries (Denmark, Ireland, the United Kingdom, and Portugal) were at the other end of the spectrum, with significantly higher levels of unnecessary mortality. SHI countries showed a slight advantage vs. all tax-funded countries (ratio of 0.92) as well as when compared to the northern tax-funded group (ratio of 0.94).

Based on the data presented, it is hard to discern any major distinctions between the SHI and the tax-funded group. The only noteworthy differential is that five of the six countries that had minimized amenable mortality by most

Table 4.2 Change in temporary life expectancy up to age 75; change in life expectancy amenable through health care in 1980s and 1990s; and age-standardized mortality from amenable conditions in 1998

	Longitudinal									Cross-sectional	
	1980–9 (change in years)				1990–8 (change in years)						
	Total up to age 75		Of which due to amenable conditions		Total up to age 75		Of which due to amenable conditions		Relative order based on change from amenable conditions	1998 amenable mortality (standardized death rates; ages 0–74)[1]	Relative order based on 1998 amenable mortality
	Men	Women	Men	Women	Men	Women	Men	Women			
Sweden	1.06	0.57	0.26	0.25	1.08	0.57	0.17	0.10	9	58.5	1
France	1.17	0.78	0.32	0.25	1.05	0.38	0.16	0.08	8	62.7	2
Spain	0.37	0.71	0.53	0.39	1.13	0.68	0.31	0.27	4	66.1	3
Norway	n.a.	n.a.	n.a.	n.a.	n.a.	n.a.	n.a.	n.a.	n.a.	66.5	4
Italy	1.62	1.07	−1.46	0.50	1.16	0.51	0.32	0.25	12	68.9	5
Netherlands	0.91	0.30	0.20	0.21	0.79	0.31	0.06	0.11	11	71.2	6
Finland	0.86	0.33	0.26	0.21	1.61	0.71	0.28	0.20	7	71.8	7
Greece	0.94	1.00	0.76	0.70	0.31	0.44	0.21	0.26	2	72.3	8
Austria	1.95	1.23	0.79	0.55	1.32	0.76	0.25	0.29	3	72.8	9
Germany[2]	1.73	1.09	0.58	0.49	0.89	0.50	0.12	0.14	6	74.4	10
Denmark	0.52	0.25	0.09	0.13	1.21	0.66	0.18	0.20	10	81.4	11
Ireland	n.a.	n.a.	n.a.	n.a.	n.a.	n.a.	n.a.	n.a.	n.a.	81.9	12
United Kingdom	1.32	0.80	0.49	0.46	1.04	0.60	0.16	0.26	5	87.5	13
Portugal	2.14	1.42	1.33	0.99	0.93	0.78	0.53	0.39	1	113.0	14
SHI countries average	1.44	0.85	0.47	0.37	1.01	0.49	0.15	0.16	–	70.3	–
Tax-funded countries average	1.10	0.77	0.28	0.45	1.06	0.62	0.27	0.24	–	76.8	–

Table 4.2 Cont.

	1980–89 (change in years)				1990–98 (change in years)				Relative order based on change from amenable conditions	1998 amenable mortality (standardized death rates; ages 0–74)[1]	Relative order based on 1998 amenable mortality
	Total up to age 75		Of which due to amenable conditions		Total up to age 75		Of which due to amenable conditions				
	Men	Women	Men	Women	Men	Women	Men	Women			
- northern	0.94	0.49	0.28	0.26	1.23	0.64	0.20	0.19	–	74.6	–
- southern	1.27	1.05	0.29	0.64	0.88	0.60	0.34	0.30	–	80.1	–
Ratio SHI/all tax	1.30	1.11	1.68	0.82	0.96	0.79	0.56	0.64	–	0.92	–
Ratio SHI/northern tax	1.53	1.74	1.72	1.42	0.82	0.77	0.76	0.83	–	0.94	–
Difference SHI to all tax	0.33	0.08	0.19	–0.08	–0.04	–0.13	–0.12	–0.09	–	–6.52	–
Difference SHI to northern	0.50	0.36	0.20	0.11	–0.22	–0.15	–0.05	–0.03	–	–4.31	–

Notes:

n.a. = not available. Countries are sorted according to age-standardized mortality form amenable conditions in 1998. Ordering is only to facilitate easy interpretation of the data. It does not reflect overall national rankings – see caveat page 82/83. No data are available for Belgium, Israel, Luxembourg and Switzerland. Amenable causes of death in the Nolte and McKee study included (mostly for all persons up to age 74, but partly with different age limits; some conditions only for particular countries): Intestinal infections, tuberculosis, diphtheria, tetanus, poliomyelitis, whooping cough, septicaemia, measles; Malignant neoplasm of colon and rectum, skin, breast, cervix uteri and body of the uterus, and of testis; Hodgkin's disease, leukaemia; Diseases of the thyroid; Diabetes mellitus; Epilepsy; Hypertensive disease, ischaemic heart disease, cerebrovascular diseases; Respiratory diseases; Peptic ulcer, appendicitis, abdominal hernia, cholelithiasis and cholecystitis; Nephritis and nephrosis, benign prostatic hyperplasia; Maternal deaths; Congenital cardiovascular anomalities, perinatal deaths (excluding stillbirths); Misadventures to patients during surgical and medical care. Averages are based on the underlying, more precise, country data.

1 1998 amenable mortality data for Denmark, Finland and Sweden include causes of deaths that had been excluded in the other data.

2 West-Germany only; total Germany for amenable mortality, standardized death rates.

Sources: Nolte and McKee (2004); for cross sectional amenable mortality: Nolte and McKee (2003) and Erratum to Nolte and McKee (2003)

between 1980 and 1998 were tax-funded countries, suggesting that SHI systems were less successful in influencing these outcomes than were their northern tax-funded counterparts. Improvement was higher in both northern and southern tax-based countries, except for men in the 1980s.

Satisfaction/responsiveness

A central aspect of health system performance is how well they meet the concerns of patients. This became an important topic over the 1990s, typically cited as a major factor in support of SHI systems by their proponents. Researchers have variously termed this the degree of 'satisfaction' and/or 'responsiveness' of the health system to patient preferences. Satisfaction is a broad, subjective category that seeks to measure patient and/or citizen opinion about the perceived acceptability of health service design, delivery and funding. Responsiveness focuses on a more detailed set of qualitative relationships that characterize the interaction between the individual and the health system (e.g. autonomy, choice, confidentiality, dignity). While the majority of categories that compose responsiveness are predominantly subjective in nature, several can be charted more objectively – for example length of waiting times and degree of patient choice.

Based on subjective opinion, the category of satisfaction is notoriously difficult to measure in a scientifically rigorous fashion. The survey research instruments utilized to assess the opinions of individual respondents can produce conclusions that change dramatically if a question is phrased differently, if the answer categories are organized differently, or if the broader context changes (e.g. a health sector scandal erupts). Moreover, survey research methodology produces even less reliable results when used comparatively across countries, since explicit answers necessarily incorporate implicit cultural preferences and expectations that vary widely across western Europe (Hofstede 1980, 1985). While these difficulties are most visible with satisfaction data, they also affect the reliability of results for the qualitative aspects included in assessments of responsiveness. These technical limitations suggest that ostensibly 'hard' data obtained through 'objective' questions provide at best an impression rather than a factual portrayal of the true state of popular attitudes and/or system responsiveness, and, consequently, should be interpreted with a healthy dose of scepticism.

This section reviews five separate statistical pathways to measuring satisfaction and/or responsiveness. The first considers results obtained from broad undifferentiated opinion questions asked to citizens in 1996, 1998 and 1999. The second reports 2003 data from an eight-part breakdown of responsiveness issues asked to opinion leaders and citizens. A third approach focuses on patient opinions about the character of hospital or general practice care. The two final sections review available data on two quantitative dimensions of responsiveness – waiting times and patient choice – each of which also may reflect political decisions to spend higher levels of funds on health care.

General population surveys (1996, 1998 and 1999)

Results from four separate administrations of the Eurobarometer survey of public opinion are presented in Table 4.3. In each administration, one broad health-related question was included. As Table 4.3 indicates, the exact phrasing of the question and the structure of possible answers was the same in 1996 (Eurobarometer 44.3) and in the first 1998 administration (Eurobarometer 49), while both question and response categories were slightly different in the second 1998 (Eurobarometer 50.1) and the presented 1999 (Eurobarometer 52.1) administrations. In all four surveys, answers were obtained from the broad citizenry rather than from either policy elites or patients.

The most striking aspect of these four sets of results is how widely they vary with slightly different phrasings of the question and/or structuring of the answer categories. On the 1996 survey and the first 1998 administration, for example, two northern tax-funded health systems showed the highest values – Denmark and Finland. They were followed by five of the six SHI countries included – all except Germany, which had slightly lower results. The four southern tax-funded countries had notably lower results. One interesting detail is that the United Kingdom, which had substantially lower results than did the Nordic countries, was given somewhat higher ratings by two lower-income groups (the poor and the elderly). Overall, the six surveyed SHI countries scored a bit lower than did northern tax-funded systems (65.7 vs. 68.9 in 1998) but substantially higher when southern tax-funded countries are included (65.7 vs. 48.8). When this 1998 satisfaction data is charted against national per capita expenditures, a similar set of relationships between SHI and tax-funded countries can be observed (Figure 4.1). Poor and elderly respondents in 1998 were more likely to be satisfied in northern tax-funded than in SHI systems.

The issue of reliability appears, however, when the results from these first two Eurobarometer surveys are compared with those obtained by a second 1998 Eurobarometer survey using a slightly different question with a slightly altered scoring system for responses. In the second 1998 survey, while some reported SHI numbers fell noticeably (e.g. Germany by 13.3 per cent and Luxembourg by 16.9 per cent), reported results from several northern tax-based systems plummeted far further (Denmark by 42.4 per cent; Ireland by 34.0 per cent). Indeed, in the same year, Denmark fell from the highest positive response rate for all countries (90.6 per cent) to a number that was nearly 50 per cent lower (48.2 per cent). This results in the SHI country average being notably higher than that of northern tax-funded countries. More importantly, however, it highlights the erratic and impressionistic character of the data that these opinion surveys generate.

Policy elite and population survey (2002)

Following from initial efforts published in the *World Health Report 2000*, WHO undertook more comprehensive surveys of the general population as well as of national policy elites. The questions asked sought confirmation about what WHO characterized as responsiveness of health care systems to individuals

Table 4.3 Eurobarometer surveys: satisfaction with the health care system

	'In general, would you say you are very satisfied, fairly satisfied, neither satisfied nor dissatisfied, fairly dissatisfied or very dissatisfied with the way health care runs in (OUR COUNTRY)?': *very or fairly satisfied*					'And, on a scale from 1 to 10, how satisfied are you with health services in (OUR COUNTRY)?': *answers 7, 8, 9 or 10*	'Please tell me whether you are very satisfied, fairly satisfied, not very satisfied or not at all satisfied with each of the following?' '(OUR COUNTRY)'s health care system in general': *very or fairly satisfied*
	1996 population (%) [E44.3]	*1998 population (%) [E49]*	*1998 poor (%) [E49]**	*1998 elderly (%) [E49]**	*Change 1996–8 population (% points)*	*1998 population (%) [E50.1]*	*1999 population (%) [E52.1]*
Austria	63.3	72.7	73	74	9.4	70.6	83.4
France	65.1	65.0	69	68	-0.1	59.4	78.2
Belgium	70.1	62.8	54	57	-7.3	56.5	77.0
Denmark	90.0	90.6	90	93	0.6	48.2	75.8
Finland	86.4	81.3	78	83	-5.1	78.0	74.3
Netherlands	72.8	69.8	68	70	-3.0	69.7	73.2
Luxembourg	71.1	66.6	69	75	-4.5	49.7	71.6
Sweden	67.3	57.5	56	66	-9.8	45.9	58.7
United Kingdom	48.1	57.0	67	69	8.9	49.3	55.7
Germany	66.0	57.5	52	57	-8.5	43.2	49.9
Ireland	49.9	57.9	65	62	8.0	23.9	47.7
Spain	35.6	43.1	47	57	7.5	30.8	47.6
Italy	16.3	20.1	22	30	3.8	14.9	26.3
Portugal	19.9	16.4	20	19	-3.5	5.7	24.1
Greece	18.4	15.5	18	22	-2.9	10.7	18.6
SHI countries	*68.1*	*65.7*	*64.2*	*66.8*	*-2.3*	*58.2*	*72.2*

Table 4.3 *Cont.*

	'In general, would you say you are very satisfied, fairly satisfied, neither satisfied nor dissatisfied, fairly dissatisfied or very dissatisfied with the way health care runs in (OUR COUNTRY)?': *very or fairly satisfied*					'And, on a scale from 1 to 10, how satisfied are you with health services in (OUR COUNTRY)?': *answers 7, 8, 9 or 10*	'Please tell me whether you are very satisfied, fairly satisfied, not very satisfied or not at all satisfied with each of the following?' (OUR COUNTRY)'s health care system in general': *very or fairly satisfied*
	1996 population (%) [E44.3]	*1998 population (%) [E49]*	*1998 poor (%) [E49]**	*1998 elderly (%) [E49]**	*Change 1996–98 population (% points)*	*1998 population (%) [E50.1]*	*1999 population (%) [E52.1]*
Northern tax-funded countries	68.3	68.9	71.2	74.6	0.5	49.1	62.4
Ratio SHI/northern tax	0.9960	0.9546	0.9012	0.8959	–	1.1863	1.1566
Difference SHI to Northern tax (% points)	-0.3	-3.1	-7.0	-7.8	-2.9	9.1	9.8
All tax-funded countries	48.0	48.8	51.4	55.7	0.8	34.2	47.6
Ratio SHI/all tax	1.4184	1.3464	1.2473	1.2006	–	1.7035	1.5157
Difference SHI to all tax (% points)	20.1	16.9	12.7	11.2	-3.2	24.0	24.6

Notes:

Countries are sorted according to the 1999 satisfaction data. Ordering is only to facilitate easy interpretation of the data. It does not reflect overall national rankings – see caveat page 82/83. Data for Israel, Norway and Switzerland were not available. *Data source:* Personal interviews, population sample size: about 600 for Luxembourg, about 1300 for the UK (of which 300 for Northern Ireland), 2000 for Germany and about 1000 for the other countries for all four Eurobarometer inquiries, n.a. = not available, E44.3 = Eurobarometer 44.3 (conducted February–April 1996), E49 = Eurobarometer 49 (conducted April–May 1998), E50.1 = Eurobarometer 50.1 (conducted November–December 1998), E52.1 = Eurobarometer 52.1 (conducted November–December 1999).

Sources: INRA (Europe) European Coordination Office (1996); INRA (Europe) European Coordination Office (1998); INRA (Europe) European Coordination Office (1999); INRA (Europe) European Coordination Office (2000); * Blendon *et al.* (2001).

Figure 4.1 Per capita expenditure on health in US$PPP as compared to satisfaction with health system, 1998

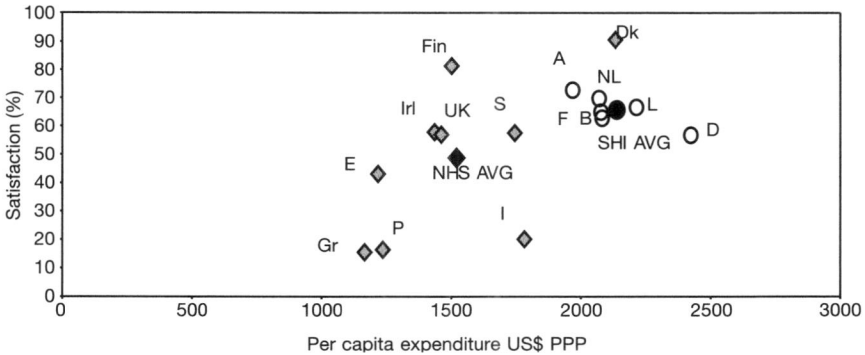

Note: Survey question: 'In general, would you say you are very satisfied, fairly satisfied, neither satisfied nor dissatisfied, fairly dissatisfied or very dissatisfied with the way health care runs in (country)?': very or fairly satisfied.

Sources: INRA (Europe) European Coordination Office (1998); OECD (2000).

(Üstün *et al.* 2001). Responsiveness was defined as embodying two major categories with a total of eight domains: respect for persons, which included respect for the dignity of the individual, confidentiality, communication and autonomy; and client orientation which consisted of prompt attention, amenities of adequate quality, access to social support networks and the choice of institution and care provider. The surveys were conducted via face-to-face or telephone interviews, but also partly by postal surveys. Interviewees were asked to rate their experiences over the past 12 months. While questions regarding seven of the eight domains were relevant for both inpatient visits and outpatient visits, social support was asked only to inpatients. Questions regarding choice of provider and institution clearly militated against those tax-funded systems where policy still stressed planned public capacity through catchment areas. All domains included a summary rating question (scaled 1 to 5, very good to very bad). In addition, several domains included questions on how often a particular experience had occurred during encounters with the health system (scaled 1 to 4, always to never). The WHO World Health Survey tried to increase cross-population comparability by using vignettes to adjust for different expectations by country, cultural background, social class, age etc. Some of the vignettes plotted did not do this adequately. In addition, some domains of health are inherently multi-dimensional, thus complicating comparability (Üstün *et al.* 2001).

Table 4.4 shows available results of the 2002 surveys for five SHI countries and eight tax-funded countries. It suggests that northern European tax-funded countries seem to do significantly better in terms of autonomy, communication, respect for dignity, and confidentiality. Northern European tax-funded countries also have equal results to those of SHI countries concerning prompt attention. Regarding choice of provider, SHI countries score clearly better.

Table 4.4 WHO's components of responsiveness, 2000–1

	Autonomy		Choice		Communication		Confidentiality		Dignity		Prompt attention		Access to family and community support	Basic amenities	Country weighted mean		Relative order	
	In	Out	In	Out	In	Out	In	Out	In	Out	In	Out	In	Out	In	Out	In	Out
Ireland	75	87	88	98	91	94	92	94	91	98	82	95	90	88	87	94	2	1
UK	81	81	93	98	85	85	90	96	94	95	82	81	95	77	88	87	1	3
Sweden	81	83	87	94	89	88	88	86	97	95	74	82	95	74	86	86	4	4
Luxembourg	83	83	88	98	90	81	83	82	92	91	83	82	94	74	87	85	2	9
Germany	74	84	85	98	74	85	83	87	85	90	85	94	89	83	82	89	8	2
Belgium	75	79	97	100	87	87	79	81	88	92	73	84	91	75	83	86	5	4
France	71	71	96	100	88	89	83	85	91	95	72	81	90	77	83	86	5	4
Netherlands	72	80	88	97	82	85	75	77	87	94	85	89	96	73	83	86	5	4
Finland	76	84	60	83	86	88	83	86	85	95	81	86	87	72	79	86	9	4
Spain	61	64	82	85	84	79	83	83	85	83	78	83	80	71	79	79	9	10
Italy	53	58	90	98	74	73	68	69	74	73	78	75	79	61	74	73	11	11
Portugal	66	67	78	85	71	76	70	71	66	71	71	76	74	65	71	73	12	11
Greece	44	48	71	72	49	53	79	81	61	63	61	71	78	59	62	64	13	13
SHI countries average	75.0	79.4	90.8	98.6	84.2	85.4	80.6	82.4	88.6	92.4	79.6	86.0	92.0	76.4	83.6	86.4	–	–
Tax-funded countries average	67.1	71.5	81.1	89.1	78.6	79.5	81.6	83.3	81.6	84.1	75.9	81.1	84.8	70.9	78.3	80.3	–	–
Ratio SHI/all tax	1.12	1.11	1.12	1.11	1.07	1.07	0.99	0.99	1.09	1.10	1.05	1.06	1.09	1.08	1.07	1.08	–	–
Difference SHI to tax countries	7.9	7.9	9.7	9.5	5.6	5.9	-1.0	-0.8	7.0	8.3	3.7	4.9	7.3	5.5	5.3	6.2	–	–
– northern	78.3	83.8	82.0	93.3	87.8	88.8	88.3	90.5	91.8	95.8	79.8	86.0	91.8	77.8	85.0	88.3	–	–
Ratio SHI/northern tax	0.96	0.95	1.11	1.06	0.96	0.96	0.91	0.91	0.97	0.97	1.00	1.00	1.00	0.98	0.98	0.98	–	–

Difference SHI to northern tax	−3.3	−4.3	8.8	5.3	−3.6	−3.3	−7.7	−8.1	−3.2	−3.3	−0.2	0.0	0.3	−1.3	−1.4	−1.8	–	–	–	–
– Southern	56.0	59.3	80.3	85.0	69.5	70.3	75.0	76.0	71.5	72.5	72.0	76.3	77.8	64.0	71.5	72.3				
Ratio SHI/southern tax	1.34	1.34	1.13	1.16	1.21	1.22	1.07	1.08	1.24	1.27	1.11	1.13	1.18	1.19	1.17	1.20				
Difference SHI to southern tax	19.0	20.2	10.6	13.6	14.7	15.2	5.6	6.4	17.1	19.9	7.6	9.8	14.3	12.4	12.1	14.2				

Notes:

In = inpatient mean, out = outpatient mean. Countries are sorted by the average of country-weighted means for in- and outpatient care. Ordering is only to facilitate easy interpretation of the data. It does not reflect overall national ranking – see caveat page 82/83. No data are available for Austria, Denmark, Israel, Norway and Switzerland.

Source: Valentine et al. (2003).

WHO's judgment of quality of amenities for outpatient care is more favourable for northern European tax-based countries, while it is slightly worse for access to family and community support. Applying WHO's weights, derived from the frequencies with which respondents ranked the different elements first (prompt attention being perceived as most important and choice of provider as less important, Valentine and Salomon 2003) to these different components of responsiveness, northern European tax-funded countries score better than SHI countries, while the picture is reversed when comparing SHI countries to southern European tax-funded countries.

A closer look at the reported results reveals large differences within the country groups. France, for example, scores lower for 'prompt attention' in inpatient care than most tax-funded countries, while the United Kingdom scores higher than almost all of the SHI countries for both autonomy and choice. These data contradict those based on other surveys among actual patients (see next section).

WHO's population surveys on responsiveness also assess the variance within countries of the answers obtained. Using the coefficient of variation (i.e. standard deviation divided by the mean) as the indicator, the five SHI countries show higher levels of responsiveness than the tax-based countries on average (cf. previous section), and the responsiveness is also more evenly distributed – both regarding outpatient as well as inpatient care (Table 4.5).

Patient surveys (1998–2000)

The following surveys assess opinions regarding satisfaction not from the general citizenry but from individual patients. Data from two different surveys are presented, one conducted by a European-level task force on general practice (EUROPEP), the second a smaller four-country study funded by the Picker Institute in London. Once again, notable disparities between the two studies in the results obtained suggest that asking different questions and using different survey methodologies can elicit widely varying responses.

The general practice study was conducted in 1998 across 17,000 patients in ten countries, including four studied SHI countries and four northern tax-funded comparison countries (the two remaining countries being Iceland and Slovenia). Table 4.6 reports results from eight of 23 highly specific questions regarding patient satisfaction with non-clinical dimensions of general practice services. On average, the four SHI countries scored higher than did the four northern tax-funded countries (Grol *et al.* 2000). Differences in these averages ranged from 4 per cent on keeping records confidential to 29 per cent and 28 per cent on two questions concerning telephone access.

The Picker Institute study surveyed patients in four countries – two SHI and two northern tax-funded – about their satisfaction with hospital services they had received (Coulter and Cleary 2001). Questions in this survey focused on various non-clinical dimensions of hospital-related services, primarily linkages to subsequent non-hospital services (e.g. coordination of care, continuity and transition, involvement of family etc). Several of the questions explored social networks and/or characteristics of the broader culture (e.g. involvement

Table 4.5 Overall, outpatient and inpatient inequality in responsiveness (coefficient of variation)

	Overall		Outpatient		Inpatient	
	Level	Relative order	Level	Relative order	Level	Relative order
Germany	0.061	1	0.055	1	0.124	8
Netherlands	0.064	2	0.063	2	0.085	1
France	0.068	3	0.067	3	0.106	5
Belgium	0.070	4	0.068	4	0.099	4
Finland	0.079	5	0.070	5	0.138	9
United Kingdom*	0.080	6	0.080	8	0.092	3
Spain	0.080	6	0.079	7	0.119	7
Ireland	0.084	8	0.074	6	0.155	11
Luxembourg	0.089	9	0.086	9	0.117	6
Sweden	0.090	10	0.092	11	0.089	2
Italy	0.095	11	0.086	9	0.174	12
Portugal	0.105	12	0.094	12	0.154	10
Greece*	0.137	13	0.128	13	0.204	13
SHI countries average	0.070	–	0.068	–	0.106	–
Tax-funded countries average	0.094	–	0.088	–	0.141	–
– northern	0.083	–	0.079	–	0.119	–
– southern	0.104	–	0.097	–	0.163	–
Ratio SHI/all tax	0.75	–	0.77	–	0.76	–
Ratio SHI/northern tax	0.85	–	0.86	–	0.90	–

Notes:
Ordering is only to facilitate easy interpretation of the data. It does not reflect overall national rankings – see caveat page 82/83. Countries are sorted according to their overall coefficient of variation. No data are available for Austria, Denmark, Finland, the Netherlands and Switzerland.
* Postal surveys, while in the other countries face-to-face or telephone interviews were used.

Source: Ortiz et al. (2003).

of family and friends, emotional support). Results were somewhat similar to those of the EUROPEP general practice study, in that the two surveyed SHI countries generally scored better (e.g. had fewer reported problems) (Table 4.7). However, on two issues (most notably continuity and transition), Sweden scored marginally better than Germany. Moreover, on the final 'recommend this hospital to others' question, almost twice as many Germans as Swedes would *not* do so. Perhaps more telling, however, responses from patients in all four countries on the continuity and transition issue were notably less satisfied than on any other issue – with 30.0 to 45.1 per cent reporting problems. Again, the results demonstrate that the data obtained regarding patient satisfaction varies considerably according to survey questions and methodology.

Table 4.6 Evaluations of general practice care in four SHI and four tax-based countries, c. 1998 (per cent)

	CH	D	B	NL	S	N	DK	UK	SHI avg.	Northern tax-fund avg.	Ratio
Overall evaluation	91	88	87	80	78	76	74	72	87	75	1.15
1 Keeping records and data confidential	96	94	97	95	88	91	96	91	96	92	1.04
2 Listening to you	96	92	93	89	85	85	79	83	93	83	1.11
3 Making you feel you had time during consultations	96	90	92	88	85	78	75	80	92	80	1.15
4 Providing quick services for urgent problems	96	95	93	85	84	83	81	71	92	80	1.16
. . . (15 other items)											
20 Offering you services for preventing disease	84	85	77	76	75	67	68	74	81	71	1.13
21 Getting through to the practice on the phone	96	95	93	71	67	56	53	62	89	60	1.49
22 Being able to speak to the GP on the telephone	91	87	90	72	65	54	59	51	85	57	1.48
23 Waiting time in the waiting room	79	70	66	61	65	57	59	50	69	58	1.19
Relative order	1	2	3	4	5	6	7	8	–	–	–

Notes:
Countries are sorted from left to right by overall evaluation. No data are available for other countries. Ordering is only to facilitate easy interpretation of the data. It does not reflect overall national rankings – see caveat page 82/83.

Source: Grol *et al.* (2000).

Table 4.7 Patients reporting problems with hospital care – two SHI countries and two tax-based northern European countries, 1998/2000 (per cent)

	Switzerland	Germany	Sweden	UK
Overall care NOT GOOD	3.7	6.6	7.4	8.5
Relative Order	1	2	3	4
Problems with . . .				
Information and education	16.7	20.4	23.4	28.7
Coordination of care	13.1	17.2	n.a.	21.9
Physical comfort	2.6	6.7	4.0	8.3
Emotional support	14.7	21.9	26.0	27.1
Respect for patients' preferences	15.6	17.9	21.2	30.7
Involvement of family and friends	11.5	16.6	14.6	27.5
Continuity and transition	30.0	40.6	40.2	45.1
Would not recommend this hospital to friends/family	3.6	5.0	2.8	7.8

Notes:
n.a. = not available
Countries are sorted from left to right by level of care reported 'not good'. No data are available for other countries.

Source: adapted from Coulter and Cleary (2001).

Waiting times

A different measure of health system responsiveness is waiting times for elective procedures. Long waiting times cause considerable distress to patients, and are often taken as a negative symbol regarding the overall functioning of a health system. In northern tax-funded countries, for example, waiting lists from several months (Finland, Sweden) to up to two years (United Kingdom), especially for certain procedures for the elderly (coronary artery bypass grafts, corneal lens transplants, hip transplants), frustrated policy-makers throughout much of the 1990s and became 'hot button' political issues (Siciliani and Hurst 2003). Conversely, of the eight studied SHI countries, only Israel and the Netherlands seem to have experienced waiting time problems for routine elective procedures (see below).

In addition to responsiveness, however, waiting lists also demonstrate efficiency dimensions. A recent OECD study suggested that higher levels of medical resources (physicians, hospital beds) as well as a fee-for-service payment structure, were negatively correlated with waiting lists, confirming that higher expenditures can reduce these lists. This inverse financial relationship (higher expenditures leads to lower waiting times) implies that the decision to reduce waiting lists may reflect a political decision about how much to spend on health service capacity (see the section on relative resource levels in SHI countries on p. 121).

As already noted, only two of eight SHI countries have queues that extend beyond four weeks for specialist care, nursing care or nursing home care (see

Table 4.8). In Israel, it has been common wisdom that since 1995 there are no significant waiting lists, hence large deficits. Some observers suggest queues are growing once again in certain specialities, especially for hospital-based outpatient specialist consultations. For nursing care, there are long waiting lists (Chinitz 2003). In the Netherlands, average waiting times in December 2002 ran from five weeks for outpatient departments to 5.8 weeks for inpatient procedures (see Table 4.9a). For several surgical procedures waiting times were more

Table 4.8 Waiting lists in the eight SHI countries, 2002

	Specialist care	Nursing care	Nursing homes	Transplantations
Austria				X
Belgium				X
France				X
Germany				X
Israel	X	X		X
Luxembourg				X
Netherlands	X	X	X	X
Switzerland				X

Note:
X = Confirmed non-exceptional prevalence waiting times longer than four weeks.

Sources: Maarse (2002/2003); Chinitz (2003); Feider (2003); Kratzer (2003); Ministerie van Volksgezondheid, Welzijn en Sport (2003a); Kletter (2003); Santé Suisse (2003).

Table 4.9 Waiting times in the Netherlands

a) Average waiting times weighted for the prevalence of the main specialties (weeks), December 2002

	December 2002
Clinical	5.8
Outpatients department	5.0
Day care	5.2

Source: Ministerie van Volksgezondheid, Welzijn en Sport (2003a).

b) Average waiting times for nursing home care (weeks), October 2001

	October 2001
Extramural nursing home care	47
Day care somatic nursing home	16
Day care psychogeriatric nursing home	24
Night care	24
Additional nursing home care	39
Short-lasting admission nursing home	14
Admission somatic nursing home	30
Admission psychogeriatric nursing home	41
Intermittering admission nursing home	39

Source: Somai and Hutten (2002).

than ten weeks on average (e.g. cataract operations, plastic surgery, surgical removal of varicose veins, cardiologic 'open heart' operations and orthopaedics) (Ministerie van Volksgezondheid, Welzijn en Sport 2003a). The average waiting time for home care and nursing home services in October 2001 varied from 14–47 weeks (see Table 4.9b). In Germany, a ministry spokesperson stated that there were no waiting lists beyond four weeks, thus no statistics were available (Kratzer 2003). A 2001 study found a mean waiting time of 35 days for cataract surgery (Wenzel *et al.* 2001). For Luxembourg, a representative of the Sickness Fund Union said it did not know of any waiting lists (Feider 2003). Also in France, national officials do not believe that waiting lists are a problem, although there are indications that this might be changing (Baubeau *et al.* 2001; E-santé, 2001; Fédération Hospitalière de France 2001; Le Quotidien du Médecin 2002; Libération 2002a, 2002b; L'Express 2003).

Waiting lists in SHI countries exist consistently only for organ transplant operations that require a donor. In Austria, for example, between 1 January 1997 and 31 December 2002 average waiting time for a kidney was 15.6 months, for a liver 3.5 months, for a pancreas 6.8 months, for a heart 5.4 months and 3.6 months for a lung (Eurotransplant 2003). Table 4.10 shows that organ transplantation waiting times increased in Germany and the Netherlands. In general they are relatively high in Germany and particularly low in Belgium. Overall, SHI countries have notably fewer and/or shorter waiting times for elective procedures than do both northern and southern tax-funded countries.

Choice

The issue of choice has traditionally played a major role in SHI systems. Moreover, much like waiting times, choice has both satisfaction/responsiveness and

Table 4.10 Waiting time (post-mortal) for organ transplants in four SHI countries, 1997 and 2001 (in months)

	Kidney[1]			Heart			Liver		
	1997	2001	Change (%)	1997[2]	2001	Change (%)	1997	2001	Change (%)
Austria	29	24	−17	9	6	−37	2	4	+91
Belgium	21	19	−11	5	5	−2	3	4	+41
Germany	37	42	+14	8	10	+27	4	8	+114
Netherlands	28	39	+38	5	8	+52	4	5	+21

Notes:
Approximations based on Eurotransplant (1998, 2002) data; for 2001 data Netherlands: Ministerie van Volksgezondheid, Welzijn en Sport (2003a), weighted averages. Changes are based on unrounded data. All organ allocations were changed from 'centre-based' to 'patient-oriented' due to newly-implemented laws on transplantation in these (Eurotransplant) countries.
1 Waiting time kidney changed from 'registration date' to 'start dialysis' in 2000.
2 Including heart/kidney transplantations; but these were only less than 1.2 per cent of total.

efficiency dimensions to it. Regarding responsiveness, the ability to choose provider – both physician and hospital – is seen as a central characteristic of these systems, and it is frequently put forward by proponents as a key aspect of why citizens in SHI countries have high satisfaction levels. Indeed, proponents often argue that choice of provider reflects an important social decision in that citizens in SHI countries willingly pay more for their health care systems in order to maintain provider choice.

During the 1990s, a relatively new dimension of choice emerged, promoted by health economists as a way to create competitive forces inside SHI systems and thus, they argued, to create greater economic efficiency. This was choice of insurer (e.g. sickness fund), which had been only a marginal part of traditional SHI models. The degree to which subscribers now change their sickness funds, as well as the impact of these changes on economic efficiency in the overall system, has been and remains a contentious political issue in a number of studied countries (see Chapter 7; also Chapter 3, page 42).

These two rather different discussions about choice – of provider as against of insurer – can be seen in Table 4.11. With regard to choice of provider, five of the eight studied countries (Austria, Belgium, France, Germany and Luxembourg) allow largely unrestricted choice of general practitioner, ambulatory specialist, hospital and nursing home. The remaining three countries (Israel, Netherlands and Switzerland) place some restrictions on choice of provider.

When one turns to the question of choice of insurer, the picture becomes substantially more complex. As a consequence of reforms introduced during the 1990s in several countries including Germany and the Netherlands, Table 4.11 indicates that five of the eight countries now allow choice of sickness fund. Three countries (Austria, France, and Luxembourg) have not modified traditional arrangements and do not allow such choice.

A further distinction between choice of insurer compared to choice of provider can be observed in figures regarding those who exercise such choice. Choice of provider is utilized nearly universally and/or within mandated restrictions by patients in SHI countries. The uptake on use of choice of insurer, however, in the five SHI countries where it is allowed, typically remains quite small.

Limited data suggest that usage of the opportunity to change insurer has grown considerably over the past decade in both the Netherlands[2] (Table 4.12) and Germany (Table 4.13). In the Netherlands from 1995 to 1999, only one sickness fund gained a considerable number of members (almost 100,000) while four others gained more than 20,000 members. Three sickness funds experienced a relatively large loss of more than 20,000 members. In total, gains were larger than losses, indicating a growing market (Greß et al. 2002). In Germany, the data indicate considerable shifting from percentage of income (AOK) to lower percentage of income (BKK) sickness funds from 1997 to 1999. For Switzerland, data indicate that 19 per cent of younger subscribers, aged 19–39, changed fund in 1996–7 while only 6 per cent of elderly subscribers aged 65–100 did so (Beck 2000). In Israel, the largest sickness fund has seen an exodus of younger and more affluent subscribers, leaving it with an increasingly large proportion of elderly, poor, and Israeli-Arab citizens (Chinitz 2002).

Three caveats may affect how one interprets this data. First, regarding choice of provider, two SHI countries (Israel and Switzerland) have adopted legislation

Table 4.11 Choice of provider and insurer in eight SHI countries in 2003

	Austria	Belgium	France	Germany	Israel	Luxembourg	Netherlands	Switzerland
GP	Yes[1]	Yes	Yes	Yes	Partly yes[2]	Yes	Partly yes[2]	Partly yes[3,4]
Ambulatory specialist care	Yes[1]	Yes	Yes	Yes	Partly yes[2,5]	Yes	Partly yes[2,6]	Partly yes[3,4]
Hospital (inpatient care)[6]	Yes	Yes	Yes	Yes	Yes	Yes	Partly yes[2]	Partly yes[3,7]
Nursing home[6]	Yes	Yes[8]	Yes	Yes[9]	Yes	Yes	Partly yes[2]	Partly yes[3,7]
Sickness fund	No	Yes[8]	No	Yes[9]	1×/12	No	Yes	Yes[8]
	(geographical/	1×/3	(occupational)	18 month	months	(occupational)	1 year	1×/6 months
	occupational)	months		interval			interval	

Notes:

Referring physicians (especially in the Netherlands) have an important say in which specialist/hospital a patient goes to. Also there is a small number of private hospitals/clinics/departments that are limited to usage by people with a private (co-)insurance (in e.g. the Netherlands and Switzerland). In addition (e.g. in Austria and Germany) there may be minimum periods of time during which you can't change GP (sometimes consent of the sickness fund is needed as in Austria and of the GPs in the Netherlands).

1 By choosing a physician who is not under contract to the scheme, reimbursement is 80 per cent of the fee of a contracted physician.

2 If the physicians/hospitals have a contract with the sickness fund (in the Netherlands only privately insured and civil servants with public sickness fund arrangements have real free choice).

3 35 per cent of the insured can choose for a HMO or PPO (preferred provider organization) that restricts the patient's choice of physician/hospital (HMOs and PPOs are not offered in every canton). About 8 per cent of the Swiss formed part of a HMO or PPO (2000 data).

4 People do not have free access to physicians outside their canton of residence (exceptions: people working outside their canton have access to physicians at the place where they work, and in case of urgency, have free access to all physicians also outside their canton).

5 The largest sickness fund limits access to specialists to five specialities, while the other three Israeli sickness funds guarantee free access.

6 Referral necessary if no emergency.

7 Only within the canton; there is a limited cantonal list of hospitals and nursing homes for which costs are reimbursed; only in emergency cases and when permission is obtained before treatment, patients can get care in hospitals not on the cantonal list of their home canton.

8 Except for railway employees.

9 Except for farmers, miners and sailors.

Sources: European Observatory's Health Care in Transition reports, Weber (2000); Österreichische Sozialversicherung (2002); Beck (2003); Belgian Federal Ministry of Social Affairs, Public Health and Environment (2003); Bundesministerium für Soziale Sicherheit und Generationen und Konsumentenschutz (2003a); Chinitz (2003); Lamers *et al.* (2003); Ministère de la Sécurité Sociale du Gran-Duche de Luxembourg (2003); Ministerie van Volksgezondheid, Welzijn en Sport (2003b; 2003c); BSV/OFAS/UFAS (2003).

Table 4.12 Dutch citizens that are insured outside their region

Year	Insured outside region of residence
1994	2.9%
1995	5.3%
1996	7.0%
1997	8.7%
1998	9.6%
1999	10.9%
2000	14.0%
2001	15.9%

Source: adapted from CVZ (1997) as in Vektis (2002a).

Table 4.13 Indicators at frequency of sickness fund change, Germany

a) net gains in membership numbers, 1997–9

Year	AOKs	BKKs
1997	−479,000	+335,000
1998	−400,000	+516,000
1999	−292,000	+971,000

Source: Busse and Riesberg (2000).

b) Insured that changed, considered to change, or did not think about changing sickness fund (%), 1998–2003

	1998	1999	2000	2001	2002	2003
Thought about change (actual change)	15(6)	15.7(7.3)	n.a	13.8	21.1	23.4
Did not think about change	85	84.3	n.a.	86.2	79.9	76.6

Notes:
n.a. = not available.
Enquiry among about 3000 insured between 16 and 65 years old. Same question over the years (except that the possibility of indicating actual change was removed in 2001; thus 1998 and 1999 data may include people that changed, but did not actually think about changing).

Sources: Wissenschaftliches Institut der AOK (1999); Zok (2003).

to enable Health Maintenance Organization (HMO) structures to be introduced by sickness funds, thus moving in the direction of restricting choice of provider. Second, regarding choice of insurer, critics have raised concerns about potential equity consequences for less healthy and/or lower-income individuals (see Chapter 7). And third, returning to choice of provider, most northern European tax-funded systems (including Sweden, Denmark, Norway, and in 2002 the United Kingdom) have adopted rules allowing choice of hospital (Denmark and the UK have traditionally had choice of GP), although the degree of implementation varies.

Equity

The concept of equity has been subject to long and often contentious debate. Questions about equity of what, compared to what, for whom, under what conditions, have occupied a range of academic minds from philosophers to economists to public policy analysts. Moreover, the rapidity with which 'equity' – what is fair – becomes transmuted into 'equality' – each treated the same – suggests the conceptual complexity of dealing with this notion in a health sector setting.

To philosophers like John Rawls (1971), *equity* occurs when all individuals are assumed to be behind a 'veil of ignorance', unable to know their own life conditions or those of their peers. In this circumstance, Rawls postulates, a social contract model will emerge which guarantees 'fair equality of opportunity' for all individuals in the pursuit of life's essential components – including health care (Daniels 1985; Churchill 1987). To economists like Tony Culyer (1991), *equality* with regard to health services is a pragmatic question which could refer to a number of different service-related outcomes: equality of status, equality of services received, equality of outcome, equality of funds expended. Other economists have sought to reduce issues of equity to two general categories: 'horizontal equity' – equal treatment of equals – and 'vertical equity' – unequal treatment of unequals (McGuire *et al.* 1988). To public policy analysts like Deborah Stone (cited in Rice 1998), equality must also incorporate environmental, cultural and social dimensions of human behaviour.

These differing assessments about the extent to which different definitions of 'equality' can be seen as providing 'equity' suggest the difficulty in assessing whether SHI systems are 'equitable'. Unfortunately, these conceptual requirements cannot be met in a comprehensive manner by currently available data. Consequently, it is necessary to adopt a partial, impressionistic view about the degree to which SHI systems in western Europe – or any health care system – are 'equitable' in their funding, structure and operation as well as their outcomes. Limited by constraints of space and data, this section does not seek to present a comprehensive view of equity in health systems. Rather, it explores two key aspects of any assessment of equity in health care systems: equity of funding and equity of access. While this limited assessment will satisfy neither philosopher nor economist nor public policy analyst, it can provide a general indication of the broad overall position of SHI systems *vis-à-vis* tax-funded health systems in western Europe, and thus serve as the basis for further debate and research.

Equity of funding

The standard statistical approach for determining the extent to which a particular funding arrangement is 'equitable' makes two simplifying assumptions. First, it presumes that equity is a relative rather than an absolute category, and renders its judgements on a comparative cross-case basis (e.g. is one arrangement 'more equitable' than another?). Second, it substitutes one particular statistical relationship – whether a particular funding arrangement is 'progressive or regressive' – for the fundamental question of whether it is 'equitable'. *Progressive*

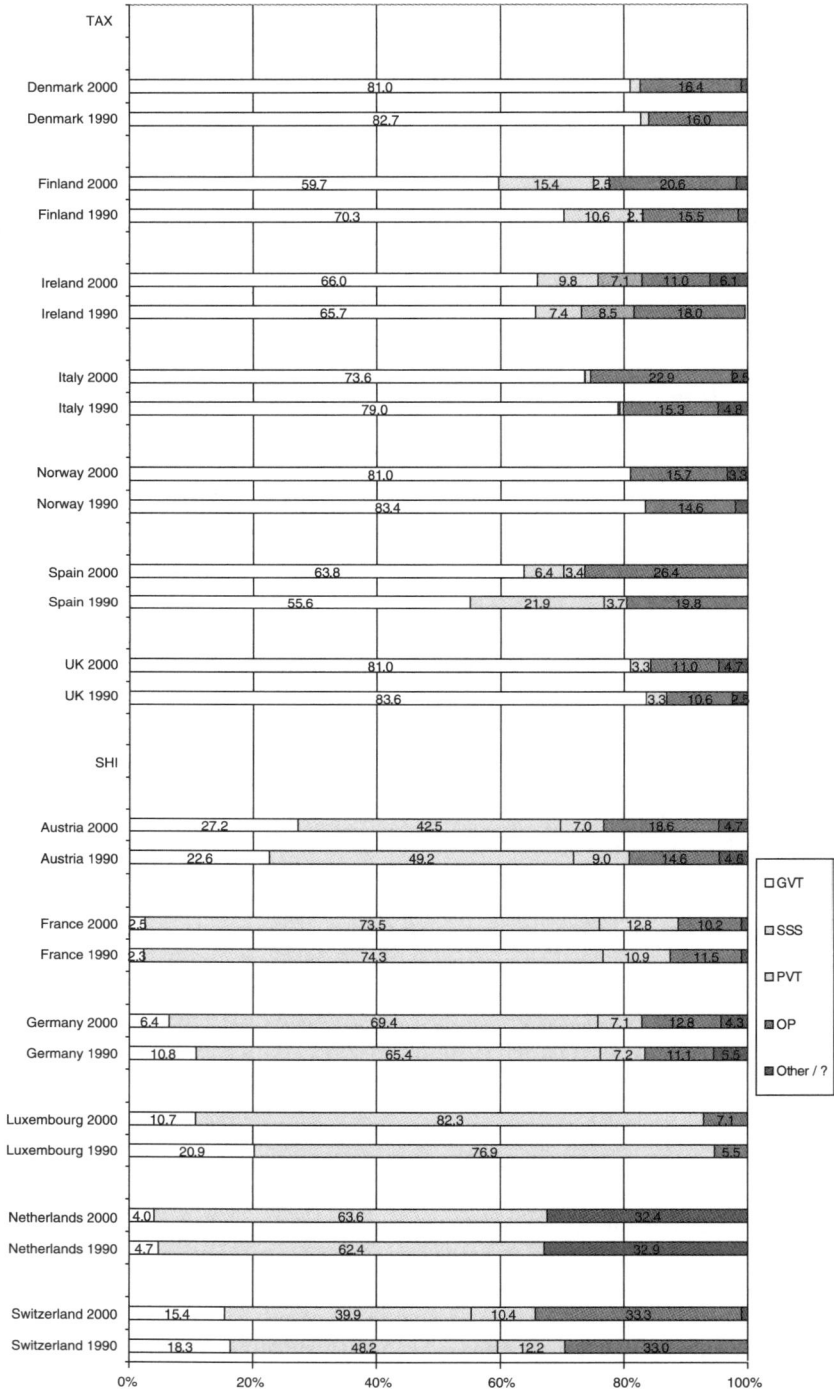

TAX					
Denmark 2000	81.0				16.4
Denmark 1990	82.7				16.0
Finland 2000	59.7		15.4	2.5	20.6
Finland 1990	70.3		10.6	2.1	15.5
Ireland 2000	66.0		9.8	7.1	11.0 6.1
Ireland 1990	65.7		7.4	8.5	18.0
Italy 2000	73.6			22.9	2.5
Italy 1990	79.0			15.3	4.8
Norway 2000	81.0			15.7	3.3
Norway 1990	83.4			14.6	
Spain 2000	63.8		6.4 3.4	26.4	
Spain 1990	55.6		21.9	3.7	19.8
UK 2000	81.0			3.3 11.0 4.7	
UK 1990	83.6			3.3 10.6 2.5	
SHI					
Austria 2000	27.2	42.5		7.0	18.6 4.7
Austria 1990	22.6	49.2		9.0	14.6 4.6
France 2000	2.5	73.5			12.8 10.2
France 1990	2.3	74.3			10.9 11.5
Germany 2000	6.4	69.4		7.1	12.8 4.3
Germany 1990	10.8	65.4		7.2	11.1 5.5
Luxembourg 2000	10.7	82.3			7.1
Luxembourg 1990	20.9	76.9			5.5
Netherlands 2000	4.0	63.6			32.4
Netherlands 1990	4.7	62.4			32.9
Switzerland 2000	15.4	39.9		10.4	33.3
Switzerland 1990	18.3	48.2		12.2	33.0

Legend:
□ GVT
□ SSS
□ PVT
■ OP
■ Other / ?

0%   20%   40%   60%   80%   100%

Figure 4.2 Funding sources of health expenditure (% of total health expenditure), 1990 and 2000

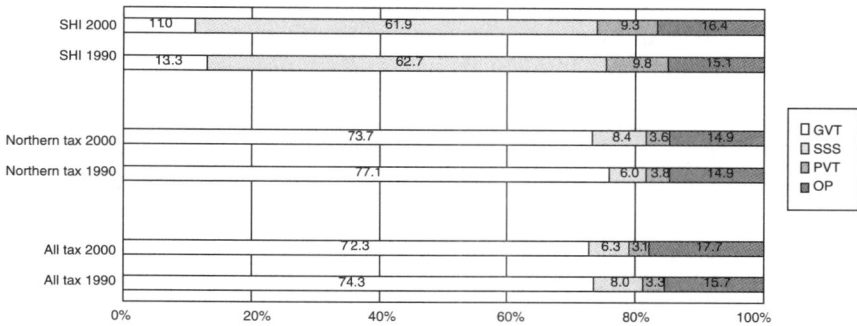

Notes: GVT = general government, excluding social security. Belgium, Greece, Israel, Portugal and Sweden are excluded because OECD data were not or too scarcely (Portugal) available, SSS = social security schemes, PVT = private insurance, OP = out-of-pocket payments. OECD and Wagstaff *et al.* (1999) use somewhat different definitions for SHI. 2000 Data: Luxembourg, Spain, Switzerland (1999), Germany (1998), Norway (OP: 1999, GVT: 1996), UK (PVT & OP: 1996). 1990 Data: Austria (GVT, SSS & OP: 1995), Spain (GVT, SSS & OP: 1991), Switzerland (PVT & OP: 1995). (for Switzerland this distorts the picture as the 1990 data add up to 111.7 per cent). 2000 data for Germany is 1998, for Luxembourg, the Netherlands, Spain and Switzerland is 1999. Data are shown when > 2.0. For some countries no data were available for SSS (Denmark, Norway), PVT (Luxembourg, Netherlands, Norway) and OP (Netherlands) – these were excluded when calculating the averages; still the percentages do not always add up to exactly 100 per cent (main reasons: exclusion in the figure of OECD's *other private funds* and not all data from 1990 and 2000).

Source: OECD (2002).

Figure 4.3 K index measuring progressivity/regressivity of health care finance, selected years

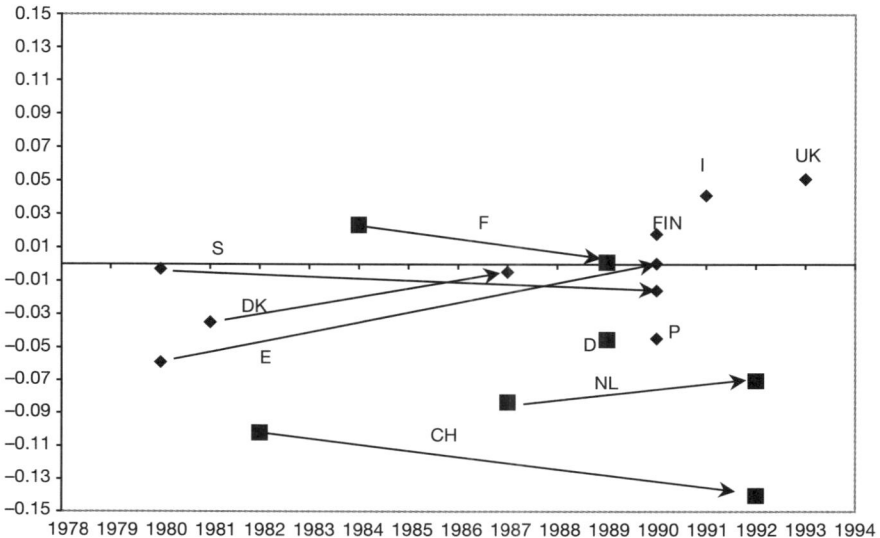

Source: adapted from Wagstaff *et al.* (1999).

is defined as higher income individuals (in theory based on both income and wealth) paying a higher proportion/percentage of their income for the same coverage than do lower income individuals (e.g. creating a cross-subsidy from wealthier to less-wealthy citizens). *Regressive* characterizes the reverse relationship (e.g. higher income individuals pay a lower proportion than do lower income citizens).

In addition to these two simplifying assumptions, the standard statistical approach tends to focus more on the overall funding framework in a country than the specific components that compose that framework. Since nearly all health care systems in western Europe utilize some mix of all four major funding arrangements – SHI, tax-funded, private insurance and out-of-pocket (Figure 4.2, see p. 106) – results presented in the statistical studies tend toward highlighting the general progressivity or regressivity of the overall mix of funding systems in SHI countries – not that of SHI mechanisms specifically.

Taken together, these simplifications reduce the usefulness of the standard statistical approach in terms of answering the question this section poses about the equity of specifically SHI funding arrangements. Consequently, after reviewing aggregate national data on 'progressivity/regressivity' (Wagstaff *et al.* 1999) and 'fairness' (Murray *et al.* 2003), this section also presents two additional data series, each of which is, technically, a sub-set of the overall national figures, but tends not to be visible within the aggregate statistics. These two are the percentages of total health system funding in each country paid by the least equitable of the four funding forms presented in Figure 4.2, namely out-of-pocket deductibles and co-payments, and how SHI premiums are charged and paid for in relation to two groups of non-working adults (e.g. the unemployed and pensioners).

Equity of system-wide funding

Two quantitative studies have included efforts to assess the degree of progressivity/regressivity and/or the 'fairness' of system-wide funding structures in western European health care systems. Wagstaff *et al.* (1999) presented revised results from an earlier study of EU countries and the United States, utilizing national accounts data from the 1980s and early 1990s. They employed a calculation known as a K index, with which a positive value of K indicates a progressive structure, while a negative value demonstrates a regressive structure. Although the data is now 12 to 15 years old, Figure 4.3 on p. 107 provides a useful historical view of previous trends in funding equity at the overall health system level for ten western European countries. It shows, as the Wagstaff study itself concludes, that generally the SHI-based health systems are mildly regressive, while the tax-based health systems are mildly progressive. Broken down by sources of funding within countries, direct taxes, general taxes and social insurance typically have positive K values on the vertical redistribution axis, though Germany and the Netherlands are exceptions in the case of social insurance as they exclude, or allow the opting-out of, higher income earners. This results in a concentration of people in the statutory SHI system with lower incomes and often higher risks, making them regressive. An exception was the long-term care component of the Dutch health care system, the AWBZ, which

Figure 4.4 K index measuring progressivity of the dominant health care finance method in four SHI countries and seven tax-funded western European countries, selected years

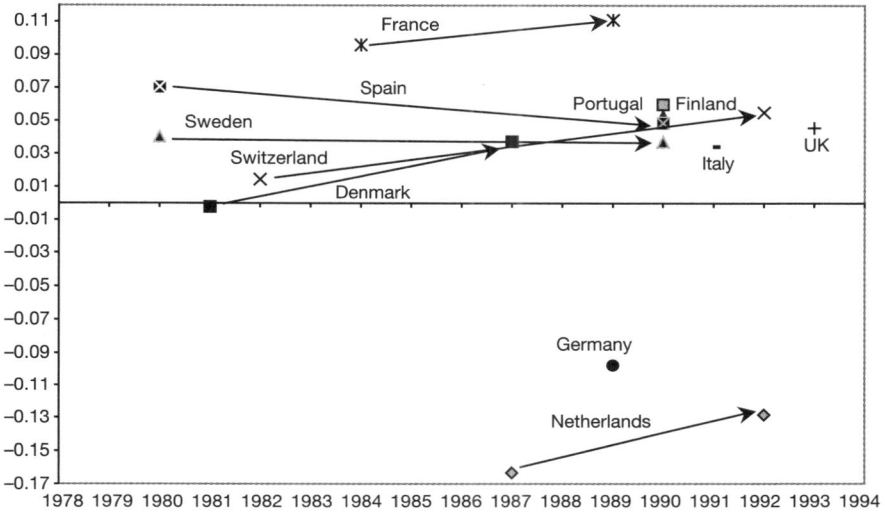

Note: Progressivity indices of, for predominantly tax funded countries, the general tax component (indirect and direct taxes) and, for predominantly SHI based countries, the social insurance component of health care finance.

Source: adapted from Wagstaff *et al.* (1999).

has universal coverage with fixed percentage premiums and thus was marginally progressive.

Figure 4.4 separates out only the SHI and tax-based elements from these systems. It indicates that tax-based funding is mildly progressive, limited in Nordic countries by reliance upon proportional rather than progressive income taxes at the regional and/or municipal level. The figure also suggests that SHI in countries with maximum contribution ceilings and opt-outs for high income earners (e.g. Germany and Netherlands) is substantially regressive. In earlier work, Wagstaff and Van Doorslaer (1997) presented simulations that the degree of progressivity differs both with upper contribution limits and exemptions for the poor. In the data by Wagstaff *et al.*, out-of-pocket payments were always, and private insurance premiums often, related to negative values.

It is important to emphasize that numerous, sometimes important, changes have taken place in both SHI and tax-funded systems since the data for the Wagstaff study was collected. Among SHI systems, two major changes already described earlier in Chapter Three should be noted. One concerns France, which in 2000 introduced a new tax-paid supplemental insurance for the lowest-income individuals. Furthermore, individuals with the lowest incomes are exempted from paying premiums for sickness insurance (up to a certain wage lower premiums often apply), and since 2001 there is only one fund left (AMPI/CANAM, the fund of the self-employed, covering less than 5 per cent of the population) which still has an income ceiling beyond which premiums are not assessed. The result, some commentators believe, is that the overall national mix of funding sources in France has become more progressive than (flat) tax-financed Denmark, Finland and Sweden, despite France's continued user charges and only partially refunded outpatient charges, as well as the role played by the private not-for-profit *Mutualités* (Evans 2002).

The second change concerns Israel, which, although it was not included in the Wagstaff study, is included in the SHI systems assessed in this volume. In 1995, Israel switched to a 'health tax', paid on a progressive basis by all income-earning citizens. As a result, Israel's funding arrangements have become substantially more progressive then they were pre-1995 when subscribers paid fixed health premiums to their sickness fund (Gross and Harrison 2001).

It should also be noted that tax-funded systems in western Europe have undergone certain changes with regard to progressivity since the early 1990s. Chief of these has been increases in out-of-pocket co-payments (particularly Finland and Sweden) which have slightly reduced previously observed levels of progressivity (as noted earlier in Evans 2002).

These caveats all suggest that, overall, SHI countries in 2003 are likely to be slightly less regressive than portrayed by the earlier Wagstaff data, while tax-funded systems may well be slightly less progressive than they previously were. Without appropriate analysis of current data, however, it is impossible to determine to what degree the gap between them has diminished.

Some (although not all) of the 1990s changes may be reflected in the 2003 fairness in financing data collected and analysed in the second broad study, conducted by the Division of Evidence and Policy at the World Health Organization in Geneva. Looking at the opposite end of the statistical continuum from the Wagstaff study, which assessed aggregate expenditures at country level, the WHO study evaluates the percentage of health-related expenditures in individual household income (after adjustment to remove subsistence costs – in particular food). 'Fair' – as defined by this study – was a situation in which all households pay the same percentage of their disposable income for health care (again a simplification of the equality issues discussed in the introduction to this section).

The WHO methodology focused on how health care is financed by households through a combination of out-of-pocket payments, tax contributions, social insurance and private insurance. The data are based on national household income and expenditure surveys, government taxation documents, national health account figures, social security and health insurance laws, and health system profiles. Several dilemmas have been raised about fairness in financing data by Navarro (2000), Shaw (2001), Szwarcwald (2002) and Wagstaff (2001) (as in WHO 2002b). Some of these concerns have been resolved in this latest data series by separately addressing the percentage of households facing catastrophic payment (Kawabata *et al.* 2001; WHO 2001), defined as households facing out-of-pocket health costs greater than 40 per cent of their total disposable income. The data also include figures on percentage of households 'impoverished due to health payments'.

The WHO data presented in Table 4.14, collected between 1993 and 2000, include five of the eight studied SHI countries (not Austria, Luxembourg or

Table 4.14 Fairness in financing, 1993–2000

	Fairness in financial contribution[1]		% of households with catastrophic health expenditures		% of households impoverished due to health payments	
	Level	Relative order	Level	Relative order	Level	Relative order
United Kingdom	0.921	1	0.33	2	0.18	8
Denmark	0.920	2	0.38	3	0.03	4
Sweden	0.920	2	0.39	4	0.31	9
Germany	0.913	4	0.54	5	0.01	3
Belgium	0.903	5	0.23	1	0.00	1
Finland	0.901	6	1.36	10	0.08	5
Spain	0.899	7	0.89	7	0.44	11
Israel	0.897	8	1.09	8	0.43	10
France	0.889	9	0.68	6	0.13	7
Norway	0.888	10	1.22	9	0.00	1
Switzerland	0.875	11	3.03	11	0.08	5
Greece	0.858	12	3.29	12	0.56	12
Portugal	0.845	13	4.01	13	1.79	13
SHI countries average	*0.90*	–	*1.11*	–	*0.13*	–
Tax-funded countries average	*0.89*	–	*1.48*	–	*0.42*	–
– northern	*0.91*	–	*0.74*	–	*0.12*	–
– southern	*0.87*	–	*2.73*	–	*0.93*	–
Ratio SHI/all tax	*1.002*	–	*0.751*	–	*0.307*	–
Difference SHI to all tax (% points)	*0.001*	–	*–0.370*	–	*–0.294*	–
Ratio SHI/northern tax	*0.984*	–	*1.514*	–	*1.083*	–
Difference SHI/northern tax (% points)	*–0.015*	–	*0.378*	–	*0.010*	–

Notes:
1 Score ranging between 0 and 1. Countries tending to 1 have fairer health financing systems. Ordering is only to facilitate easy interpretation of the data. It does not reflect overall national rankings – see caveat page 82/83. Countries are sorted according to their fairness in financial contribution level. No data are available for Austria, Ireland, Italy, Luxembourg and the Netherlands.

Source: Murray *et al.* (2003).

Netherlands), five of six northern tax-funded countries (not Ireland), and three of four southern tax-funded countries (not Italy). These data reflect household surveys, which varied in number from 1,103 in Sweden to 48,270 in Germany (Xu *et al.* 2003). Based on this partial representation, the mix of funding in SHI countries (including all forms of health-related payment) is slightly less progressive than that in the northern tax-funded countries (0.90 vs. 0.91) but a bit more progressive than the mix in southern tax-funded countries (0.90 vs. 0.87). The third column – percentage of households impoverished by out-of-pocket health costs – shows a similar relationship, although the figure for southern tax-funded countries is notably higher. Much wider differences appear in the middle column, concerning percentage of households forced to spend more than 40 per cent of their disposable income on health costs. Here, the SHI country average is notably higher than northern tax-funded countries – 1.11 vs. 0.74 – but notably lower than the figure of 2.73 for southern tax-funded countries.

Overall, the WHO data suggests that in the late 1990s, the overall mix of funding in SHI-based countries was slightly more regressive than the overall mix in the northern tax-funded countries that have roughly equivalent per capita incomes (southern tax-funded countries having significantly lower per capita incomes than either SHI or northern tax-based countries).

Out-of-pocket payments

Out-of-pocket payments incorporate a range of charges that individuals must pay at the point of service or purchase. These can include co-payments (fixed fee at point of service), so-called 'nominal premiums' (e.g. monthly co-payments as part of SHI premiums in the Netherlands), residual payments (un-reimbursed expenses as for outpatient physician visits in France), and initial up-front deductibles. They also include payments for non-covered services, drugs and medical supplies. Current data is not available for aggregate co-payment levels in western Europe, but exists for the broader category of out-of-pocket expenditures.

All out-of-pocket expenditures by definition decrease equity, in that they necessarily put a greater strain on the household budgets of lower income as against higher income individuals (Barer *et al.* 1998; Kutzin 1998; Evans 2002; Robinson 2002). Such charges have been shown to discourage lower income individuals from seeking necessary care (D'Onofrio and Muller 1977; Lohr *et al.* 1986 as in Louckx 2002; Kutzin 1998) and thus reduce equity of access (Rice 1998).

There is some anecdotal country evidence regarding the impact of co-payments and other direct charges. In Belgium, the reduction of some co-payments for certain vulnerable (so-called VIPO) groups has made a marginal improvement (Kerr 2000), however, the less-well-off and elderly still have to make considerable large payments both for co-payments and in bearing the full cost of non-reimbursable medicines (Peys 2001). The first Belgian Health Survey of 1997 revealed that one-third of the Belgian population claimed to experience difficulty in paying for medical care (Belgische Senaat 1999 as in Louckx 2002). The survey also showed that 8 per cent of the families questioned occasionally postponed medical care for financial reasons, with visits to the dentist most likely to be sacrificed. One should also mention that the poverty percentage in families with a sick or invalid breadwinner doubled between 1985 and 1997, from 8.3 to 16.4 per cent (Vranken *et al.* 1999 as in Louckx 2002).

Available statistical evidence shown in Figure 4.2 suggests that out-of-pocket expenditure (summarized in Table 4.15) varies considerably among western European countries. Among the five SHI countries assessed, the variation is much greater (in 2000 7.1 per cent for Luxembourg contrasted with 33.3 per cent for Switzerland) than it is among five northern tax-funded countries (in

Table 4.15 Out-of-pocket expenditures in 1990 and 2000 (data from Figure 4.2)

SHI:	1990	2000
Austria	14.6 (1995)	18.6
France	11.5	10.2
Germany	11.1	12.8 (1998)
Luxembourg	5.5	7.1 (1999)
Switzerland	33.0 (1995)	33.3 (1999)
Northern tax-funded:		
Denmark	16.0	16.4
Finland	15.5	20.6
Ireland	18.0	11.0
Norway	14.6	15.7 (1999)
UK	10.6	11.0 (1996)
Southern tax-funded:		
Italy	15.3	22.9
Spain	19.8 (1991)	26.4 (1999)
SHI Average	*15.1*	*16.4*
Northern tax-funded average	*14.9*	*14.9*
All tax-funded	*15.7*	*17.7*

2000 11.0 per cent for Ireland contrasted with 20.6 per cent for Finland). The data also indicate that between 1990 and 2000, the percentage of out-of-pocket expenditures fell dramatically in one tax-funded country (Ireland by 7.0 per cent) and only slightly in one SHI country (by 1.5 per cent in France – although the 2000 tax-based changes in funding in France would be felt more strongly since then). It is also noteworthy that, while Finland's figure increased by 5 per cent over the ten-year period, its absolute percentage at 20.6, as the highest northern European tax-funded system, is only two-thirds of the absolute figure in the highest SHI country (e.g. Switzerland at 33.3 per cent). These wide variations are, not surprisingly, subsumed within the average figure for each category, which, while showing in 2000 SHI as higher (16.4 per cent) than northern tax-funded (14.9 per cent), it is lower once Italy and Spain are added into the overall tax-funded figure (17.7 per cent). One additional equity-related figure is that most countries in both categories witnessed increases in this highly regressive form of health care funding over the 1990s: four of five SHI, four of five northern tax-funded, and the two southern tax-funded.

Unemployed, pensioners, and low-waged

The equity implications of how the eight studied SHI countries treat these three categories of non- or low-waged individuals are complex and somewhat contradictory. As Table 3.5 indicates (see p. 48), each of these three categories demonstrates a mix of progressive as well as regressive measures, typically depending upon the country and the specific circumstances. Of the three groups, the unemployed receive fairly progressive treatment, often remaining insured with all required payments made by the unemployment agency (e.g. Germany) or public tax-raised funds (e.g. France). One exception is the Netherlands, where the unemployed must pay the normal percentage on their social benefits as well as the nominal out-of-pocket premium. Since these social benefits are relatively low, this requirement is mildly regressive. Another exception is Switzerland, where the unemployed must themselves pay the regular fixed premium – a regressive approach – however, local social agencies will pay the premium for those below a fixed threshold who file a formal petition – a progressive approach.

The overall equity implications of measures for accommodating the second of these three groups – pensioners – are mixed. Some formulas are mildly regressive, requiring the retired to pay the same fixed percentage of their pension as employees pay of their wages (Germany, Netherlands) while others include special exemptions (Belgium) or lower annual ceilings (Israel). Switzerland again is an exception: as in the treatment of the unemployed, pensioners must pay the regular fixed premium from their typically lower monthly incomes; however, social agencies will pay if petitioned by those who fall below a certain threshold.

Of the eight countries, two have measures in place that lower the amount the worker pays either partially (Israel) or completely (France). A third country (Switzerland) will pay the low income worker's fixed premium from mixed federal/cantonal funds under certain tightly constrained circumstances. These count as progressive measures. Conversely, however, five of the eight countries require low income workers to either pay the same contribution rate (and fixed nominal premium) as do higher income workers (the Netherlands) or exempt the worker from mandatory health insurance payments but then exclude those workers from health insurance coverage (Austria, Germany, Luxembourg, the Netherlands). If these excluded workers are not covered either by another (primary) job or by a family-tied arrangement (e.g. spouse or parent), they may be eligible to have cover by public funds (Austria, Germany). While not providing cover to low income workers is highly regressive, the number of workers affected (e.g. not covered by another job or family-tied arrangement, or by special public funds) is not clear.

Equity of access

The provision of adequate access to necessary care sits at the core of an equitable health system. However, the definition of what is a suitable level of access can (and often does) depend on varying interpretations of what is equitable, as well as sometimes widely divergent views of what is understood as 'necessary'. Moreover, the concept of access itself extends to a wide range of organizational dimensions.

Since they have well-developed and articulated health care systems, nearly all SHI countries can provide reasonable physical access to curative providers such as GPs and hospitals. However, there often remain less apparent barriers such as inconvenient office hours, appointment requirements, visit lengths and a variety of other non-financial obstacles.

One example of recent redirection in these non-financial barriers can be seen in Israel. In the first three years of implementation of its 1995 national health insurance law, older patients reported an improvement in waiting times, physician office hours and services provided (Bentur and Gross 2001). An example of decidedly less improvement was Switzerland, where, despite the availability of reduced premiums after passage of the 1996 Federal Law on Health Insurance, lack of information to some target groups led fewer lower income individuals to apply in some cantons (Balthasar *et al.* 2001). Moreover, legal provisions regarding compulsory claims are so detailed that it is difficult for insurers to verify claims at a reasonable cost, and the legal obligation to reimburse is so ambiguously defined that different insurers interpret their responsibilities quite differently – both provisions resulting in uneven, occasionally unequal reimbursement across the insured population (Hornung *et al.* 2001). There also appeared to be reduced access to preventive health measures for groups at risk (Sager *et al.* 2001). There are large differences in waiting lists across regions in the Netherlands (Hurst and Siciliani 2003; Ministerie van Volksgezondheid, Welzijn en Sport 2003a; RIVM 2003). In France and Germany, known for having practically no waiting lists for specialist care, there are cases of waiting lists respectively up to six months for ophthalmologist appointments in the French countryside (*Le Quotidien du Médecine* 2002) and a mean of 35 days for cataract surgery in Germany (Wenzel *et al.* 2001 as in Siciliani and Hurst 2003).

Some commentators have also argued that a central obstacle to receiving needed care is social class, for one instance in France (Bocognano *et al.* 2000). Considerable research exists on this issue in tax-funded countries in northern Europe. Several reports in Sweden and in the UK (e.g. Black *et al.* 1982; Whitehead 1988; Dahlgren and Whitehead 1992) found that lower social class was directly correlated with poorer health status, despite the availability of all necessary health care services without charge at the point of provision. A similar research finding in France, coupled with data suggesting lower income individuals in Switzerland have difficulty in penetrating obstacles created by the need to enrol in social health insurance (SHI) plans, suggests that a class-based access problem likely also exist in other SHI countries such as Austria, Belgium or Germany. Two recent studies suggest that there may be age-related access problems due to discrimination in writing health insurance policies in the Netherlands (LBL 2002; Unie KBO 2003). The lack of availability of adequate research on these questions, however, makes it difficult to make any broader judgements.

Efficiency

A central dimension of health sector policy-making and debate in Europe is the efficiency with which different health care systems operate. While concepts of efficiency were initially developed by economists for use in the industrial sector, these instruments are being increasingly adopted for application in the health sector. There continues to be considerable controversy surrounding the appropriateness of applying available measurement tools to a complex human service sector like health.[3] A wide range of efforts have been made to develop more suitable measures that can incorporate quality-related dimensions at both aggregate national and cross-national levels (e.g. QUALYs and DALYs).

In economic theory, a main measure of efficiency is technical efficiency (Rice 1998). Reinhardt (2003) emphasizes that technical efficiency has little if any correlation to distributional appropriateness. This reflects the fact that technical efficiency is concerned with outputs, while distribution is a normative category that is concerned not with outputs but with the socially desired objective that the system is seeking to satisfy (e.g. improved health status for certain vulnerable groups). As Reinhardt pointedly explains, the distinction between outputs and outcomes, 'a resource allocation that would be said by economists to be more "efficient" than another is not necessarily "better" than the other' (Reinhardt 2003: xvii).

The discussion in this section focuses exclusively on the technical or operating efficiency of SHI systems. It is concerned with the outputs achieved – the intermediate products – rather than the purpose or value of the overall outcome. This approach has several data-related limitations. As noted in this chapter's introduction, current statistical systems do not always collect resource-related data across countries according to the same criteria. Moreover, regarding resource levels, the available data series often do not provide sufficient corroborating information to determine if higher levels of resources (e.g. number of CT scanners or MRIs) are correlated to higher or lower utilization rates, or whether utilization rates reflect clinically necessary or clinically unnecessary (for instance, duplicate) procedures.

This section presents four different categories, each of which has some bearing on overall health system efficiency. The first two provide information on the level of resources committed to the health system – cost/expenditures and relative resource levels and utilization rates. Subsequently information is presented on one particular type of expenditure – administrative costs. Finally, the section briefly presents several comparative studies of the quality of services provided – relative clinical performance. It is important to note that, while all four of these categories have a bearing on the overall efficiency with which a health system delivers care, none of these four can be directly tied to the prior three parameters of activity – health status, satisfaction/responsiveness and equity – and thus they are unable to generate unambiguous judgements about the specific technical efficiency of the different health systems assessed.

Costs/expenditure

Total expenditure on health care is perhaps the most visible measure of health system activity in the developed world. It is also the most politically volatile, turning up in national election campaigns and in the national news media.

These figures, as noted earlier, are notoriously difficult to calculate. The OECD's latest data set (2003) indicates that a substantial number of western European countries vary considerably from the OECD's May 2000 guidance in how they calculate their national health expenditures. One particularly thorny issue is the degree of inclusion of elderly care services, including nursing home, residential living and home care services (Saltman *et al.* 2001).

Given this combination of intense political interest yet substantial difficulty in both the definition and calculation of the actual data, this section will present four separate sets of OECD-generated statistics that illustrate different dimensions of the cost/expenditure issue: percentage of GDP expended on health; per capita expenditure on health; the rate of increase in expenditures during the 1990s; and the percentage of total health expenditures that run through publicly controlled or publicly accountable institutions.

System-level expenditure figures for the eight studied SHI countries tell an interesting tale. However calculated, SHI systems cost more to run than do their tax-funded northern European counterparts.[4] For example, using 2000 data (Table 4.14), Germany expended 10.6 per cent of GDP on health and Switzerland expended 10.7 per cent, while the same OECD sequence indicates that Sweden spent 8.4 per cent, Finland spent 6.7 per cent and Ireland spent 6.4 per cent. Conversely, however, the Netherlands spent 8.6 per cent, Belgium spent 8.6 per cent, and Austria spent 7.7 per cent,[5] which is very close to the annual GDP percentage of expenditure of Denmark at 8.3 per cent and Norway at 7.6 per cent. Constructing a ratio of the percentage of GDP expenditures in the eight SHI countries as contrasted with six northern European tax-funded systems, average SHI systems spending in terms of GDP as a ratio to northern European tax-based systems' spending was substantially higher at 1.16 in 2000 (Table 4.16).

A review of per capita expenditure figures (2000 or latest year available) tells a similar although somewhat more muted tale (Table 4.17). Switzerland's (PPP adjusted) $3,160 is nearly double Finland's $1,699 or the United Kingdom's $1,813. Yet, conversely, the Belgian ($2,260), Dutch ($2,348), Austrian ($2,170) and Israeli ($1,777) figures are substantially less than Norway's $2,755 and Denmark's $2,398. The more compressed relationship between SHI and tax-funded health systems on this per capita measure does not appear in the overall ratio, however, which at 1.16 is equal to the GDP figure.

Two further aggregate series concern the rate of increase in expenditures over the 1990s, and the percentage of total health expenditures that run through publicly controlled or publicly accountable institutions. Here, the data provide some nuance to the above two headline statistics. Regarding the rate of growth in expenditures, annual figures show that between 1990 and 1995 total health expenditures (in 1995 GDP prices) in the eight SHI countries increased by an average of 5.1 per cent per year, while between 1995 and 2000, the average increase was only 3.1 per cent per year (Table 4.18). These data suggest that cost constraining mechanisms put in place during the reform period in the mid-1990s had started to have limited success. This perception also conforms to certain country-based evidence. In Switzerland, for example, the introduction by the largest sickness fund of a premium rebate based on prior year utilization appears linked to a low growth rate in per capita costs (Beck 2000). In France, stronger price controls appear to be having the desired effect (Le Pen 2003). In general it appears that those countries which had introduced both price and volume controls (Germany and the Netherlands) have been more successful in containing drug cost growth. There is no clear empirical evidence that volume controls alone have had any decreasing effect on the aggregate level (see Chapter 9). Furthermore, a portion of the observed cost

Table 4.16 Total health expenditure as a percentage of GDP 1980–2000

	1980 (% of GDP)	1985 (% of GDP)	1990 (% of GDP)	1995 (% of GDP)	2000 (% of GDP)	Change 1980–2000 (% points)
Switzerland	7.6	8.0	8.5	10.0	10.7	3.1
Germany (West until 1990)	8.7	9.0	8.5	10.6	10.6	1.9
Greece	6.6	7.4[1]	7.4	9.6	9.4	2.8
France	7.4*	8.3*	8.6	9.5	9.3	1.9
Portugal	5.6	6.0	6.2	8.3	9.0	3.4
Belgium	6.4	7.2	7.4	8.6	8.6	2.2
Netherlands	7.5	7.3	8.0	8.4	8.6	1.1
Sweden	8.8	8.5	8.2	8.1	8.4	−0.4
Denmark	9.1	8.7	8.5	8.2	8.3	−0.8
Israel	6.1*	6.2*	7.3*	7.8*	8.3*	2.2
Italy	7.0*	7.0*	8.0	7.4	8.2	1.2
Austria	7.6	6.6	7.1	8.2	7.7	0.1
Norway	6.9	6.6	7.7	7.9	7.6	0.7
Spain	5.4	5.5	6.7	7.6	7.5	2.1
United Kingdom	5.6	5.9	6.0	7.0	7.3	1.7
Finland	6.4	7.1	7.8	7.5	6.7	0.3
Ireland	8.4	7.6	6.1	6.8	6.4	−2.0
Luxembourg	5.9	5.9	6.1	6.4	5.6	−0.3
SHI countries average	*7.2*	*7.3*	*7.7*	*8.7*	*8.7*	*1.5*
Northern tax-funded average	*7.5*	*7.4*	*7.4*	*7.6*	*7.5*	*−0.1*
Ratio SHI/ Northern tax	*0.95*	*0.99*	*1.04*	*1.15*	*1.16*	*–*
Difference SHI/ Northern tax (% points)	*−0.4*	*−0.1*	*0.3*	*1.1*	*1.2*	*1.6*
All tax-funded average	*7.0*	*7.0*	*7.3*	*7.8*	*7.9*	*0.9*
Ratio SHI/all tax	*1.02*	*1.04*	*1.06*	*1.11*	*1.10*	*–*
Difference SHI – all tax (% points)	*0.2*	*0.3*	*0.4*	*0.8*	*0.8*	*0.6*

Notes:
1 1987 data.
Ordering is only to facilitate easy interpretation of the data. It does not reflect overall national rankings – see caveat page 82/83. Countries are sorted by the expenditure level in 2000.

Sources: OECD (2003); * WHO (2003) and, for Israel 1980 and 1985, Ben Nun (2003).

containment could have been produced by the implementation of capitation (Jönsson 2002).

The percentage of total health expenditures spent by publicly controlled bodies provides an insight into the public-private mix in the source of health care

Table 4.17 Rate of increase of total health expenditure in the 1980s and 1990s, $PPP per capita

	1980 ($ PPP)	1990 ($ PPP)	2000 ($ PPP)	Change 1980s (%)	Change 1990s (%)
Switzerland	891	1836	3160	106.1	72.1
Germany (West until 1990)	824	1600	2780	94.2	73.8
Norway	632	1363	2755	115.7	102.1
Luxembourg	606	1501	2719	147.7	81.1
Denmark	819	1453	2398	77.4	65.0
France	701*	1509	2387	115.3	58.2
Netherlands	668	1333	2348	99.6	76.1
Belgium	576	1245	2260	116.1	81.5
Sweden	850	1492	2195	75.5	47.1
Austria	662	1204	2170	81.9	80.2
Italy	579*	1321	2060	128.2	55.9
United Kingdom	445	977	1813	119.6	85.6
Ireland	452	719	1793	59.1	149.4
Israel	n.a.	947	1777	–	87.6
Finland	509	1295	1699	154.4	31.2
Greece	348	695	1556	99.7	123.9
Portugal	265	611	1519	130.6	148.6
Spain	328	813	1497	147.9	84.1
SHI countries average	*704*	*1397*	*2450*	*98.4*	*75.4*
Northern tax-based average	*618*	*1217*	*2109*	*96.9*	*73.4*
Ratio SHI/Northern tax	*1.14*	*1.15*	*1.16*	*–*	*–*
Difference SHI/northern tax (% points)	*86*	*180*	*341*	*1.5*	*2.0*
All tax-based average	*523*	*1074*	*1929*	*105.5*	*79.6*
Ratio SHI/all tax	*1.35*	*1.30*	*1.27*	*–*	*–*
Difference SHI – all tax (% points)	*181*	*323*	*522*	*–7.0*	*–4.2*

Notes:
n.a. = not available.
Ordering is only to facilitate easy interpretation of the data. It does not reflect overall national rankings – see caveat page 82/83.
Countries are sorted by the expenditure level in 2000.
1 1987 data.

Sources: OECD (2003),* WHO (2003) and, for Israel, Ben Nun (2003).

resources. OECD figures indicate that the overall public role in SHI funding (which had been considerably lower than in tax-based countries) decreased further in a number of countries over the 1990s (Table 4.19). The Netherlands, for instance, showed a decrease of 7.6 per cent in publicly-controlled funding between 1995 and 2000. However, reflecting major reforms introduced in the mid-1990s, Belgium and Switzerland had an increased public role between 1995 and 2000 of 1.6 percentage points and 1.8 percentage points respectively. The OECD data also show that the percentage of public expenditure also

Table 4.18 Percentage mean annual growth rates for total health expenditure

Percentage mean annual growth rates of total health expenditure in selected European countries based on national currency units at 1995 GDP prices (the GDP price deflator is used because data are available and health care price deflators are biased towards pharmaceutics), 1980–5, 1985–90, 1990–5 and 1995–2000.

	1980–1985	1985–1990	1990–1995	1995–2000	Relative order based on 1995–2000 data
Ireland	0.6	0.3	7.9	9.8	1
Portugal	2.7	7.0	9.2	6.3	2
Netherlands	0.7	5.7	3.3	4.6	3
Luxembourg	2.5	9.7	5.2	4.4	4
Italy	n.a.	n.a.	−0.4	4.3	5
Sweden	1.0	1.9	0.6	4.2	6
United Kingdom	3.0	4.1	5.2	4.1	7
Spain	1.7	10.3	4.6	3.7	8
Switzerland	2.7	4.4	3.2	3.5	9
Greece	1.6[1]	2.8[2]	7.7	3.2	10
Denmark	0.9	0.9	1.3	3.2	10
Belgium	3.3	4.2	4.9	3.1	12
Norway	2.2	5.4	4.7	2.8	13
Finland	5.9	5.8	−1.5	2.6	14
France	n.a.	n.a.	3.4	2.4	15
Germany	2.1	2.2	10.3	1.9	16
Austria	−1.3	5.2	5.5	1.7	17
Israel	n.a.	n.a.	n.a.	n.a.	–
SHI average	*1.7*	*5.2*	*5.1*	*3.1*	–
Tax-funded average	*2.2*	*4.3*	*3.9*	*4.4*	–
– northern	*2.3*	*3.1*	*3.0*	*4.5*	–
Difference SHI all tax (% points)	*−0.5*	*1.0*	*1.2*	*−1.3*	–
Difference SHI – northern tax (% points)	*−0.6*	*2.2*	*2.1*	*−1.4*	–

Note:
Ordering is only to facilitate easy interpretation of the data. It does not reflect overall national rankings – see caveat page 82/83. Countries are sorted by mean annual growth rates between 1995 and 2000.
1 1980–1987.
2 1987–1990.

Sources: OECD (2003); based on Mossialos and Dixon (2002a).

decreased during this period of northern tax-funded health systems, although by a substantially smaller rate.

Overall, one concludes from these four different sets of aggregate expenditure statistics that, while the level of spending is higher in SHI than in tax-funded

Table 4.19 Public expenditure on health as percentage of total health expenditure

	1990	1995	2000	Relative order based on 2000 data	Change 90–5 (% points)	Change 95–00 (% points)
Luxembourg	93.1	92.4	87.8	1	−0.7	−4.6
Norway	82.8	84.2	85.2	2	+1.4	+1.0
Sweden	89.9	86.7	85.0	3	−3.2	−1.7
Denmark	82.7	82.5	82.5	4	−0.2	+0.0
United Kingdom	83.6	83.9	80.9	5	+0.3	−3.0
France	76.6	76.3	75.8	6	−0.3	−0.5
Finland	80.9	75.6	75.1	7	−5.3	−0.5
Germany	76.2	76.7	75.0	8	+0.5	−1.7
Italy	79.3	72.2	73.4	9	−7.1	+1.2
Ireland	71.9	71.6	73.3	10	−0.3	+1.7
Belgium	n.a.	70.5	72.1	11	n.a.	+1.6
Spain	78.7	72.2	71.7	12	−6.5	−0.5
Austria	73.5	70.9	69.4	13	−2.6	−1.5
Israel	71.0	74.0	69.0	14	+3.0	−5.0
Portugal	65.5	61.7	68.5	15	−3.8	+6.8
Netherlands	67.1	71.0	63.4	16	+3.9	−7.6
Greece	53.7	52.0	56.1	17	−1.7	+4.1
Switzerland	52.4	53.8	55.6	18	+1.4	+1.8
SHI average (7/8 countries)	*72.8*	*73.2*	*71.0*	*–*	*+0.4*	*−2.2*
Northern tax-funded	*82.0*	*80.8*	*80.3*	*–*	*−1.2*	*−0.4*
Difference SHI to Northern tax (% points)	*−9.1*	*−7.6*	*−9.3*	*–*	*+1.6*	*−1.8*
All tax-funded	*76.9*	*74.3*	*75.2*	*–*	*−2.6*	*+0.9*
Difference SHI to all tax (% points)	*−4.1*	*−1.1*	*−4.2*	*–*	*+3.0*	*−3.1*

Notes:
Ordering is only to facilitate easy interpretation of the data. It does not reflect overall national rankings – see caveat page 82/83. Countries are sorted by 2000 public expenditure.

Sources: OECD (2003), Israel: WHO (2003).

systems, the recent rate of growth has been equal (per capita) or lower. This assessment also has been reached by other calculations (Barros 1998).

Relative resource levels and utilization rates

Given higher aggregate expenditures on health care, it is to be expected that SHI countries often have higher absolute levels of physical resources than do tax-funded systems. For example, OECD data (although from mixed years

1995–2001) suggest that SHI systems often have higher population-adjusted numbers of expensive high technology diagnostic equipment such as CT scanners (although not for MRI units) (Table 4.20). As noted earlier, however, the number of units provides no information about the efficiency with which they are operated (utilization rates), or the medical or administrative appropriateness of the procedures carried out. Rates of CT scanners in SHI countries run from Austria with 25.8 CT scanners per million population, Luxembourg 25.1, Switzerland 18.5 and Germany 17.1. Rates for the group of tax-funded countries

Table 4.20 MRI and CT units per million population, 2001

	CT units/ million population	Relative order	MRI units/ million population	Relative order
Switzerland	17.6	4	12.9	1
Austria	26.3	1	11.6	2
Finland	13.7	8	11.0	3
Italy	21.9	3	8.6	4
Sweden	14.2[2]	6	7.9[2]	5
Denmark	13.2	9	6.6[1]	6
Germany	17.1[4]	5	6.2[4]	7
Spain	12.5	10	5.7	8
United Kingdom	6.2[2]	13	4.6[2]	9
Luxembourg	24.9	2	4.5	10
Netherlands	n.a.	–	3.9[5]	11
Belgium	n.a.	–	3.2[4]	12
Portugal	12.1[4]	11	2.8[4]	13
France	9.6[1]	12	2.6[1]	14
Greece	13.8[4]	7	2.0[3]	15
Ireland	n.a.	–	n.a.	–
Israel	n.a.	–	n.a.	–
Norway	n.a.	–	n.a.	–
SHI countries average	*19.1*	–	*6.4*	–
Northern tax-funded average	*11.8*	–	*7.5*	–
Ratio SHI/northern tax	*1.62*	–	*0.85*	–
Difference SHI/northern tax	*7.3*	–	*−1.1*	–
All tax-funded average	*13.5*	–	*6.2*	–
Ratio SHI/all tax	*1.42*	–	*1.04*	–
Difference SHI/all tax	*5.7*	–	*0.3*	–

Notes:
Countries are ordered by MRI units/million population in 2001. Ordering is only to facilitate easy interpretation of the data. It does not reflect overall national rankings – see caveat page 82/83.
n.a. = not available.
1 2000.
2 1999.
3 1998.
4 1997.
5 1995.

Source: OECD (2003).

differed considerably: from 19.6 in Italy, 14.2 in Sweden and 13.5 in Finland to 3.6 in the United Kingdom. Regarding MRI units, the picture is more mixed: Switzerland has 13.0 units per million population, followed by Finland with 11.0, Austria with 10.8 and Sweden with 7.9. Low numbers exist in the United Kingdom (3.9) but also in France (2.8). Overall, SHI countries have an average 19.1 CTs and 6.4 MRIs per million population, contrasted with 11.8 CTs and 7.5 MRIs for northern tax-funded countries.

One instance where some utilization data are available is for inpatient care beds (Table 4.21). Looking at levels of physical resources, SHI countries had on average 7.6 beds per 1000 population in 2001, while northern tax-funded countries had 4.8 and all tax-funded taken together, 4.6. Thus, SHI systems have a substantially larger number of beds, in total 64 per cent higher (on a population-adjusted basis) than the tax-funded countries. Turning to utilization, hospital admissions in SHI countries (adjusted per 100 population) are on average at 20.0 slightly higher than northern tax-funded countries at 18.2, but notably higher when southern tax-based countries are included (16.4).

Length of stay in SHI countries is, on average, substantially higher than for all northern tax-funded countries, except Norway. On average the figure for SHI countries in 2001 (dropped considerably by Austria at 7.6) is 11.7 days, with Germany at 11.9, Netherlands at 12.5 and Switzerland at 13.0. Conversely, the average for northern tax-funded countries is 8.0 days, with the lowest figures being Sweden at 6.3 and Denmark at 6.6 (both Denmark and Sweden reformed their hospital payment arrangements during the 1990s to encourage home care and nursing home services to accept hospital patients as soon as clinically possible) (Johansson 1997). Thus, although SHI countries have 64 per cent more (population-adjusted) beds, the higher admission rates and longer lengths of stay result in essentially the same overall bed occupancy rate in SHI as in all tax-funded countries (78.1 versus 79.3 per cent). On a per capita basis, however, the higher utilization rates result in average number of bed days per capita in SHI countries that, at 2.3 vs. 1.4, are 72 per cent higher than on average in all tax-funded countries.

These data suggest that SHI systems have more physical resources and cost more to run than do tax-funded systems, and that some of this additional cost can be attributed to greater use of inpatient hospital services (more bed days per capita and longer length of stay). Based on the data provided, it is hard to explain why this might be true. One cause could lie in a lower degree of operating and budgetary integration in SHI systems between hospitals and primary care, nursing home and especially home care. It is not possible to tell from this data set, however, whether resource utilization rates in SHI hospitals reflect higher rates of elderly 'finished' patients waiting for placement; a higher proportion of less acutely ill patients who might be treated more appropriately on an outpatient basis; a lower proportion of day surgery patients; or any of a number of other factors.

In sum, the data tells us that SHI hospitals have substantially higher capacity and much higher per capita utilization rates than in northern tax-funded countries. Yet it only provides hints as to possible reasons why. Thus these data do not allow for a determination as to whether SHI hospitals are more or less technically efficient than those in northern tax-funded countries.

Table 4.21 Indicators in inpatient care and physicians, 2001

	1) Hospital beds/100,000 population	2) Inpatient care admissions/100 population	3) Average length of stay, all hospitals (days)	4) Inpatient care bed days/capita**	5) Bed occupancy rate, acute care hospitals (%)	6) Physicians/100,000 population	7) Doctors' consultations/capita*
Austria	861[1]	29.2[1]	7.6[1]	2.2	75.5[1]	323	6.7
Belgium	699	19.7[3]	11.5[3]	2.3	79.9[3]	419	7.4
Denmark	434[2]	18.9	6.6[1]	1.2	83.5[1]	342	6.2
Finland	737	26.0	10.3	2.7	74.0[6]	311	4.3
France	820[1]	23.0[2]	10.8[4]	2.5	77.4[2]	330	6.9[1]
Germany	912[1]	23.5[1]	11.9[1]	2.8	81.1[1]	363	6.5[5]
Greece	484[1]	15.4[3]	8.3[3]	1.3	n.a.	451	2.5[3]
Ireland	357	14.8	7.5	1.1	83.8	239	n.a.
Israel	616	18.7	11.1	2.1	93.0	375	n.a.
Italy	450[1]	16.5[1]	7.6[1]	1.3	75.5	567[2]	6.1[1]
Luxembourg	1100[7]	19.4[7]	15.3[5]	3.0	74.3[7]	254	6.2
Netherlands	466	9.3	12.5	1.2	58.4	328	5.8
Norway	440	17.6	7.7	1.4	87.2	356	n.a.
Portugal	392[2]	12.0[3]	9.0[3]	1.1	75.5[3]	318[1]	3.4[3]
Spain	401	11.5[4]	9.7[4]	1.1	76.2[4]	329[1]	8.7
Sweden	522[4]	16.6	6.3	1.0	77.5[5]	287[2]	2.9
Switzerland	618[1]	16.9[3]	13.0[1]	2.2	85.0[1]	350[1]	n.a.
United Kingdom	417[4]	15.1[3]	9.8[5]	1.5	80.8[3]	164[8]	4.9[1]

Average SHI countries	*762*	*20.0*	*11.7*	*2.3*	*78.1*	*343*	*6.6*
Average northern tax-funded countries	*485*	*18.2*	*8.0*	*1.5*	*81.1*	*283*	*4.6*
Ratio SHI/northern tax	*1.57*	*1.10*	*1.46*	*1.53*	*0.96*	*1.21*	*1.44*
Difference SHI/ northern tax	*277*	*1.8*	*3.7*	*0.8*	*-3.1*	*60*	*2.0*
Average all tax-funded countries	*463*	*16.4*	*8.3*	*1.4*	*79.3*	*336*	*4.9*
Ratio SHI/all tax	*1.64*	*1.21*	*1.41*	*1.66*	*0.98*	*1.02*	*1.35*
Difference SHI/all tax	*298*	*3.5*	*3.4*	*0.9*	*-1.3*	*6*	*1.7*

Notes:
1 2000 data.
2 1999 data.
3 1998 data.
4 1997 data.
5 1996 data.
6 1995 data.
7 1994 data.
8 1993 data.
** = calculated using the following columns: C4 = C3×C2/100.
n.a. = not available.

Sources: WHO (2003); *OECD (2003).

Administrative costs

Total administrative costs reflect a component of health care funding consumed on non-health improving activities. The definition of health administration and insurance costs used by the OECD (2003) comprises activities of private insurers and central and local authorities and social security. Included are the planning, management, regulation and collection of funds and handling of claims of the delivery system. Public administration costs borne by health care providers (e.g. patient records and hospital management) are not included.

Although data are available only for a limited number of countries, Table 4.22 suggests that administrative costs as measured by the OECD (2003) are higher in SHI countries than in countries with a tax-based system. Similarly, Janssen (2002) mentions that transaction costs in the Danish tax-funded system are low compared to those of health care systems based on social insurance. Administrative costs from providers are not included in the data, but there are several reasons to believe that these may be larger in SHI countries. In particular, providers have to maintain contact with multiple sickness funds, to follow the different procedures required by the different insurers, and often to negotiate with a larger number of entities.

One factor that may help explain the difference in administrative costs among SHI countries is whether there is choice of sickness fund. The evidence in this regard is circumstantial and somewhat mixed. The two countries without choice of sickness funds (Austria and France) show the lowest administration costs of the eight studied SHI countries (Table 4.22). Luxembourg is an

Table 4.22 Total expenditure on health administration and insurance as a percentage of total health expenditure, 1990, 1995, 2000

Country	Dominating system	Administrative costs (% THE)		
		1990	1995	2000
Luxembourg	SHI	–	–	6.7
Germany	SHI	6.3	5.3	5.4
Switzerland	SHI	6.1	5.0	5.1
Netherlands	SHI	4.9	4.5	4.4
Austria	SHI	–	3.7	3.7
UK	Tax-funded	–	–	3.3[1]
Spain	Tax-funded	–	2.7	2.3
Finland	Tax-funded	2.0	2.3	2.1
France	SHI	1.6	1.7	1.8
Denmark	Tax-funded	0.8	0.9	0.9
Italy	Tax-funded	0.3	0.3	0.3
Portugal	Tax-funded	–	0.1	0.1

Notes:
1 1999 data. Countries are ordered by 2000 costs. Ordering is only to facilitate easy interpretation of the data. It does not reflect overall national rankings – see caveat page 82/83.

Source: OECD (2003).

exception. The correlation between the number of sickness funds per capita and administrative cost provides some prima facie support for this interpretation (Tables 4.22,4.23,4.24). France has by far the largest average number of members per sickness fund (almost 3.5 million) and the lowest reported administrative costs, while the Netherlands (428,000) and Austria (336,000) had considerably lower administrative costs than Germany (199,000), Switzerland (79,000) and Luxembourg (63,000). The fact that Austria – with 21 per cent less subscribers per fund – has considerably lower costs than the Netherlands also reinforces the interpretation that choice of sickness fund might be an important factor in higher overall administrative costs. Data regarding administrative cost in Germany (Table 4.25), however, only show a slight increase from 1992 to 2001 as the process of individual choice of sickness fund was implemented.

Since 1990, administration cost has decreased slightly in some SHI countries as a percentage of total health care costs, but it remains high compared to tax-funded systems (Schieber 1995; OECD 2003). While OECD data in Table 4.22 show cost reductions for some countries that have had sick fund mergers in the mid-1990s (Germany, Netherlands), in other countries these costs have not been reduced. Moreover, German government data show a slight increase not a decrease over the period 1992–2001. In France, recent ministry policy has sought to incorporate the small corporate sickness funds into the *Régime Général* (Cambus 2003), and in 1988 added the sickness branch of *cultes* (CAMAC) and in 1991 the sickness insurance of *Compagnie Génerale des Eaux* (RSSS 'CGDE') to it (Ministère des Affaires Sociales du Travail et de la Solidarité 2003; Schaller 2003).

While in general the merging of sickness funds may help to decrease administrative costs, there have also been cost increasing factors due to growing competition. In Israel, for example, competition among sickness funds increased administrative costs significantly after the 1995 reforms. Sickness funds increased their expenditures for advertising, marketing and administration, and their marketing budgets jumped from 51.5 million NIS in 1994 to 91.2 million NIS in 1996 (Gross and Harrison 1998 as in Gross and Harrison 2001). Similarly, in Switzerland, an analysis of seven sample cantons indicated that the greater complexity of the reformed system made management more difficult and increased costs (Haari *et al.* 2002). According to Mossialos and Dixon (2002b), higher administrative costs also appear to be correlated with the presence of private funders. German government data in Table 4.25 show private health insurers to have costs approximately three times higher than do the statutory sickness funds.

Relative clinical performance

A related picture of how SHI systems perform can be drawn from data concerning their comparative clinical performance. While formally more of a quality than an efficiency indicator, these data provide one measure of how well resources are utilized to obtain specific medical outcomes. Several recent studies have compared outputs for specific clinical conditions across both SHI and tax-funded systems in western Europe. Gandjour *et al.* (2002a), using a sample of

Table 4.23 Number of sickness funds, 1990–2002

	1990	1991	1992	1993	1994	1995	1996	1997	1998	1999	2000	2001	2002	Change 1990–2002[2]
Austria	26	26	26	26	26	26	26	26	26	26	26	25	24	-7.7%
Belgium[1]	119	127	127	121	121	114	116	111	109	107	103	95	94	-21.0%
France	18	17	17	17	17	17	17	17	17	17	17	17	17	-5.6%
Germany[2]		1209	1223	1221	1152	960	642	554	482	455	420	396	355	-70.6%
Israel	4	4	4	4	4	4	4	4	4	4	4	4	4	0%
Luxembourg	9	9	9	9	9	9	9	9	9	9	9	9	9	0%
Netherlands[3]	37	31	27	26	26	27	29	30	28	28	27	25	24	-35.1%
Switzerland	220	203	191	207	178	166	145	129	118	109	101	99	93	-57.7%

Notes:

1 Forming part of seven national associations which are financially responsible for the compulsory health insurance system.

2 For Germany: 1991–2002. 1990 is difficult to compare being from before German reunification. Data from 1 January of the corresponding year. 2002 data take into account the 1 January 2002 merger of Groene Land and PWZ (even though they were still not fully merged).

3 Only counted as one sickness fund if merged; 2002 data take into account the 1 January 2002 merger of Groene Land and PWZ (even though they were still not fully merged).

Sources: Austria: Bundesministerium für Soziale Sicherheit und Generationen und Konsumentenschutz (2003b); Belgium: RIZIV (2003) and Schokkaert and Van de Voorde (2003); France: Meftah (2003); Germany: Bundesministerium für Gesundheit und Soziale Sicherung (2003); Israel: Gross and Harrison (2001); Luxembourg: Union des caisses de maladie (2003); Netherlands: Vektis (1996, 1998, 2000, 2002b) and CVZ/CTZ (2003); Switzerland: BSV/OFAS/UFAS (2003) and estimation by BSV/OFAS/UFAS for 2002.

Table 4.24 Average number of insured per sickness fund (thousands), 1990–2002

	1990	1991	1992	1993	1994	1995	1996	1997	1998	1999	2000	2001	2002	Change 1990–2002[1]
Austria	294	298	301	304	306	306	307	307	308	308	309	322	336	+14.3%
Belgium	81	77	78	82	82	88	87	91	92	94	98	107	108	+32.8%
France	3132	3331	3347	3360	3371	3382	3393	3403	3415	3445	3461	3478	3495	+11.6%
Germany		59	59	59	62	75	112	129	148	157	170	179	199	+238.3%
Israel	1075	1115	1178	1238	1269	1301	1373	1416	1455	1497	1540	1582	1615	+50.2%
Luxembourg	47	48	48	49	51	52	53	54	56	57	59	62	63	+35.1%
Netherlands	248	298	346	363	368	359	337	330	354	355	382	411	428	+72.2%
Switzerland	31	34	37	38	40	43	50	56	61	67	72	74	79	+152.9%

Notes:
1 For Germany 1991–2002. The data are based on the data in Tables 4.23 and 3.3.

Table 4.25 Administrative costs in the German health care system

	1992	1993	1994	1995	1996	1997	1998	1999	2000	2001
Number of sickness funds	1223	1221	1152	960	642	554	482	455	420	396
Administrative costs of sickness funds (€ billion)	5.3	5.5	5.8	6.4	6.4	6.3	6.6	6.9	7.0	7.6
% of SHI expenditure	5.3%	5.6%	5.4%	5.7%	5.5%	5.4%	5.6%	5.7%	5.6%	5.9%
Administrative costs of private health insurers (€ billion)	2.0	2.1	2.4	2.5	2.5	2.7	2.8	3.0	3.1	3.1
% of PHI expenditure	17.0%	16.7%	17.1%	17.2%	16.6%	16.9%	17.4%	17.3%	17.1%	16.4%
All administrative costs (€ billion)	8.7	9.2	9.8	11.0	11.0	11.2	11.7	12.2	12.4	12.9
% of total health expenditure	5.3%	5.5%	5.4%	5.7%	5.4%	5.5%	5.6%	5.7%	5.7%	5.7%

Sources: Federal Ministry of Health (1993, 1994, 1995, 1996, 1997, 1998, 1999, 2000, 2001, 2002); Federal Statistical Office (2002, 2003).

208 hospitals in four SHI and three tax-based countries, evaluated quality and costs in the treatment of acute myocardial infarction. As Table 4.26 shows, quality was not correlated with the type of health system. With 0.96, Germany scored highest but both France and the United Kingdom scored lowest with 0.89. Using country-specific unit costs, total treatment costs were higher in SHI countries. When average costs were used (i.e. when only differences in the intensity of resources used were taken into account), costs were more similar, suggesting higher unit prices in the SHI countries as the main source for cost differences.

A similar methodology was applied by the same group of authors for evaluating quality and costs of care for patients with Type 2 diabetes treated in 188 practices (Table 4.27). Both variation of quality and of costs is larger than for AMI, with costs varying by more than a factor of 4. Again, there is no correlation between the quality and the system type. Noticeably, the order of the countries is nearly reversed from that found in the AMI study, suggesting that countries do not have the same degree of quality across all types of health care.

Table 4.26 Average quality ratings and acute myocardial infarction (AMI) costs in Euro, 2000/1

Country	Average quality rating (1.0 = max.)	Total AMI costs using country-specific unit prices	Total AMI costs using average unit prices
Germany	0.961	2462	2239
Sweden	0.919	843	1153
Netherlands	0.918	1612	1508
Italy	0.916	1808	2349
Switzerland	0.914	2670	1787
France	0.889	1375	1900
United Kingdom	0.888	1393	1598

Source: Gandjour *et al.* (2002a).

Table 4.27 Average quality ratings and total annual costs of patients with Type 2 diabetes in Euro, 2000/1

Country	Average quality rating (1.0 = max.)	Diabetes care costs using country-specific unit prices	Diabetes care costs using index fees
United Kingdom	0.62	n.a.	122
France	0.54	n.a.	386
Switzerland	0.53	475	348
Sweden	0.50	n.a.	166
Germany	0.49	381	522
Italy	0.47	281	350
Netherlands	0.40	n.a.	157

n.a. = not available.

Source: Gandjour *et al.* (2002b).

Cost-effectiveness appears to be worse in SHI countries than in other countries, primarily due to high costs (France, Germany, Switzerland) or to low quality (Netherlands) respectively.

A third study (EUROASPIRE I and II Group 2001) focused on the quality of the post-inpatient care of patients with coronary heart disease once discharged to ambulatory care (Table 4.28). Based on the three SHI countries and the three tax-based countries in this study,[6] SHI countries seem, on average, to do worse when it comes to treating patients according to coronary prevention guidelines, especially if the improvement over the second half of the 1990s is taken into account. However, the example of the Netherlands also demonstrates that it is possible within SHI countries to reach results comparable with more centrally determined tax-funded systems.

Table 4.28 Therapeutic control of blood pressure and cholesterol in patients with coronary heart disease, 1995/6 and 1999/2000

Country	Therapeutic control of blood pressure		Therapeutic control of cholesterol	
	1995/6	*1999/2000*	*1995/6*	*1999/2000*
Finland	44.3%	47.4%	16.7%	57.4%
Netherlands	44.2%	46.2%	8.8%	55.7%
Spain	44.8%	50.6%	19.6%	47.0%
Italy	42.3%	43.4%	7.4%	43.1%
France	49.4%	45.0%	15.2%	39.8%
Germany	42.1%	34.2%	15.9%	33.7%

Source: EUROASPIRE I and II Group (2001).

Summing up

Interpreting the data examined in this chapter is a complicated task, made more difficult by definition and/or collection dilemmas in several of the data series. The best current available information does not allow one to draw a firm judgement about whether the overall performance of SHI systems is 'better' or 'worse' than that of their northern tax-funded counterparts.[7] Instead, the data point toward different relative relationships depending upon the parameter of performance being assessed. This less than clear cut assessment is underscored by the existence on several dimensions (health status; satisfaction/responsiveness) of one or more data series that appear to diverge or even lead in the opposite direction from that of most other information concerning that dimension. Moreover, the overall differences on many of these data series are small, definitions are sometimes debatable (e.g. equity), and some series (e.g. satisfaction/responsiveness) are methodologically of uncertain reliability.

Summarized in a nutshell, the reviewed data appears to suggest the following. Outcomes regarding health status are similar between SHI and northern tax-funded countries, although health status has only a weak correlation with the activities of health systems. Outcomes regarding equity are slightly worse in SHI countries. However, outcomes regarding satisfaction/responsiveness are slightly higher in SHI countries when one takes all the measures (including level of choice and waiting times) into consideration. Outcomes regarding efficiency vary according to the data series, but do not show a clear trend overall. Ultimately, the central question that emerges from the available data is whether the apparent additional satisfaction is justified by the additional money and resources spent, despite the fact that not much more health is obtained. This requires, clearly, a societal rather than a technical judgement, leading back to the main point in Chapters 1 and 2 that SHI systems are a 'way of life', a way of understanding the world, and a framework for making policy based on that societal perspective.

Notes

1 Unweighted averages have been used since the unit of interest is countries rather than the total population within the groups of countries.
2 For the Netherlands an indication of the rate of change is given by the percentage of citizens that are insured outside their region. Insurance outside the region of residence was allowed only from 1992 on; until that date sickness funds were strongly regionally affiliated.
3 For early examples of the difficulties in adapting such measures to the health sector, see the Swedish Finance Ministry's (1985) report on productivity in the Swedish health system (ESO 1985); also the State of New York's 1992 ranking of hospital outputs (New York State Department of Health 1992). A more recent Swedish assessment can be found in Federation of Swedish council counties (2002).
4 Since this section focuses on observed data, it does not consider various theories as to whether these higher expenditures represent conscious choice by SHI governments, inadequate expenditure controls or some mix of both.
5 Luxembourg has imbalances due to its tiny population as well as a large 'offshore' banking income that distorts its figures for comparative purposes. The Austrian figure is viewed as controversially low by some Austrian analysts (Hofmarcher and Röhrling 2003).
6 There were three more countries from central and eastern Europe (CEE) included as well, namely Hungary, Czech Republic and Slovenia. Regarding the therapeutic control of blood pressure, these three countries actually scored highest in 1999/2000 with 58.6 per cent, 53.6 per cent and 50.6 per cent respectively. For therapeutic control of cholesterol the respective figures in 1999/2000 were 39.8 per cent, 27.5 per cent and 47.0 per cent.
7 As noted earlier, northern tax-funded countries tend to be similar to SHI countries in important aspects including overall per capita income and longevity of the current health system structure.

References

Balthasar, A., Bieri, O. and Furrer, C. (2001) Evaluation de l'application de la réduction de primes (Analyse des effects de la LAMal). Research rapport number 5/01, BSV/OFAS/ UFAS.

Barer, M., Evans, R.G., Hertzman, C. and Johri, M. (1998) *Lies, Damned lies, and Health Care Zombies: Discredited Ideas that will not Die.* HPI discussion paper #10 (March). Texas: Health Policy Institute, University of Texas – Houston Health Science Center, pp. 1–73.

Barros, P.P. (1998) The black box of healthcare expenditure growth determinants, *Health Economics*, 7(6): 533–44.

Baubeau, D., Bousquet, F. and Joubert, M. (2001) Le traitement chirurgical de la cataracte en France: un développement encore limité de la chirurgie ambulatoire, *DREES Études et Résultats*, 101.

Beck, K. (2000) Growing importance of capitation in Switzerland, *Health Care Management Science*, 3(2): 111–19.

Beck, K. (2003) Personal communication, 16 September.

Belgian Federal Ministry of Social Affairs, Public Health and Environment (2003) *Beknopt overzicht van de sociale zekerheid in België.* http://socialsecurity.fgov.be/overzicht/2003/ (accessed 17 September 2003).

Belgische Senaat (1999) *De toegang tot de gezondheidszorg voor patiënten met zware pathologische verschijnselen en chronische aandoeningen: verslag over de hoorzittingen namens de Commissie voor Sociale Aangelegenheden* [Accessibility to healthcare by patients with serious pathological disorders and chronic diseases: report of the hearings ordered by the commission for social affairs]. Brussels: Belgische Senaat.

Ben Nun, G. (2003) Reviewer's comments, 1 April.

Bentur, N. and Gross, R. (2001) Clinical investigations – the reform of the Israeli healthcare system: a comparison between older and younger consumers, one year and three years after its implementation, *Journal of the American Geriatrics Society*, 49(1): 56–64.

Black, D., Townsend, P. and Davidson, N. (1982) *Inequalities in Health: The Black Report.* Harmondsworth: Penguin.

Blendon, R.J., Kim, M. and Benson, J.M. (2001) The public versus the world health organization on health system performance, *Health Affairs*, 20(3): 10–20.

Bocognano, A., Couffinhal, A., Dunesnil, S. and Grignon, M. (2000) Which coverage for whom? Equity access to health insurance in France. Paris: oral presentation prepared for the European Public Health Association Congress, CREDES.

BSV/OFAS/UFAS (2003) *Assurance obligatoire des soins: assurés et assureurs de 1990 à 2001.* http://www.bsv.admin.ch/statistik/details/f/svs/am_5_1.pdf (accessed 19 September 2003).

Bundesministerium für Gesundheit und Soziale Sicherung (2003) *Zahl der Gesetzliche Krankenkassen.* http://www.bmgs.bund.de/download/statistiken/stattb2002/09/9.04. pdf (accessed 18 September 2003).

Bundesministerium für Soziale Sicherheit und Generationen und Konsumentenschutz (2003a) Personal communication with H. Rack, January and 29 August.

Bundesministerium für Soziale Sicherheit und Generationen und Konsumentenschutz (2003b) Personal communication with J. Stefanits, 20 February and 22 May.

Bunker, J.P., Frazier, H.S. and Mosteller, F. (1995) The role of medical care in determing health: creating an inventory on benefits, in B.J. Amick, S. Levine, A.R. Tarlov and D. Chapman Walsh (eds) *Society and Health*, pp. 305–41. New York: Oxford University Press.

Busse, R. and Riesberg, A. (2000) *Health Care Systems in Transition: Germany.* Copenhagen: European Observatory on Health Care Systems.

Cambus, P. (2003) (Spokesperson Ministry of Health) Personal communication, 5 December.

Chinitz, D. (2002) Personal communication, 22 June.

Chinitz, D. (2003) Personal communication, 4 February.

Churchill, L.R. (1987) *Rationing Health Care in America.* Chicago: University of Notre Dame Press.

Coulter, A. and Cleary, P.D. (2001) Patients' experiences with hospital care in five countries, *Health Affairs*, 20(3): 43–53.

Culyer, A.J. (1991) Reforming health services: frameworks for the Swedish review, in A.J. Culyer, R.G. Evans, J.-M. Graf von der Schulenburg, W.P.M.M. van de Ven and B.A. Weisbrod (eds) *International Review of the Swedish Health Care System*, pp. 1–50. Stockholm: SNS.

CVZ/CTZ (2003) Personal communication with M. Hagen on behalf of C. Oranje, 27 February.

D'Onofrio, C. and Muller, P. (1977) Consumer problems with prepaid health plans in California, *Public Health Reports*, 92: 121–34.

Dahlgren, G. and Whitehead, M. (1992) *Policies and Strategies to Promote Equity in Health*. Copenhagen: World Health Organization.

Daniels, N. (1985) *Just Health Care*. Cambridge: Cambridge University Press.

Den Exter, A., Hermans, H., Dosljak, M. and Busse, R. (2002) *Health Care Systems in Transition: The Netherlands*. Copenhagen: European Observatory on Health Care Systems (to be published).

E-Santé (2001) Adultes autistes: un manqué honteux de structures, by I. Herbert, 2 July 2001, http://www.e-sante.fr/francais/article_4786_30.htm (accessed 16 September 2003).

Eco-Santé France (2003) *Les données de la base*. http://www.credes.fr/ecosante/francedata.htm (accessed 16 September 2003).

ESO (1985) *Produktions-, kostnads- och produktivitetsutveckling inom offentligt bedriven hälso- och sjukvård 1960–1980* [*Production, cost and productivity development within public health and care*] DsFi 1985: 3.

EUROASPIRE I and II Group (2001) Clinical reality of coronary prevention guidelines: a comparison of EUROASPIRE I and II in nine countries, *Lancet*, 357: 995–1001.

Eurotransplant (1998) *Annual Report 1997*. Leiden: Eurotransplant, International Foundation.

Eurotransplant (2002) *Annual Report 2001*. Leiden: Eurotransplant, International Foundation.

Eurotransplant (2003) www.oebig.at, quoted by S. Hruby, personal communication 17 March.

Evans, R.G. (2002) Funding healthcare: taxation and the alternatives, in E. Mossialos, A. Dixon, J. Figueras and J. Kutzin (eds) *Funding Health Care: Options for Europe*, pp. 31–58. Buckingham: Open University Press.

Faisst, K., Fischer, S. and Schilling, J. (2001) *Monitoring 2000 von Anfragen an PatientInnen- und Versichertenorganisationen (Wirkungsanalyse KVG)*. Research report. Bern: OFAS.

Federal Ministry of Health (1993, 1994, 1995, 1996, 1997, 1998, 1999, 2000, 2001, 2002) *Statistisches Taschenbuch (Gesundheit)*. Bonn: Federal Ministry of Health, http://www.gbe-bund.de (accessed 13 August 2003).

Federal Statistical Office (2002) *Gesundheitsausgabenrechnung der Gesundheitsberichterstattung des Bundes 1992–2000*. Bonn: Statistisches Bundesamt, http://www.gbe-bund.de (accessed 13 August 2003).

Federal Statistical Office (2003) *Health Expenditure (Gesundheitsausgaben)*. Bonn: Federal Statistical Office, http://www.destatis.de/themen//thm_health.htm (accessed 13 August 2003).

Fédération Hospitalière de France (2001) L'Avenir de l'hospitalisation publique au service des Français, 5 December: 33.

Federation of Swedish Council Counties (2002) *Swedish Health Care in the 1990s*. Stockholm: Federation of Swedish council counties, http://www.lf.se/lfenglish/download/Healthcare.pdf (accessed 26 September 2003).

Feider, J.M. (2003) (Head of the law department Union des Caisses de Maladie) Personal communication, 3 February.

Gandjour, A., Kleinschmit, F., Lauterbach, K.W. and the INTERCARE International Investigators (2002a) European comparison of costs and quality in the treatment of acute myocardical infarction (2000–2001), *European Heart Journal*, 23: 858–68.

Gandjour, A., Kleinschmit, F., Lauterbach, K.W. and the INTERCARE International Investigators (2002b) European comparison of costs and quality in the prevention of secondary complications in Type 2 diabetes mellitus (2000–2001), *Diabetic Medicine*, 19: 594–601.

Greβ, S., Groenewegen, P., Kerssens, J., Braun, B. and Wasem, J. (2002) Free choice of sickness funds in regulated competition: evidence from Germany and the Netherlands, *Health Policy*, 60: 235–54.

Grol, R., Wensing, M, Mainz, J. *et al.* (2000) Patients in Europe evaluate general practice care: an international comparison, *British Journal of General Practice*, 50: 882–7.

Gross, R. and Harrison, M. (1998) *Competitive Strategies in a Regulated Environment: The Israeli Case* (AHSR 15th annual meeting abstract book). Washington, DC: Association for Health Services Research.

Gross, R. and Harrison, M. (2001) Implementing managed competition in Israel, *Social Science and Medicine*, 52: 1219–31.

Haari, R., Haari-Oberg, I., Schilling, K. and Torrisi, M. (2002) *Analyse des effets de la LAMal: Différences intercantonales en matière de coûts de la santé. Analyse des politiques cantonales*. Research report. Bern: OFAS.

Hofmarcher, M.M. and Rack, H. (2001) *Health Care Systems in Transition: Austria*. Copenhagen: European Observatory on Health Care Systems.

Hofmarcher, M.M. and Röhrling, G. (2003) Health expenditure in the EU: comparability is ailing. Focus: forecast of health expenditure in Austria, *Soziale Sicherheit*, I(spring): supplement.

Hofstede, G. (1980) *Culture's Consequences: International Differences in Work-Related Values*. London: Sage.

Hofstede, G. (1985) The interaction between national and organizational value systems, *Journal of Management Studies*, 22: 347–57.

Hornung, D., Röthlisberger, T. and Stiefel, A. (2001) Praxis der Versicherer bei der Vergütung von Leistungen nach KVG (Wirkungsanalyse KVG). Research report number 12/01, BSV/OFAS/UFAS.

Hurst, J. and Siciliani, L. (2003) *Tackling Excessive Waiting Times for Elective Surgery: A Comparison of Policies in Twelve OECD Countries*. Paris: OECD.

INRA (Europe) European Coordination Office (1996) *Eurobarometer 44.3*. Brussels: INRA (Europe) European Coordination Office.

INRA (Europe) European Coordination Office (1998) *Eurobarometer 49*. Brussels: INRA (Europe) European Coordination Office.

INRA (Europe) European Coordination Office (1999) *Eurobarometer 50.1*. Brussels: INRA (Europe) European Coordination Office.

INRA (Europe) European Coordination Office (2000) *Eurobarometer 52.1*. Brussels: INRA (Europe) European Coordination Office.

Janssen, R. (2002) Evaluation of the organization and financing of the Danish healthcare system, *Health Policy*, 59: 145–59.

Johansson, L. (1997) Decentralization from acute to home care settings in Sweden, *Health Policy*, 41(supplement): S131–44.

Jönsson, B. (2002) *Macroeconomic Analysis of the Differences in Expenditure*. Stockholm: School of Economics, Centre for Health Economics.

Kawabata, K., Knaul, F., Xu, K. and Lydon, P. (2001) *WHO Fair Financing Methology* (draft, 17 July). Geneva: World Health Organization.

Kerr, E. (1999) *Health Care Systems in Transition: Luxembourg*. Copenhagen: European Observatory on Health Care Systems.

Kerr, E. (2000) *Health Care Systems in Transition: Belgium*. Copenhagen: European Observatory on Health Care Systems.

Kletter, H. (2003) Personal communication with spokesperson of the Internationales Büro der Österreichische Ärztekammer, 21 January.

Kratzer, A. (2003) (Bundesministerium für Gesundheit und Soziale Sicherung) Personal communication, 15 January.

Kutzin, J. (1998) The appropriate role for patient cost-sharing, in R.B. Saltman, J. Figueras and C. Sakellarides (eds) *Critical Challenges for Health Care Reform in Europe*, pp. 78–112. Buckingham: Open University Press.

Lamers, L.M., Van Vliet, R.C.J.A. and van de Ven, W.P.M.M. (2003) Risk adjustment premium subsidies and risk sharing: key elements of the competitive sickness fund market in the Netherlands, *Health Policy*, 65: 49–62.

LBL (2002) *Leeftijdsgrenzen in polisvoorwaarden van ziektekostenverzekeringen [Age restrictions in policy conditions of health insurance]*. http://www.leeftijd.nl/p0113.html (accessed 25 September 2003).

L'Express (2003) Il faut sauver l'hôpital (by Vincent Olivier), 27 February 2003.

Le Pen, C. (2003) The drug budget silo mentality: the French case, *Value in Health*, 6 (s1): 10–19.

Le Quotidien du Médecin (2002) La journée d'action des ophtalmos: dépistage à l'œil du glaucome (by Henri de Saint Romain). Issue 7177, 16 September.

Libération (2002a) Un choix de société (editorial), 2 November.

Libération (2002b) A Paris, l'hôpital Saint-Louis ferme des blocs opératoires, 4 December.

Lohr, K.N., Brook R.H., Kamberg, C.J., *et al.* (1986) Effect of cost-sharing on use of medically effective and less effective care, *Med Care*, 24(supplement): 31.

Louckx, F. (2002) Patient cost sharing and access to healthcare, in J. Mackenbach and M. Bakker (eds) *Reducing Inequalities in Health – A European Perspective*. London: Routledge.

Maarse, H. (2002/3) The politics of waiting lists in Dutch healthcare, *Eurohealth*, 8(5): 27–9.

McGuire, A., Henderson, J. and Mooney, G. (1988) *The Economics of Health Care: An Introductory Text*. London: Routledge & Kegan Paul.

McKee, M. (2001) Health Status in the EU and Central and Eastern European (CEE) Countries, in M. Garcia-Barbero (ed.) *Appraisal of Investments in Health Infrastructure*, pp. 37–56. Barcelona: World Health Organization.

McKeown, T. (1976) *The Role of Medicine – Dream, Mirage or Nemesis?* Rock Carling Lecture, Nuffield Trust.

Meftah, V. (2003) Personal communication with French sickness fund representative, May 2003.

Minder, A., Schoenholzer, H. and Amiet, M. (2000) *Health Care Systems in Transition – Switzerland*. Copenhagen: European Observatory on Health Care Systems.

Ministère de la sécurité sociale du Gran-Duche de Luxembourg (2003) Personal communication with L. Falchero, Chef de bureau adjoint, 23 January.

Ministère des Affaires Sociales du Travail et de la Solidarité (2003) *Les comptes des régimes autres que le régime genéral*. http://www.social.gouv.fr/htm/dossiers/ccss/a99-00/comptes2000/camac.htm (accessed 7 December 2003).

Ministerie van Volksgezondheid, Welzijn en Sport (2003a) *Landelijke databank wachttijden*. Utrecht: NVZ.

Ministerie van Volksgezondheid, Welzijn en Sport (2003b) Personal communication with M. van Uchelen, August.

Ministerie van Volksgezondheid, Welzijn en Sport (2003c) Personal communication with E. van den Berg, 24 and 25 September.

Mossialos, E. and Dixon, A. (2002a) Funding health care: an introduction, in E. Mossialos, A. Dixon, J. Figueras and J. Kutzin (eds) *Funding Health Care: Options for Europe*, p. 7. Buckingham: Open University Press.

Mossialos, E.A. and Dixon, A. (2002b) Funding healthcare in Europe: weighing up the options, in E.A. Mossialos, A. Dixon, J. Figueras and J. Kutzin (eds) *Funding Health Care: Options for Europe*, pp. 272–300. Buckingham: Open University Press.

Murray, C.J.L., Xu, K., Klavus, J. *et al.* (2003) Assessing the distribution of household financial contributions to the health system: concepts and empirical application, in C.J.L. Murray and D.B. Evans (eds) *Health Systems Performance Assessment: Debates, Methods and Empiricism*, pp. 513–23. Geneva: World Health Organization. http://whqlibdoc.who.int/publications/2003/9241562455_(part4)_(chp34–42).pdf (accessed 13 November 2003).

Navarro, V. (2000) Assessment of the *World Health Report 2000*, *Lancet*, 356(9241): 1598–601.

New York State Department of Health (1992) *Coronary Artery Bypass Surgery in New York State: 1989–1991*. Albany: New York State Department of Health.

Nolte, E. and McKee, M. (2003) Measuring the health of nations: analysis of mortality amenable to healthcare, *British Medical Journal*, 327: 1–5.

Nolte, E. and McKee, M. (2004) Does healthcare save lives? Avoidable mortality revisited. London: The Nuffield Trust.

OECD (2000) *OECD Health Data 2000: A Comparative Analysis of 30 Countries*. Paris: OECD.

OECD (2002) *OECD Health Data 2002: A Comparative Analysis of 30 Countries*. Paris: OECD.

OECD (2003) *OECD Health Data 2003: A Comparative Analysis of 30 Countries*, 2nd edn. Paris: OECD.

Or, Z. (1997) Determinants of health outcomes in industrialized countries: a pooled, time-series analysis. OECD Working Party on Social Policy Ad Hoc Meeting of Experts in Health Statistics, Document No. 8. Paris: OECD.

Ortiz, J.P., Valentine, N.B., Gakidou, E. *et al.* (2003) Inequality in responsiveness: population surveys from 16 OECD countries, in C.J.L. Murray and D.B. Evans (eds) *Health Systems Performance Assessment: Debates, Methods and Empiricism*, pp. 653–68. Geneva: World Health Organization. http://whqlibdoc.who.int/publications/2003/9241562455_(part4)_(chp43–49).pdf (accessed 7 December 2003).

Österreichische Sozialversicherung (2002) Soziale Sicherheit, *Fachzeitschrift der Österreichischen Sozialversicherung*, 2002 Special Issue. http://www.sozialversicherung.at/media/12458.PDF (accessed 16 September 2003).

Peys, F. (2001) The pharma sector and its financing in Belgium, *Health Economics in Prevention and Care*, 2: 33–8.

Rawls, J. (1971) *A Theory of Justice*. Cambridge: Belknap Press of Harvard University.

Reinhardt, U. (2003) Foreword, in T. Rice (ed.) *The Economics of Health Reconsidered*. Chicago: Health Administration Press.

Rice, T. (1998) *The Economics of Health Reconsidered*. Chicago: Health Administration Press.

RIVM (2003) *Zorg in de grote steden*. Bilthoven: Rijksinstituut voor Volksgezondheid en Milieu.

RIZIV (2003) Personal communication with L. Van Damme, RIZIV (Rijksinstituut voor Ziekte- en invaliditeitsverzekering), Dienst bijdragebescheiden, Administratieve cel en Ledentallen, February.

Robinson, R. (2002) User charges for health care, in E. Mossialos, A. Dixon, J. Figueras and J. Kutzin (eds) *Funding Health Care: Options for Europe*, pp. 161–83. Buckingham: Open University Press.

Rosen, B. (2003) *Health Care Systems in Transition: Israel*. Copenhagen: European Observatory on Health Care Systems.

Rutstein, D.D., Berenberg, W., Chalmers, T.C. *et al.* (1976) Measuring the quality of medical care, *The New England Journal of Medicine*, 294(11): 582–8.

Sager, F., Rüefli, C. and Vatter, A. (2001) Politik-forschung und Beratung: Auswirkungen der Aufnahme von präventiv-medizinischen Leistungen in den Pflichtleistungskatalog. Politologische Analyse auf der Grundlage von drei Fallbeispielen. (Wirkungsanalyse KVG). Research rapport number 10/01, BSV/OFAS/UFAS.

Saltman, R.B., Berleen, G. and Larsson, B.A. (2001) A methodological note on combining health and social care expenditures into a single statistic for policy-making purposes, *European Journal of Public Health*, 11(1): 93–6.

Sandier, S., Polton, D. and Paris, V. (2004) *Health Care Systems in Transition: France*. Copenhagen: European Observatory on Health Care Systems.

Santé Suisse (2003) Personal communication with M. Kocher, 2 October.

Schaller, J-C. (2003) Personal communication with J-C Schaller (Compagnie Générale des Eaux), 24 April.

Schieber, G.J. (1995) Preconditions for health reform: experiences from the OECD countries, *Health Policy*, 32: 279–93.

Schokkaert, E. and Van de Voorde, C. (2003) Belgium: risk adjustment and financial responsibility in a centralized system, *Health Policy*, 65: 5–19.

Shaw, R.P. (2001) The conceptual basis and the scope of health systems performance assessment in the *World Health Report 2000*. Invited commentary: Regional consultation of the Americas on health system performance assessment 8–5 2001, Washington, DC.

Siciliani, L. and Hurst, J. (2003) *Explaining Waiting Times Variations for Elective Surgery Across OECD Countries*, OECD health working papers No. 7. Paris: OECD.

Somai, D. and Hutten, J.B.F. (2002) *Brancherapport Cure '98–'01*. Ministerie van Volgsgezondheid, Welzijn en Sport.

Szwarcwald, C.L. (2002) On the World Health Organization's measurement of health inequalities, *Journal of Epidemiology and Community Health*, 56: 177–82.

Unie KBO (2003) *Uitkomsten belronde acceptatie aanvullende ziektekostenverzekeringen* [*Results telephone inquiry acceptance supplemental health insurance*]. 's-Hertogenbosch: Unie KBO.

Union des caisses de maladie (2003) Personal communication with Jean-Marie Rossler on behalf of Robert Kieffer, February, June and 19 September.

Üstün, T.B., Chatterji, S., Villanueva, M. *et al.* (2001) WHO multi-country survey study on health and responsiveness. Global Programme on Evidence for Health Policy Discussion Paper Series No. 37. World Health Organization, 30 November.

Valentine, N.B. and Salomon, J.A. (2003) Patient experiences with health services: population surveys from 16 OECD countries, in C.J.L. Murray and D.B. Evans (eds) *Health Systems Performance Assessment: Debates, Methods and Empiricism*, pp. 643–53. Geneva: World Health Organization. http://whqlibdoc.who.int/publications/2003/9241562455_(part4)_(chp43–49).pdf (accessed 7 December 2003).

Valentine, N.B., Ortiz, J.P., Tandon, A., Kawabata, K., Evans, D.B. and Murray, J.L. (2003) Patient experiences with health services: population surveys from 16 OECD countries, in C.J.L. Murray and D.B. Evans (eds) *Health Systems Performance Assessment: Debates, Methods and Empiricism*, pp. 643–53. Geneva: World Health Organization. http://whqlibdoc.who.int/publications/2003/9241562455_(part4)_(chp43–49).pdf (accessed 13 November 2003).

Vektis (1996) *Zorgmonitor 1996*. Zeist: Vektis.

Vektis (1998) *Zorgmonitor 1998*. Zeist: Vektis.

Vektis (2000) *Zorgmonitor 2000*. Zeist: Vektis.

Vektis (2002a) *Werkgebieden en verre verzekerden.* Internal document faxed by Marije Schwitters, 16 January. Zeist: Vektis.

Vektis (2002b) *Zorgmonitor 2002.* Zeist: Vektis.

Vranken, J., Geldof, D. and Van Menxel, G. (1999) *Armoede en sociale uitsluiting: jaarboek 1999 [Poverty and social exclusion: yearbook 1999].* Leuven: Acco.

Wagstaff., A. (2001) Measuring equity in healthcare financing: reflections on and alternatives to the World Health Organisation's Fairness of Financing Index. Development Research Group and Human Development Network, World Bank.

Wagstaff., A. and Van Doorslaer, E. (1997) Progressivity, horizontal equity and rearranging in healthcare finance: a decomposition analysis for the Netherlands, *Journal of Health Economics,* 16: 499–516.

Wagstaff., A., Van Doorslaer, E., Van der Burg, H. *et al.* (1999) Equity in the finance of healthcare: some further international comparisons, *Journal of Health Economics,* 18: 263–90.

Weber, A. (2000) HMOs und Hausartzmodelle [HMOs and GP models] *Lehrgang Gesundheitswesen Schweiz,* Chapter 4.4, http://www.medpoint.ch/other/lehrgang/44_HMO. pdf (accessed 7 November 2003).

Wenzel, M., Reuscher, A. and Aral, H. (2001) Zum Stand der Katarakt – und refraktiven Chirurgie Umfrage von DGII und BVA 2000 im internationalen Vergleich, *Ophtalmo-Chirurgie,* 13: 137–43.

Whitehead, M. (1988) *Inequalities in Health: The Health Divide,* 2nd edn. London: Penguin.

WHO (2000) *World Health Report 2000.* Geneva: World Health Organization.

WHO (2001) *Technical Consultation on Fairness on Financial Contribution to Health Systems: Background Paper,* 4–5 October. Geneva: World Health Organization.

WHO (2002a) WHO European Health for All Database. Copenhagen: WHO Regional Office for Europe, June.

WHO (2002b) *Report of the Scientific Peer Review Group on Health Systems Performance Assessment.* Geneva: World Health Organization. http://www.who.int/health-systems-performance/sprg/report_of_sprg_on_hspa.htm (accessed 17 September 2003).

WHO (2003) *WHO European Health for All Database.* Copenhagen: WHO Regional Office for Europe, June.

Wissenschaftliches Institut der AOK (1999) *WIdO- Frühjahrsstudie 1998 ff.* Bonn: AOK- Bundesverband.

Xu, K., Evans, D.B., Kawabata, J., Zeramdini, R., Klavus, J. and Murray, C.J.L. (2003) Understanding household catastrophic health expenditures: a multi-country analysis, in C.J.L. Murray and D.B. Evans (eds) *Health Systems Performance Assessment: Debates, Methods and Empiricism,* pp. 565–72. Geneva: World Health Organization. http://whqlibdoc.who.int/publications/2003/9241562455_(part4)_(chp34–42).pdf (accessed 11 February 2004).

Zok, K. (2003) Immer mehr Versicherte wollen wechseln, *Gesundheit und Gesellschaft,* 9/03: 38–41.

chapter five

Assessing social health insurance systems: present and future policy issues

Richard B. Saltman

This chapter focuses on the policy lessons to be taken from the preceding four chapters in Part One, as well as the key conceptual and operational issues raised in the eight chapters in Part Two. It begins by presenting three different, complementary approaches to assessing the available evidence about current trends and performance levels in the eight studied social health insurance (SHI) countries. The chapter then explores some of the key dilemmas that this evidence raises for the future direction of policy-making for SHI systems, and the complex trade-offs that decision-makers face. A short concluding section suggests that a comprehensive process of what can be termed 'strategic incrementalism' may provide a useful way forward.

Reviewing the available evidence

The overall picture that emerges from Chapters 1–4 is complex and complicated. The eight studied SHI systems vary considerably along organizational and structural dimensions, reflecting differing histories and, often, different national norms and values that underpin these organizational arrangements. This is not surprising given the range of countries reviewed, and speaks to the broadly diverse character of SHI as a conceptual model.

As diverse as these particular national arrangements are, however, this review has also demonstrated several central underlying commonalities that link these eight systems together. Prominent among these is the assumption that SHI is first and foremost a 'way of life', a stable, tradition-bound social institution in which economic implications play an important role but do not exercise primary influence over decision-making. A second shared assumption is that the specific structure and organization of SHI is grounded in the bedrock of social solidarity, of a system of social cohesion that reflects national culture and social preferences. Solidarity is seen as the touchstone of social insurance, and is the core principle around which policy-making has (or is at least expected to) orient itself.

A third commonality reflects the complicated governance arrangements in SHI systems. SHI's pluralist, corporatist, participatory model of enforced (e.g. statutory) self-regulation, grounded in the private but cooperative realm of civil society, is seen as an alternative form of democratic control parallel to (if not entirely independent of) the state (Altenstetter 1999). Although this alternative democratic dimension is stronger in some countries (Austria, Belgium, Germany, Netherlands) than in others (France, Israel, Switzerland), it is an important factor in the psychology of the citizenry in SHI countries, and in their understanding of what makes an SHI system different from a state-run, tax-funded framework.

These three common characteristics of SHI countries have been strengthened and reinforced by a number of the recent organizational and structural reforms reviewed in Chapter 3. This first, qualitative, approach to assessing the overall status of the eight studied SHI systems reviewed the character and consequences of recent structural and organizational reforms. Among the reform measures taken over the past decade by the eight studied SHI systems, considerable expansion occurred in coverage, extending solidarity to all citizens (Israel, Switzerland) to the self-employed (Netherlands) and to remaining lower income groups (Belgium, France). Similarly, coverage of long-term care was expanded through new programmes (Austria in 1993, Germany in 1996, Luxembourg in 1999) or new coverage initiatives (France, Netherlands). Both types of increased coverage are consistent with the traditional momentum of SHI systems, in which over time solidarity is extended incrementally to new groups and new categories of care (Abel-Smith 1988).

There were, however, other areas of reform activity which appeared to have a less supportive impact on traditional SHI patterns of stable, solidaristic and, most notably, self-regulatory behaviour. One key example concerns state-imposed efforts regarding the financial sustainability of SHI systems. These finance-related measures can be divided into two quite different categories. As Chapter 3 discussed, one series of measures taken during the past decade sought either to expand the available revenue base for SHI (France's new CSR wealth-based tax) or, conversely, to constrain the flow of available funds into the SHI system (Germany's coupling of increases in SHI premiums to increases in overall employee salary levels). A number of states also strengthened their regulatory efforts to rein in growth of pharmaceutical costs (Mossialos *et al.* 2004 forthcoming). Such measures are, broadly speaking, consistent with traditional SHI structures, in that they seek either to supply more funds or, conversely, to restrict funds as a device to create an incentive for more cost-effective behaviour and/or to impose more decision-making discipline on existing, long-standing organizational patterns of funds and providers.

Cost-constraining measures also included, however, finance-related efforts that could put at risk some measure of existing solidarity or which sought, in principle, to radically restructure existing sickness fund and provider relationships. These quite different measures revolved around a desire to introduce more market-influenced, entrepreneurial, even for-profit style initiatives and mechanisms into what was seen not so much as a traditional but rather as an anachronistic and obsolescent structure of SHI arrangements. Among the package of measures that some SHI systems sought (with varying degrees of success) to introduce have been patient choice of sickness fund (Germany, Israel, Netherlands); increased financial risk-bearing for sickness funds (Belgium, Israel, Netherlands, Switzerland); enhanced collective retrospective (Germany) and individual prospective (Netherlands) risk adjustment formulas; the introduction of non-income-related, flat rate premium payments (Netherlands); and increased cost-sharing and co-payments (Austria, Belgium, Germany, Netherlands). Dixon *et al.*, in Chapter 7, caution that the use of competitive mechanisms without enhanced regulatory measures runs the risk of damaging traditional norms of solidarity within SHI structures. Similarly, van de Ven *et al.* (2003), in a five-country study of risk adjustment formulas, conclude that, as currently constructed, competitive mechanisms create incentives for increased risk selection in the future unless there are 'substantial improvements' in the structure of existing state regulations and the risk adjustment formulas being utilized.

The above assessment of the present status of trends and patterns in SHI systems can be supplemented by a second analytic approach, utilizing available quantitative techniques to evaluate the present level of performance of SHI systems and to compare that performance with the outcomes obtained among peer counterpart but tax-funded northern European health systems. This approach was explored in Chapter 4. Within the limitations of available data and methodological techniques, Chapter 4 identified not only areas where SHI systems performed slightly better than northern tax-based systems, but also several areas of activity within present-day SHI structures where future reform efforts in SHI systems might seek to make improvements.

With regard to health status, for example during the 1990s, SHI systems showed less improvement than tax-funded northern European systems on conditions amenable to medical intervention. With regard to access issues, ongoing reform in at least one country (Switzerland) appeared to create new administrative obstacles to necessary care. With regard to equity issues, comparative statistics from the early 1990s suggest that the current mix of funding sources within six of eight SHI systems (France and Israel are exceptions) likely remains broadly if mildly regressive. This likelihood is reinforced by recent OECD data indicating that SHI systems have higher out-of-pocket payments than do northern European tax-funded systems. Indeed, increased co-payments (Germany, Israel) and the introduction of flat-rate premiums (Netherlands) raise concerns that some SHI systems may be becoming more rather than less regressive in character – an outcome which runs directly contrary to stated principles of social solidarity.

Beyond issues of health status and regressivity of funding, the statistical review in Chapter 4 also explored a series of potential efficiency issues. In terms of total expenditure on either a GDP or a per capita basis, SHI systems spend significantly more. As noted earlier, proponents of SHI have traditionally attributed these higher expenditures to patients' ability to choose physician and hospital, arguing that, although this SHI approach costs more, it eliminated queues and produced greater levels of responsiveness and patient satisfaction. Interestingly, however, the available data on satisfaction and responsiveness presented in Chapter 4 indicates that SHI systems are only somewhat more responsive and/or produce higher levels of overall satisfaction than do northern tax-funded systems. This suggests that other cost drivers such as higher resource levels and (in some countries) insufficient coordination between different levels of care may also play a role in SHI systems. More complexly, SHI's pluralist, participatory structure of governance, rather than patients' ability to choose doctor and hospital, may also contribute to SHI's higher cost structure. While the extra cost attributed to the traditional governance model may be seen as necessary and acceptable to SHI policy-makers, costs associated with other administrative factors may be appropriate areas to address in future reform measures.

A third approach to assessing the current status of SHI systems can be found in the commissioned chapters in Part Two. Some of the most insightful observations about the structure and performance of SHI systems can be found in the topic-based chapters grouped under 'Key organizational issues'. Gibis *et al.* (Chapter 8) suggest that the future development of benefit catalogues will depend on the abilities of government and SHI agencies to promote both greater citizen participation but also the elaboration of evidence-based clinical practice guidelines. Hofmarcher and Durand-Zaleski (Chapter 9) find that collective rather than selective contracting continues to predominate in SHI systems, attributable largely to an unwillingness to incur the higher transaction costs associated with individual contracts. Wasem *et al.* (Chapter 10) conclude that, while strict separation between SHI and supplementary private health insurance (PHI) is preferable, state regulatory efforts over these two insurance areas should be harmonized. Lastly, Wildner *et al.* (Chapter 11) suggest that existing levels of patient choice (what in the past has often been trumpeted as a successful dimension of SHI systems) are insufficient and will require substantial strengthening.

Similarly, the two chapters in the 'Beyond acute care' section of Part Two raise important issues regarding current practices in SHI systems in preventive public health and in long-term care for the elderly. McKee *et al.* (Chapter 12) suggest that SHI systems have yet to grapple adequately with the need to develop new networks to implement population-based public health measures. De Roo *et al.* (Chapter 13) conclude that SHI systems need to make greater efforts to coordinate and integrate long-term care services into the overall focus of the service delivery system.

Taken together, the observations from these three different analytic approaches – current trends and patterns, statistical performance, and the issue-based chapters – sketch out a broad assessment of the current status of key policy issues within the eight studied SHI countries. These observations can provide a useful framework for the ongoing health reform debate about making organizational and institutional improvements within existing SHI systems, as well as raising a variety of issues that require additional research.

The broader policy challenge

The process of health reform in the studied SHI systems can be broadly characterized as one of careful incrementalism (funding reforms in Israel and Switzerland are exceptions). Most steps have been measured and their impact limited. Outcomes from any individual reform measure have rarely affected the overall social or economic nature of the system itself. In many ways, this limited impact can be considered a success of recent SHI policy-making. Maarse and Paulus (2003) conclude their recent study of solidarity in four SHI countries by stating 'reform proposals that would threaten solidarity never achieved a political majority' (p. 610).

Yet, when one looks beyond the impact of specific individual reform measures to consider the overall pattern of change and the potential implications that this pattern could hold in the foreseeable future, the central policy dilemma that SHI systems face appears to be not technical or incremental in nature but rather fundamental and strategic. Moreover, considered as a pattern, the current careful process of small technical reforms may well itself be helping to generate some of the more serious strategic risks that SHI systems currently confront.

As explored in Chapter 1, the key challenge for future policy-making in the studied SHI countries revolves around complex interrelationships among questions of economic, political and social sustainability. The central imperative of reinforcing future financial sustainability in a period of rapid technological advance, ageing populations and rising economic volatility, while (for six of the eight countries) accommodating an ongoing process of political integration within the European Union (EU), involves a complicated mix of often contradictory measures. To be successful, this reoriented policy process must be undertaken without fatally weakening the core social solidarity-based foundation upon which these health systems have been constructed – that is, without undermining the very social configuration that national policy is dedicated to defending.

The danger that lies just below the surface in present-day SHI policy-making is that the long-standing priority of defending the social character of these health systems will be replaced by a new economic priority of achieving sustainable funding regardless of the structural consequences. This inversion of current policy priorities, this substitution of economic concerns for the 'non-economic benefits' that inhere within traditional SHI arrangements, need not – and probably will not – reflect a consciously adopted change of strategic direction. Rather, the shift may well occur through a process of accretion, in which technical economic measures, each seemingly reasonable and unthreatening by itself, add up over time to a change of fundamental proportions. The concern is that the accumulation of technical mechanisms such as selective contracts, risk-bearing sickness funds, flat-rate rather than income-proportional premiums, patient co-payments, 'no use' rebates, and a host of similar instruments will aggregate into not a technical but a strategic change that reduces or eliminates important dimensions of SHI as a 'way of life'.

A critical aspect of this strategic challenge reflects the unusually configured roles of public and private, and of social and market, in SHI systems. In the civil society-based structure of SHI systems, the dimension of social solidarity and accountability is associated with the 'private' (not-for-profit) sickness funds. Conversely, the role of the 'public' sector (e.g. the state) has recently become in considerable part associated with national policies to introduce more market-oriented mechanisms into the health sector, potentially worsening existing levels of regressivity and reducing social solidarity more generally. This creates a pattern of relations that is the converse of what is typically seen in tax-funded health care systems (Saltman 2003). In the current framework of SHI decision-making, the private not-for-profit funders rather self-consciously see themselves as the defenders of social responsibility, while the public sector has been cast as having prioritized economic efficiency, to be achieved through socially disruptive market mechanisms. There is the further dimension that SHI systems feel increasingly threatened by growing national-level state intervention in health-related decisions that previously had been allocated to self-regulating private arrangements. Combining these two elements, the strategic dimension of the current dilemma is seen by a variety of SHI stakeholders as pitting 'state/economic' concerns against traditional 'private/social' interests, with a not unfounded fear that 'state/economic' will eventually come to dominate in overall health sector decision-making.

The worry about the long-term aggregate consequences of market-oriented reform measures reflects the degree to which these seemingly reasonable financial mechanisms can potentially fragment both the organizational and the social cohesion of traditional SHI structures. Many of these concerns are discussed directly in Part Two both by Chinitz et al. (Chapter 6) and Dixon et al. (Chapter 7). There are also concerns that, at least in some contexts, certain market-oriented mechanisms may not be very efficient in the health sector. Among other concerns, there may be increased transaction costs associated with these approaches – as noted in Chapter 4, administrative costs are already higher in SHI countries than in their tax-based counterparts. Similarly, when funders become risk-bearing, they may decide to adopt both visible and less visible mechanisms to pick among potential and, ultimately, existing subscribers – something Germany already began to experience in the late 1990s (Pfaff 2001). Ultimately, an unrestrained commitment to cost-focused economic incentives could potentially lead to a situation in which not-for-profit private entities slowly jettison their social role while simultaneously creating new financial costs to the health care system.

Concern about long-term social and organizational fragmentation caused by the introduction of technical mechanisms of financial efficiency is neither new nor restricted to western European SHI systems. A large literature exists regarding the inability of market-based efficiency mechanisms to incorporate moral or social dimensions, including highly regarded work by Arrow (1963), Daniels (1985), Etzioni (1988), Sen (1992) and Rice (1998). Moreover, the substitution of public/economic for private/social priorities has occurred previously, in other health care systems, although under quite different national, political and cultural circumstances. On this issue, the United States can serve as a worst case example. In the 1960s, its health care system also was predominantly private not-for-profit (though not statutory) in nature (Starr 1983), with the large majority of funders (Blue Cross/Blue Shield) and hospitals formally committed to an organizational mission to improve health in the local community. This social dimension of the US health care system changed irrevocably over the next two decades. Although no official national or regional legislation was ever adopted, the accumulated weight of individual mechanisms designed to increase technical efficiency ultimately generated a fundamental shift to a fully market-based, for-profit system.

It is, of course, difficult to imagine that western European SHI systems, with their very different organizational, cultural and statutory arrangements, could undergo such a transformation. The point here is thus not that continued incremental accumulation of economic efficiency measures in western Europe threatens to push these systems into a US-style health sector transformation. Rather it is that the uncalculated, step-by-step introduction of seemingly reasonable efficiency measures has the potential to result in undesirable strategic consequences for both the social and economic characteristics of the overall health system.

One important caveat to this argument concerns the importance of differentiating between those market-oriented measures that have the potential to aggregate into a serious problem for SHI health systems, in notable contrast to the particular market-oriented mechanisms recently introduced within tax-funded health systems across northern Europe. Two crucial distinctions need to be made, reflecting not only the actual market-oriented mechanism itself, but, equally as important, the regulatory context within tax-funded health systems in which these measures were adopted, and the consequent constraints upon their impact on the overall health system. First, market-oriented mechanisms in tax-funded systems have been utilized exclusively on the supply or production side, typically to create more efficient behaviour among hospitals (Busse *et al.* 2002). Second, tax-funded systems are utilizing these mechanisms exclusively among publicly-owned and publicly-operated hospitals, generating forms of 'public competition' that intentionally exclude privately-owned institutions or the accumulation of private capital (Saltman and Von Otter 1992). By contrast, the developing pattern of market-oriented instruments within SHI systems has had a substantially broader, system-wide character. Depending on the SHI system, they may be introduced on the demand or funding side as well as the production side, and allow for participation by for-profit as well as not-for-profit private funders and/or provider institutions. In short, in tax-funded systems, market-oriented instruments have been strategically deployed to reinforce existing publicly-operated structures, and carefully separated from equity-sensitive aspects of the demand side of the system. This strategic character, combined with careful hedging of regulations around the use of market-oriented mechanisms to ensure that they act in service to broad system-level objectives, is not always apparent in how some SHI systems have sought to employ market-oriented initiatives. These are important distinctions which can have major implications for the outcomes obtained.

Strategic incrementalism

The discussion-making landscape within SHI systems is densely layered and historically conditioned. In historical terms, the SHI model has been both organizationally and financially stable. The tightly focused notion of solidarity upon which it has been constructed remains a central component of present-day health policy, and continues to generate fierce loyalty from the citizenry these systems serve. Overall, as noted in Chapter 1, SHI is closely woven into the social fabric of the studied countries, viewed not just as a technical mechanism to fund health services but rather as an overarching and pre-eminent 'way of life'.

The recent process of reforms in SHI countries has served largely to reinforce this broad historical and normative pattern. As reviewed in Chapter 3, reforms have been predominantly technical and incremental in nature, seeking to maintain financial sustainability without making major alterations to existing structural or organizational arrangements. Moreover, the two countries which enacted more major finance-related reforms – France and Israel – did so with the explicit intention of enhancing solidarity as well as the financial sustainability of their funding systems.

This same pattern of technical and incremental reform emerges from the assessment of the current status of SHI systems presented in the first section of this chapter. While each of the three approaches to the available evidence about SHI systems leads to a set of concerns and/or potential policy changes, those changes largely point toward adjustments and refinements of existing policies and structures rather than a need for more fundamental change.

Yet this overall stability and success does not alter the core strategic dilemma that SHI systems currently confront. As the discussion above emphasized, the long-term danger arises not so much from the specific technical mechanisms introduced in pursuit of financial sustainability, but from the broader process of change itself and from the cumulative impact of individual measures on the core characteristics of the overall system. The critical issue is one of unintended consequences from the reform process, rather than of intentional consequences created by the adoption of any specific reform measure.

The central policy challenge thus becomes to develop a broader strategic framework within which to assess the longer-term implications of each incremental proposal, and through which to harness the overall change process in a direction that remains consistent with the underlying features and values of SHI systems. In support of such a framework, policy-makers in SHI countries might find it useful to consider the following two linked concepts.

The first concept can be termed 'strategic incrementalism'. It involves articulating a long-term set of objectives for the health system that is consistent with its current aims and organization, and that can provide guidance to the necessary incremental reforms that will be required over the next period of years. Proposals for specific reforms could then be evaluated in terms of their likely longer-term strategic impact on the overall system, and where appropriate, adjustments in their design or application could be made prior to their introduction. This process could ensure that short-term, small-scale changes are considered in terms of their likely long-term systemic impact.

The second concept, operationalizing the first, would be to establish a mandatory system of 'solidarity impact assessments'. These assessments would be formal in nature, following a clear set of administrative procedures that tie these reports directly to the objectives established by the long-term strategic framework just described. Much like environmental impact assessments in a number of countries (on which this concept is modelled), these solidarity impact assessments would be a required part of the national legislative and/or rule-making process. With such a regulatory procedure in place, no technical change (beyond a certain financial or organizational threshold) could be adopted without first mapping its likely impact on the broader objectives of the entire health care system. Experience in the environmental area indicates that such impact assessments would rarely stop the proposed activity entirely, but rather they would likely lead to valuable modifications to ensure closer compatibility of the proposed measure with the long-term stability and sustainability of the overall system. These solidarity impact assessments could be particularly useful to ministries of health when evaluating the likely long-term implications of reform proposals put forward by ministries of finance.

Taken together, these two concepts suggest that national policy-makers in SHI countries should consider establishing a targeted and goal-oriented regulatory framework through which to steer the ongoing process of incremental health sector reform. Such a new regulatory process would enable decision-makers to build upon and reinforce the strengths of existing SHI systems without sacrificing the ability to introduce needed future changes. It holds the promise of introducing a greater degree of systemic thinking into ongoing reform activities at various levels of these health care systems. Most of all, it would put in place a routine administrative arrangement to ensure that the long-term strategic result of short-term technical reforms is in fact one that is politically and socially desirable.

References

Abel-Smith, B. (1988) The rise and decline of the early HMOs: some international experiences, *Milbank Memorial Fund Quarterly*, 66(4): 694–719.

Altenstetter, C. (1999) From solidarity to market competition? Values, structure, and strategy in German health policy 1883–1997, in F.D. Powell and A.F. Wessen (eds) *Health-Care Systems in Transition: An International Perspective*, pp. 47–88. London: Sage.

Arrow, K. (1963) Uncertainty and the welfare economics of medical care, *American Economic Review*, 53(3): 941–73.

Busse, R., Van der Grinten, T. and Svensson, P-G. (2002) Regulating entrepreneurial behaviour in hospitals: theory and practice, in R.B. Saltman, R. Busse and E. Mossialos (eds) *Regulating Entrepreneurial Behaviour in European Health Care Systems*, pp. 126–45. Buckingham: Open University Press.

Daniels, N. (1985) *Just Health Care*. Cambridge: Cambridge University Press.

Etzioni, A. (1988) *The Moral Dimension: Toward a New Economics*. New York: The Free Press.

Maarse, H. and Paulus, A. (2003) Has solidarity survived? A comparative analysis of the effect of social health insurance (SHI) reform in four European countries, *Journal of Health Politics Policy and Law*, 28(4): 585–614.

Mossialos, E., Mrazek, M. and Walley, T. (eds) (2004 forthcoming) *Regulating the Cost and use of Pharmaceuticals in Europe*. Maidenhead: Open University Press.

Pfaff, M. (2001) Comment at the Authors' Workshop, Storkow, Germany, 6 October.

Rice, T. (1998) *The Economics of Health Reconsidered*. Chicago: Health Administration Press.

Saltman, R.B. (2003) Melting public-private boundaries in European health systems, *European Journal of Public Health*, 13(1): 24–9.

Saltman, R.B. and Von Otter, C. (1992) *Planned Markets and Public Competition: Strategic Reform in Northern European Health Care Systems*. Buckingham: Open University Press.

Sen, A. (1992) *Inequality Re-examined*. Cambridge: Harvard University Press.

Starr, P. (1983) *The Social Transformation of the American Health System*. New York: Basic Books.

Van de Ven, W.P.M.M., Beck, K., Buchner, F. *et al.* (2003) Risk adjustment and risk selection on the sickness fund insurance market in five European countries, *Health Policy*, 65(1): 75–98.

part two

The challenge to solidarity

chapter six

Governance and (self-)regulation in social health insurance systems

David Chinitz, Matthias Wismar and Claude Le Pen

Introduction

Long before 'the Third Way' became the reformist buzzword of 1990s public policy, social health insurance (SHI) systems had evolved as a uniquely structured institutional arrangement that inhabited the social space between purely public (e.g. state) as against purely private (e.g. for-profit) modes of health sector organization. Although no western European health care system has accepted the social, economic or political risks inherent in relegating health care finance and delivery to a totally private market, nearly as many countries have chosen to adopt a social insurance approach as have adopted a tax-funded framework – i.e. to be a Bismarck- rather than a Beveridge-type system.

This chapter is, however, about one of the main components of SHI systems, the structure for governance and regulation. It seeks to explore a number of key issues that influence the basis for, and the legitimacy of, SHI systems. Among these are the following: What is the distribution of authority among public, not-for-profit private and for-profit private entities? What are the relative roles of legislative, executive and judicial bodies? What is the legal structure and how are health care funding and delivery regulated? What challenges are posed for coordination among various agencies involved in this policy-making and regulatory network, and between the regulatory agencies and the professionals and provider groups in the health system? What are the mechanisms of accountability in such systems and how well do they function? Moreover, what impact do alternative SHI frameworks have on outcomes of the system such as equity, efficiency and responsiveness? Finally, what is the likely future of such

SHI systems in view of the evolving role of the European Union (EU) in health-related realms of economy, politics and law?

On governance

The decade of the 1990s has been described as the decade of 'governance' in political science and public policy (Plumptre and Graham 2000). For an increasing range of public and social activities, traditional distinctions between government, the private sector and the non-profit sector, which had become quite well developed and accepted, were no longer adequate for either analysis or management. The lines between sectors have become increasingly blurred, so that even when one discusses the public-private mix in health care, reference is no longer to a mix between two clearly defined sectors, but to a variety of inter-organizational arrangements (Saltman 2003). These arrangements are often fluid and arise to meet the contingencies of complex public managerial challenges (Øvretveit 2001).

One useful definition of governance suggests that it is 'the art of steering societies and organizations' (Plumptre and Graham 2000: 3). As Plumptre and Graham recognize, however, this captures only part of the concept. A broader concept would hold that 'Governance is the process whereby, within accepted traditions and institutional frameworks, interests are articulated by different sectors of society, decisions are taken, and decision makers are held to account' (Plumptre and Graham 2000). In this view, government is more a 'process than an institution'. The process of governance does differ noticeably across different sectors: international, national, local, non-profit and private. A realm which has received a great deal of attention in recent literature on governance is that of 'civil society' (Fukuyama 1995; Putnam 2000). Civil society, with its close conceptual affinity to voluntary action and involvement of citizens in public affairs, has come to be seen as a source of social capital and trust which in turn can lead to better performance of both government and private markets. This approach provides an overarching context somewhat lacking in alternative approaches, currently in fashion, which take a decidedly microanalytic approach to fundamental issues of governance and social contract. For example, some have sought (with some merit), to tackle issues of health system finance and delivery through the lens of the 'new institutional economics' (Preker *et al.* 2000), and its operational embodiment: comparative institutional analysis. As articulated by Williamson (1993), institutional economics is concerned with governance, thought of as 'good order and workable arrangements'. However, Williamson's approach captures only part of a much broader picture that has not just technical economic but also strong historical and cultural overtones. Comparative institutional analysis seeks to explain why certain institutional arrangements appear to survive organizational evolution. The 'action', from Williamson's perspective (1993), lies in microanalysis of the transactions in question, seeking to explain how the interaction of human behavioural tendencies with fixed technical qualities inherent in the production or exchange process can lead to the emergence of different organizational forms. This is a kind of positivist, game theory approach which can usefully assess the governance of specific transactions as well as governance arrangements at the level of individual health system transactions. Such approaches, however, need to be supplemented with attention to what Williamson himself refers to as the 'institutional environment' of society, and the social 'atmosphere' within which transactions take place.

Thus, governance can be viewed as the process of accountable decision-making in society that interlinks the various sectors mentioned above. But, as the literature suggests, the nature of governance will alter across different social endeavours. Internal corporate governance of private enterprises will differ from governance of non-profit organizations. Government relations with, and regulation of, these two sectors will likely differ as well in the components and style of the governing process.

In this respect, SHI can be expected to display unique characteristics of governance. First, SHI combines elements of civil society, institutional mechanisms for negotiation and decision-making among stakeholder groups, and government regulation. This mix evolved long before the phenomenon of governance was 'discovered' by policy analysts during the 1990s. The historical and cultural roots of SHI within countries are essential to an understanding of current governance arrangements in these systems. Moreover, since the impact of history and culture vary across countries and locales, it becomes important to consider not only the common characteristics of governance across SHI systems – the generic dimensions of 'social embeddedness' (Saltman 1998) – but also the variations through which those common dimensions are expressed.

The field of comparative health systems is an appropriate context within which to capture the more elusive part of comparative institutional analysis – namely, the role of cultural or 'atmospheric' factors in moulding institutional structures. Williamson's institutional environment cannot be taken for granted. When considering social policy, it is untenable to hold the surrounding atmosphere 'constant'. One observes, rather, a symbiotic relationship between the institutional environment and the institutions of governance. Especially in the current European era with trends toward regional responsibility, such as the role of the EU, it is critical to consider whether there can be a 'one size fits all' way of organizing social services such as health, or whether cultural as well as institutional diversity will continue to be necessary, appropriate and respected. Comparative assessment of SHI frameworks can shed light on this emerging issue.

The first section of this chapter expands on this comparative assessment of SHI systems, laying out the main parameters of SHI governance structures and examining patterns of interaction among those parameters. The second section discusses examples from various SHI health systems that can shed light on how the transactional and governance issues are structured within them. The third section then explores the dynamic relationship between the institutional environment on the one hand, and the mechanisms of governance on the other, relating, among others, to the evolving role of the EU. The concluding section suggests lessons and policy options for SHI systems and propositions for future research.

The essence of governance in SHI systems

One way to probe the essence of governance in SHI systems is to compare the latter with the traditional Beveridge model in which 'action' in governance is hierarchical and intended to follow the basic Weberian conception of bureaucratic organization. Of course, the realities of organizational politics belie the neat theory and in many cases regional/county and local/municipal levels of the Beveridge model have an independent political and financial foundation, and are thus far from simply the 'long arm' of central government. Nonetheless, the underlying orientation in Beveridge-type health systems, whether highly centralized or decentralized, is one of substantive rationality associated with a national, regional or local command and control system (Saltman and Von Otter 1992). In contrast, SHI systems focus more on procedural rationality, reflected in aspects of corporatism, legislation and the role of the private sector to be discussed below. In SHI systems, the action centres on plural actors whose activities and decisions are aligned through corporatist techniques deployed under the aegis of government statute.

The stakeholders that are the subject of governance in SHI are many and varied. Employers (and their associations), employees (and their unions), insurers (both private not-for-profit and for-profit) and providers (in some cases even doctors are unionized) come together to set the rules of the game regarding health insurance, *collectively* (Evans 1991). The interplay among these stakeholders has induced action at the macro level of national governments to regulate the system. Stakeholders operate in an environment mandated by government. Going beyond technical regulatory interventions, European governments in SHI countries shape health insurance arrangements in a more organic way, which is what makes them SHI systems. Bringing the stakeholders together for structured negotiations, establishing public consensus, nurturing social solidarity; these are the roles of government in SHI systems. In other words, the macro level of central government is integrally involved in governing SHI, through establishment of the mechanisms by which the interests of all the stakeholders will be coordinated at all levels of the system.

The management of the interactions between stakeholders in SHI systems contributes to the fabric of society. Governance in SHI systems goes beyond the 'make or buy' decision that some have emphasized (Preker *et al.* 2001). The relationship is also not captured by a straightforward classification as government involvement to correct for market failures (Williamson 1985), or by characterizations of the distinct attributes of different sectors: public, private and not-for-profit (Cohen 2001). Different countries have evolved different modes of institutionalizing and organizing this network, and the attributes of these alternatives will be considered below. First, we take a look at the partners to the governance process.

The stakeholders

The stakeholders in SHI systems include employers, employees, citizens, patients, insurers, providers and government. The stakeholders are not monolithic. There are small and large employers, high and low income insurees, large insurers and small insurers. Moreover, stakeholders, especially insurers, may vary in terms of whether they are for-profit or not-for-profit entities. Stakeholders may be grouped into various umbrella organizations, for example consumers' associations representing different age groups or disease categories. The possibilities for coalitions among these stakeholder groups are many. Providers and patients may line up and militate against 'stingy' sickness funds; employers and sickness funds may combine to restrain expansion of health insurance benefits; insurers and providers may join into integrated organizations, seeking greater efficiencies, but perhaps at the cost of limiting choice.

The challenge for governance of these interactions is to create mechanisms by which all parties may come out of the game feeling that they have not been taken advantage of. Governance mechanisms must, for example, see to the availability and distribution of relevant information regarding the transactions in question. Are the sickness funds providing adequate access to care at acceptable levels of quality? Are benefits accurately costed and premiums adjusted accordingly? Who is making coverage decisions and what mechanisms exist for appealing such decisions?

Governance mechanisms

Governance by history and tradition

It is important, especially in comparative analysis, to be sensitive to the degree to which the social atmosphere interacts, limits and is, in turn, influenced by SHI governance. Historical antecedents constitute an inheritance likely to have a strong hold on the governance mechanisms which emerge. Cultural predilections – for example, to voluntarism and reliance on non-governmental organizations – are part of the constellation of governance. Strongly-held social or professional norms may lead to a system that is more self-regulating than governed by the various organizational, legal and technical mechanisms alluded to above. Moreover, overreliance on any of the above may have a negative impact on norms, as partners to transactions come to behave in accordance with external governing mechanisms and become weaned from the control of their own values. As Williamson points out, extreme reliance on legal remedies has the potential to corrode less adversarial forms of mutual adaptation, which may, impose high transactions costs.

SHI systems cannot be understood without reference to fundamental issues of social contract that typically characterize the countries which choose SHI as the organizing principle of their health systems. It should be remembered that in almost all countries some form of health delivery system existed before health became a public issue inviting government intervention. As such, health services were nested within the fabric of civil society, linked to other social and economic functions crossing the voluntary, private and government sectors. In some countries, health finance and delivery began as being integrated with employment or labour organizations, sometimes in conjunction with political orientations or parties. Belgium, France and Israel are prime examples. In all of these countries, health insurance began under the auspices of guilds or labour unions. Israel differs from Belgium and France in that a single labour federation developed its own provider network in addition to the insurance and reimbursement function. In each of these countries there are political links between the health insurance funds and political parties. This means that some of the governance issues will be cast differently depending on which political party is in power.

For example, in Belgium, health insurance arrangements began in the early nineteenth century with the creation, by groups of workers, of 'mutualities' providing health insurance coverage to different professional groups. In the latter part of the nineteenth century the government intervened, granting recognition to the mutualities which enabled them to receive government subsidies. During the twentieth century the mutualities segmented ideologically and formed national unions such as the National Union of Christian Mutual Funds (today about 45 per cent of the population) and the National Union of Socialist Mutual Funds (about 29 per cent of the population). These health insurance associations became subject to national law, making membership compulsory in 1943. At that time, representatives of employers and trade unions met and, under government aegis, it was decided that health insurance would be compulsory for salaried workers and to create the National Office of Social Security (Nonneman and Van Doorslaer 1994; Kerr 2000).

Another aspect of governance that seems rooted in history and tradition is that different countries appear to strike a different balance between the verticality of government intervention in SHI and more reliance on horizontal mechanisms of accommodation among the stakeholders. Of the countries examined here, Israel has, perhaps, an SHI system most constrained by central government directive. Despite the fact that the country's 1994 National Insurance Legislation appears to emphasize competition, the financing mode (in which general tax monies, channeled through the state budget, account for half or more of SHI finance), leads to 'regression to the mean' (or, some would say, the lowest common denominator) on the part of the sickness funds. The situation is one in which the sick funds feel that the government, more than they, is financially accountable for SHI. Governance turns more on political demands for increased funding, with sickness funds, providers, patients and consumers lobbying the government for increased funding from general revenues (Chinitz *et al.* 1998; Shadmi 2003).

This is quite different from the situation in Germany, in which government attempts to resolve these matters through structured negotiations over the level of premiums. Participants in these negotiations include sickness funds, providers, employers and unions (Schwartz and Busse 1996). While government clearly provides the auspices for these negotiations, in Germany it is important to emphasize, at least in rhetoric, that the goal is 'concerted action', not imposed top-down control by central government.

Showing the importance of historical and cultural traditions, France, like Germany, governs the SHI system through structured negotiations among the stakeholders. But, in keeping with the traditionally strong centralization of French government, there is one large sickness fund, CNMATS, which has been created more or less by government to represent that sector (Rodwin

2003). This is different from the associations of sickness funds in Germany and the Netherlands which come to the negotiating table, and is more similar to the situation in Belgium, where sickness funds are largely under the umbrella of large labour unions. Thus, Germany and the Netherlands retain, within the framework of structured negotiation, more of a tendency towards the pluralism of the SHI governing system than do Belgium and France.

Law

The SHI system is often governed by a set of statutes which constitute the main rules of the game. Who is qualified to provide insurance? What is the minimum set of benefits that must be provided? Who is required to pay SHI premiums and what mechanism shall be used to determine the rates? Laws are intended to be clear and binding, and aimed at clarifying lines of accountability. However, total reliance on the legal system to govern SHI may be deleterious in two ways: creating lack of flexibility in the system; and encouraging the debilitating affects of resort to the court system to remedy perceived violations of the law.

Structured negotiations

By requirement of SHI statutes, or by agreement among the stakeholders, a framework for joint decision-making may be created. This is the case in Germany. Here, all of the stakeholders are required to come to the table to negotiate the overall SHI budget, premium rates to be paid by employers and employees, provider reimbursement and benefits to be covered, among others (Schwartz and Busse 1996; Worz and Busse 2002). Such negotiations, especially when given high public visibility, may contribute to social consensus and trust, but are also subject to the rising and flagging strength of different interest groups and their representatives at the bargaining table.

Market competition

Within the rules set by the governing system – for instance, law and negotiation as discussed above – the stakeholders may decide to use market mechanisms to help govern aspects such as choice of provider by the patient, or modes of reimbursement between sickness funds and providers. One of the most controversial governance issues in SHI is the degree to which premiums paid by the insured should be determined by market competition. A related question is the role of co-payments and deductibles and who determines whether and how to deploy these modes of exchange between insured and insurers (Maarse and Paulus 2001). The degree of competition is a measure of the degree to which the national or regional level dominates in SHI. If all prices, benefits and reimbursement rates are decided on at the national level, SHI begins to look like a unitary hierarchical health system. At the other extreme lies the US model: a wide variety of different forms of private collective insurance with little social governance involved. An interesting middle ground is the case where government subsidizes the social insurance system in a significant way, using general revenues to do so. In such a case the governance mechanisms will feature a tension between the horizontal and vertical modes of control and coordination. Switzerland and Israel feature particularly interesting developments in this connection, but every SHI system exhibits this tension.

Technocratic planning

Related to this last point is the possibility that the SHI system will be governed largely by technical guidelines issued by government and translated into directives. These guidelines may concern prices, reimbursement and the content of benefits. Again, extreme reliance on technocratic guidance of the system tends to move the system towards a unitary top-down mode of governance. The SHI approach is based on restraining such an outcome, and seeks to maintain a balance between technical management of the system and necessary and unavoidable political processes.

SHI governance: social and political capital

In considering the outcomes of alternative governance modes, the usual questions of efficiency, quality and equity are posed (dealt with elsewhere in the volume). Since SHI inherently must coordinate diverse and pluralistic partners to transactions, the accountability, transparency of the process, and the degree to which the process itself contributes to social solidarity are major outcomes of concern. Some observers appear to assume that political input is likely to be deleterious to social solidarity (Maarse and Paulus 2001), but it would appear that politics has a legitimate and possibly productive role to play in the governance of SHI systems. For some outcome measures, such as responsiveness, it may be difficult to separate between responsiveness of the governance system and the implications of governance for responsiveness at other levels of the system – for example, of insurers to consumers or physicians to patients. For example, if the politics of the priority setting process are perceived as fair, patients may more readily accept decisions of insurers and providers to deny access to specific treatments, rather than just viewing this as a form of lack of responsiveness (Tyler and Degoey 1996; Daniels 2000; Sabin 2000; Chinitz and Israeli 2001).

Previously, we alluded to the subject of social capital. The latter has come to be perceived by many prominent analysts as leading to better government (Fukuyama 1995; Putnam 2000). Some writers see a symbiotic relationship between civil society and government (Evans 1996; Fox 1996; Potapchuck *et al.* 1997). However, in these instances, reference is usually to local government, i.e. that level most likely to correspond to the usual locus of social capital. Relatively small, intimate organizations such as religious groups, sports clubs, neighbourhood associations etc., are the incubators for social capital. Local government can encourage the creation and maintenance of social capital by, for example, concerted efforts at citizen involvement.

SHI systems appear to constitute a variation of this model at higher systems levels. They have developed, perhaps, as part of a social learning process that led to recognition that social capital is difficult to maintain beyond the relatively intimate context of community and municipality. This could be the social intuition that leads to having peak organizations come together under the auspices of national government to negotiate and agree basic principles, major rules of the game and key operating procedures for the health system. The manner in which government frames the negotiations and leads the system towards outcomes it values affects the levels of trust and social capital in the system, thus making government and social capital reciprocal and mutually enhancing.

SHI systems suggest, therefore, that social capital interacts with what might be called political capital. The latter includes the ability of government leaders to promote trust in governmental institutions and processes. The underlying social solidarity that lies at the heart of SHI is not to be replaced by government involvement, but rather promoted by it. This can only be accomplished if politics is enacted not as simply a game of brute power, but, rather, within rules of the game that contribute not only to achievement of consensus, but also to its legitimacy. We propose that this is an overarching ethos in the governance of SHI systems, seeking to demonstrate this through some examples provided in the next section.

Perhaps the best way to grasp the essence of SHI governance is not through the lens of a static description, but, rather, by looking at the dynamics of the system. Recent changes in SHI systems, far from casting doubt on their viability, serve to demonstrate the vitality of the governing mechanisms of SHI. Moreover, as systems adjust to new exigencies, governance of SHI seeks to maintain the fundamental values that lie at the base of SHI.

Governing SHI: current challenges

SHI systems, like all health systems, have been subjected to efforts at major reform over the last decade. While many analysts have focused on the details of financing, allocation and production mechanisms related to these reforms, less noticed but at the core of the changing system is the governance system and the core values it reflects.

An example is the repeated attempt to introduce so-called managed or regulated competition into Dutch health insurance arrangements. This direction for reform began with the 1987 Dekker plan, persisting through the Simons plan of the early 1990s and up to attempts of the current government to restructure health insurance by 2005 (Maarse 2002). These dynamics highlight the three main structural elements of governance in an SHI system: the underlying historical and traditional infrastructure of voluntary health insurance arrangements; technocratic proposals for structural reform; and the intervention of government, ranging from a guiding hand to imposition of clear 'rules of the game'.

Voluntary health insurance arrangements, such as union- or professional-based sick funds, reflect the principle of *subsidiarity*, according to which responsibility for decision-making should be vested in the lowest possible level in society. Subsidiarity coincides with social capital in the sense that authority is delegated to organizational frameworks much closer to the community level, encouraging grass roots involvement. On the other hand, subsidiarity may undermine social capital in so far as local-level organizations seek the welfare of their own members at the expense of other groups and associations. This is part of the insight of the government's attempts to reform the Dutch health insurance system; namely, to get local organizations, such as regional sick funds, operating on the subsidiarity principle, to agree to rules of the game that will ensure the survival of social solidarity throughout the nation state in question. Thus, the current Dutch reform seeks to eliminate the distinction between sick funds and private insurers, by mandating them both to play by the same rules.

These rules are intended to nurture solidarity: eliminating selection bias practised by private insurers by obligating them to accept all individuals seeking insurance; requiring that all health insurers charge community rates; and standardizing the basket of services to be provided by insurers (Maarse 2002).

But, even as these rules seek to use 'fair competition' to preserve social solidarity, the new rules of the game encourage evasive behaviour by insurers that eats away at both solidarity and social capital. Behaviour aimed at discouraging enrolment by undesirable, problematic categories of citizens becomes attractive to insurers who now perceive themselves as being in a cat and mouse game with government regulators. Following Gouldner's model of direct exercise of authority in organizations, government responds by tightening regulation and a potentially vicious cycle might ensue.

This degeneration from a situation of high social and political capital can be avoided if a conscious effort is made to retain trust among various subsidiary actors and between them and government. Corporatism is a key tool used by SHI systems to produce consensus in a manner that does not eat away at trust among the various stakeholders and between the stakeholders and government. A scheme of regulated competition among sickness funds cannot be based on structural design and technical management tools alone, but also requires adequate stores of social and political capital that nurture each other.

One form of encouraging the availability of social and political capital was the creation, in 1999, of a Commission on Corporate Governance in health care in the Netherlands (Maarse 2002). The Commission dealt, among other things, with the roles of executives and supervisory boards in health care organizations, and its recommendations were discussed by almost all health care organization governing bodies in the Netherlands. A key element of the Commission's work was to trace the lines of accountability in health care organizations. While executive boards were said to be more or less accountable to supervisory boards, it was not clear who would supervise the latter. The Commission suggested that the solution lay in 'openness, transparency and accountability'.

Issues of good governance are especially salient in systems where government is not the owner and operator of health care organizations. This is particularly true in SHI systems, leading to reliance on mechanisms of self-governance in a system based on the complexity of interaction among clients, providers and health insurers. Thus it is no surprise that the Dutch Commission on Governance arose. At the same time, it is telling that a similar commission did not arise to deal with governance of sick funds. That is because, in most SHI systems, mechanisms of governance at that level are already quite 'thick' even without government intervention. Managers, providers and clients sit together on boards which oversee the activities and behaviour of insurers. Moreover, sickness funds, as well as providers and, to some extent, clients, are associated at the intermediate (regional) level to represent their interests within the network of actors comprising the SHI system and in structured negotiations overseen by government.

An interesting issue is whether the recent emphasis on competitive reforms in SHI systems encourages or discourages these forms of governance. After all, if, for example, sickness funds are going to compete for members and selectively contract for providers, then the logic of 'voice', as exercised through joint decision-making bodies seems to be replaced by 'exit' in a competitive market. It seems, perhaps ironically, that the move towards competitive mechanisms has only strengthened collective forms of governance. Questions of accountability for the cost and quality of health care appear to only encourage the deployment of various mechanisms for citizen involvement, joint decision-making among health insurers and government over issues such as the extent of coverage, and resolution of complex matters such as risk adjustment and cross-subsidization of insurance programmes.

The danger to SHI systems, however, is the desire, especially of elected officials, to avoid political accountability for value-laden health policy decisions. This leads to the temptation to transform SHI arrangements, for example by introduction of market-like competition, into systems that 'run on their own', without government involvement. Under such conditions, the mechanisms of governance at the meso level may be 'stretched' beyond their suitable degree of accountability. So, for example, government may seek to absolve itself of responsibility for matters such as 'cream-skimming' by relying on the formal rules of the game and turning away from more political mechanisms such as structured negotiations and agreements brokered under government auspices. Sick funds may retreat, under the guise of market rhetoric, from open and transparent joint decision-making to ostensible reliance on the 'letter of the law' of competition and more subtle collaboration – for example, in price and premium determination.

What this implies is that to preserve what Deborah Stone has called the 'soul' of health insurance, SHI systems moving in a competitive direction, perhaps for good reasons, should pay self-conscious attention to preserving the social capital inherent in SHI arrangements. The move to competition (exit) must be accompanied by collaboration (voice) under the guiding hand of government (political capital) if SHI systems are to avoid conversion into private insurance arrangements lacking social solidarity. Self-governance, collaborative associations and structured negotiations at the meso level take place within the institutional environment moulded at the macro level. This is discussed in the next section.

The institutional environment and governance of SHI

As trust in governmental institutions has declined throughout western democracies, solutions to governance of areas of social policy such as health have naturally been sought in mechanisms that appear to be 'non-governmental' or 'depoliticized'. Thus the current emphasis on social capital in the US, and the slippery slope of the 'new public management' and the 'Third Way', even in countries with a strong base of social solidarity, such as in western Europe. The question is whether perceived depoliticization contributes to, or eats away at, social solidarity.

It is widely recognized that the move to competition, say, in the form of internal or public markets, requires new forms of government regulation. It is unlikely that such regulation can, especially in health systems, be based solely on technical control of prices and measurement of outcomes. In some areas regulation will need to look more like governance. For example, setting priorities for health care and determining the contents of benefits packages requires creation not only of sophisticated technical methods for evaluating the utility of health interventions, but also mechanisms for public deliberation on these difficult ethical issues. National governments that seek to avoid involvement in these discussions in deference to the subsidiarity principle, may, nonetheless, need to provide the umbrella under which they take place. SHI systems can, if they choose, rely on their tradition of structured negotiations to create the institutional environment for such deliberations. This would be a good example of social and political capital complementing each other. Interestingly, recent survey evidence from Israel demonstrates that public trust in government health institutions is significantly higher than trust in government in general. In addition, Israelis place high trust in their sick funds. If this is true in other countries as well, such trust constitutes a source of political and social capital that should be carefully considered as a resource for governing health systems.

In the European context, however, national governments are now faced not only with the possibility of seeking to avoid playing this role by devolving it, but also of deferring to the new authority of the EU. EU involvement, for example, in making coverage decisions through resolution of cross-border care issues (Mossialos and McKee 2002), takes health policy one more level further away from the local roots of social capital which lie at the base of SHI systems. This further highlights the question of whether national governments have the political capital to maintain social solidarity in health systems. SHI systems may have much to offer in a globalizing world in terms of techniques for structured negotiation among stakeholders on difficult, value-laden issues. The question is whether the fiscal emphasis of the EU, and its tendency to resort to court resolution of health coverage issues, will leave sufficient room for an adaptation at the European level of the mechanisms of government and self-regulation that have traditionally characterized SHI systems.

Conclusion

On a descriptive level, this chapter has explored how SHI systems in western Europe combine self-governance at the micro level with government regulation. One of the key elements of SHI systems is the reliance on a network of stakeholders, negotiating the determination of health policy under the auspices of government. SHI systems are characterized by a delicate balance of social solidarity derived from social capital at the local level with social trust based on political capital at the government level. Current dynamics, especially the move towards more streamlined competitive behaviour in SHI systems, may threaten the underlying social and political capital in the system. Therefore, self-conscious attention should be paid to the implications of the introduction of markets in health care, even if not privatization, on the one hand, and the rising role of the EU, as an imposer of new 'rules of the game', not necessarily grounded in social solidarity, on the other.

In all health systems, new issues of accountability and transparency are being posed as cost pressures have lead to pressures for new efficiencies in health care that sometimes take the form of cutbacks in access to care, or rationing. Different systems have evolved different types of mechanisms – for example, various forms of deliberative bodies – to cope with making these tough decisions. SHI systems have built into themselves a tradition of mutual aid and solidarity that derives from the local origins of many of the health insurance arrangements extant in these systems. One of the challenges for SHI systems has been to maintain self-governance and central guidance of the system simultaneously. The outcomes of SHI in terms of quality and cost, compared to other types of financing systems such as the Beveridge system, may be debated. However, it cannot be denied that SHI is linked with a type of social capital, and consequently different forms of political capital, that characterize non-SHI systems. The question is whether these attributes are worth the cost of the complex networking and negotiation in which government is called upon to engage and whether the social and political capital aspects of SHI are a resource that all health systems should seek to emulate.

Finally, the comparative institutional analysis of SHI systems has implications for the new institutional economics. The latter has been applied usefully by others in seeking to understand the organization of health care, especially at the level of micro organizations and, to a certain extent, in relation to regulatory policy (Chinitz 2002). Application to SHI, however, challenges institutional economics to deal systematically with what Williamson has called 'atmosphere'. It is not possible to understand the technicalities of SHI transactional modes, such as global budgeting of physician groups, without understanding the larger social context. The success of technical modes of management or regulation depends on the level of social and political capital extant in society. These types of 'atmospheric' considerations have generally been treated as a residual and, in any event, as a given rather than subject to policy intervention. Comparative institutional analysis of SHI suggests that microanalytic and atmospheric parameters exist in a symbiotic relationship. Further study of SHI systems promises conceptual and theoretical developments in the field of institutional economics.

References

Chinitz, D. (2002) Good and bad health sector regulation: an overview of public policy dilemmas, in R.B. Saltman, R. Busse and E. Mossialos (eds) *Regulating Entrepreneurial Behaviour in European Health Care Systems*. Buckingham: Open University Press.

Chinitz, D. and Israeli, A. (2001) Health care rationing and the uninsured: diagnosis and cure in international perspective, in E. Loewy and R. Loewy (eds) *Ethics, Rationing and Health Reform*. New York: Springer-Verlag.

Chinitz, D., Shalev, C., Galai, N. and Israeli, A. (1998) Israel's basic basket of services: the importance of being explicitly implicit, *British Medical Journal*, 317: 1005–7.

Cohen, S. (2001) A strategic framework for devolving responsibility and functions from government to the private sector, *Public Administration Review*, 61(4): 432–40.

Daniels, N. (2000) Accountability for reasonableness in private and public health insurance, in A. Coulter and C. Ham (eds) *The Global Challenge of Health Care Rationing*. Buckingham: Open University Press.

Evans, R.G. (1991) Life, death, money and power: the politics of healthcare finance, in T.J. Litman and L.S. Robins (eds) *Health Politics and Policy*. Albany: Delmar.

Evans, P. (1996) Government action, social capital and development: reviewing the evidence of synergy, *World Development*, 24(6): 1119–32.

Fox, J. (1996) How does civil society thicken? The political construction of social capital in rural Mexico, *World Development*, 24(6): 1089–103.

Fukuyama, F. (1995) *Trust*. New York: The Free Press.

Kerr, E. (2000) *Health Care Systems in Transition – Belgium*. Copenhagen: European Observatory on Health Care Systems.

Maarse, H. and Paulus, A. (2001) Can solidarity survive? Paper presented at the Conference of the European Health Management Association.

Maarse, H. (2002) Health Insurance Reform (again) in the Netherlands: will it Succeed, *Euro Observer*, 4(3): 1–3.

Mossialos, E.A. and McKee, M. (2002) *EU Law and the Social Character of Health Care*. Brussels: PIE – Peter Lang.

Nonneman, W. and Van Doorslaer, E. (1994) The role of the sickness funds in the Belgian healthcare market, *Social Science and Medicine*, 39: 1483–95.

Øvretveit, J. (2001) Private healthcare in the Nordic countries, *Health Management*, November: 22–4.

Plumptre, T. and Graham, J. (2000) *Governance in the New Millenium: Challenges for Canada*. Ottawa: Institute On Governance.

Potapchuk, W., Crocker, J., Schechter, W. and Boogaard, D. (1997) Building community: exploring the role of social capital and local government. Washington, DC: Program for Community Problem Solving.

Preker, A.S., Harding, A. and Travis, P. (2000) Make or buy decisions in the production of healthcare goods and services: new insights from institutional economics and organizational theory, *Bulletin of the World Health Organization*, 78(6): 779–90 (http://www.who.int/docstore/bulletin/pdf/2000/issue6/bu0606.pdf, accessed 19 April 2004).

Putnam, R. (2000) *Bowling Alone*. New York: Simon & Shuster.

Rodwin, V.G. (2003) The healthcare system under French national health insurance: lessons for health reform in the United States, *American Journal of Public Health*, 93(1): 31–7.

Sabin, J.E. (2000) Fairness as a problem of love and the heart: a clinician's perspective on priority setting, in A. Coulter and C. Ham (eds) *The Global Challenge of Health Care Rationing*. Buckingham: Open University Press.

Saltman, R.B. (1998) Convergence, social embeddedness and the future of health systems in the Nordic Region, in D. Chinitz and J. Cohen (eds) *Governments and Health Systems: Implications of Differing Involvements*. Chichester: Wiley.

Saltman, R.B. (2003) Melting public-private boundaries in European health systems, *European Journal of Public Health*, 13(1): 24–9.

Saltman, R.B. and Von Otter, C. (1992) *Planned Markets and Public Competition: Strategic Reform in Northern European Health Systems*. Buckingham: Open University Press.

Schwartz, F.W. and Busse, R. (1996) Fixed budgets in the ambulatory care sector: the German experience, in F.W. Schwartz, H. Glennerster and R.B. Saltman (eds) *Fixing Health Budgets: Experience from Europe and North America*, pp. 93–108. London: Wiley.

Shadmi, H. (2003) Bribes are not only in the pocket, *Haaretz Daily Newspaper*, 29 April.

Stone, D. (1993) The struggle for the soul of health insurance, *Journal of Health Politics, Policy and Law*, 18 (2 , summer): 289–315.

Tyler, T.R. and Degoey, P. (1996) Trust in organizational authorities: the influence of motive attributions on willingness to accept decisions, in T.R. Tyler (ed.) *Trust in Organizations: Frontiers of Theory and Research*. Thousand Oaks, CA: Sage.

Williamson, O.E. (1985) *The Economic Institutions of Capitalism*. New York: Free Press.

Williamson, O.E. (1993) *The Mechanisms of Governance*. Oxford: Oxford University Press.

Worz, M. and Busse, R. (2002) Structural reforms for Germany's healthcare system? *Euro Observer*, 1–3.

chapter *chapter* seven

Solidarity and competition in social health insurance countries

Anna Dixon, Martin Pfaff and Jean Hermesse

Introduction

Social health insurance (SHI) was founded on the principle of solidarity. Despite the political motivations of Bismarck, namely to suppress socialist opposition among the workers, the model adopted in Germany brought workers together for mutual benefit. Developing out of the voluntary sickness funds, the national SHI established solidarity between the healthy and the sick, the young and the old, the childless and those with children, the better-off and the worse-off members of the funds and between men and women. With the expansion of insurance to cover other groups, including the non-working population, dependants and pensioners, solidarity has also been extended. Solidarity remains the key feature of the present SHI systems of western Europe.

During the 1990s, health care systems were subject to major reforms. One of the main thrusts of these reforms was the introduction of competition into health care. Heavily influenced by 'market romantics' (Morone and Goggin 1995), European health care policy-makers experimented in a variety of ways with the market in public health systems. SHI systems were not immune to the influence of pro-market policies.

This chapter focuses on the introduction of competition on the financing side, between insurance funds in the SHI systems of western Europe. It begins by defining solidarity and competition followed by a brief history of competition in Belgium, Germany, Israel, the Netherlands and Switzerland. The next section analyses why competition was introduced and the extent to which competition actually operates in practice. The tension between competition and solidarity is mediated by a number of mechanisms that are then discussed. An assessment of the impact of competition follows. Finally the chapter concludes with a discussion of future policy directions in all eight countries covered by this book and the policy implications for other countries with competing funds or considering reform in this area.

Solidarity and competition – conflict or complement?

Solidarity is fundamental to the social welfare vision of universal benefits shared by all citizens. It is based on interpersonal transfers. The extent of solidarity between these groups depends on the structure of, and participation in, the social insurance system. This solidarity exists on the revenue side because contributions are neither tied to the actual cost of the services used nor the expected cost. On the expenditure side, entitlements are equal so that the benefits received are according to need and irrespective of ability to pay or other characteristics of those individuals. Therefore, groups that utilize more but pay less will benefit from the transfers. Furthermore, if dependants and non-working spouses (more usually women) are covered without additional contribution, transfers from those without children to those with children and from men to women are larger. However, if people with incomes above a certain threshold are excluded from the SHI or can opt out, the transfers from rich to poor are reduced. Finally, where pensioners pay a lower rate, this increases transfers from the young to the old. Solidarity, then is at the very heart of SHI. This differs from voluntary and private insurance where normally the costs of insurance are risk-rated and entitlements vary, thus limiting solidarity.

In contrast to solidarity, competition is based on self-interest and 'encourages individuals and institutions to do whatever they can to maximise their own gain' (Light 2000: 969). In this light, competition appears as the antithesis of solidarity, although aspects of it exist in several SHI systems. Economic theory suggests that competition will exist when there is perfect information, no positive or negative externalities of consumption and consumer tastes are predetermined (Rice 1998). A number of analysts believe that these features do not exist in the market for health care services (Stone 1993; Light 2000; Rice 2003). So what role does competition play in SHI systems?

Competition may operate at different levels within the health care system: between public insurance and private insurance; between purchasers; and between providers. Competition between purchasers (i.e. insurance funds offering SHI) is the focus of this chapter. Direct competition between social insurance and private insurance exists only in those countries where membership of the statutory system is voluntary for part of the population. For example, in Germany those earning over €41,400 per annum (2003; raised to €46,350 in 2004) have the right to opt out. However, due to the irreversible nature of this decision, competition cannot really be seen in practice.[1]

Competition policies in SHI systems

Before analysing the extent and impact of competition it is important to understand the policies which have been implemented in each of the five SHI countries where choice between sickness funds exists (Belgium, Germany, Israel, Netherlands, Switzerland). In Austria, France and Luxembourg there is no competition between the sickness funds as people cannot choose between funds, since sickness fund membership is dependent on occupation or/and region of residence.

Belgium

Choice of fund has existed in Belgium since the establishment of SHI in 1945. There are about 100 mutualities (this number is rapidly reducing due to mergers), which are mostly grouped into five alliances (the National Alliance of Christian mutualities, National Union of Neutral mutualities, National Union of Socialist mutualities, National Union of Liberal mutualities and the National Union of the Free and Professional mutualities), one railway association and one public fund (the Auxiliary Fund) among which citizens may choose. They have the right to change fund every three months. All funds operate nationally. The funds receive a per capita allocation for administrative costs (Kerr and Siebrand 2000). Until 1995, despite legal provision that funds should be financed prospectively from contributions and subsidies, in fact all costs were reimbursed and funds faced no budget constraint. All surpluses and deficits were pooled across funds and any overall deficit was covered by subsidies from state finances. Legislative reform passed in 1995 introduced risk-adjusted capitation in order to finance funds on a prospective basis. This has been implemented gradually: 10 per cent of fund income 1995–7, 20 per cent in 1998–2000, and 30 per cent since 2001. However, the funds are protected from full financial risk and are only responsible for a proportion of any deficit which is not due to external factors: 15 per cent in 1995–7, 20 per cent in 1998–2000, 25 per cent since 2001. Since 1995 insured persons have to pay in order to cover eventual deficits. As deficits can vary among funds, this individual contribution may vary from one fund to the other. Although the amount of this contribution remains very small, it may rise in the future to cover rising expenditures and growing deficits and increase differences between the funds.

Germany

Up until 1996, choice of funds only existed for white-collar workers but not for the majority of blue-collar workers who were assigned membership according to occupation and region. Thus there were large differentials in contribution rates between the sickness funds (i.e. high-risk occupational groups were subject to the highest rates). The Health Care Structure Act (GSG), passed in 1992 and which came into effect in 1993, marked a major structural change in SHI. It granted equal legal status to manual and salaried workers (i.e. extended the right to change funds) and introduced cross-subsidization between funds. Contribution rates are set by the funds and collected directly by them. A risk adjustment mechanism, called the Risk Structure Compensation Scheme, calculates the financial transfers to be made between funds to compensate them for both the difference in contribution income and in expected expenditures of enrollees. Enrollees initially had the right to change fund annually with three months notice. However, from the beginning of 2000, enrollees can change fund at any time but must stay with the fund for a minimum of 18 months after changing. In 2000 there were 420 funds operating in Germany, however many operate at a regional level (Busse 2001).

Israel

Competition between insurance funds was introduced in Israel in 1995 under the National Health Insurance Law. The majority of the population (96 per cent) were enrolled in one of four not-for-profit sickness funds prior to 1995. These operated with integrated providers and received revenues directly from members and indirectly from employers via government. The main fund, Kupat Holim Clalit (KHC), covered 70 per cent of the population and had a higher proportion of elderly, chronically ill and low income than the other smaller funds. As a result KHC suffered from chronic financial deficits and relied on regular government subsidies (Shmueli and Chinitz 2001). The source of revenues was changed to a health tax (accounting for about 40 per cent of fund income) and general taxation. An annual budget is set by the Ministry of Finance and this is used to calculate a capitation to the funds adjusted only for age. The only additional sources of revenue come from co-payments and the sale of supplementary insurance policies (Gross and Harrison 2001).

Netherlands

In the Netherlands the introduction of competition was part of an evolving debate on the role of competition which had been reflected in earlier reform proposals (Schut 1995). The concrete proposals were put forward in the report of a government commission in 1987, chaired by Wisse Dekker, former chief executive of Philips and passed by government in 1988. The changes to the health insurance sector formed part of a wider restructuring of sick leave and disability insurance. Not all of the committee's recommendations were adopted due to doubts about the ability of the new system to contain costs as well as strong opposition from interest groups such as the private insurers and employers. However, the following proposals were adopted:

- insurers were able to directly levy a flat-rate contribution set by them, in addition to the proportional income-based contribution which was collected by the Central Fund and is the same for everyone regardless of insurer;
- the abolition of the regional restrictions on sickness fund activity (which had

resulted in natural monopsonies) and new entrants including private insurers were allowed in to the market;

- insurers were allowed to contract selectively with providers and negotiate reimbursement prices lower than those set by the Central Tariff Authority;
- insurers were able to restrict the purchase of supplementary insurance products to those subscribers who already had their main insurance from them (Schut 1995; Schut and Van Doorslaer 1999).

These reforms, which became known as the Dekker-Simons reforms after a change in government, created a model of 'competition among purchasers' – i.e. between health insurance funds. Risk adjustment in the Netherlands is performed by the Central Fund which collects contributions from employers and employees. It then makes capitation payments to the funds adjusted for age, sex, social security/employment status, region of residence and pharmaceutical cost groups (since 2002). Citizens have the right to change fund once a year. In 1999 there were 30 funds in the market operating at a national level (Okma and Poelert 2001).

Switzerland

Since the Health Insurance Law came into force in 1996, all permanent residents in Switzerland are legally obliged to purchase health insurance policies. The reform contained a number of measures:

- premiums are community rated (i.e. the same for each person taking out insurance with a particular company within a canton or sub-region of a canton); previously risk rating of premiums was permitted;
- subsidies from the cantons are means-tested and allocated directly to the enrollees;
- all willing provider contracting of physicians was abolished;
- a risk adjustment mechanism based on the age and sex of enrollees.

Before the introduction of the law, the purchase of health insurance in Switzerland was voluntary. Thus the introduction of 'managed competition' has increased government control. There are 93 funds operating in Switzerland (2002 data) though many operate within cantons. Citizens may change fund annually.

This brief description of insurance competition in each country provides the background for the following examination of the reasons why competition was introduced.

The logic for competition in SHI systems

The theory of 'managed competition', most famously described by Alain Enthoven (see for example Enthoven 1998), suggests that properly regulated competition will lead to more efficient use of resources, restrain health care expenditure and improve quality. These ideas were particularly resonant at a time when governments across Europe were keen to reduce public expenditures and 'roll back' the welfare state: 'Governments deployed market mechanisms in an attempt to push ossified health service bureaucracies into becoming more efficient and responsive' (Morone 2000: 960).

In the European context, managed competition is most commonly used to describe the use of competitive or market-like mechanisms within the public sector. These were advocated for the United Kingdom and found expression in the introduction of the internal market in the National Health Service which aimed to promote competition between suppliers. Separation of purchaser and provider has traditionally existed within SHI systems, though due to all-willing provider contracts not on the provider side. The expression of managed competition in SHI systems was to enhance competition between purchasers (i.e. insurance funds). This was to be achieved primarily by offering choice of funds. Both the stated policy objectives of competition and the political motivations, however, differed between countries.

Choice of funds was not an explicit policy decision in Belgium. However, the introduction of reforms to increase the financial responsibility of the funds was intended to shift the financial risk onto insurance funds, in order to increase efficiency, reduce deficits and government subsidies.

In Germany, the main policy objective was that competition combined with risk adjustment would lead to convergence of contribution rates, thus reducing the variation in rates between funds. This reflected concern about equity. Occupational funds with lower than average incomes and higher than average risks were charging higher contribution rates than the company funds with higher than average incomes and lower than average risks. In addition, there was growing concern at the escalating contribution rates and the consequences for labour costs. By increasing incentives for efficiency, it was hoped that competition would result in reduced contribution rates across the board.

In Israel, competition was seen as the solution to the problems of deficits in the insurance funds, particularly KHC, as well as a lever to enhance the performance of funds – for example, by offering additional benefits. However, the main political thrust (led by the Ministry of Finance) was to constrain government expenditures through enhanced central control (Gross and Harrison 2001).

In the Netherlands, the impetus was to drive up efficiency by breaking the natural monopolies formed by the exclusivity of regional funds and making health insurance funds more active purchasers. It was hoped this would precipitate a process of rationalization within the SHI system. The insurer was expected to develop into an active 'purchaser of care' on behalf of the insured person, i.e. it would organize a network of physicians, paramedics, health care establishments etc. to take care of an 'insured' patient, for which it would receive a per capita fee from the public payer (Bocognano *et al.* 1998: 194).

In Switzerland the stated objective of managed competition was to 'marry efficiency with equity'. However, the political context was that the reforms shifted the costs of health care onto consumers by relieving federal and cantonal governments of the burden of health care expenditure (Zweifel 2000).

The underlying objectives of the reforms to some extent reflected the theoretical expectations of managed competition. However, in practice there were other national political objectives which mediated the policies and adapted the ideal type of managed competition to the existing structures, organizations and interest groups in each country. Thus any evaluation of the impact of competition must also recognize the accompanying institutional and historical constraints (Gross and Harrison 2001).

The extent of competition in SHI

There are a number of dimensions that can be used to measure the extent of competition. First, an assessment of market structure: the number of funds, their concentration and the numbers of mergers, acquisitions and new market entrants. Second, the activity of funds: marketing costs, innovative products, cartel formation and price setting. Third, the behaviour of consumers: frequency and numbers moving funds and the information used to choose funds.

Market structure

In the Netherlands, one effect of the changes has been the emergence of private insurers who are active in the statutory insurance market. The established sickness funds, however, continue to dominate regional markets for statutory insurance. The choice of fund has prompted an accelerated process of mergers and acquisitions – between 1985 and 1993 the number of insurers fell from 53 to 26. By 1999, there were 30 funds operating nationwide, with an average membership of about 300,000 persons (with a large variation in membership, ranging from less than 1000 to over 1 million). This suggested that when faced with competition, multiple insurers merged to benefit from economies of scale (Normand and Busse 2002). In Israel there have been no new market entrants. The market share of the funds has, however, shifted. The market share of the largest fund (KHC) was 70 per cent prior to the reforms and has fallen to 59 per cent (Gross and Harrison 2001).

Response of funds

The expected results of competition were that sickness funds would increase efficiency (by strengthening their purchasing power or improving their administrative efficiency) and reduce their price (either contribution rates or other charges). In practice the behaviour of sickness funds had some negative effects on both equity and efficiency. Covert risk selection, collaboration and price fixing have been observed. In their evaluation of managed competition in Israel, Gross and Harrison observed: 'Rather than striving to improve clinical quality or publicize information on their services and quality of care, the SFs [sickness funds] concentrated on making service improvements that would readily impress patients and used aggressive and even illegal marketing methods to attract members' (2001: 1220).

In Belgium, competition between mutualities for members was intense prior to 1995 when per capita allocations were made for administrative costs.

Response of consumers

The necessary prerequisite for competition between funds is the unimpeded choice of funds by consumers. The extent to which this choice is exercised varies between countries and between groups. As well as presenting data on the scale of the movement between funds this section discusses some of the factors which influence consumer choice. For example, in some countries price competition is enabled either through the setting of different contribution rates or a per capita premium. In other cases there is no price competition, but rather quality competition in terms of the services offered to members.

Data on the movement of individuals between funds in Germany reflects the net gains and losses of the different funds rather than the actual number of people who have moved. However, it gives an indication of the magnitude of the movement in terms of the impact on fund membership. Recent data released by the Ministry of Health indicates that this trend continues (Greß *et al.* 2002). Population surveys carried out in Germany in spring 1999 showed that 7.3 per cent of the population had changed funds since 1996. Those who switched are more likely to have no dependants, to be from the former East Germany, under 40 and without chronic conditions.

In the Netherlands, the number of people who exercise their right to move funds is very small but has been increasing since the introduction of competition (Müller *et al.* 2000).

In Israel, total switching amounted to (as a percentage of total population): 1995 (second half), 4.2, 1996, 3.9, 1997, 4.2 and 1998, 1.7 (Shmueli *et al.* 2003).

Price competition

In Israel there is no competition on price. In Belgium and the Netherlands contribution rates are uniform for the whole population, but in the Netherlands the only price mechanism is an additional flat-rate premium (nominal premium) set and levied directly by the insurance fund. However, the value of these is small when compared with the amount of money collected centrally through the income-related contributions. It is likely that other factors – for example, a conveniently located insurance office or choice of fund of other family members – will have more impact. For example, in the Netherlands (2001) about 85 per cent of people chose the fund in their local area (Vektis 2002). Approximately 90 per cent of the expenditure of the health insurance funds is covered by this financing mechanism. The remainder and any deficit must be made up by the insured persons by means of a nominal premium which, in 1999, ranged between about €134 and €162 per year. In 2003 this amount was almost double: € 239.4 – € 390 per year (Ministerie van Volksgezondheid, Welzijn en Sport 2003).

In Germany, where each fund sets its own contribution rate, price competition has been more evident. Price was mentioned most frequently by respondents as the reason for switching fund. Other reasons frequently mentioned were changing job, recommendation of a friend or acquaintance, not happy with the service and better coverage through new fund (Zok 1999). Other evidence shows that the funds with the lowest contribution rates (namely the company funds) had the largest net gain of members in 2001–2 (Greß *et al.* 2002). Data shows a shift away from the AOKs (general funds) (a net loss of 1.2 million members 1997–9) to BKKs (occupational funds) (a net gain of 1.8 million members over the same period) which correlates with contribution rates (Busse 2000). Contribution rate levels are being regulated to prevent further reductions: from 2002 they must charge a contribution rate of at least 12.5 per cent (Busse 2001).

In Switzerland, the insurance companies compete within each canton based on the level of the premium. There is no premium fixing by the state; instead, price competition appears to work, with many people changing companies on an annual basis depending on the premiums offered (Minder *et al.* 2000).

Quality competition

Basic benefit package

Funds in Switzerland are not allowed to compete on the basis of benefits offered, as a package of health care benefits is defined which all companies must provide. Opportunities for competition based on the quality of care are very limited. Managed care and quality competition are allowed under compulsory health insurance but are still not very common in Switzerland (less than 10 per cent of policies in 2000) (Minder *et al.* 2000; Zweifel 2000). Swiss sickness funds attract people by offering rebates for higher deductibles (Beck *et al.* 2003). In Germany the law fixes more than 95 per cent of the benefits package. Only for some services (e.g. alternative medicine) it is up to the sickness funds to decide whether or not and to what extent to include these services in the benefits package (Schut *et al.* 2003). In Belgium, the law imposes that the compulsory insurance cover is identical for all sickness funds, so as to avoid it being used as an instrument for competition (Schokkaert and Van de Voorde 2003). In Israel, sickness funds compete on quality of services, but the basic package of benefits offered is fixed by law. Since 1998 Israeli sickness funds can compete on the basis of the level of co-payments (Shmueli *et al.* 2003).

Supplementary insurance

Funds in all countries except Germany compete on the basis of supplementary insurance products which they can offer at special rates to those people who also subscribe for insurance for the basic benefits package. In the Netherlands, sickness funds are not allowed to sell any supplementary insurance (as in Germany) and most sickness funds have a very close relation with a private insurer because they are both part of one holding company (Van de Ven *et al.* 2003). The most frequently reported reason for changing fund in the Netherlands was the benefit package of the supplementary insurance (Kerssens and

Groenewegen 2003). In Israel, about 50 per cent of the population has bought supplementary insurance from their sickness fund. In the Netherlands and in Belgium, 90 per cent of the sickness fund enrollees, and in Switzerland 70 per cent of the population has bought supplementary insurance (Van de Ven *et al.* 2003).

Retaining solidarity

Multiple competing insurers may engender greater efficiency but may also bring potential difficulties in ensuring equal access to care for all. Therefore, a number of regulatory mechanisms are used in order to protect solidarity:

- Open enrollment – insurers are required to accept all applicants. The obligation of individual funds to accept all applicants was considered to be a necessary condition if competition was to work in the direction of efficiency.
- Risk adjustment mechanisms – to stop some insurers from bearing a disproportionate part of the risk or adopting covert forms of cream-skimming, allocations are adjusted according to the risk profile of the members. These are described extensively elsewhere (Rice and Smith 2001). According to economic theory, risk adjustment mechanisms can encourage competitive behaviour and offer choice to the population without allowing opportunistic behaviour such as risk selection (Saltman 2001). Risk adjustment is essential to protect solidarity from the ravages of competition. Otherwise competition will become an instrument to promote cream-skimming by attempting to attract the better risks (namely, higher-income individuals, singles, young men and the childless). The basic aim of such risk adjustment measures is to neutralize the effect of those factors that the individual fund cannot influence by its own actions at least in the short run.
- Mandatory contracting with all willing providers – used to ensure equality of benefits and equity of access to providers. These oligopolistic or even monopolistic supply structures (often set in law) have been maintained with corresponding cost effects to be borne by the insured. Rather than pass on the increased pressure to act competitively to their providers – thereby enhancing the efficiency of the health care system as a whole – funds concentrate on inter-fund competition and on increasing marketing and risk-selection efforts (Pfaff and Wassener 2000).
- Uniform contribution rates – used to ensure equity of financing.
- Uniform benefits package – used to ensure equality of benefit. Some countries allow competition through variation in additional benefits or supplementary insurance policies.
- Compulsory for most/all citizens – if solidarity is to operate between groups, all low and moderate income citizens must be mandatorily insured. In the Netherlands, where all those with an income of above €31,750 (2003) are excluded from the social insurance scheme, there is no cross-subsidization from rich to poor. Proposals are now being discussed to make SHI compulsory for everybody (Maarse 2002). In Germany, where all those with an income above €41,400 (2003; raised to €46,350 in 2004) are allowed to choose whether

to opt out, and where all civil servants and the self-employed are excluded, the extent of solidarity within the SHI system is limited. In Belgium, the self-employed are excluded from insurance for major risks.

Competition in SHI operates in an environment that is heavily regulated or managed. These mechanisms are intended to preserve solidarity but may hinder competition.

The impact of competition in SHI

Some feared that competition would 'corrode the old logic of social solidarity' (Morone and Goggin 1995: 559). However, early assessments concluded that where solidarity was a long-entrenched institutionalized principle, it held its own against the impulses of the market (Peterson 2000). The extent to which competition might conflict with wider societal objectives depends largely on how and at what level it is implemented: 'In most healthcare sectors, market allocation is not compatible with the health and social policy aims of social health insurance (SHI) systems. Competition on the other hand may be employed in certain subsystems without endangering the health and social policy aims which gave rise to regulatory measures in the first place' (Pfaff 1990: 116).

To date, empirical evaluations of the impact of competition on the outcomes of health care systems are limited. From this brief review of the secondary literature it is however possible to identify some early indications of the impact on efficiency and equity.

The fact that citizens have a right to choose is not necessarily a sufficient driver for competition to ensue. However, it has been used as one of the main tools for driving competition within the so-called internal markets, not only within health but within other public sectors such as education (Le Grand *et al.* 1998). Some argue that choice has intrinsic value. However, this is disputed (Rice 2001).

Efficiency and effectiveness

There are a number of factors which have prevented efficiency gains from being realized.

First, in most systems the allocation formula is based on average costs, thus insurance funds still have an incentive to select members whose risk is lower than the average person in their age and sex category. In fact, risk adjustment has accelerated the process of 'de-solidarization'. For example, a 'virtual' company-based health insurance fund that is able to attract either younger persons who are healthier than the average or even older persons who are healthier than the average, will get allocated an average or standardized amount which is greater than the actual expenses incurred. The difference between the average amount allocated and actual expenditure acts like a subsidy, making possible a further reduction in the contribution rate, thereby leading to concentration of low risks in certain funds and larger transfers having to be made between funds each year. In Germany, this has had an adverse effect on overall health care revenues. On average over the past three years, DM 1.7 billion (€0.87 billion) per annum less has been collected by the funds. This has severe consequences for the established insurance funds with wider networks and services and with an older and/or sicker membership.

Second, the transition to full introduction of genuine care-purchaser behaviour by the health insurance funds is still not complete. This is mainly because the supply of care is patchy and strictly organized and the public authorities maintain their overall control of the system (especially pricing). The funds should be made to act more decisively in the interests of the enrollees, above all by actively influencing the quality and efficiency of health care services. However, success in this respect is difficult to measure.

Third, transaction costs in the system are high due to higher costs of marketing and selection by funds, and the costs of information for the public authorities to ensure that a sophisticated risk adjustment can't be implemented.

Equity

The outcomes of competition in terms of improving equity are mixed. The risk adjustment system has led to a narrowing of contribution rates for the majority of the insured in Germany. In 1994, 27 per cent of all members paid a contribution rate differing by more than 1 per cent from the average. This had reduced to only 7 per cent of all members in 1999, following enactment of the legislation (Busse 2001). In addition, the same rights to choose have been extended to all members of the SHI system, whatever their socio-professional status or place of residence.

However, not all groups have benefited from the right to choose equally. Mostly, consumer information about different funds relies on the funds own marketing. This might leave out some groups such as the elderly – for example, if it is only via the internet – thus making them less likely to exercise their right to move fund. Behavioural changes on the part of older and sick persons are required if they are to utilize elements of choice more actively and to search for health insurance funds which have currently lower contribution rates. In practice, these conditions were not satisfied within the German context: the older, the less healthy a person is, the more risk-averse he or she is likely to be and the less likely this person is to look out for other health insurance funds with lower contribution rates. In this way, loyalty to a particular health insurance fund works to the detriment of a competition-based social policy: mainly the young and the healthy move to other funds. This opens the opportunity to found funds solely for the purpose of generating lower contribution rates. Furthermore, the treatment of those with chronic illnesses has been inadequate, with little or no incentives for funds to provide specifically tailored services such as disease management programmes.[2]

Risk selection by insurers has not been eliminated despite the fact that it is illegal in most cases. The managers of SHI funds have to respect social policy aims and therefore avoid outright strategies of cream-skimming. Some so-called corporate health insurance funds were founded solely with the aim of offering low contribution rates, particularly to the young and the healthy. This was attained for example by not having any service network in the area, by announcing the founding of such funds via internet. By exercising their right to move, the young and the healthier of course improve their own financial position. But at the same time this leads to a drain of financial resources from the total system and correspondingly to an increase of contribution rates of the older and sicker members who remain in the traditional health insurance funds.

Conclusions

Table 7.1 presents a summary overview of current competitive mechanisms in the five countries that have introduced such measures. In those countries, it is unlikely that there will be any reversal of this policy. It would be very difficult to remove a citizen's right to choose. Further refinements of the risk adjustment mechanisms can be expected in most countries, including the use of morbidity indicators. It should be noted that the information requirements to implement such a scheme will be costly. Attempts to increase competition on the provider side will be furthered, including selective contracting with individually negotiable tariffs. Given the strength of the corporatist provider bodies in most of these countries, breaking up provider cartels will be extremely difficult and a politically contentious policy. However, without competition on the provider side, many of the potential efficiency gains from competition on the insurance side will not be realized.

In Austria and France, which currently do not have competition, there is likely to be debate on the introduction of competition. France does have some transfers between funds, due to the differences in the risks of the populations covered, but this is not explicit. As greater fiscal pressure is put on the funds by government and they are made more responsible for deficits, government might come under pressure to make the transfers more transparent. Currently the market structure in France matches that found in Israel prior to the introduction of competition, i.e. most people are covered by one fund. Unless there is more significant action to break up the large fund, the market conditions for competition are unlikely to develop. Luxembourg has a single collection fund and multiple funds. As in Austria and France, sickness fund basic package insurance in Luxembourg is attached to occupation and there is no competition.

Zweifel makes an optimistic assessment of the implementation of competition in Switzerland where he believes that 'the idea of choice is now firmly rooted in the thinking of all parties concerned' (2000: 940). He observes that consumers compare managed care products with traditional policies; funds compete for enrollees; and doctors and hospitals have become more aware of quality and cost (Zweifel 2000). Whether competition has embedded itself as deeply in other systems where choice did not traditionally exist prior to the 1990s can only be seen with time. The applicability of competition in other contexts is not only dependent on the capacity of government to regulate the behaviour of the funds and to ensure their financial solvency, but also on the values embedded within the health care system and the society. Where providers are resistant to competition and wish to maintain their strong

Table 7.1 Competitive practices of SHI funds in each country

	Belgium	Germany	Israel	Netherlands	Switzerland
Setting contribution rates (compulsory insurance)	No, uniform rate set by law	Yes, increases limited to projected increases in expenditure	No, health tax plus budget allocation from general revenues	No, for income related premiums, but can set nominal flat-rate premium	Yes, community rated per capita premium
Open enrolment (compulsory insurance)	Yes	Yes, all 'open' funds includes all general regional funds (AOKs) and all substitute funds, most company (BKKs) and guild funds (IKKs). Not farmers', miners' or sailors' funds which retain assigned membership	Yes	Yes	Yes
Selective contracting of providers	No	No, except pilot projects	Yes	Yes	Yes
Differentiating benefits	Yes, offer supplementary service e.g. home care, hospital insurance, preventive medicine, health care abroad	Yes, offering some additional benefits (such as homeopathic medicine or benefits when travelling abroad)	Different co-payments and supplementary insurance	Different nominal premiums and supplementary insurance	Different co-payments and supplementary insurance
Integrated care arrangements	No	Pilots (projects involving doctors, social services, long-semicare, etc.)	Yes	No	Yes

negotiating position in relation to purchasers and continue to influence the levels of reimbursement it will be very difficult for insurance funds to strengthen their position.

In order for risk adjustment to be effective it is important that the system is administratively feasible and robust. Also, its success will depend largely on the availability of data at an individual level.[3] Risk adjustment must be based on objective criteria that are not open to manipulation by providers, insurance funds or government. However, the objective measurement of health is notoriously difficult. Further adjusters may increase the accuracy of the model but they may also increase the cost and administrative complexity.

In summary, competition and solidarity are not incompatible but a good deal of regulation is required if competitive processes are to be introduced into SHI systems without undermining the founding principle of solidarity.

Notes

1 Less than a quarter of those eligible to do so actually opt out, mainly because private health insurance (PHI) is less comprehensive, does not cover dependants, is more expensive and is risk-rated so premiums rise with age (Mossialos and Thomson 2002).
2 This issue is being addressed in the latest reform of the German risk compensation scheme.
3 Aggregate data applicable in the context of regional resource allocation is not appropriate where the membership of a fund is dispersed nationally.

References

Beck, K., Spycher, S., Holly, A. and Gardiol, L. (2003) Risk adjustment in Switzerland, *Health Policy*, 65: 63–74.
Bocognano, A., Couffinhal, A., Grignon, M. Mahieu and R. Polton D. (1998) *Mise en concurrence des assurances dans le domaine de la santé; théorie et bilan des expériences étrangères [Introducing competition into insurance in the health field: theory and an appraisal of experiences abroad]*. Paris: CREDES.
Busse, R. (2000) *Health Care Systems in Transition: Germany*. http://www.observatory.dk/hit/images/hits_pdf/germany.pdf (accessed 25 February 2001).
Busse, R. (2001) Risk structure compensation in Germany's statutory health insurance, *European Journal of Public Health*, 11(2): 174–7.
Enthoven, A.C. (1998) Managed competition: an agenda for action, *Health Affairs* (Millwood), 7(3): 25–47.
Greß, S., Groenewegen, P., Kerssens, J., Braun, B. and Wasem, J. (2002) Free choice of sickness funds in regulated competition: evidence from Germany and The Netherlands, *Health Policy*, 60: 235–54.
Gross, R. and Harrison, M. (2001) Implementing managed competition in Israel, *Social Science and Medicine*, 52(8): 1219–31.
Kerr, E. and Siebrand, V. (2000) *Health Care Systems in Transition – Belgium*. Copenhagen: European Observatory on Health Care Systems.
Kerssens, J. and Groenewegen, P. (2003) Consumer choice of social health insurance (SHI) in managed competition, *Health Expectations*, 6(4): 312.
Le Grand, J., Mays, N. and Mulligan, J. (1998) *Learning from the NHS Internal Market*. London: King's Fund.

Light, D.W. (2000) Sociological perspectives on competition in healthcare, *Journal of Health Politics, Policy and Law*, 25(5): 969–74.

Maarse, H. (2002) Health insurance reform (again) in The Netherlands: will it succeed? *Euro Observer*, 4(3): 1.

Minder, A., Schoenholzer, H. and Amiet, M. (2000) *Health Care Systems in Transition – Switzerland*. Copenhagen: European Observatory on Health Care Systems.

Ministerie van Volksgezondheid, Welzijn en Sport (2003) *Ziektekostenverzekeringen in Nederland: Stand van zaken per 1 Januari 2003* [*Sickness fund insurances in the Netherlands: current state per 1 January 2003*]. Den Haag: Ministerie van Volksgezondheid, Welzijn en Sport.

Morone, J.A. (2000) Citizens or shoppers? Solidarity under siege, *Journal of Health Politics, Policy and Law*, 25(5): 959–68.

Morone, J.A. and Goggin, J.M. (1995) Health policies in Europe: welfare states in a market era, *Journal of Health Politics, Policy and Law*, 20(3): 557–69.

Mossialos, E. and Thomson, S. (2002) Voluntary health insurance in the EU: a critical assessment, *International Journal of Health Services*, 32(1): 19–88.

Müller, R., Braun, B., Greß, S. and Lukas-Nülle, M. (2000) *Allokative und distributive Effekte von Wettbewerbselementen und Probleme ihrer Implementation in einem sozialen Gesundheitswesen am Beispiel der Erfahrungen in den Niederlanden* [*Allocative and distributional effect of competition and problems with its implementation in a social healthcare system, the example of the Netherlands*]. Bremen: University of Bremen.

Normand, C. and Busse, R. (2002) Social health insurance (SHI) financing, in E. Mossialos, A. Dixon, J. Figueras and J. Kutzin (eds) *Funding Health Care: Options for Europe*, pp. 59–79. Buckingham: Open University Press.

Okma, K.G.H. and Poelert, J.D. (2001) Implementing prospective budgeting for Dutch sickness funds, *European Journal of Public Health*, 11(2): 178–81.

Peterson, M.A. (2000) Editor's note: is there a future in your market? *Journal of Health Politics, Policy and Law*, 25(5): 807–14.

Pfaff, M. (1990) Market elements and competition in the healthcare system of the Federal Republic of Germany, background and developments, in A.F. Casparie, H.E.G.M. Hermans and J.H.P. Paelinck (eds) *Competitive Health Care in Europe, Future Prospects*. Dartmouth: Aldershot.

Pfaff, M. and Wassener, D. (2000) Germany, *Journal of Health Politics, Policy and Law*, 25(5): 907–14.

Rice, N. and Smith, P.C. (2001) Strategic resource allocation and funding decisions, in E. Mossialos, A. Dixon, J. Figueras and J. Kutzin (eds) *Funding Health Care: Options for Europe*. Buckingham: Open University Press.

Rice, T.H. (1998) *The Economics of Health Reconsidered*. Chicago: Health Administration Press.

Rice, T.H. (2001) *Should consumer choice be encouraged in healthcare?* in J.B. Davis (ed.) *The Social Economics of Health Care*. New York: Routledge.

Rice, T.H. (2003) *The Economics of Health Reconsidered*. Chicago: Health Administration Press.

Saltman, R.B. (2001) EJPH Policy Forum: risk adjustment strategies in three social health insurance (SHI) countries, *European Journal of Public Health*, 11(2): 121.

Schokkaert, E. and Van de Voorde, C. (2003) Belgium: risk adjustment and financial responsibility in a centralized system, *Health Policy*, 65: 5–19.

Schut, F.T. (1995) Healthcare reform in the Netherlands: balancing corporatism, etatism, and market mechanisms, *Journal of Health Politics, Policy and Law*, 20(3): 615–52.

Schut, F.T. and van Doorslaer, E.K. (1999) Towards a reinforced agency role of health insurers in Belgium and the Netherlands, *Health Policy*, 48(1): 47–67.

Schut, F.T., Greß, S. and Wasen, J. (2003) Consumer price sensitivity and social health insurer choice in Germany and the Netherlands, *International Journal of Health Care Finance and Economics*, 3(2): 117–38.

Shmueli, A. and Chinitz, D. (2001) Risk-adjusted capitation: the Israeli experience, *European Journal of Public Health*, 11(2): 182–4.

Shmueli, A., Chernichovsky, D. and Zmora, I. (2003) Risk adjustment and risk sharing: the Israeli experience, *Health Policy*, 65: 37–48.

Stone, D.A. (1993) The struggle for the soul of health insurance, *Journal of Health Politics, Policy and Law*, 18(2): 287–318.

Van de Ven, W.P.M.M., Beck, K., Buchner, F. *et al.* (2003) Risk adjustment and risk selection on the sickness fund insurance market in five European countries, *Health Policy*, 65: 75–98.

Vektis (2002) *Werkgebieden en verre verzekerden*. Internal document faxed by Marije Schwitters, 16 January. Zeist: Vektis.

Zok, K. (1999) *Anforderungen an die Gesetzliche Krankenversicherung: Einschatzungen und Erwartungen aus Sicht der Versicherten [Demands on statutory health insurance: assessments and expectations of insurees]*. Bonn: Wissenschaftliches Institut der AOK.

Zweifel, P. (2000) Switzerland, *Journal of Health Politics, Policy and Law*, 25(5): 937–44.

Key organizational issues

chapter eight

Shifting criteria for benefit decisions in social health insurance systems

Bernhard Gibis, Pedro W. Koch-Wulkan and Jan Bultman

Introduction

Historically, social health insurance (SHI) systems were established on the principles of solidarity and equity, rather than on the basis of free market insurance. The implementation of social health care systems, dating back to the 1880s, was seen as a national undertaking. It is still an emotional item in many of the SHI countries. Discussions surrounding the unwanted effects of a 'two tier' medicine which could possibly divide society still reflect, to some extent, this emotional character and point at the principal understanding of SHI systems: entitlement to appropriate health care for all, regardless of financial or social status.

The legal framework surrounding these health insurance systems reflects this intention. In Germany, all insured citizens are entitled to receive all 'reasonable and effective' health services necessary for the treatment of diseases. Services and technologies should be 'medically necessary, effective and cost-effective' – terms which are not described in detail by legislation. However, the understanding of these concepts has changed over the years and they are being redefined by each generation throughout the eight SHI countries. Table 8.1 shows the broad characteristics of the framework within which decision-makers have to decide upon particular technologies. Not all countries consider economic aspects to be of core importance for the definition of health benefits, while the criteria of 'medical necessity' and 'effectiveness' are frequently named.

The ways and measures to define 'effective' are changing constantly and evidence-based medicine is only the latest approach. The definition of medical necessity is also under reconsideration. Health conditions that were considered

Table 8.1 Legal framework for accepting services and technologies to the benefit package

Country	Terms	Legal base
Austria	Medically necessary, sufficient, appropriate	General Social Insurance Act (ASVG), §133(2)
Belgium	Medical necessity, activity, cost-effectiveness, safety	Published by Royal Decree
France	Inscription of new medical and surgical procedures after advice of ANAES on efficacy and safety	Decree to be published very soon
Germany	Medically necessary, effective, cost-effective	Social Code Book (SGB) V, §135(1)
Israel	Effective, appropriate, cost-efficient	National Health Insurance Law (1995)
Luxembourg	1 Sufficient, appropriate	1 Code des assurances sociales, art. 17,1
	2 Medically necessary, effective, efficient	2 Code des assurances sociales, art. 23,1
The Netherlands	Medically necessary	Sickness Fund Act (ZFW), preamble
Switzerland	Effective, appropriate, cost-efficient	Swiss Insurance Law (KVG), §32

'physiological' are now treatable – for example, menopause in women. The definition of illness is also changing over time and is influenced by differences in culture.[1] 'Quality of life' has increasingly become important and each society must decide whether a certain health status is defined as a disease or not – for example, infertility or depression due to seasonal mood swings. The understanding of the term 'cost-effectiveness' of a treatment has always been a consideration of legislators and decision-makers, but due to increased financial pressures this term has gained importance – to the point where it virtually dominates health care debates. In addition, an arsenal of study types and measures to quantify economic benefits has been developed for use in decision-making. This also shaped the redefinition of the term 'cost-effectiveness' considerably. Furthermore, there are driving pressures that have forced legislators and decision-makers to reconsider the broad frame of SHI-health care systems. Among others these are:

- rising demand by patients ('technology pull')
- supplier-induced demand ('technology push')
- the 'medicalization' of society
- rising healthcare costs and
- the changing perception of health.

The entitlement to specific health care services and the regulation of these is controlled in SHI systems in various ways. Depending on the sector of the health care system, both implicit (such as negative lists) or explicit regulations (such as positive lists) are in place – and often, both are used in combination. In the following section, emphasis will be given to benefit catalogues which are one of the characteristics of SHI systems, particularly in ambulatory health care. Benefit catalogues serve different roles and functions which will be explored later on.

Delegation of decision-making to self-governing bodies

In the Bismarck-type health care systems, the task of establishing and maintaining benefit catalogues has generally been delegated to self-governing bodies (exceptions apply for instance for France,[2] Israel, the Netherlands and Switzerland). Self-governing bodies are under public law and are not-for-profit organizations (see also Chapter 3). Typically, they represent health care providers (such as physicians) and sickness funds (insurers), rather than patient organizations or citizens. Since the decisions of these self-governing bodies can easily affect the majority of citizens in the eight countries, discussions arose around the legitimacy of these self-governing bodies and their decision-making procedures. Is it, for example, justifiable that a few persons decide on whether pre-implantation diagnostics (PID), a highly controversial issue, should be offered to insured citizens? When politicians, as democratically elected representatives, are not integrated in the decision-making process, ways and measures are needed to ensure proper citizen and patient participation. This seems to be of paramount importance for future public acceptance of SHI systems and their self-governing bodies.

In some SHI countries, political involvement has grown steadily in recent years. In Switzerland, all decisions regarding the benefit catalogue are passed through the Swiss Federal Department of Home Affairs. Self-governing bodies still have an advisory role to inform the Ministry of Internal Affairs, but they do not independently make decisions regarding the introduction of health care interventions. In Germany, the Minister of Health has the right to reject decisions of the Federal Committee of Physicians and Sickness Funds – however, this very seldom takes place. The history of SHI systems is marked by times with more and with less political interference (see also 'trends', p. 200). An example of a dramatic change regarding self-governance is the Netherlands. All decision-making powers were stripped from established self-governing bodies in 1996 (primarily because of a scandal in the social benefit funds which were regulated in a similar way as the sickness funds). In France, all decisions are largely supported, influenced and controlled by the Ministry of Health.[3] The government traditionally played a dominant role, however until now physicians and sickness funds have negotiated the fees for medical services.

Depending on the perspective of the observer, the relation between government and self-governing bodies can be described either as government involvement or interference. The necessity for governments to interact and, if required, to be involved on a regular basis in the decision-making process can depend on various aspects.

- Public dissatisfaction with self-governing bodies demands political interference (e.g. when scandals have occurred).
- Rising health care costs demand reduction of health care spending – a task which self-governing bodies cannot fulfil without political backup (e.g. exclusion of dental care from the benefit package).

- Competence and public confidence in the ability of self-governing bodies to fulfil their task. Related to this is the apparently diminishing role of sickness funds as representatives of patients, and the discussion concerning the state's role as regulator/steward of the health care sector.

An optimal balance is achieved by a comprehensive legal mandate and sufficient power of self-governing bodies to organize and provide appropriate health care (according to the principles of good governance, responsibility, accountability and transparency), while government still sets the frame but is involved only in cases of importance. Government, for example, would regulate whether long-term care is part of the health care system or should be regulated in a different manner. If this power is not given to self-governing bodies, then governmental structures have to be in place, which may be supported by the self-governing bodies. Such a model can be observed in France where self-regulation was gradually reduced in some health care sectors. Governmental institutions such as the Agence Nationale pour l'Accreditation et l'Evaluation en Santé (ANAES) or the Agence Française de Sécurité Sanitaire des Produits des Santé (AFSSAPS) issue legally binding clinical practice guidelines (Références medicales opposables, RMO)[4] (OECD 2002). However, there is also a 'nomenclature' in place which regulates reimbursement in the ambulatory care sector. The process to develop and maintain this benefit catalogue is currently under reconstruction (Fleurette and Banta 2000).

This also shows one important function of benefit catalogues: they serve as fee-for-service lists which tell the health care provider the payment that will be made for his or her efforts. The need for benefit catalogues is therefore partially linked to the installation of health care providers who provide services on a contract basis (with different contract types, such as fee-for-service payments) and who are not directly employed by the sickness funds or government. The close connection between available techniques and services and costs also implies that benefit catalogues can be used as a vehicle for cost containment and ultimately for quality control. These examples clarify why benefit catalogues are health policy instruments whose original intention of a simple service and reimbursement list became broadened (and to some extent overburdened) with additional tasks. It also explains to a good degree the traditionally strong position of physicians in SHI systems.

Today, many benefit catalogues provide the insured with a clear description of their entitlements, though this consumer-friendly approach was not the original intent. However, since all services are explicitly listed in the benefit catalogue, fundamentally, new innovations and technologies cannot easily diffuse into the health system. If patients ask for certain treatments (such as intracytoplasmatic sperm injection) the reimbursement is linked to the listing in the benefit catalogue. If the treatment is not listed, reimbursement is declined.[5]

Benefit catalogues are thus, to a certain extent, positive lists that protect insurers from uncontrolled expansions of health care coverage (Rutten and Van Busschbach 2001). On the other hand, they are time-consuming and costly to maintain. The decision-making process necessitates the involvement of the partners who constitute the self-governing bodies and, depending on the arrangement, of the government. Benefit catalogues can easily comprise several thousand interventions and procedures which have to be constantly checked for their current necessity and appropriateness. Increasingly, this requires additional resources in order to monitor and reflect technological progress and innovations. Furthermore, the monetary value of each intervention listed in the benefit catalogue has to be calculated ('microcosting') and finally balanced in such a way that the monetary equivalent mirrors the efforts necessary to provide the technology itself as well as relative to other services ('relative value scale').

As a rule, countries do not only use positive lists across all sectors of health care, i.e. they do not have an explicitly defined benefit catalogue across the board. Rather, there is a combination with negative lists which regulate technologies in a more implicit way as they explicitly list only those technologies which are *not* covered. This approach leaves all other technologies inside the thus implicitly regulated benefit package. Negative lists are easier to handle than positive lists and require selective action only on important issues. However, negative lists require a close surveillance of the health market in order to avoid constant broadening of the range of covered benefits. Instruments such as early warning systems or horizon scanning can be useful to identify costly innovations at an early stage. This approach has been developed within the field of health technology assessment and serves policy-makers as an information tool to enhance prospective policy-making (Mowatt *et al.* 1998).

A shortcoming of benefit catalogues derives from their orientation towards particular technologies and procedures. They do not usually reflect treatment chains or complex treatment patterns in a way necessary for the establishment of disease management programmes or for reimbursement for episodes of illness. No examples could be identified where benefit catalogues were reshaped in order to adapt them to the needs of disease management programmes.

In order to compare the decision-making environments in the eight health care systems, information was retrieved via a structured, semi-open questionnaire which was sent out to key informants in each country. After receiving the questionnaire responses, telephone interviews were conducted to clarify any outstanding questions. The questionnaire focused on the following issues:

1 What types of health care are covered by the SHI system?
2 How are the individual services/technologies regulated (implicitly or explicitly)?
3 Who decides on the introduction or exclusion of health care services and technologies?
4 Can that decision be challenged?

What types of health care are covered?

The coverage of European SHI systems revolves around the provision of curative hospital and ambulatory health care (Kupsch *et al.* 2000: 49–156). This can be explained by the historical development of these systems which were originally installed in order to regain and maintain the ability of diseased workers. Until today, preventive services and other medical interventions that are not directly linked to therapy have often not been a central component of health care provision (Kupsch *et al.* 2000: 40–7).

In almost all countries, ambulatory health care is provided by physicians operating on a fee-for-service basis. Consequently, benefit catalogues were introduced. In the Netherlands, this applies for specialists only, since general practitioners (GPs) receive a capitation-based payment (Bos 2000). While the Sickness Fund Act only defines the services available through GPs as those which are 'customary', the GPs themselves (or rather their association, the Landelijke Huisartsen Vereniging) defined a basic GP care package in the 1980s (Groenewegen and Greß 2003). It was their intention to clearly define their role in order to prevent a shifting of risks, by increasing their workload, from the sickness funds to them.

It appears that thus far no detailed comparison of the various benefit catalogues has been undertaken in respect to their contents and differences.[6] Increasing mobility within the European Union (EU) could stimulate this comparison in order to provide citizens with comparable health care packages. Hospital care is usually organized in a decentralized way and without the use of benefit catalogues. Some countries, such as Germany, are implementing diagnosis-related group (DRG) systems. This could subsequently lead to benefit catalogues where all approved interventions are listed and grouped around the relevant diagnoses. In defining such an inpatient benefit catalogue, the government's role will most likely be larger than for the ambulatory care benefits.

Coverage of pharmaceuticals differs considerably among the compared countries. While in some countries, such as Germany or Switzerland, licensure by the European Medicines Evaluation Agency (EMEA), or the national equivalent, allows reimbursement in the SHI system, other countries, for example France, Israel and the Netherlands, have established positive lists of drugs covered. This also applies for the actual coverage. Coverage of dental care has been reduced, or at least restricted (despite the technical progress in this field), in almost all observed SHI systems (Kaufhold and Schneider 2000). Dental care is mostly of a preventive or elective nature and is provided in a fee-for-service environment. Detailed benefit catalogues regulate the types of dental care covered and the associated reimbursement. Dental emergency treatments are generally covered, with the exception of Switzerland and the Netherlands, where citizens subscribe to private insurance schemes. Co-payments are frequent, treatments are paid by the patients who later get some (and rather little) compensation from their sickness funds. The amount differs considerably between countries (Holst *et al.* 2002).

Long-term care has been included in many SHI benefit catalogues or has been covered by establishing a separately financed social insurance scheme, as in Germany (Geraedts *et al.* 2000). This also applies to preventive services. Since the borders between curative and preventive medicine are somewhat vague, sickness funds also cover some preventive services – for example, for early detection of cancers or childhood disabilities, which are covered in France and Germany ('secondary prevention'). The regulation of complementary medicine has a specific and strong cultural background in each SHI system. In Switzerland for instance the coverage for complementary medicine (acupuncture, anthroposophy, homeopathy, phytotherapy, neural therapy and traditional Chinese medicine) was mandated by the Swiss Federal Department of Home affairs; a similar step was taken by the German parliament. Examples of such coverage include anthroposophy, homeopathy and phytotherapy. Other countries, such as the Netherlands, exclude this field almost entirely, or require co-payments (such as in all fields in France).

Table 8.2 shows which types of benefits are covered in the eight health insurance systems.

What shapes the benefit package of European SHI systems? Decision-making characteristics

It is a characteristic of SHI systems that health care providers and sickness funds are entitled to influence or make decisions with respect to the content of publicly-provided health care packages (Table 8.3). Most countries have created agencies which either make proposals to the Ministry of Health (e.g. in the Netherlands and Switzerland), or which decide on their own (e.g. in Germany – though the government can override any decisions). Others have agencies that work together with and under the auspices of governmental administration (e.g. in France). There is a distinction between the definition of the healthcare package and the monetary value of these services. This latter is the task of separate agencies or committees in all eight countries (with some exceptions, such as for the fee list for dental services in the Netherlands) (Kaufhold and Schneider 2000).

The introduction of new health care technologies is influenced by various factors, including the efficacy of the technology, its costs and cost-effectiveness, the medical necessity, the availability of the treatment, public opinion, the structure of the health care system needed to provide the new technology and finally – political issues. Thus far the cost-effectiveness of a treatment has not appeared to be the most important factor in the overall decision-making process, but recent developments have led to a reconsideration of the deliberation process when it comes to the determination of the virtues of a treatment (Eddy 1996).

Depending on the health care system, decision-makers are able to use from two (yes and no) to many (usually introduction of health technologies under certain conditions) different decision options when deciding on a particular health care technology (Table 8.4). Either an unconditioned yes or no are rarely adequate options and it is advisable to implement a range of measures in order to allow differentiated decisions.

During the last few decades, decision-making on particular medical technologies was largely dominated by expert advice. In general, the physicians provided 'evidence' regarding new interventions which were thought to be appropriate for inclusion in the benefit package. To provide written information regarding a technology is a fairly new approach, termed 'health technology assessment'. Traditionally, the 'best' national experts of a specialty or field were gathered, interrogated and the results compiled for subsequent decision-making. This system has been re-evaluated for various reasons. First, medical knowledge is

Table 8.2 Explicit and implicit coverage of benefit types in the eight SHI countries

Technology	Austria	Belgium	France	Germany	Israel	Luxembourg	Netherlands	Switzerland
Ambulatory care	ER	ER	ER	ER	ER	ER	IR[2]	NR
Inpatient care	ER	ER	NR	NR[7]	ER	ER	ER, IR	NR
Pharmaceuticals	ER	ER	ER	IR	ER	ER	ER	ER
Medical devices	ER	ER	ER	ER	ER	ER	ER	ER
Dental care	ER	ER	ER[4]	ER	NC	ER	NC, IR[3]	ER
Complementary medicine	NR	NC	NC[5]	ER	NC	NC	NC	ER
Prevention	ER	ER	ER	ER	ER	NR[6]	IR, ER[1]	ER
Long-term care	IR	ER	ER	ER, NR[8]	NC	ER	ER	ER

ER: explicit regulation (benefit catalogue, positive list). Austria: not closed, additional benefits on an individual basis possible.

IR: implicit regulation (such as negative list).

NR: no explicit regulatory decision on usage of a particular technology or service, such as case-by-case decision on the insurance and/or provider level. Switzerland: only cases where providers (such as physicians) and payers (such as sickness funds) cannot agree are regulated in a normative decision, all other services are included.

NC: not covered by health insurance (may be covered by a different type of social insurance or is not covered at all and left to private insurance).

Notes:

1 Vaccines and pharmaceuticals regulated in positive lists, other preventive measures regulated implicitly.

2 Negative list for specialists, not for GPs.

3 Broadly defined positive list for children up to 18 years, for adults only few treatments covered (such as prescription of drugs by dentists, preventive treatments).

4 In general not covered, exceptions apply for some basic treatments (e.g. treatment of caries).

5 Prevention in general is not part of the health care package and covered by the so-called 'social budget', although preventive measures get increasingly introduced by sickness funds.

6 Specific programmes are initiated and covered by the Ministry of Health (such as mammography programme).

7 DRG-introduction from 2003/4 may transform it into an explicitly regulated area.

8 Positive list for ambulatory long-term care, no specific list for inpatient care.

Table 8.3 Role of self-governing bodies

Country	Status
Austria	Strong role in all areas of the health care sector
Belgium	Self-governing bodies consisting of physicians and sickness funds (RIZIV) regulate health care, ministry of health 'sets the frame'
France	Decision-making power is left in part to the sickness funds and physicians, however, most decisions are left to the Ministry of Health under advice of independent assessment agencies such as ANAES
Germany	Still important role for self-governing bodies: 'Gemeinsamer Bundesausschuss' regulates ambulatory and hospital health care and is built by physicians, sickness funds and Federal Hospital Association
Israel	Strong role in all areas of the health care sector
Luxembourg	Union des Caisses de Maladie (UCM) regulates health care, only limited intervention by government
The Netherlands	No, since the Ziekenfondsraad (Sickness Fund Council) was abolished
Switzerland	All decision-making takes place in Swiss Federal Department of Home Affairs, advisory role for sickness funds and physicians

Table 8.4 Decision options: can decisions on the content of benefit catalogues be varied (i.e. time limit, confined to specific indications etc.)?

Country	Status
Austria	In general yes or no; decisions can be accompanied by various limitations
Belgium	In general yes or no regulation; in certain cases individual decisions can be made by the sickness fund depending on the evidence provided. There is a special budget for orphans and people with diseases that require expensive treatments
France	In general yes or no regulation on a national level; exceptions apply for pharmaceuticals where temporary authorization is possible and for medical devices which can be included in a trial or a prospective survey in order to grant reimbursement. This will also be true for some emerging medical and surgical procedures under evaluation. They will have a temporary code until reassessment
Germany	In general only yes or no decisions apply; increasingly quality assurance measures are introduced in order to specify yes decisions
Luxembourg	In general yes or no; decisions can be accompanied by various limitations or guidelines
The Netherlands	Sickness funds can subsidize treatments which are not introduced within research settings. CVZ can subsidize treatments if at developmental stage; sickness funds can pay for additional, not covered benefits if efficiency is enhanced (limited to 1–2% of total expenditure)
Switzerland	Several decision options, yes decision: total within a certain time limit; with the necessity to install and maintain monitoring registries or data collections with other monitoring designs; confined to centres of excellence; confined to specific indications; and combinations of the above-mentioned limitations

increasingly not the exclusive privilege of the medical profession. Sources such as health technology assessments provide relevant and useful information in a transparent and reproducible way. Second, the independence of experts is increasingly questioned. Very often such experts will benefit from changes in reimbursement decisions. They may also have developed ties to industry during their medical career – for example, through research funding. Finally, advice presented in an oral manner has often not proven to be reliable when later revisited in the courts, as has been the case in Germany. Consequently, almost all health insurance systems have introduced some elements of evidence-based decision-making. In Germany, the Federal Committee of Physicians and Sickness Funds (*Bundesausschuss der Ärzte und Krankenkassen*) increasingly uses evidence for decision-making and publishes its decision reports on the internet (Jung *et al.* 2000). In Switzerland, applicants who ask for a decision regarding a 'disputed' new technology must present an extensive health technology assessment report which is further revised by the government (Swiss Federal Social Insurance Office). The Netherlands has developed various mechanisms for the preparation of health technology assessments and the evaluation of particular technologies of unclear benefit (Bos 2000). In France, the development of the 'nomenclature' will be linked to ANAES – which will provide the scientific evidence to the medical unions and the sickness funds. Other countries, such as Austria, Belgium and Luxemburg, have not yet developed a process to incorporate scientific evidence from assessments. However, on the European level, initiatives are underway to foster and harmonize European health technology assessment initiatives. The EU-funded ECHTA project (European Collaboration on HTA) has proposed to establish a clearing house to gather and distribute such evidence to decision-making bodies (Jonsson *et al.* 2002).

The evaluation of health care technologies in SHI systems increasingly leads to a 'fourth hurdle' – accreditation by EMEA or the respective national accreditation bodies is no longer a guarantee for the introduction of a pharmaceutical into an SHI system. Traditionally, EMEA has looked at the efficacy of a treatment in comparison with a placebo, however, SHI system decision-makers are concerned with the value added by a new technology when compared to existing ones. The comparative efficacy is becoming the dominant factor in the decision-making process – causing industry to fear that the already cumbersome and expensive regulation of new developments will be further aggravated by restricted access to the public health care market. This applies not only to pharmaceuticals but also to medical devices and procedures. Since the majority of all citizens of European SHI systems are insured with the statutory health system, access to the public health care system is of crucial importance for industry. Consequently, reimbursement decisions, particularly those concerning technologies developed and marketed by domestic companies, can have political implications. However, concrete examples where political interference caused the introduction of a scientifically unproven intervention were not identified in the questionnaires.

Patient and citizen participation are constant issues in health care planning and decision-making. Greater levels of choice and influence for patients was one of the three central objectives in European health care reform declared by the World Health Organization (World Health Organization 1997).[7] However, a direct integration of patients or their representatives in the decision-making process has not happened in most European SHI systems. Also, in most countries (with the exception of Switzerland), patients or other interested parties, such as industry, have no legal mandate to make an application for the consideration of a new technology. This does not mean that a proposal from a patient organization would not be considered by the decision-making agency, however, an obligation to pursue this application is not in place. The right to submit an application is usually confined to the corporatist bodies and/or the respective government. The Swiss approach allows scientific medical societies or patient organizations or industry to issue a formal application. In order to raise the acceptability of those decision-making bodies this approach can be seen as an innovative way (among others) to overcome often autistic and bureaucratic self-governing structures. An interesting approach was chosen in Israel in 1997 when, after a public outcry, US$35 million were additionally allocated to the SHI system and since then, each year, the government adds a limited amount of money to fund new technologies. The minister of health installed a National Advisory Committee as a decision-making body for the update of the National List of Health Services (NLHS).[8] The Committee numbered 14 members and more than a third were public representatives, mostly without a medical background. The Committee based its recommendations on health technology assessment reports and the proposed technologies were finally added to the NLHS (Shani *et al.* 2000).

Only a few countries have formal structures in place to challenge decisions regarding benefit catalogues (Table 8.5).

In Germany, if patients seek post hoc reimbursement for a treatment which is denied by the sickness funds, they may apply to the 'social' courts which exclusively deal with all public insurance matters, regardless of the sector (pension fund, health care, long-term care etc.). While the courts generally

Table 8.5 Can decisions be challenged?

Country	Status
Austria	Pharmaceuticals: yes; other sectors: so-called social courts
Belgium	No specific system in place except civil courts
France	No specific system in place
Germany	So-called, 'Widerspruchststellen' at sickness funds; so-called social courts which deal exclusively with social insurance matters
Israel	Yes, district labour courts
Luxembourg	Inquiries at the Ministry of Health (medical control unit) or at 'Conseil arbitral des Assurances Sociales'
The Netherlands	Patients can ask for a review of the decision by their sickness fund, and take it to civil court if unresolved; if the specific technology is regulated in a positive list usually no exceptions apply
Switzerland	Only rules on pharmaceuticals can be challenged (regulated at the Federal Social insurance office, FSIOS, which is part of the Swiss federal administration)

follow the normative decision of the Federal Committee, some do make changes in rulings for individual cases. In other countries, patients as individuals have limited options to receive treatments not included in the benefit package. There are other, informal ways to influence benefit catalogues, such as lobbying political parties or using other methods to influence public opinion, in particular via the media.

While it is not possible to legally challenge a decision in most countries, other means allow patients to get specific treatments. Since explicit regulation is in place only for the ambulatory sector, patients can sometimes obtain a treatment which is not available in the ambulatory sector in hospitals due to the implicit benefit packages which are in place there. However, not all systems' sickness funds are allowed to offer services that are not part of the statutory benefit catalogue. If there is a market for such treatments, physicians, who in general work also for the sickness funds, may provide these services to their patients. This leaves the individual physician in the potentially dubious situation of being in the business of providing unproven or not medically necessary health care. For example, a physician may inform his or her patient that PSA-screening is not offered within the public health care package, but that it is available if the patient will pay out-of-pocket for the test. Although patients are nowadays, often through the internet, but also through the sickness funds, often better informed than before, the information gap between physicians and patients is still wide enough to put the physician in a principally better position to negotiate such extra treatments. This situation could increase pressures to introduce unproven treatments in order to avoid creating a private health care market that would undermine the basis of the SHI system. Thus if decision-makers opt for a health care basket that contains only treatments which are proven according to the standards of evidence-based medicine, popular treatments may have to be removed – a decision which will be perceived by the public as rationing. The alternative is to tolerate interventions whose benefits are not clearly proven but which are popular with the insured in order to maintain the popularity of the SHI system and its benefit catalogue. Both options are problematic and underline the difficulties of composing a health care basket which is both affordable and comprehensive. Ways to deal with this pivotal situation point in two different directions: first, to grant reimbursement for SHI patients only for those physicians who work exclusively for the sickness fund, without offering private services, and second, to allow statutory sickness funds to offer special health care packages which cover these extra services.[9]

Trends

In order to cope with ever-increasing demands, plans to establish so-called core catalogues that provide only basic, medically necessary services are being debated throughout the compared countries. So far, no country has been able to reduce the health care package to a minimal, undisputed level of services. The ideas surrounding such a core package are intriguing: such a package would ensure that illness will not result in personal financial hardship and that standard treatments are ensured. If patients choose to have more extensive health care coverage it is left to them to purchase additional insurance. However, for various reasons this approach does not work properly: first, there is no method for clearly differentiating between necessary and less necessary treatments in two (or more) categories. Although health technology assessment (HTA) can be a useful tool to broaden the knowledge base of decision-makers, it does not offer choices for rationing health care. At least, no attempt has been made to use HTA for this purpose in European SHI systems. Second, often the treatment or service is in itself useful, but its inappropriate use is the problem. In other words, very rarely are treatments and services totally obsolete[10] – it is more often that the conditions and indications to use them are changing.

Third, restricting the benefit catalogue without tangible advantages is not popular among voters. Even with a reduced contribution, citizens would need to purchase additional insurance to regain the old benefits status and would likely end up with the same or, more probably, higher insurance premiums. This can be seen in the reduction of dental services, such as in the Netherlands and Switzerland, which are not thought to be part of the core package. This gives the term 'core package' a different meaning, as, rather than determining specific benefits, whole areas of care such as dental care or pharmaceuticals are excluded from the benefit package. Since it is difficult to define medical necessity and benefit to health, this approach is undoubtedly effective in reducing statutory health care costs. However, it leaves the citizen with higher personal costs for health care since additional private insurance schemes will be required to replace the former statutory health plan. A possible cure for the problem could be the systematic development of guidelines. SHI countries such as the Netherlands have taken this route and it appears that this tool can be successfully used for cost-containment and restriction of treatment usage. It is crucial to ensure that these guidelines are developed in collaboration with practitioners and are not seen as bureaucratic measures imposed from above. However, so far it is not clear how many guidelines are necessary to organize the core of statutory medicine. Furthermore, the costs of updating and maintaining such guidelines are not known and impact studies demonstrating a clear benefit derived from the introduction of guidelines are lacking. The alternative of regulating all technologies listed in a benefit catalogue is less attractive: this would require an immense (bureaucratic) apparatus and one which would likely be perceived as a means of government rationing.

A loss of identification with the principles of equality and equity, i.e. a rise of individualism with respect to maximizing one's own benefits, is often claimed, but so far no convincing empirical evidence is available that insured citizens prefer a fundamentally different health care system. Insurance mentality ('I get what I pay for') seems to be one manifestation of increasingly individualistic societies. This trend is fostered by the changing perception of health, which includes wellness and well-being, as described through the definition of health by the World Health Organization. This changed perception is also influenced by the 'medicalization' of society where every disturbance of the physiological state is regarded as a potentially treatable condition. To distinguish between these different, constantly changing meanings of health and to choose a benefit package which is affordable and useful is a task which requires broad political and societal support.

Consequently, the legitimacy of non-elected, corporatist decision bodies is increasingly under question and traditional 'closed shop' mentalities will further erode the public support for the, thus far, fairly successful approach of statutory health insurance systems. The public is also increasingly doubtful of the legitimacy of self-governing bodies, particularly as they are not the product of democratic elections. Since the majority of citizens are members of statutory health insurance schemes they cannot choose between private or statutory health care and have to accept what is offered to them. In order to facilitate and foster the identification of future generations with the statutory health insurance principles, increased options for participation and influence by insured citizens are needed. To enable citizens to have more influence on the funding and delivery of health care will therefore be one the major challenges in future. The examples of Israel and Switzerland demonstrated earlier in this chapter show ways to ensure citizen participation.

It is often claimed that freedom of choice is regarded as an important good in the SHI system. Freedom of choice refers to several characteristics: freedom to choose the physician or hospital; choices of treatment options; and/or direct access to specialist care. Freedom of choice is not just a choice between different insurance schemes but also a choice from a broad basket of health care services. Since the health care packages are already comprehensive in European SHI systems, freedom to choose between insurance plans would have to be combined with considerably reduced insurance premiums. It may not be possible to reduce the health care package in order to offer various insurance plans (which must still include a basic health care package). A different situation is present when it comes to an extension of the already comprehensive health care packages. For example, should acupuncture be covered within the regular benefit catalogue? Some countries (such as France or Switzerland) do cover acupuncture, but if it is not already included, the discussion around additional insurance schemes arises once again.

Despite many similarities, there are many differences between the eight countries with SHI systems. One difference lies in the provision of health care to the insured citizens. In Germany, it is seen as a major achievement that patients do not have to pay the physician or the hospital directly. It is almost seen as a *conditio sine qua non* that the doctor-patient relationship is not compromised by direct payment from the patient. Benefit catalogues in this system, besides their functions as 'entitlement' lists, do not fulfil a financial function for patients. Whereas, in France or Switzerland for example, this principle does not apply and patients must pay their doctors (and get compensation from their sickness fund). In France, this is true except for low income patients that are immediately and completely covered and do not have to pay anything. It is often claimed that this cost transparency causes expenditure reductions; in other words, citizens are more cost-conscious when seeking medical care. Empirical studies have not been undertaken to prove this hypothesis, but comparing the (rather high) expenses of these two health care systems with other countries does not seem to provide evidence for this premise.

If European citizens increasingly take advantage of health care services in a unified Europe, the French system for physician reimbursement might be more compatible with such a situation than the benefit-in-kind schemes used in

Germany or the Netherlands, as the latter require contracts between sickness funds and providers. Europeans could visit doctors or physiotherapists outside their own country and receive compensation from their domestic sickness funds after having paid the health care provider directly. This can also be achieved through cumbersome and difficult to negotiate bilateral contracts between the countries and requires an elaborate bureaucracy. This trend may be fostered by recent rulings of the European Court of Justice (ECJ). For example, in the Kohll-Decker ruling, the ECJ determined that ambulatory benefits that are insured in a specific European health care system can be obtained by the insured person in all European countries without obtaining an approval from their sickness fund. In the Peerbooms decision of July 2001, a patient received an inpatient treatment in Austria which was not covered in the Netherlands (in this case only within a controlled trial with enrolment limited to participants below the age of 25). The ECJ ruled that the requirement for a patient to get authorization for reimbursement from his or her social security system before going abroad for hospital treatment is indeed an obstacle to EU rules on the freedom to provide services. However, it stated that such a restriction on free movement was justified in order to protect the financial balance of the health care system and to ensure the planning and provision of hospital services. Nevertheless, it ruled that member states must comply with two key conditions if they wish to restrict access to hospital services in other parts of the EU. First, authorization cannot be refused simply because a treatment is not considered 'normal' in the patient's home country; instead this must be judged by international medical standards. Second, permission to go abroad cannot be denied if the treatment is unable to be provided without 'undue delay' in the patient's home country. These decisions point to an interesting development: if this Europe-wide entitlement to 'scientifically proven' health care is really used to their advantage by citizens and respected by health planners in the different national health care systems, a European benefit catalogue looms on the horizon (Wismar and Busse 2002). Two groups might typically use this option: first, retired Europeans who prefer to reside in southern European countries, and second, patients who seek elective treatment with high cost or new technologies (such as new methods of hip replacement, minimally invasive surgical techniques etc.). It is difficult to predict to what extent European citizens will travel to neighbouring countries for health care. Language, culture and distance from relatives and friends may limit the number of potentially interested patients.

Conclusion

We have seen that benefit catalogues are an essential part of SHI systems and that they fulfil various functions: clarifying entitlements to health care for citizens, facilitating reimbursement for medical professionals and 'controlling' the influx and diffusion of new technologies into the health care system. This explicit approach of defining healthcare necessitates a timely and extensive monitoring process – one which makes decision-makers aware of the benefits of technologies and the corresponding needs. Benefit packages can be connected (in legal and practical terms) with supply-side regulations (capacity planning and tariff regulations), and demand-side regulations (i.e. co-payments; pre-services review of need and approval by sickness funds). Benefit catalogues appear to be an appropriate approach to specify entitlements to healthcare and to regulate public medicine. Their future development will depend on the ability of self-governing bodies and governments to undertake further initiatives, such as the promotion of citizen participation in health care and the development of evidence-based clinical practice guidelines to ensure the appropriate delivery of the services included in the benefit catalogue.

Acknowledgements

We are in particular indebted to C. Wild and G. Endel (Austria), P. Meus and J. Hermesse (Belgium), D. Polton, M.J. Moquet and J. Orvain (France), G. Ben Nun (Israel), G. Holbach (Luxembourg) and R. Boekart (Netherlands) for their valuable contributions.

Notes

1 An interesting example is the treatment of low blood pressure in otherwise healthy persons in Germany, a health state which is in other countries not even seen as a disease (Lee Robin and Orvain 2003).
2 The model is that self-governing bodies should establish the catalogue but the actual situation is that the minister has a strong role, especially for the hospital sector.
3 However, the government makes decisions after discussion with the different partners (Lee Robin and Orvain 2003).
4 This approach has not proven to be successful. Problems were legitimacy, monitoring compliance and missing sanction mechanisms. No further inspections are carried out by health insurance funds. ANAES states efficacy and safety and not the reimbursement itself (Lee Robin and Orvain 2003).
5 There are exemptions from the rule: sometimes new services can be sub-summarized under existing services. This is often done when the new technology is a slight variation of an existing one or a subsequent development. This type of 'implicit' regulation of benefit catalogues is used as a less formal tool to control the influx of innovations. In Germany, this happens when the so-called Evaluation Committee (*Bewertungsausschuss*) changes the description of an existing service in a way that a new technology is *de facto* covered.
6 An exception is the comparison of the Swiss benefit catalogue with those of France, Germany, Israel, Luxembourg and the Netherlands on behalf of the Eidgenössisches Departement des Inneren in 2000 (Polikowski *et al.* 2000; Polikowski and Santos-Eggimann 2002). The evaluation showed a great degree of similarity in covered services, with some differences e.g. in the field of complementary medicine (in part covered) and dental care (in general not covered).
7 The other two objectives were greater efficiency in deploying resources and greater effectiveness in achieving health outcomes.
8 All services in the list must be available for every patient through every sickness fund.
9 It has to be kept in mind that many of the medically unnecessary services derive from the so-called wellness sector and are often not based on a mortality risk and have more of the characteristics of consumer goods.

10 One of the rare examples: pneumocystencephalogram for the diagnosis of spinal disc protrusion has been replaced by MRI and CT. Usually innovations do not replace older ones but are used in addition.

References

Bos, M. (2000) Health technology assessment in the Netherlands, *Int J Tech Assess Health Care*, 16(2): 485–519.

Eddy, D.M. (1996) Benefit language: criteria that will improve quality while reducing costs, *JAMA*, 275(8): 650–7.

Fleurette, F. and Banta, D. (2000) Health technology assessment in France, *Int J Tech Assess Health Care*, 16(2): 400–11.

Geraedts, M., Heller, G.V. and Harrington, C.A. (2000) Germany's long-term-care insurance: putting a social insurance model in practice, *The Milbank Quarterly*, 78(3): 375–401.

Groenewegen, P. and Greß, S. (2003) *Der Hausarzt in den Niederlanden, in Jahrbuch für Kritische Medizin 38*. Hamburg: Argument.

Holst, D., Sheiham, M. and Petersen, P. (2002) Regulating entrepreneurial behaviour in oral health services, in R.B. Saltman, R. Busse and E. Mossialos (eds) *Regulating Entrepreneurial Behaviour in European Health Care Systems*, pp. 215–31. Buckingham: Open University Press.

Jonsson, E., Banta, H.D., Henshall, C. and Sampietro-Colom, L. (2002) Summary report of the ECHTA/ECAHI project, *Int J Technol Assess Health Care*, 18(2): 218–37.

Jung, K., Gawlik, C., Gibis, B. *et al.* (2000) Bundesausschuss der Ärzte und Krankenkassen: Ansprüche der Versicherten präzisieren, *Deutsches Ärzteblatt*, 97(7): A365–70.

Kaufhold, R. and Schneider, M. (2000) *Preisvergleich zahnärztlicher Leistungen im europäischen Kontext*. Köln: IDZ.

Kupsch, S., Kern, A., Klas, C., Kressin, B., Vienonen, M. and Beske, F. (2000) *Health Service Provision on a Microcosmic level – An International Comparison. Results of a WHO/IGSF Survey in 15 European Countries*. Kiel: Institute for Health Systems Research.

Lee Robin, S.H. and Orvain, J. (2003) Personal communication, October.

Mowatt, G., Thomson, M.A., Grimshaw, J. and Grant, A. (1998) Implementing early warning messages on emerging health technologies, *Int J Tech Assess Health Care*, 14(4): 663–70.

OECD (2002) *Improving the Performance of Health Care Systems: From Measures to Action (A Review of Experiences in Four OECD Countries)*. Paris: Directorate for Education, Employment, Labour and Social Affairs.

Polikowski, M. and Santos-Eggimann, B. (2002) How comprehensive are the basic packages of health services? An international comparison of six health insurance systems, *J Health Serv Res Policy*, 7: 133–42.

Polikowski, M., Lauffer, R., Renard, D. and Santos-Eggimann, B. (2000) *Analyse de la LAMal: Le 'catalogue des prestations' est-il suffisant pour que tous accèdent à des soins de qualité?* Lausanne: IUSMP.

Rutten, F. and Van Busschbach, J. (2001) How to define a basic package of health services for a tax funded or social insurance based healthcare system? *European Journal of Health Economics – HEPAC*, 2(2): 45–6.

Shani, S., Siebzehner, M., Luxenburg, O. and Shemer, J. (2000) Setting priorities for the adoption of health technologies on a national level – the Israeli experience, *Health Policy*, 54: 169–85.

Wismar, M. and Busse, R. (2002) Scenarios on the future of healthcare in Europe, in R. Busse, M. Wismar and P. Berman (eds) *The European Union and Health Services – The*

Impact of the Single European Market on Member States, pp. 261–72. Amsterdam: IOS Press.

World Health Organization (1997) *European Health Care Reform: Analysis of Current Strategies*, WHO regional publications, European series No. 72. Copenhagen: World Health Organization.

chapter nine

Contracting and paying providers in social health insurance systems

Maria M. Hofmarcher and Isabelle Durand-Zaleski

Introduction

A wide range of contracting and payment methods have been adopted in social health insurance (SHI) systems with the main purpose of providing the several actors with incentives to restrict provider costs. This chapter explores the type of contractual relationships that sickness funds can create with providers of care. By contractual relationships we mean that the purchaser(s) of health care (often SHI in a position of monopsonistic payer) will negotiate with health care providers a set of commitments on both parts. These commitments may be informal or formal, the latter resulting in signed agreements.

Contracts are mechanisms to deal with asymmetric information. Encompassing adverse selection and moral hazard, asymmetric information is a common problem in health systems. It is found in the relation between providers and patients as well as between payers and providers. Economic situations involving asymmetric information can be referred to as agency problems (McGurie 2000), in that the principal (the insured patient/payer) is affected by an action (effort) taken by the agent (the doctor/provider). This chapter focuses on contracting as a means to deal with asymmetric information between insurer and provider: the principal (sickness fund) is unaware of what exactly the agent is doing, and of all the other factors determining performance, so it is not possible to directly observe whether the provider (physician) has made the desired effort. Asymmetric information creates a relationship between the principal and the agent where the agent has incentives to shirk at any task and the principal cannot precisely detect that shirking. This makes it difficult to design an optimal contract, especially when providers are risk averse. In this case it will not be optimal for the principal to fully penalize the provider for shortfalls in observable outcomes, since the poor performance may not necessarily be the result of agent shirking, but rather due to random shocks. This means that a contract, although optimal given the information structure, will not be fully based on observable outcomes (Gaynor and Mark 1999). Moreover, the fact that a dimension of quality is observed does not imply that it is verifiable. Verifiability requires that it can be specified and enforced in a contract, whereas observability indicates only that subjective assessments can be made about it (Chalkely and Malcomson 2000).

In addition to these basic obstacles, the general objective of contracting should be to improve medical practice and ultimately the quality of care. Historically however, many contracts have been simply about paying providers. With the increasing complexity of medicine and the emergence of managed care, providers are forced into fulfilling a double agent role – providing high quality care to patients while defending own income interests – and containing costs on behalf of insurers. Performance contracting and/or incentive contracts have become the mode to balance the challenges for providers. Recent evidence suggests that quality of care is improved with the implementation of financial incentives within contractual relationships in managed care settings (Gaynor *et al.* 2001). It was further found that the use of group incentives could lead to a more efficient allocation of resources among Health Maintenance Organization (HMO) patients rather than incentives geared towards individual physicians.

Most European SHI systems focus on the cross-pressures of combining near universal coverage with freedom of choice. This combination, in a context of technological progress and supplier-induced demand, is seen as inherently inflationary. As a consequence, SHI decision-makers have sought to introduce cost-saving contractual relationships for service provision while ensuring quality. Such a process is not easy and has not been uniformly successful in the different countries, owing to different demographic, cultural and economic factors. Most SHI countries combine a mix of private and public service provision, with private provision being mainly focused in primary care and/or office-based physicians, and public provision being predominantly rendered in inpatient and outpatient settings (Hofmarcher and Riedel 1999). This mix is often part of a sincere attempt to design contract terms and payment mechanisms to contain costs while preserving/improving quality and coverage. Nevertheless, other motivations, such as the influence of particular politically active interest groups or short-term budget objectives, might also play a role and, as a result, the weights attached to cost, quality and coverage might vary widely.

The contract terms and payment systems in the different SHI countries and their implications are examined below. Subsequently, the leverage of sickness funds (as SHI countries' figureheads) over these two features is discussed.

Range of contract terms

Since physicians and other primary care providers are mostly self-employed individuals, working in either single or group practices, contracting them as private self-employed individuals (entrepreneurs) has been the foremost challenge for sickness funds. Equally if not more important in terms of expenditure burden are contracts for inpatient and/or outpatient care, however these services receive less attention since, in these sub-sectors, public provision of services is predominant. This division between private provision in primary care and public provision in inpatient care has created incentives for various forms of cost shifting in either direction. Thus, designing contracts to coordinate and optimize the interface between primary care and inpatient care has also been a common issue, particularly in the two SHI countries where a portion of speciality services are provided in the private sector (Austria and France). In the pharmaceutical sector, contracts take on various forms ranging from inclusion/exclusion of drugs (positive/negative list) to agreements with wholesalers and retailers, mostly accompanied by price measures enforced by law.

Physician services

Contracts with private self-employed physicians are very diverse across SHI systems, within these systems and over time. Historically many contracts have been simply about paying physicians. Medical progress in combination with accelerating costs and high relative prices in the health sector accompanied by revenue shortfalls have challenged sickness funds/government to negotiate with providers more proactively. Other dimensions such as obligation and collectiveness vary widely.

Pay agreement versus innovation

Apart from challenges for sickness funds resulting from either inclusion of new services in benefit packages or physician supply, some SHI countries (France, Switzerland) have started to experiment with European-style managed care models. These are an expression of the drive for proactiveness. In Switzerland, the physicians' role as double agents in combination with patients' desire to see any provider has been viewed as responsible for the slow growth of an HMO insurance model (Bundesamt für Sozialversicherung 2000). Comprising only 7 per cent of all insured, growth of enrollment in HMOs has been only moderate in the last couple of years. Although new organizational entities have been created between provider and insurer, the implementation of the 1995 law did not boost the development of alternative insurance models. Insurers claim that managed care models are only appropriate in urban areas. Apart from concerns about coping with the double agent role, physicians have little incentive to join managed care models since regular SHI contracts are available to all providers in Switzerland.

In France, SHI is now evolving towards agreements by type of provider (primary care physicians, opticians, dentists), at the micro level, by defining the type of care to be provided in a given situation. The state and the regions are working at the macro level, establishing a desired level of supply by region and for every type of provider (hospitals, clinics, physicians in private practice). A voluntary contractual agreement is being tested between GPs, patients and sickness funds to limit the use of medical services via improved co-ordination of health care delivery and better medical practice. GPs volunteer to become *médecin référent*. The contract between the GP and the SHI is that the GP will receive additional funds in exchange for charging the standard fee, prescribing generic drugs, attending continuing medical education sessions, following practice guidelines and using computerized patient records. The impact of these arrangements on health care cost and quality seems to be marginal so far (Or 2002). The relatively small number of patients that did volunteer belonged to two specific population groups, the elderly and patients with chronic diseases (Aguzzoli *et al.* 1999). Also in Germany managed care models are allowed by the government, but have not been implemented as yet. Population inquiry suggests that, even when offered a rebate, there is little interest in limitation of freedom of choice of physician (Emphasis 1999). In Austria, any services not regulated by contracts are subject to authorization by supervising head doctors. They also have the function of checking the prescribing habits of contract doctors and may, if these deviate greatly from the usual standard, initiate audits. This means that SHI can exert some control over the use of resources in primary care, a central task rather successfully implemented in managed care models (Glied 2000).

Thus, there is experience with managed care models for nearly 15 years in SHI countries, however there does not exist clear evidence of their success in containing costs or improving quality. Moreover, sluggish implementation suggests that sickness funds are not convinced of the cost containing effects of managed care. Empirical evidence and patient inquiries show that patients are only interested in specific cases when their normal health consumption behaviour will not be affected and if rebates are large enough.

Compulsory versus selective contracting

The freedom to choose any physician depends on regulations regarding market entry. For instance, contracting with all physicians is compulsory for SHI insurers in Germany and Switzerland. In the Netherlands and Austria, though, selective contracting is the rule. Selective contracting does not necessarily restrict access to any particular physician. In Austria, an individual may visit any physician and be reimbursed 80 per cent of the rates agreed with contract doctors. The difference between seeing a contract physician and a so-called private physician concerns the reimbursement mode and the amount of co-payment. Whereas contacting a contract physician implies provider reimbursement, the visit to a private physician involves both patient reimbursement and mostly substantial co-payments. Depending on which delineation is applied, co-payments in Austria account for between 4 to 18 per cent of total health expenditure. This share has not only been increasing over time but is also highest among SHI countries (Hofmarcher and Röhrling 2003).

Collective versus individual contracting

In addition to different approaches to market entry, SHI countries have developed varying ways to structure contracts. In Germany, Austria and Switzerland, collective contracting is typically based on collective bargaining about fees and prices, while in the Netherlands, Belgium and France, fees are set centrally.

Switzerland is an interesting example regarding current attempts to disentangle purchaser and provider cartels in order to promote more competition. One aim of the 1996 Health Insurance Law (KVG) was to encourage individual contracting (*Sonderverträge*). However, until now only an insignificant number of individual contracts have been awarded. This reflects concerns that the administrative outlays for multiple contracts will be high (Bundesamt für Sozialversicherung 2000). Nevertheless, the number of contracts awarded has increased some 30 per cent since 1995. The boost is attributed to new primary care services and new contracts in the hospital sector (Bundesamt für Sozialversicherung 2000). In Israel, only the second largest sickness fund (*Maccabi*) provides primary care predominantly through independent practitioners, supplemented by the fund's own local clinics offering nursing services, physiotherapy, diagnostic facilities and physician consultation. In 1997 *Maccabi* spent 23 per cent of its budget on physician services, which roughly compares to the SHI budget share spent on physician services in Austria.

Entrepreneurship versus civil servants

Payments to physicians in some SHI countries contain a component for investment and costs. Since doctors in their role as entrepreneurs are often also employers, the tension created between 'labour and capital' may influence some contract negotiations. Self-governing SHI bodies in some countries (e.g. Austria, France and Israel) represent the labour faction, and, given their structural information disadvantage as purchaser of services, they may become rather defensive.

In their role as entrepreneurs, practising doctors and other health personnel often seek a target income. Negotiations of contracts (fee levels) are sometimes driven by explicit reference to certain income levels, like in the Netherlands where the income of specialists should not exceed the income of civil servants in higher income brackets (College Tarieven Gezondheidszorg 2000). However, Dutch specialists are predominately practising in public hospitals. Thus, the consideration of capital costs is not always relevant. Specialists in particular (with their income relying more on fee-for-service payments) are seen as entrepreneurs, even though they are often physically located in hospitals. The confusing situation regarding physicians' claims in Austria seems to be illustrative of the problem. When electronic accounting was implemented in 2003, physicians demanded financial support from the sickness funds for investment in computers to administer their billing. This request appears paradoxical to the self-perception of doctors as independent self-employed individuals.

Inpatient/outpatient care

Whereas contracting with physicians and other primary care providers is common in SHI countries, it appears to be less widespread in the inpatient sector.

Since sickness funds often have various historical and/or geographical links to secondary/tertiary care level providers, contracting individually with hospitals is rather the exception than the rule. Similar to the primary care sector, collective contracting dominates. Individual contracting appears to occur more frequently with private sector and/or non-profit hospitals. Contracting in this sector of the health care systems must address the interface between the predominantly private provision of services in primary and secondary care and the mostly public provision of services in the hospital sector. Additionally, due to current legislation, capital costs are mainly borne by hospital owners with little or no involvement of sickness funds. Budgeting of the sickness funds' share of hospital financing appears to deepen the resulting defensive role and thus inhibits active purchasing.

Outpatient/primary care and inpatient interface

Though sometimes promoted by policy-makers in the search for cost-effective service provision, integrated service provision appears to be crowded out in some SHI countries. One reason may be the power of the medical profession. Another may be a lack of competition (X-inefficiencies), i.e. the political commitment that health care is a public good. Integrated service provision may also be threatening for private practice as prices may differ.

In Austria, for example, the number of both general and dental clinics owned by sickness funds has been reduced by 50 per cent since 1975. This decline is due to efforts by the social security funds to shut down small, unprofitable clinics and concentrate on larger units. Integrated service provision in the inpatient sector is rather low in Austria: sickness funds maintain about 8 per cent of the total bed capacity. About 19 per cent of independent outpatient clinics are operated by sickness funds across the country. Health insurance funds concentrate on operating dental clinics: 98 per cent of dental clinics operating in 1997 were run by a health insurance fund. Prior to 1998, law prohibited dental clinics run by sickness funds to render any fixed dentures not included in the sickness fund's benefit package. The provision of this service was reserved to contract dentists in private practice. The 1998 amendment to the General Social Security Act (ASVG) sets out that social health insurers' dental clinics may also provide fixed dentures under certain conditions. This has lowered the prices of dentists as dental crowns made at the social insurers' own clinics are much cheaper than those made by dentists. This is an indication that removing these kinds of supply restrictions might have a cost-containing effect.

In Israel, although a purchaser-provider split was introduced after the introduction of the 1995 law, primary care appears to be predominately provided in integrated outpatient clinics. The ownership structure of hospital beds suggests that the majority of inpatient services are being 'contracted' by the sickness funds from either the government or the private (non-profit) providers.

Partitioning of operating costs

Partitioning of operating costs has important consequences for the allocation of the total hospital budget. If providers are paid a lump sum fee per hospital day, as predominantly is done in Germany and Switzerland, partitioning creates the incentive for hospital owners to minimize their financing burden by maximizing revenues generated from sickness fund flows. This rational behaviour by hospital owners may be inefficient however, as length of patient stays may exceed the medically justified threshold and thus waste resources. In addition to lacking transparency, this payment approach can encourage cost shifting, which can be hard to trace and thus is in itself costly. As opposed to the literature (Dranove 1988; Dor and Farley 1996), cost shifting reflects in our context the behavioural built-in incentive of sickness funds to benefit from shifts of patient flows to the inpatient sector.

In some SHI countries (e.g. Austria, Germany, Switzerland), mostly federal law rather than contracts defines a split in responsibilities for covering hospital operating costs. In a number of SHI countries (e.g. Austria, France, Switzerland), private non-profit providers are given subsidies if they take on public responsibilities and provide services to SHI beneficiaries. In fulfilling these tasks, the managerial discretion of non-profit hospital owners is bound by regulations concerning access and capacity provisions, at least for emergency care and quality assurance. These restrictions protect patients as particular fixed payments per case may generate incentives to avoid treating more costly patients. In Switzerland and Austria, to improve their negotiating power and to utilize economies of scope and scale, non-profit hospitals increasingly merged into holding companies or associations. After the implementation of the 1995 Swiss Health Insurance Law, the number of contracts, in particular with provider associations, has increased. Due to the broadening of the benefit package, nursing home organizations providing nursing and other services were increasingly contracted (Bundesamt für Sozialversicherung 2000). The partitioning of operating costs has been nationally regulated since 1995 in Switzerland, with the amount paid by sickness funds not to exceed 50 per cent of total operating costs (Eugster 1998).

Pharmaceutical sector

As the majority of drugs in industrial nations are paid for from public funds, there is no other sector in the health service that is as greatly affected by the public/private mix as the pharmaceutical market. Contract arrangements in the pharmaceutical sector of SHI health systems appear to be influenced by the power of the industry in the respective countries. Major pharmaceutical industries are located in Germany, France and Switzerland. Particularly in those countries, health policy goals of making drugs with high therapeutic quality available as quickly as possible at the lowest possible price coexist with the aim of maintaining drug company profits in order to encourage innovation and growth.

Agreements about rational prescription

Monitoring prescription behaviour has become a standard measure to contain costs and reduce growth in drug consumption in SHI countries. Agreements rather than contracts are mostly enforced and in some countries physicians are not necessarily obliged to join those agreements.

Rational prescription behaviour is being monitored in Belgium and Germany where, in addition, the prescription of generic drugs is being promoted (in Belgium, generics represent less than 1 per cent of total drug consumption). Physicians in Luxembourg have to write up a formal justification if they prescribe more than three drugs per prescription. The Netherlands introduced pharmaco-economic guidelines in the 1990s and also promotes the use of generic drugs (Rosian *et al.* 2001). Prescription guidelines are also being issued from the Austrian sickness funds. In addition, some sickness funds started to cooperate with contract physicians to promote 'reasonable use' of drugs. By law, Austrian sickness funds may monitor prescription behaviour and have introduced sanctions, the most common of which is to require contract physicians to discuss their prescription patterns if they deviate from their peers.

In France, prescription-related expenditures (drugs mainly, but also tests) have been subjected to two major contractual experiments (see www.cnamts.fr/secu/fichiers/rmo.pdf). The first one began in 1993 and is known as 'regulatory medical references' or 'mandatory practice guidelines' (Durand-Zaleski *et al.* 1997). A containment policy for health care expenditure became law in 1993. This introduced mandatory medical practice guidelines, known as *références médicales opposables*. These form a negotiated contract signed by the social security administration and unions representing doctors in private practice. The guidelines limit prescriptions by fining physicians who over prescribe. The guidelines were applied immediately after their publication and the enforcement procedures after a two-month observation period. The number of violations per doctor was determined by sampling prescriptions over a two-month period. Roughly 10 per cent of the physician population was surveyed over two years, of which less than 0.6 per cent was eventually fined. The fine, however, was never paid because an appeals court did not uphold the first ruling. These mandatory practice guidelines do not apply to hospital practice. Only a centralized health care system with relatively weak medical unions could introduce such a system, since guidelines have to be universal and the paymaster has to have leverage over doctors' and the government's support.

Agreements with distributors, retailers and manufacturers

In practically all SHI countries, laws regulate margins for the distribution and retailing of drugs. Whereas wholesale margins for all circulating drugs are regulated in Belgium, Germany (only for drugs sold in pharmacies), Luxembourg and Austria, the regulation of wholesale profits is restricted to reimbursed drugs in France and also in the Netherlands. In France and the Netherlands, the regulation of pharmaceutical margins is again restricted to reimbursed drugs; in all other SHI countries pharmaceutical margins are regulated for all circulating drugs (Rosian *et al.* 2001). In France, an attempt to link the diffusion of technical progress to a contractual relationship between the manufacturer and the payer was developed in 2000. It concerned the drug 'celebrex', used in the treatment of rheumatic disease. This contract was a price-volume agreement; the manufacturer was granted reimbursement and a high price, providing that, if sales increased, the unit price would decrease accordingly. This is the most innovative type of contract regarding technical change.

Payment mechanism

Approximately 70 per cent of total health expenditures in SHI countries comes from public sources. Of this share, approximately 90 per cent is paid by sickness funds (Table 9.1).

In all countries, the largest expenditures are payments for physician services (approximately 30 per cent) and hospitals (approximately 30 per cent), followed by expenses for drugs (up to 20 per cent). Traditionally, payment of providers was fee-for-service for physicians in private practice, per diem for hospitals and negotiated prices for drugs. In each case, the SHI system had control over unit price but not over volume, which meant an open-ended system without adequate cost containment. In the last 20 years, payment methods have changed mainly towards a mixed payment scheme (i.e. fee-for-service, capitation) for physicians, prospective payments and/or capped budgets for hospitals and/or a mix for hospitals, and price regulations accompanied by (capped) budgets for the provision of drugs. Theory on optimal contracting suggests that fixed payments like salary or capitation are not optimal payment contracts (Holmström 1979). Nevertheless, holding physicians entirely responsible for adverse events is also not optimal (Gaynor and Gertler 1995). By increasingly introducing mixed payment schemes, SHI systems have responded to real-world experiences with contracting.

Table 9.1 Health care expenditure in SHI countries, 2000

	Public expenditure (% of GDP)	Public expenditure (% of total expenditure on health)	SHI expenditure (% of public expenditure on health)
Austria	5.4	69.4**	61.0**
Belgium	6.2	72.1	48.6
France	7.1	75.8	96.8
Germany	7.9	75.0	91.7
Israel	5.7	69.0	66.9*
Luxembourg	4.9	87.8	88.5*
Netherlands	5.5	63.4	94.1
Switzerland	5.9	55.6	72.7
SHI average	6.1	71.0	89.1
EU15 average	6.0	74.0	n.a.

* 1999
** Underestimated due to the underestimation of reported public expenditure on health calculated according to SNA 1995 (IHS HealthEcon estimate: 81.6 per cent).

Sources: IHS HealthEcon Calulations (2003); Kerr (2000); OECD (2003); Israel: Israel Yearbook and Almanac (1999), WHO (2003).

Table 9.2 Remuneration

Remuneration	Types of payment	Main incentives
Fee-for-service	• Patient reimbursement • Provider reimbursement • Remuneration according to previously fixed charges	The more services the higher the revenue
Capitation	Flat periodic payment fixed according to the medical needs of the patients enrolled; may comprise: • services by GPs • all medical services • all health care services	If spending exceeds the expected amount, financial losses occur. If less money than previously expected is spent, providers might receive additional profits
Salary	Salary according to legal requirements for employees	Salary is independent of performance

Physician services

Different payment schemes (Table 9.2) coexist in primary care, but are mostly different from the scheme for specialists. Salaried employees dominate the primary care sector in Israel (many are employed by the sickness funds). In Belgium, Luxembourg, Switzerland and France, fee-for-service remuneration and patient reimbursement are still the common payment mode, although recently there have been experiments with mixed payment methods in France and capitation is expected to increase in Switzerland (Wyler *et al.* 2001). However, combinations of payment methods are common, and innovative payment methods have been tested with only limited success.

Mixed payments

Experience in the Netherlands is illustrative of empirical developments with mixed payments. Capitation payments to physicians is common for sickness fund enrollees as is fee-for-service remuneration for privately insured individuals. Policy-makers in the Netherlands discovered that complete reliance on fee controls as an instrument failed to achieve effective cost containment in the area of specialist care. Specialists could respond to a cut in their fees with an increase in the volume of health services. In order to counteract such a response, an expenditure target (cap) has been introduced. The specialists' revenues are now part of the hospital budget. There is a budget for each speciality. Medical specialists, however, are still paid on a fee-for-service basis. If their service volume is lower than agreed, they will then receive less remuneration than anticipated. If the volume is higher, the hospital can negotiate an additional production volume with the insurer. This arrangement has only been introduced in 2001 and is based on the government's policy of reducing lists. Provider reimbursement prevails. The Tariffs Act (WTC) determines the price that may be declared by those providing care to the health care insurers. The WTG not only sets the prices and budgets for institutions but also the fees charged by independent professionals, through guideline tariffs for GPs, specialists, chemists, physiotherapists etc. (College Tarieven Gezondheidszorg 2000). However, insurers and suppliers may agree on a rate lower than the maximum rate given by the guidelines. Guidelines must be approved by the Ministry of Health and may be changed according to procedures set down by law. The formula used to calculate tariffs for professional individuals contains standard income plus standard costs divided by standard workload. The standard income contains elements such as salary, holiday bonus, insurances, social premiums and pension facilities. The government derives salaries from salary scales applied for civil servants employed by the national government. The guidelines also give the method employed to adjust these amounts each year.

In France, price and volume contracts, operational in hospitals since 1998, were shifted onto physicians in private practice in 1999 but were a spectacular failure. The SHI fixed a ceiling for global ambulatory expenditures (doctors' fees plus expenditures from doctors' prescriptions) by region. If a region overspent, doctors responsible for the additional expenditures were to pay back out of their pockets, while doctors in under-spending regions would receive additional payments. This bylaw was repealed by the French Supreme Court on the grounds that it created inequities, violated the constitution and was unethical in that it rewarded doctors for prescribing less than might be necessary (Or 2002). In Austria, it is also theoretically possible that physicians whose average 'consumption' is permanently above their colleagues' have to reimburse the differential amount. This measure has, however, rarely been applied in practice.

Austria provides a good example of the large variation within countries. Most health insurance agencies pay for primary care services provided to insured persons under a mixed compensation system of flat rates (remuneration for basic services) and fee-for-service payments. For the large majority of insured people, a flat rate is paid for a three-month period, regardless of how often services are required. The amount of the flat payment varies by specialty and state. Figure 9.1 shows the large spread of the fees per case across the nine regions relative to the Austrian average. Some of the differences might be due to incentives to attract physicians to rural areas. Some regions began to allocate a fixed percentage of the budget, earmarked for primary care, to the regional physicians association. This budgeting of primary care providers may be interpreted as a response to relatively higher fee levels. Doctors thus share the risk of fluctuations in the labour market with the insurance funds and thereby of contribution revenue.

Inpatient/outpatient care

As in primary care and consistent with theoretical findings (Ellis and McGurie 1986), supply-side cost sharing measures are increasingly used to enhance efficient allocation of hospital budgets in SHI countries. Budgets for individual

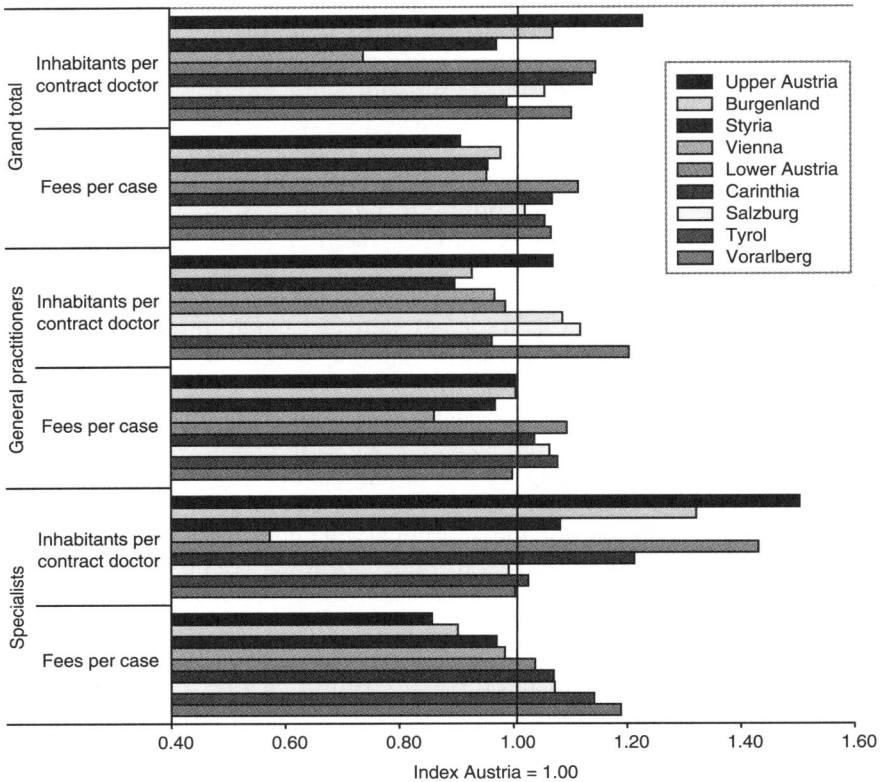

Figure 9.1 Population ratios and fees per case of contract physicians in Austrian states, 2000

Source: Federation of Austrian Social Security Institutions (HVSV) (2001).

hospitals are being calculated nationally and on a yearly basis in the Netherlands and Luxembourg. Germany, Israel and Switzerland have a mixed payment system combining per diem rates and case rates. In Switzerland, the implementation of DRGs has increased since 1995 replacing per diem rates (Bundesamt für Sozialversicherung 2000). In Austria, about half of the yearly budget for public hospitals is fixed. Of this share, 80 per cent is financed by the sickness funds and is also fixed. In general, flexible budgets or budgets that can be avoided (e.g. by referring to private hospitals in France) are not very effective. If budgets are well designed and fixed, though, they may affect quality (as in the Netherlands, where they created waiting lists).

Global budgets?

Evidence from France, Israel and the Netherlands suggests that budget restraints might not have been successful in containing cost and might have affected quality. In France, when a device has not received reimbursement approval but is considered medically useful, it will be used preferentially in public hospitals, which can use their global budget to purchase it, while devices with reimbursement approval and a high cost will be widely used in private clinics. Other types of contracts have been tested with limited success. Hospitals run large budget deficits and there are signs of hospital underinvestment. In the Netherlands, in the case of budget overruns, the funds must be compensated in the subsequent year. However, hospital budgets did not keep pace with the increase in demand for hospital care. Budgeting was considered to have eroded the fundamentals of insurance and it was decided to replace it with performance-related payments (Den Exter *et al.* 2002). Similarly, in Israel, huge budget overruns occurred and in the late 1990s the government provided extra funds. In Austria, although hospital cost growth rates slowed recently, there remains doubt as to whether this slow-down is attributable to the introduction of fixed-cost payment per case since the deceleration had begun in advance of the reform (Hofmarcher and Riedel 2003). In addition, case-load increased. Only some regions in the western part of Switzerland have introduced prospective global budgets. In those regions, hospital cost growth has stabilized; however, global budgets were initially set rather high, and thus their real relevance might be doubted. In almost all regions, regional hospital budgets for the share to be financed by canton were implemented. It has been found that global budgets have increased the cost awareness of physicians.

Capital costs

Hospital capital cost payment mechanisms are very diverse among SHI countries, but in general (local) governments maintain relatively large importance in the payment of these costs. Capital investments are seen as a responsibility of the governments because of the collective importance attached to adequately equip the diverse hospitals, the need for rational planning and the large cost involved.

In Austria, in addition to a portion of the current operating costs, investment and maintenance costs are borne by the owners (*Länder*, the federal government, public non-profit and other) and financed mainly via taxes. In Switzerland, while capital costs are mainly financed by the cantons, national legislation stipulates that in addition to the 50 per cent of total operating costs borne by the regions/hospital owners, provisions for investment and maintenance are also the responsibility of suppliers. Capital costs for Israeli hospitals are being borne by the sickness funds that own 9 per cent (2001) of the hospitals, however the major part is funded by the Ministry of Health in its capital budget. Capital costs in outpatient clinics in Israel are mainly borne by the sickness funds. The non-profit owners pay for the remaining share. In Luxembourg, the government finances up to 80 per cent of investments in the hospital sector. In Belgium, regions finance 60 per cent of capital costs, the remaining share being financed by federal taxes via per diem hospital payments. In the Netherlands, capital costs are paid for by the government. Location costs as a component of Dutch hospital budgets are concerned with the infrastructure of the institution, i.e., the costs of buildings and installations, such as depreciation and interest. The depreciation periods have been standardized. The costs of depreciation are also partly standard, and partly geared to reality (based on former approved investments). The interest paid is included in the institution's budget.

Pharmaceutical sector

In most countries, pharmaceutical spending has reached 10–15 per cent of the total health care budget. In the last decade, growth in drug spending has in most countries outpaced the rate of growth for both expenditure on inpatient care and ambulatory care (Hofmarcher *et al.* 2003). There is no uniform drug policy in SHI countries, and reimbursement and pricing varies considerably between the countries (Nuijten *et al.* 2001). Regarding drug reimbursements, SHI countries introduced various measures during the 1990s to contain accelerating increasing costs in this sector of their health systems. Although reimbursement modes differ widely, there are some similarities in actions taken including drug lists, budgets, monitoring of prescription behaviour and reference pricing (Rosian *et al.* 2001).

Contractual agreements for drugs are either negotiated for a given molecule (typically a new expensive one) or by supplier. In certain countries, the social health insurers will set a reimbursement price based on the sale price of the generic drug. This applies only to drugs with expired patents, but those may represent 50–60 per cent of sales volume. For innovative drugs, there are sometimes price-volume agreements whereby the manufacturer is granted reimbursement and a high price, providing that, if sales increase, the unit price will decrease accordingly. While the Netherlands and Germany have free – and thus higher – drug prices, France and Belgium have state-regulated prices (Pelen 2000). In France, the unit price is negotiated with the *Comité Economique des Produits de Santé* on the basis of *Amélioration du Service Médical Rendu* and the drug budget impact, while in Belgium the Ministry of Economic Affairs' Pricing Committee for Pharmaceutical Specialities sets the maximum price. These price controls seem to have had a cost-containing influence (Pelen 2000).

Whereas only Austria, Belgium and Germany have introduced a negative list (of only small scope), all SHI countries have established some kind of positive list. Table 9.3 shows that full reimbursement of reimbursable drugs is granted in Austria, Germany and the Netherlands. In Austria and the Netherlands co-payments such as a fixed amount per prescription for the compulsory insured were introduced in the 1980s and earlier. When co-payments started in the Netherlands, the number of prescriptions decreased, but the number of items per prescription increased and any cost-containing benefits from co-payments were offset by an increase in volume (Van Andel and Brinkman 1997). In France, private (and also some public) hospitals buy drugs through tenders. Private hospitals negotiate with the local sickness fund payer according to their activities to receive a fixed budget per patient for drugs (Nuijten *et al.* 2001). Budgets that provide incentives for volume controls are common and have been implemented in all SHI countries except in Luxembourg and Austria. In Germany, regional budgets are used to influence drug consumption. Generally, since budget overruns were not fully penalized – in spite of formal provisions – the

Table 9.3 Reimbursement rules in SHI countries 2000/1

| Country | Drug lists | | | Other reimbursement regulations | | | Price and volume indicators, 1999 | |
	Positive list(s)	Reimbursement rates (%)	Negative list(s)	Prescription guidelines	Budgets	Change in the number of prescriptions, index: 1990 = 100	Change of public expenditure on drugs, index: 1990 = 100
Belgium	X	100, 80, 75, 50, 40, 20	–	X	National planned budgets, sanctions possible with repayments	n.a.	106
Germany	X (planned)	100	X	X	Regional drug budgets for physicians (collective and individual liabilities)	–25	26
France	X	100, 65, 35	–	X	National planned budgets, repayment clause vs. individual contracts to fix turnovers	–	84
Luxembourg	X	100	–	–	–	4	19
Netherlands	X	100	–	–	National planned budgets without liability conditions	24	74
Austria	X	100	X	X	–	19	161

Source: Rosian *et al.* (2001).

effectiveness of this measure was limited (Rosian *et al.* 2001). Also in Belgium budgets are not enforced as there is an annual budgetary overspending.

It appears that those countries which have introduced both price and volume controls have been more successful in containing drug cost growth (Germany, the Netherlands). Further, the growth of public expenditure on drugs appears to outpace the increase in the number of prescriptions. Overall, average expenses per prescription have increased more than the number of prescriptions. This disproportionate growth may be attributable to the introduction of new, innovative high-price drugs, for which measures taken to contain cost growth apparently could not compensate.

Limited decision-making options for sickness funds

The health care package reimbursed by SHI is defined in a negotiating process between government, sickness funds and physicians, with the first generally having the decisive power. At the macro level, this process creates difficulties due to the absence of a clear relationship between expenditures and outcomes, while at the micro level problems arise from the limited scope of evidence-based medicine and the difficulty in assessing providers' performance. Other factors such as the number of specialist physicians influence the choice of contractual agreements. When the ratio of specialists to GPs is high, for example, gatekeeping systems are difficult to implement. When hospital and ambulatory care budgets are separated and allocated through different mechanisms, effective management of care requires complicated coordination measures. Decision-making options for sickness funds are constrained by national laws stipulating the services to be provided within a specified benefit package. While the government is the final financial decision-making power, sickness funds have obtained more autonomy in several countries in designing patient and physician payment mechanisms.

In Austria, for instance, the regional sickness funds, being a principal partner of the HVSV in regular volume and price negotiations, are rather strong. Generally, however, the scope of autonomy of insurance funds is rather limited as federal law largely determines their obligations towards beneficiaries. It appears that big regional sickness funds exert the greatest autonomous power. As a consequence, regional interest may prevail over general price and volume policies as pursued by the Federation.

In Israel, decision-making by sickness funds regarding providers is influenced by overall government policies, as the health insurance budget is largely financed by taxes. However, sick funds retain considerable authority, exercised through closure of clinics on evenings and weekends, restrictions on referrals to outside therapists and hospital outpatient clinics, cutbacks in non-insured services and increases in drug prices beyond the limits set by the Knesset Finance Committee. Also, to collect the co-payments previously authorized, they charged members full prices and promised refunds for which they had not created a mechanism.

Supplemental coverage

In addition to traditions within each welfare state regarding the scope and the type of contracting (see above), the degree of freedom to contract with providers is further bound by political goals regarding comprehensiveness and universality of coverage. This would not be an issue in Beveridge systems but is a feature of almost all SHI systems (see Chapter 1). This is particularly true in France, where the SHI system covers 100 per cent of the population but only for a limited share of their health care expenditures. Since supplemental insurance is believed to be a necessary mechanism to prevent overuse of health care services, the SHI funds step in to offer supplemental insurance in addition to core insurance. Supplemental insurance vouchers are offered to the population under a certain ceiling of resources and the insurer could be either the core insurer or any other. As it happens, persons in the less favoured population groups tend to know about the SHI funds and naturally turn to them when having to choose supplemental coverage. In most SHI systems a baseline fee is negotiated and used to set the reimbursement rate by the public insurance, while supplemental insurance reimburses a complement to the baseline fee plus some or all of the extra money that providers charge. When the SHI steps in as a provider of supplemental insurance, contracts with providers in private practice seek to reduce or eliminate the ability of health care providers to charge above the baseline fee or to be paid for it. One type of such negotiation ended up by mandating that health care providers accept the baseline fee for all patients whose supplemental insurer is an SHI provider and not directly bill patients (who may not be able to pay) but bill the SHI provider. In exchange, providers are guaranteed speedy payment.

The advantage of providing access to supplemental insurance for needy persons is to fulfil the mission of public service and solidarity. The risk of such contracts with providers in private practice is creating adverse selection in the patient population: providers who are 'successful' and charge considerably above the baseline fee have no incentive other than compassion to treat (particularly in the case of chronic conditions) this group of poorly financed and often medically demanding patients.

Conclusion

Contracts vary widely among SHI countries and within SHI countries' health care systems. In addition, the degree of dissemination of contracts differs greatly. Whereas sickness funds are most likely to have the greatest leverage upon individual, self-employed providers in primary care, their options for contracting in inpatient care as well as in the pharmaceutical sector are constrained. Moreover, sickness funds' defensive role resulting from both the implementation of federal laws with regard to new services to be rendered and from their structural information disadvantage as purchasers appears to be aggravated when budgeting is introduced. In addition, collective contracting appears to have prevailed at least in the public sector of SHI countries' health systems.

Reasons for this may be found in the likelihood of high transaction costs (including cost for information gathering) for sickness funds when contracting with individual providers. However, individual contracting seems to be more common with private hospitals and institutions.

With regard to payment mechanisms, SHI countries increasingly introduced mixed schemes in the primary care sector and some countries have started to experiment with managed care models. However, performance-oriented contracting nevertheless appears to be rather the exception than the rule. Utilization reviews, a tool which was found to help contain costs and which in addition strengthens ties between providers and sickness funds to facilitate contracting more effectively, appear not to be evenly and regularly implemented in SHI countries. Further, even though theoretical and empirical evidence suggests that fixed cost per case payments (i.e. DRGs) are superior to cost reimbursement in the hospital sector, only one SHI country has so far introduced this scheme on a comprehensive and nationwide basis. Budgets to accompany drug provision appear to help sickness funds more effectively in containing cost growth for reimbursed drugs than solely reimbursement rules to follow and/or price negotiations.

References

Aguzzoli, F., Aligon, A., Com-Ruelle, L. and Frérot, L. (1999) Questions d'économie de la santé, *Bulletin d'information en économie de la santé*, 23 November.

Bundesamt für Sozialversicherung (2000) *Auswirkungen des KVG im Tarifbereich*. Zürich: INFRAS.

Chalkely, M. and Malcomson, J.M. (2000) Government purchasing of health services, in A.J. Culyer and J.P. Newhouse (eds) *Handbook of Health Economics*, Vol. 1A. Amsterdam: Elsevier Science, 462–874.

College Tarieven Gezondheidszorg (2000) *What is the National Health Tariffs Authority?* Utrecht: College Tarieven Gezondheidszorg (until January 2000: Centraal Orgaan Tarieven Gezondheidszorg).

Den Exter, A.P., Hermans, H., Dosljak, M. and Busse, R. (2002) *Health Care Systems in Transition – the Netherlands*. Copenhagen: European Observatory on Health Care Systems (to be published).

Dor, A. and Farley, D.E. (1996) Payment source and the cost of hospital care: evidence from a multiproduct cost function with multiple payers, *Journal of Health Economics*, 15: 1–21.

Dranove, D. (1988) Pricing by non-profit institutions, the case of hospital cost-shifting, *Journal of Health Economics*, 7: 47–57.

Durand-Zaleski, I., Colin, C. and Blum-Boisgard, C. (1997) An attempt to save money by using mandatory practice guidelines in France, *British Medical Journal*, 315: 943–6.

Ellis, R.P. and McGurie, T.G. (1986) Provider behaviour under prospective reimbursement: cost sharing and supply, *Journal of Health Economics*, 5: 129–51.

Emphasis (1999) *Der Patient im Mittelpunkt-Einstellungen und Erwartungen der Bevölkerung zum Gesundheitswesen der Zukunft*. Munich: Emphasis (Institut für Marktforschung im Gesundheitswesen).

Eugster, G. (1998) Krankenversicherung, in H. Koller, G. Müller, R. Rhinow and U.

Zimmerli (eds) *Schweizerisches Bundesverwaltungsrecht.* Basel/Genf/München: Helbing und Lichtenhahn Verlag AG.

Federation of Austrian Social Security Institutions (HVSV) (2001), IHS HealthEcon calculation 2001. Vienna: Federation of Austrian Social Security Institutions.

Gaynor, M. and Gertler, P.J. (1995) Moral hazard and risk spreading in medical partnerships, *Rand Journal of Economics*, 26(4): 591–613.

Gaynor, M. and Mark, T. (1999) *Physician Contracting with Health Plans: A Survey of the Literature.* Pittsburgh, PA: Carnegie Mellon University.

Gaynor, M., Rebitzer, J.B. and Taylor, L.J. (2001) *Incentives in HMOs.* Pittsburgh, PA: Carnegie Mellon University.

Glied, S. (2000) Managed care, in A.J. Culyer and J.P. Newhouse (eds) *Handbook of Health Economics*, Vol. 1B, pp. 462–517. Amsterdam: Elsevier Science.

Hofmarcher, M.M. and Riedel, M. (1999) Rather healthy and rich than ill and much less well off: development of the age structure within the European Union. Core subject: Managed care – Part 2, in Institute for Advanced Studies, *Health System Watch*, III/fall, http://www.ihs.ac.at/departments/fin/HealthEcon/watch/hsw99_3e.pdf (accessed 18 August 2003).

Hofmarcher, M.M. and Riedel, M. (2003) *Impact of Case-Mix Hospital Payment Reforms on Health Systems: Case Study Austria.* Vienna: Institute for Advanced Studies (Research Report commissioned by the World Bank, January 2003).

Hofmarcher, M.M. and Röhrling, G. (2003) Health expenditure in the EU: comparability is ailing. Focus: forecast of health expenditure, in Institute for Advanced Studies, *Health System Watch*, I/Spring, http://www.ihs.ac.at/departments/fin/HealthEcon/watch/hsw03_1e.pdf (accessed 18 August 2003).

Hofmarcher, M.M., Riedel, M. and Röhrling, G. (2003) Resourcenverbrauch in der EU: 'Wachstumspillen' für die Gesundheitsausgaben. Schwerpunktthema: Fallpauschalen im ambulanten Sektor, in Institute for Advanced Studies, *Health System Watch*, II/Summer, http://www.ihs.ac.at/departments/fin/HealthEcon/watch/hsw03_2d.pdf (accessed 18 August 2003).

Holmström, B. (1979) Moral hazard and observability, *The Bell Journal of Economics*, 10(1): 74–91.

IHS HealthEcon (2003) www.ihs.ac.at (accessed 18 August 2003).

Israel Yearbook and Almanac (1999) *Health chapter.* Jerusalem: IBRT Translation/Documentation Ltd.

Kerr, E. (2000) *Health Care Systems in Transition – Belgium.* Copenhagen: European Observatory on Health Care Systems.

McGurie, Th. G. (2000) Physician agency, in A.J. Culyer and J.P. Newhouse (eds) *Handbook of Health Economics*, Vol. 1A, pp. 462–517. Amsterdam: Elsevier.

Nuijten, M.J.C., Berto, P., Berdeaux, G., Hutton, J., Fricke, F.-U. and Villar, F.A. (2001) Trends in decision-making process for pharmaceuticals in Western European countries: a focus on emerging hurdles for obtaining reimbursement and a price, *Health Economics in Prevention and Care*, 2: 162–9.

OECD (2003) *OECD Health Data 2003: A Comparative Analysis of 30 Countries*, 2nd edn. Paris: OECD.

Or, Z. (2002) *Improving the Performance of Health Care Systems: From Measures to Action: A Review of Experiences in Four OECD Countries*, Labour Market and Social Policy, Occasional papers no. 57. Paris: OECD.

Pelen, F. (2000) Reimbursement and pricing of drugs in France: an increasingly complex system, *Health Economics in Prevention and Care*, 0: 20–3.

Rosian, I., Habl, C. and Vogler, S. (2001) *Arzneimittel: Steuerung der Märkte in neun europäischen Ländern.* Vienna: Austrian Health Institute (ÖBIG).

Van Andel, F.G. and Brinkman, N. (1997) Government policy and cost containment of pharmaceuticals, in A.J.P. Schrijvers (ed.) *Health and Health Care in the Netherlands: A Critical Self-assessment by Dutch Experts in the Medical and Health Services*, pp. 152–62. Maarssen: Elsevier/De Tijdstroom.

WHO (2003) *WHO European Health for All Database*. Copenhagen: WHO Regional Office for Europe, June.

Wyler, D. (2001) Tarife, in G. Kocher and W. Oggier (eds) *Gesundheitswesen Schweiz 2001/2002*. Basel: Konkordat der Schweizerischen Krankenversicherer.

chapter ten

The role of private health insurance in social health insurance countries[1]

Jürgen Wasem, Stefan Greß and Kieke G.H. Okma

Introduction

Private health insurance (PHI) serves three distinct functions in western European health systems (Timmer 1990; Schneider 1995; Wasem and Greß 2002).[2] The first is as an *alternative* for mandatory (statutory) social health insurance (SHI) arrangements. In some countries (Netherlands), certain population groups not covered by the mandatory social insurance can opt to seek insurance in the private market. In other countries (Germany), insured persons have a choice between joining PHI and remaining in SHI when their incomes surpass the eligibility ceiling. The second function is to *supplement* statutory insurance, providing coverage for services not covered by social insurance, for example dental care for adults, homeopathic drugs or cosmetic surgery. In some countries (Belgium, France), insured persons take out supplementary insurance to cover the financial risks of co-payments and co-insurance. A third function of PHI is to provide what can be termed *complementary* coverage, in which insured persons purchase additional private insurance even while they have to participate in existing social schemes. This form is mostly found in tax-financed countries that have a separate, privately-financed system parallel to the public sector, and thus we do not cover it here.

The countries studied in this chapter all have a mix of social and private funding of their health care systems with a dominant role for SHI. There is alternative PHI only in Germany and the Netherlands.[3] Supplementary PHI for services not covered in the basic benefits package of SHI is available in all countries.[4] Supplementary PHI to cover co-payment is common only in Belgium and

France. Not only form and function but also extent of PHI differs quite significantly. Expenditures of PHI measured as share of total health care expenditures vary from less than 5 per cent in Belgium and Luxembourg to more than 15 per cent in the Netherlands (2000 data) (Comité Europeén des Assurances 2000; OECD 2003).

Health policy-makers face several key challenges when regulating PHI markets, depending on the function PHI fulfils. The need for regulation is usually much higher for alternative PHI than for supplementary PHI (Jost 2001). If PHI is to be compatible with prevalent solidarity-based value systems, regulation has to ensure access to private insurance cover for bad risks such as the chronically ill. At the same time, premiums have to be affordable, especially for ageing policy-holders (Wasem and Greß 2002). The second section of this chapter reviews how regulation in Germany and the Netherlands has sought to solve these problems for alternative PHI.

The market for supplementary health insurance depends very much on the extent of the basic benefits package in SHI – both in terms of services and in terms of co-payments (see Chapter 8). If benefits of SHI are rather comprehensive and of good quality and if co-payments are low, supplementary PHI typically covers only luxury goods (e.g. more comfortable board and lodging in hospitals). As a consequence, a smaller degree of regulation for supplementary PHI as opposed to alternative PHI is justifiable in terms of social acceptability. The third section reviews supplementary PHI in Austria, Belgium, Germany, Israel, the Netherlands and Switzerland, paying close attention to access problems resulting from supplementary PHI.

Alternative PHI

In both Germany and the Netherlands, governments regulate alternative PHI quite extensively in order to assure access and affordable premiums for bad risks. Both governments require private health insurers to offer standard contracts, and both also regulate market activities in many other ways. Before considering these regulations and their effect, it is useful to describe the manner of premium calculation in PHI as opposed to calculation of contributions in SHI.

Calculation of premiums in PHI vs. calculation of contributions in SHI

One of the most important differences between social and private health insurance (PHI) is the setting of premiums (private health insurers) and contributions (social health insurers). Figure 10.1 displays the basic methods of premium calculation.

Pay-as-you-go means that premiums or contributions of all insured persons of this year finance the benefits of health insurance of the same. Since health care costs typically rise with age, this model usually leads to a redistribution from the young to the elderly over time. In *age-group-specific pay-as-you-go* systems, premiums of all insured within one age group of this year are used to finance the

	Income-related contributions	*Community rating*	*Risk-related premiums*
Pay-as-you-go	SHI Germany Long-term care insurance AWBZ Netherlands	PHI Netherlands (standard contracts of the WTZ scheme, and collective contracts for employed)	
	SHI Netherlands (income related contribution plus nominal payment)		
Age-group-specific pay-as-you-go			PHI Netherlands
Capital funded			PHI Germany
		Private mandatory long-term care insurance Germany PHI Germany (standard contracts)	

Figure 10.1 Calculation of premiums for alternative PHI and SHI contributions

Source: Wasem (2000).

benefits of the private health insurer for this age group. Since healthcare costs rise with age, the younger age groups pay lower premiums than older age groups, so that the benefits are covered by the premiums. In such an approach there is no redistribution from the young to the elderly. In *capital funded* systems, premiums paid by the young finance their health care benefits today, but also include a saving component in order to finance part of the higher health care costs of older age. This system is only used in some PHI systems, most predominantly in Germany. With this approach, premiums typically rise with the age in which the insured person enters the contract.

Income-related contributions are not related to individual health risks but to the income of the insured. A certain percentage of income is paid as a contribution to the social health insurer. Higher income people therefore pay higher amounts than lower income people, such that this method of premium calculation leads to income solidarity. There is also risk solidarity – when healthy people pay the same percentage of contributions as sick people – and solidarity between generations since social health insurers usually calculate on a pay-as-you-go basis. *Community-rated* premiums or contributions are the same for all insured of one health insurer. This method realizes risk solidarity because it leads to redistribution between the healthy and the sick. However, particularly when the pools of insured are relatively small, it does not achieve income solidarity. *Risk-related* premium calculation is typically applied by private health insurers. Individuals pay a premium according to individual risk – people with high health risks (typically, the old, sick and chronically ill) pay high premiums, people with low health risks (typically, the young and healthy) pay low premiums.

Social health insurers in Germany and the Netherlands charge income-related contributions on a pay-as-you-go basis. However, a small part of contributions in the Netherlands are community-rated. Private health insurers charge risk-related premiums, either capital funded (Germany) or on an age-group-specific pay-as-you-go basis (Netherlands). However, in both countries private health insurers are influenced by society's and consequently government's view of solidarity and thus have to offer standard contracts with community rating (Netherlands) or limited risk rating (Germany).[5] As the premiums of standard contracts, on average, do not cover all health expenditure of the insured, all other private insured face an additional premium to pool towards excess costs.

Markets for alternative PHI

Although Germany and the Netherlands share some common characteristics of alternative PHI, there are also some important differences. This section reviews common characteristics as well as differences with regard to the extent of the market for alternative PHI, the determination of premiums and benefits in non-standard as well as in standard contracts and the relationship of alternative PHI to providers.

Market structure

In the Netherlands, most higher-income residents who are not eligible for sickness fund insurance opt out to take PHI with one of the 40 or so private health insurance (PHI) companies.[6] Less than 1 per cent of Dutch residents do not have any health insurance at all, consisting mostly of illegal residents and groups refusing insurance due to religious reasons. Like sickness funds, private health insurers are legally independent enterprises. By law, they cannot produce or sell other services outside PHI. In mid-2001, there were 24 for-profit and 17 not-for-profit private health insurers offering alternative PHI. There are no significant differences of actual market behaviour between these groups.

In the last decade, private health insurers have strengthened their collaboration with the sickness funds for several reasons. Although obliged to keep separate legal entities due to different supervisory regimes, they have joined forces under the umbrella of larger finance banking and insurance conglomerates. In doing so, they have gained access to the addresses of the sickness fund insured to whom they can offer other insurance. They also benefit from the long experience of sickness funds in local and regional contracting with health care providers. Similarly, sickness funds have benefited from the administrative experience of the PHI business. They have expanded traditional health insurance to a wider range of collective insurance and employee benefits packages, both for the sickness fund insured and privately insured, under the umbrella of the larger conglomerates. Such packages have gained importance in the Dutch market, in particular after recent changes in other social insurance legislation shifted some of the financial risks for sickness and disability from social insurance to the employers, who in turn started seeking insurance coverage for their risks (Greß 2000).[7]

In Germany, the border between SHI and PHI has been stable since the 1970s when the last major occupational group (agricultural workers) was brought into the system of SHI. While about 90 per cent of the population is socially insured, around 8 per cent (or 7.5 million persons in 2000) are covered by alternative PHI. They consist of three major groups: the self-employed, civil servants and those employees above the income threshold. There is a significant difference to the situation in the Netherlands – in Germany all three groups can choose to stay as voluntary members in SHI when their income surpasses the income ceiling. If they opt for private insurance when becoming self-employed, civil servants or when surpassing the income threshold (or later on), they are more or less prohibited from returning to a social insurer in the future.

In 1999 there were 30 for-profit and 22 not-for-profit private insurers in Germany. However, there are no significant differences in the market strategies of these groups. Both groups have about the same market share. Private and social insurers both compete for high-earning employees with incomes above the income threshold. Due to the manner of premium calculation, private health insurers (for-profit as well not-for-profit) compete extensively for new contracts but it is not profitable for insured persons to switch to another private health insurer after having been insured privately for some time, because they lose the capital which has been built up in the capital-funded scheme.

Premiums and coverage

In the Netherlands, private insurers can decide to accept or decline applicants, set financial conditions, determine their range of benefits and adjust their premiums according to the risk structure of the insured. They offer a wide range of insurance policies, with varying coverage, deductibles and eligibility criteria. In general, the coverage is at least as wide as that of the SHI ZFW and includes medical care, hospital stay, drugs and medical aids, and some other services. As there is no standardized package of entitlements, coverage varies. Furthermore, private health insurers can exclude pre-existing conditions from coverage. There is no government regulation of premiums or coverage, but the most important association of the health insurers, *Zorgverzekeraars Nederland*, consults each year with its members in an effort to avoid excessive cost increases.

In practice, Dutch private insurers have never charged fully risk-related premiums.[8] Until the 1970s, most if not all charged community-based premiums for all of their insured. In the early 1970s, one of the private companies started to offer cheap policies to students. Other companies followed and then charged higher rates to elderly insured. They also started to refuse high-risk groups and to exclude pre-existing conditions from coverage. This triggered a spiral of premium differentiation and risk selection. After the private insurers failed to implement an informal agreement to solve these problems, the Dutch government felt obliged to step in and take measures to counteract the newly-created access barriers to PHI (Okma 1997).

Incentives for cream-skimming are further reduced by the fact that so-called catastrophic risks and long-term care are not covered by the insurance policies offered by private health insurers or by sickness funds. These risks are covered by a separate 'exceptional' insurance scheme, AWBZ, which is obligatory for the whole population (see Chapter 13). Social as well as private health insurers simply administer this scheme on behalf of their insured but face no financial risk in doing so. AWBZ premiums are income-dependent and uniform across the country. Since insurance agencies receive full compensation for their costs, they have no incentive for risk selection.

In Germany, premium calculation of alternative PHI is capital funded and risk related. Although in theory premiums are not supposed to be increased in later life, in fact they are adjusted from time to time to account for increasing health care expenditures, since the first premium calculation (when joining the insurance) is done on the then existing level of health care costs. In order to avoid an excessive increase of premiums, especially for the elderly, since 2000 private health insurers have had to add a flat 10 per cent on individual premiums for new contracts to compensate for increasing health care expenditures. This additional premium is to be saved by the insurer and shall be used to finance rising health care costs when the insured have passed the age of 65. Government regulation restricts the degree of risk rating. The insurer assesses the risk of the insured *once*, at the beginning of the insurance contract, in a process called *underwriting*. However, insurers are not allowed to reassess the health risk during the insurance contract or to cancel the contract. Consequently, changes in health risk after the start of the contract cannot lead to changes in the premiums to be paid by the insured.[9]

In Germany, high income employees and (under certain conditions) the self-employed can leave SHI and opt for alternative PHI (whereas average and low income employees must remain in the statutory system). Not surprisingly, high income employees and the self-employed in poor health normally do not leave SHI, since they would have to pay higher premiums in alternative PHI. Among the self-employed in good health, only high income people leave SHI, because for low income people SHI provides the cheaper benefit package. It is also unattractive to switch to alternative PHI if there are several children and a non-working spouse in the family. In SHI, these dependants are covered by the contributions of the employee or self-employed, while in PHI they are covered individually and according to risk. Thus, PHI is more attractive to single people and double-income couples – at least, when they are young and healthy. While it is quite easy to switch to PHI for those who are no longer mandatorily insured with SHI, since the 2000 Health Reform Act it has become extremely difficult to switch back to SHI. However, in the same Health Reform Act, coverage for the standard policy has been expanded (see below). Less than a quarter of persons with earnings above the income ceiling actually switch to private insurance (Mossialos and Thomson 2001). Half of the individuals who opt for alternative PHI are young, single, high earners or married couples with double incomes, and half are civil servants (Mossialos and Thomson 2001).[10]

While private insurers are free to offer a large variety of benefit packages, cost-sharing arrangements and premiums, the policy conditions of health insurance policies must be approved by an independent trustee. An independent trustee also checks if the premium calculation complies with the legal provisions on calculations designed to ensure that the interests of the insured are protected. Waiting periods may last three months before coverage begins.[11] Newborns of insured are covered immediately, regardless of their health status. No waiting periods are allowed with regard to persons switching from SHI funds. In general, children are charged a fixed premium.

Standard contracts

In principle, all applicants have a choice of insurers of alternative PHI in either Germany or the Netherlands. However, in practice this freedom is curtailed by risk selection practices of the insurers. Since there is no legal obligation to accept anyone seeking insurance, private insurers may refuse individuals trying to get cover, charge higher premiums to high-risk groups or exclude pre-existing conditions altogether. Insurers also offer collective contracts to certain groups they see as attractive (e.g. white-collar office workers). This means that in practice, freedom of choice is limited to young and healthy persons. Thus, the elderly and other persons perceived as high risk because of genetic disposition, family history of chronic illness or past experience, face access barriers in seeking alternative health insurance.

In the Netherlands, private insurers have engaged in selection activities, but they have also shown restraint in this regard, realizing that such practice is viewed negatively in egalitarian Dutch society. Reflecting this public perspective, the Dutch government passed regulation concerning standard contracts with private insurers.[12] The government determines coverage and cost-sharing arrangements of the WTZ (*Wet op de Toegang tot Ziektekostenverzekering*, Health Insurance Access Act) standard contract scheme. Benefits are (almost) identical to the sickness fund insurance coverage. Illustrating the importance of the WTZ as a risk-pooling mechanism for high-risk groups in the private market, the share of PHI expenditure financed by PHI under the standard contract was approximately 30 per cent in 1998 (Vektis 2000).

Eligible for the standard contract are:

- Persons who are required to leave the SHI programme when their incomes surpass the eligibility ceiling; they have to register within one year.
- Persons who are uninsured and did not know or reasonably could not be expected to know that they presented above-average risks.
- Persons moving to the Netherlands previously insured elsewhere.
- Persons over the age of 65 who previously had some other kind of private insurance.
- Privately insured persons who pay more than the maximum standard policy premium for their age group.
- Privately insured students.

The insured with standard contracts pay government-controlled premiums. As this premium does not fully cover the average cost of the WTZ insured, all other privately insured participate in a mandatory cost-sharing system by paying an additional premium each year. The government adjusts the premium each year by looking at the average costs over a moving three-year average, but may deviate from this adjustment because of other financial considerations. In 2001, government-controlled premiums were at a maximum of €115 per person per month. As a consequence of mandatory cost-sharing, private health insurers do not have any incentive to improve cost-effectiveness of health care provision for standard contracts. For a substantial part of their customers they have become purely administrative bodies – even more so than sickness funds.

In Germany, private health insurers are not obliged to offer standard contracts by law. However, they are only eligible to receive half of the premium for employees by their respective employers if they do so. Eligible for the standard contract are (Verband der privaten Krankenversicherung e.V. 2000b):

- Persons 65 years of age and older. They have to have pre-insurance in any alternative PHI of at least ten years (supplementary insurance does not count).
- Persons 55 years of age and older if they have pre-insurance (same as 1) or have an income below the income ceiling (c. €40,000).
- Civil servants under the same conditions as 1 and 2.
- Persons under the age of 55 if they receive a pension of any kind (e.g. disability pension), have an income below the income ceiling as in 2 and have pre-insurance as in 1.
- High-risk civil servants who would have to pay risk premiums for alternative PHI.

Deficits incurred by standard policies are compensated across all private health insurers, although the pooling mechanisms leave some incentives for efficiency for the insurers. According to the law, benefits of the standard policy have to be comparable to the standard package of SHI.[13] In fact they are not exactly the same but quite similar and uniform across all private health insurers. The Federal Insurance Supervisory Office controls the comparability of the benefits package as well as the pooling mechanism.

While at the end of 1999 only 1400 persons were covered by the standard policy, this number had increased to 3000 (or 0.04 per cent of all persons with alternative PHI) by the end of 2000 (Verband der privaten Krankenversicherung e.V. 2001). The small number of insured covered by the standard policy is probably due to the fact that the maximum premium for the standard policy is pegged to SHI levels and is based on the average contribution rate of SHI of the year before. The maximum premium of the standard contract is calculated by applying the average contribution rate to the income ceiling of SHI. Spouses pay 50 per cent of the maximum premium if household income is below the income ceiling.

Relationship with providers

Private insurers in the Netherlands, unlike sickness funds, are not obliged to contract with providers (see Chapter 9). However, they increasingly do so. If they do contract providers they face the same kind of price regulation as sickness funds. Within legal limits (maximum prices), private insurers and sickness funds negotiate with health care providers about prices and fees. In practice they usually agree on the maximum price. Following the rules of social insurance, many private insurers require that patients obtain a referral from a GP for medical treatment by specialists or in a hospital. However, due to competitive pressure they have been reluctant to enforce that rule. Referrals are quite difficult to control (Okma 1997). Traditionally, privately insured persons themselves pay their GP, medical specialists and other health care services by fee-for-service, handing in their bills to their insurer for reimbursement. In recent years, PHI companies in the Netherlands have increasingly arranged to pay the providers directly. The fees for the medical specialists used to be more than twice as high as for SHI but in 1997 government passed a law eliminating this difference.

In Germany, private health insurers do not have contractual relationships with health care providers. Thus, insurers do not negotiate with providers about tariffs and prices. However, the Ministry of Health regulates the maximum fee physicians or dentists may charge for the treatment of privately insured persons. This maximum amount is much higher than the payments health care professionals receive from social health insurers.[14] In hospital, charges are the same for standard treatment, but extra charges have to be paid for a private room and for seeing the chief medical officer privately. With regard to drugs, prices for those privately insured are 5 per cent higher than for SHI patients, since pharmacies must give a rebate of 5 per cent to SHI. With regard to long-term care insurance, prices for standard treatment are the same for insured of SHI and PHI. Payment modalities of health care providers are the same for all private insurers. The insurer reimburses the expenses of the patient. Thus, the patient can choose a provider without the need for approval of the health insurer.

Market outcome of alternative PHI

This section assesses the market outcome of alternative PHI. It focuses on equity in finance as well as in delivery of health care services. It also considers effects on cost containment.

Effects on fairness in health care finance

Health care in Germany and in the Netherlands is funded out of a complex mix of sources. Privately insured persons pay risk-related premiums that in general have a regressive effect. In the case of individual insurance contracts, there is no income solidarity and little, if any, risk solidarity. There is risk solidarity but still no income solidarity if premiums are community-rated.

In Germany, self-employed and high-income insured in poor health who have chosen to stay in SHI may be subsidized by those average and low income employees who are mandatorily insured in social insurance and cannot switch to private insurance.[15] It is likely that those who profit individually from opting out are the young and healthy, thus increasing the burden of high-cost groups for social insurance. In terms of fairness and social justice the consequences of this situation are rather undesirable.

In the Netherlands it is also clear that forcing all high income employees to leave SHI has redistributive consequences as the risk pooling of social insurance is limited to lower income groups. In order to compensate for the over-representation of elderly insured under the sickness fund scheme, private insured have to pay a solidarity contribution.

Effects on equity in health care delivery

In the Netherlands, actual health services are almost identical for sickness fund members and private insured. Dutch society values equality very highly.[16] In the second half of the 1990s, there was a quite heated discussion about preferential access to health care facilities for employees. Employers facing increased financial risks of absenteeism of disabled and sick workers were seeking ways to circumvent waiting lists for specialist and for some elective procedures in hospitals (Brouwer and Hermans 1999; Brouwer and Schut 1999). In some cases, the cost of such priority access was covered by the wider employee benefit schemes offered by the health insurance conglomerates.

Although there is no clear evidence available, privately insured persons in Germany appear to receive more comprehensive and faster treatment than persons with social insurance than is the case in the Netherlands. This is due to the fact that in Germany there are tight budgets for ambulatory and hospital care financed by sickness funds. Providers have substantial incentives to treat privately insured patients preferentially since they can charge higher prices and this income does not decrease their budget. Of course, the behaviour of health care professionals is not determined by economic incentives only, but several surveys point out that privately insured persons feel that their relationship with providers is less determined by economic constraints than socially insured persons do (Braun 2000).

Effects on cost containment

It is not uncommon in countries with a large private health care sector that providers charge higher prices for privately insured persons in order to compensate for lower prices for socially insured persons (Germany, USA). This is not common practice in the Netherlands, since reimbursement of private insurers to providers is regulated by government and private insurers are not allowed to pay higher fees for their insured. This also reduces the incentives for preferential treatment of privately insured compared to socially insured.

In Germany, cost containment of social health insurers is affected by the existence of alternative PHI in several ways (Greß and Wasem 2001; Klingenberger 2001). However, the net effect is unclear: private health insurers are quite successful in picking good risks while the bad risks remain in SHI. As mostly the young and healthy with higher incomes above the income ceiling will opt out of the public scheme, loss of income for social health insurers is quite substantial. People who switch on average incur less expenses than persons who do not and social health insurers have to cover the bad risks remaining. Consequently, the financial situation of social health insurers would improve substantially if all people above the income ceiling had to remain in SHI.

However, there are several factors counteracting this tendency. First, providers are reimbursed by private health insurance (PHI) on a much higher level than by social health insurers. This in fact leads to cross-subsidies back to SHI, as many providers would be hard pressed financially if they had only patients covered by social health insurers. Second, all civil servants including high-risk civil servants are privately insured. Since civil servants have a lower than average income this leads to relief for SHI. Third, the standard policy, especially for older persons, as well as severe restrictions on returning to SHI when reaching the age of 55, increases the share of older persons in PHI. Finally, people leaving SHI now may decrease the financial burden on SHI in 2030/2040, when contribution rates will grow due to the demographic developments in the SHI system (Hof 2001). Unfortunately, there are no reliable calculations to show whether alternative PHI in Germany leads to higher or lower contribution rates for social health insurers.

It is quite clear, however, that alternative PHI is less effective with regard to cost containment than SHI, especially in ambulatory care. Between 1991 and 1999 per capita expenditure for ambulatory care rose by 62 per cent in the private sector compared to 25 per cent in the public sector, while pharmaceuticals rose by 56 per cent and 13 per cent respectively. Hospital expenditures increased more or less to the same degree (Verband der privaten Krankenversicherung e.V. 2000c). The reasons for this disparate development seem to be quite clear – higher prices for services and less budgetary restraints in alternative PHI. Administrative and marketing costs for private insurance range between 11 and 13 per cent of premium income (Verband der privaten Krankenversicherung e.V. 2000a). Administrative costs for sickness funds are about five per cent.

Supplementary PHI

Whereas alternative PHI is available only in the Netherlands and Germany, supplementary PHI is available in the other SHI countries covered by this chapter as well. This section consists of two parts. First, it summarizes the way supplementary PHI is organized in Austria, Belgium, France, Germany, Israel, the Netherlands and Switzerland following common criteria. Second, it assesses the effects of supplementary PHI, especially with regard to access.

Markets for Supplementary PHI

The size of the market for supplementary PHI differs significantly in the seven countries. The share of supplementary PHI of total health care expenditures in 1998 was less than 5 per cent in Belgium, Germany, Israel and the Netherlands (Comité Européen des Assurances 2000; Vektis 2000; Verband der privaten Krankenversicherung e.V. 2000c; Gross 2001). The respective shares of expenditures are much higher in France and in Switzerland – between 10 and 13 per cent of total health care expenditures (2000 data) (Colombo 2001; OECD 2003). Austria is in between these two groups of countries – the share for supplementary PHI in this country is around 7 per cent (OECD 2003). Data for annual growth rates of supplementary PHI are incomplete and there is no uniform development in the seven countries. Annual premium income is increasing steadily in France, in Germany and to a lesser extent in the Netherlands. There is an exorbitant increase of premium income of supplementary PHI in Belgium. Annual growth rates from 1995 to 1998 were around 15 per cent. Premium income is decreasing slowly in Austria although coverage for SHI has been

238 Social Health Insurance Systems

reduced – which may be due to a high propensity of Austrians to accept out-of-pocket payments (Hofmarcher and Riedel 2001). The introduction of a new Health Insurance Law in Switzerland has led to an increased basic benefits package in SHI and to a subsequent decrease of premium income of supplementary PHI of 15 per cent (Colombo 2001).

The market structure of supplementary PHI also differs in the seven countries. Both for-profit and not-for-profit insurers offer supplementary PHI in Belgium, France, Germany, Israel and the Netherlands. In Austria, for-profit insurers dominate the market completely.[17] In other countries, the market shares of for-profit insurers range from around 25 per cent (Belgium, France, Israel) to 50 per cent (Germany, Netherlands).[18] There is no general tendency as to market behaviour of for-profit insurers and not-for-profit insurers. In France, non-profit mutual insurance companies (*mutuelles*) existed long before the social security scheme was created in 1945 and their traditional market was partially taken away from them at that time. They claim to be less inclined toward risk selection. For-profit insurers came into the market only in the 1980s. They position themselves as risk managers and their premiums seem to vary more with risk than those of the *mutuelles* (Couffinhal 2001). The situation is very similar in Belgium. *Mutuelles* (sickness funds) usually apply the same principles in supplementary PHI as in SHI (community-rated premiums, acceptance of all applicants) whereas for-profit insurers calculate risk-related premiums and offer individual or collective contracts (Hermesse 2001). In Germany and the Netherlands, there are no significant differences in market behaviour of for-profit and not-for-profit insurers.

In most countries, both specialist health insurers and non-specialist insurers offer supplementary PHI. In Austria and Germany by law only specialist health insurers may offer supplementary PHI. Regulation does not allow sickness funds to offer supplementary PHI in Austria, Germany and the Netherlands.[19] In all other countries, sickness funds offer supplementary PHI. Group contracts are rare in Germany, while they are rare but growing in the Netherlands, more common in Austria, Switzerland (around 20 per cent) and Israel (60 per cent of all contracts of for-profit insurers) and very common in France (61 per cent) and Belgium (74 per cent) (Comité Européen des Assurances 2000).

Public regulation in European Union (EU) countries differs significantly from non-EU countries. The third non-life directive of the EU allows only financial regulation in supplementary PHI.[20] Most countries have adapted national regulation, although the French government has been quite reluctant to let go of tax exceptions for not-for-profit insurers (*mutuelles*) and the requirement for the notification of new policies (Europäischer Gerichtshof 1999). In contrast, non-EU Switzerland requires even the approval of new policies. In Israel, regulation requires the approval of new policies, proscribes surcharges for bad risks and does not allow not-for-profit insurers to reject new applicants (Shmueli 2001). In all countries, insurers calculate risk-related premiums for supplementary PHI and make available a large variety of arrangements for co-payments and deductibles. Only in Israel are there no deductibles available. In Switzerland, there can be a time limit for contracts and insurers are allowed to terminate contracts in case of damages.[21] In all other countries, only the insured can cancel the individual insurance contract.[22]

Benefits in supplementary PHI differ widely and mostly depend on the extent of coverage in SHI. The most common benefit is upgraded hospital accommodation which is prevalent to a different degree in all countries. Also very common are benefits for dental care which are not part of the benefits package in SHI in a number of countries (e.g. Switzerland) or are only partly covered (France, Germany, Israel, the Netherlands). With the exception of France and Belgium, the market for supplementary PHI to cover co-payments is not substantial. Switzerland even prohibits coverage of SHI co-payments by supplementary PHI.[23] However, increases in cost sharing which were implemented in the hope of curbing consumption and expenditures have stimulated growth of supplementary PHI in France (Imai *et al.* 2000), with coverage for reimbursement of co-payments rising from 69 per cent of the population in 1980 to 85 per cent in 1997 (Bocognano *et al.* 2000).

In most countries, insurers covering supplementary PHI do not have direct contractual relations with providers. Usually, providers charge fee-for-service and patients are reimbursed by their insurers (Belgium, France, Germany, Netherlands). In Austria, insurers mostly pay providers directly based on regional contracts. In Switzerland, insurers apply a mix of methods and some insurers in France provide quality incentives in contracts with providers of dental care. In Israel, not-for-profit insurers offer benefits in kind while for-profit insurers reimburse patients.

Market outcome of supplementary PHI

In this section we discuss effects of supplementary PHI on equity in health care delivery, consumer mobility in SHI and cost containment in SHI.

Effects on access to health care

Access problems to supplementary PHI are common in France, since access to supplementary PHI varies according to income and social class. Low income groups comprise 63 per cent of the uninsured (with regard to supplementary insurance) and only 13 per cent of them have access to high coverage supplementary insurance for dental care. As a consequence, consumption of ambulatory care, dental care and eye glasses is much smaller in low income-groups. The French system also appears to discriminate against foreigners, young people aged between 20 and 24, and those over 70 years, all of whom are less likely to be covered by supplementary health insurance. While 59 per cent of unskilled workers have little or no supplementary PHI, the same is true for only 24 per cent of all executives (Bocognano *et al.* 2000).

In Israel, individuals with supplementary PHI are healthier, have higher economic status and are more highly educated. Eighteen per cent of the lowest income quintile has supplementary PHI, compared to 42 per cent of the other income groups (Gross *et al.* 2001). Furthermore, men and employed individuals are over-represented among those with supplementary PHI. Individuals with poor health are much more likely to apply for supplementary PHI but are also more likely to be rejected by the insurers (Shmueli 2001).

In response to access problems, the French government in 2000 introduced a means-tested, public supplementary insurance programme called CMU (*Couverture maladie universelle*) to ensure access to health care for the poor. For those whose income is below a certain threshold (about 10 per cent of the population is eligible), this insurance covers all public co-payments and offers lump-sum reimbursements for glasses and dental prostheses (Imai *et al.* 2000). Health professionals are not allowed to charge more than the public tariff or the lump-sum for CMU beneficiaries, which means that in theory, access to care is free of charge (Couffinhal 2001). There still are access problems for people with income just above the level allowing access to CMU, especially the so-called 'working poor' (Yahiel 2001). Some 4.5 million people (around 7 per cent of the population) had benefited from the CMU at the end of June 2001.

In contrast to this public solution in France, in Belgium some not-for-profit market actors have found an innovative approach to the access problem. There has been an increase in health care costs that are not covered by SHI and thus have to be paid by patients. Supplementary PHI covering co-payments for hospital costs is very popular. An example is a new insurance for hospital co-payments that has been introduced by the Walloon branch of the not-for-profit Christian sickness funds. This insurance is called *Hospi solidaire*. It provides coverage for additional hospital costs with a deductible of €400 and covers accommodation in a two-person room. This *Hospi solidaire* is part of the supplementary PHI that every insured person of the sickness funds is obliged to purchase. All applicants have to be accepted and premiums are community-rated (Hermesse 2001).

Another market solution to mitigate access problems is the establishment of group contracts. The exclusionary effects of risk-related premiums and underwriting procedures for individual contracts in supplementary PHI are mitigated to a considerable degree when insurance is sold to employment-related groups with community-rated premiums (Jost 2001). The risks of the individuals concerned are pooled. Moreover, the average risk structure of employees is better than that of non-employees so that group contracts are attractive for insurers.

Effects on consumer mobility in SHI

The Belgian, Dutch, German, Israeli and Swiss governments have implemented a limited degree of regulated competition in SHI (Schut and Van Doorslaer 1999; Greß *et al.* 2001; Gross and Harrison 2001). Sickness funds are supposed to compete for consumers by providing good services at low costs. However, the tie-in of SHI with supplementary PHI may undermine some of the policy measures in SHI by providing greater opportunities for risk selection by insurers and resulting in low mobility of consumers. In SHI, sickness funds can risk select if they tie the conditions of supplementary PHI cover to the possession of an SHI contract with the same insurer. Bad risks may face a substantial premium increase if they switch sickness funds for basic or supplementary insurance, which may discourage them from switching altogether. If individuals want to buy cover for SHI as well for supplementary PHI, sickness funds can assess individual risks through the questionnaire compiled when individuals apply for complementary health insurance (Shmueli 1998). They can discourage bad risks in SHI by reducing service quality selectively, delaying reimbursements, reducing information disclosure and deteriorating customer assistance in supplementary insurance (Colombo 2001).

Immediately after the introduction of the new Health Insurance Law in Switzerland, some sickness funds forced individuals who were changing their basic insurer to terminate their contracts for supplementary PHI as well. While such strategies are now forbidden explicitly in Switzerland, interviews with consumer associations suggest that some people continue to experience similar problems. Many people complained that reimbursement times deteriorated after they separated SHI and supplementary PHI (Colombo 2001).[24] Additionally, this kind of separation is inconvenient for providers who prefer not to bill separately for services included under two different covers (Stürmer *et al.* 2000). Evidence from the Netherlands also points to a certain degree of tie-in of supplementary PHI and SHI, although sickness funds are formally forbidden to sell supplementary PHI. Therefore, they have to set up subsidiaries. Consumers are more aware of differences with regard to price and coverage in supplementary PHI than in SHI because those premiums are more 'visible' to families than the income-related contributions that are deducted from gross income by employers (Schut 2001; Greß *et al.* 2002). In Belgium, sickness funds require their insured to take out supplementary insurance at the same sickness fund with which they hold basic SHI (Vandevoorde 2001).

Effects on cost containment in SHI

The effects of supplementary PHI on cost containment in SHI are difficult to measure. Existing evidence is rather ambiguous. On the one hand, governments in all seven countries increasingly rely on supplementary PHI to fill gaps left by the decreasing share of public expenditures of total health care expenditures. Further, PHI generates additional revenues for providers who face tight budgets in SHI and thus decreases opposition from providers. Profits from supplementary PHI in Israel, for example, are used to partly cover deficits in the SHI budget of sickness funds (Gross 2001). In Germany, the hospital financing regulation relies on charges for better amenities in hospitals which are covered by supplementary PHI to subsidize general hospital budgets.

On the other hand, due to cost containment measures, it sometimes takes a long time before new drugs, treatments or a new technology are included in SHI. Supplementary PHI puts pressure on SHI in Belgium and France, since insurers covering supplementary PHI include these innovative therapies in their coverage (Vandevoorde 2001; Yahiel 2001). This tendency may in fact act as a cost driver in SHI. Also, the coverage of co-payments by supplementary PHI obviously counteracts the intention of reducing expenditure in the SHI sector (in Belgium and France), since the prime motivation behind the increase of co-payments was to curb public health expenditures. Governments argued that co-payments were intended to make patients consume more responsibly. However, as supplementary PHI increasingly covers public co-payments, any impact these measures may have had will be counteracted.

Policy implications

All seven countries struggle to balance the need for universal access to good quality care, fairness in the allocation of the financial burden and the need to control public expenditure and they have developed a variety of actual arrangements to reach underlying policy goals. There is no single best model. This is particularly true for the regulation of PHI.

The need for regulating alternative PHI is particularly large since an unregulated market might not safeguard access to adequate health insurance for persons without access to SHI (Schut 1995; Wasem 1995a; Jost 2001). Accordingly, governments in Germany and the Netherlands regulate alternative PHI extensively. The higher degree of regulation in the Netherlands does reflect the fact that a larger share of the population does not have access to SHI – while in Germany there is only an option to exit SHI. Moreover, the clear separation between alternative PHI and SHI in the Netherlands prevents some of the market outcomes of alternative PHI in Germany. Private health insurers in the Netherlands are unable to attract actively or passively insured from SHI with good health and high income – as German private health insurers are able to, and do so intensively. Also, there are no indirect subsidies of alternative PHI to SHI in the Netherlands via providers. This is due to the fact that providers are not able to charge higher rates for PHI patients than for SHI patients – as can providers in Germany. Direct subsidies to SHI such as the MOOZ scheme in the Netherlands are more transparent than indirect subsidies. Additionally, equal remuneration schemes for PHI and SHI insured to a certain degree prevent access problems that are prevalent in Germany due to preferential treatment of PHI patients.

In regulating alternative PHI, there is a trade-off between autonomy of consumers and degree of regulation (Wasem and Greß 2002). Regulation seems to follow a progression – beginning with restrictions on pre-existing conditions exclusion clauses or minimal coverage mandates through community ratings requirements or other bans on risk underwriting and ending up with high-risk pooling between insurers. The arguable potential benefits of PHI – its flexibility and potential for innovation – are constrained as governments increasingly dictate the terms of insurance contracts. To their already considerable administrative costs, private health insurers must now add regulatory compliance costs (Jost 2001). Moreover, the more regulated alternative PHI becomes, to safeguard access and to attain cost-effective care, and the less regulated SHI becomes, to make it more cost-effective without jeopardizing access, the less distinguishable the two types of insurance become. This is true more so in the Netherlands than in Germany and is reflected in the persistent attempts of the Dutch government to integrate SHI and alternative PHI.[25] But also in Germany there is a discussion on convergence of the systems (Wasem 1995b).

In all EU countries, there is extensive debate on the consequences of EU law on both PHI and SHI, and that debate may well reshape the health insurance landscape. The French government only recently introduced a scheme to increase the access of low-income persons to supplementary PHI. In Israel, in some areas the quality of care in SHI is not satisfactory, thus regulation of the market of supplementary PHI to avoid risk selection and to control premiums is justified (Shmueli 2001). Further regulation may actually transform supplementary PHI into some kind of SHI.

In both alternative and supplementary PHI, the link between the legal status of insurers (for-profit or not-for-profit) and market outcomes is surprisingly low. The link is much stronger between the regulation allowing sickness funds to offer supplementary PHI and market outcomes. While the market behaviour of sickness funds may mitigate access problems on the one hand (e.g. Belgium) it may also counteract policy measures in SHI by such contrasting mechanisms as choice by consumers.

In order to avoid risk selection of social health insurers via supplementary PHI, there are two major policy options. First, a strict separation of SHI and supplementary PHI is preferable to a situation where social health insurers or their subsidiaries can use supplementary PHI for attracting good risks. The formal or informal conglomerates of private and social health insurers in the Netherlands are more suitable for implementing socially undesirable risk selection strategies than are the strictly separated sickness funds and private insurers offering supplementary PHI in Germany. Second, regulation for supplementary PHI and SHI can be equalized (no pre-existing conditions exclusion clauses, minimal coverage mandates through community ratings requirements or other bans on risk underwriting, risk pooling etc.) in order to reduce incentives for risk selection. However, *de facto* this can transform supplementary PHI into a form of SHI.

Notes

1   The authors would like to thank Francesca Colombo, Agnes Couffinhal, Revital Gross, Maria M. Hofmarcher, Ralf Kocher and Michel Yahiel for their valuable comments on earlier versions of this chapter.
2   It is important to note that historically, social and PHI have similar roots in the income protection schemes of the medieval guilds and the eighteenth- and nineteenth-century friendly societies and mutual funds.
3   There is one exception: self-employed persons in Belgium do not have access to SHI for non-catastrophic risks and may take out alternative PHI at sickness funds or for-profit insurers (Hermesse 2001). However, we do not feel that this minor exception warrants special consideration in this chapter.
4   Switzerland is a special case with regard to this distinction, because basic health insurance is obligatory for the whole population and every individual can choose between social and private health insurers. In fact, only a small minority of insured take that mandatory insurance with private health insurers – mostly since only one private health insurer has chosen to offer basic insurance which by law must be written on a not-for-profit basis. Thus, we do not deal with Switzerland as a case of alternative PHI in this chapter.
5   Another special case is the obligatory private long-term-care insurance in Germany. People with private (alternative) insurance have to take out long-term care insurance with a fixed benefits package and fixed maximum premiums. This is another illustration that private insurance can be heavily regulated.
6   This is partly due to the fact that the Dutch population is highly risk averse. Also, alternative PHI is not very expensive (at least compared to alternative PHI in

Germany) and the legal provision for standard contracts provides affordable access even for bad risks.

7 For example, the employer is responsible for paying cash benefits for sick days and for prevention at the workplace.

8 This is due to three main factors. First, private health insurers were keen to deprive government of arguments to expand the scope of statutory SHI. Second, for-profit, non-specialist health insurers preferred a quiet market in order to focus on more profitable lines of business – PHI for them is mainly a means to sell other products. Finally and maybe most importantly, health insurers founded by sickness funds have a significant market share in alternative PHI and refrain from applying strict risk rating and underwriting. For an in-depth analysis of the PHI market in the Netherlands in terms of structure, behaviour and conduct see Chapter 4 of Schut (1995).

9 A 'maximum' version of risk rating would imply that the insurer may reassess the health risk at any time, at least at regular intervals (for instance, once a year). The more completely the model is applied, the less *risk solidarity* is in the system; *income solidarity* is by no means achieved (and not intended).

10 There is no separate insurance scheme for civil servants. All of them are accepted by private insurers regardless of risk. However, surcharges of up to 100 per cent are charged to high-risk applicants.

11 There are some exceptions for certain kinds of care such as maternity care or psychotherapy where waiting times may last up to eight months.

12 For an in-depth analysis for the process leading to the implementation of this regulation see Chapter 5 of Okma (1997).

13 SGB V, § 257.2b.

14 Prices in ambulatory care can be up to three times as high for privately insured as for socially insured persons (by law this is not possible for insured persons with a standard policy).

15 Due to a lack of data, this cannot be proven clearly.

16 From an economic point of view, there are some incentives for preferential treatment of patients with PHI by GPs due to differences in remuneration (fee-for-service for alternative PHI, capitation for SHI). However, there are no incentives for preferential treatment by specialists, since the same fee-for-service tariffs apply for both groups.

17 Formally this was also true for Switzerland where the complete market for supplementary PHI is for-profit. However, sickness funds dominate the market for supplementary PHI, who are not allowed to make profits in basic insurance.

18 Different agencies are responsible for supervising for-profit insurers and not-for-profit insurers in most countries (e.g. France, Israel and Switzerland).

19 In the Netherlands, sickness funds have found creative ways to circumvent this regulation by creating separate legal entities (Greß *et al.* 2001).

20 Material regulation is based on the premise that if insurers are sufficiently controlled in the type of business they operate and the level of premiums they charge, there can be no doubt of insolvency. Financial regulation attempts to ensure that the insurance company remains solvent; the regulatory body's role is restricted to examining detailed financial data of the insurer. Only if national governments can invoke a *general good* to justify premium and coverage regulation can there be exceptions. Usually regulation on alternative PHI, which is given special status through Article 54 of the third directive, is considered within the realm of the general good while regulation on supplementary health insurance is not. However, the absence of a clear definition of the *general good* has led to confusion and tension between the European Commission, member states and insurance companies (Mossialos and Thomson 2001).

21 However, both for-profit and not-for-profit insurers refrain from doing so (Kocher 2001).
22 This is not the case in group contracts; however in some countries (e.g. Germany) the individual has a right to continue the contract.
23 One major sickness fund started to offer supplementary PHI policies for the coverage of co-payments in SHI in 1997. The supervising authority immediately banned such policies. They have been banned by law since 2001 (Kocher 2001).
24 In Switzerland, only 7 per cent of individuals keep supplementary PHI at an insurer different from the sickness fund providing SHI. Individuals with both covers at the same fund often receive one contract where SHI and supplementary PHI are not clearly separated (Colombo 2001).
25 The Swiss government has already done so by allowing private health insurers to cover basic health insurance and by allowing social health insurers to offer supplementary health insurance.

References

Bocognano, A., Couffinhal, A., Dumesnil, S. and Grignon, M. (2000) *Which Coverage for Whom? Equity of Access to Health Insurance in France*. Paris: Presentation at the European Public Health Association Congress, 14–16 December.

Braun, B. (2000) *Rationierung und Vertrauensverlust im Gesundheitswesen – Folgen eines fahrlässigen Umgangs mit budgetierten Mitteln?* St. Augustin: Asgard.

Brouwer, W. and Hermans, H. (1999) Private clinics for employees as a Dutch solution for waiting lists: economic and legal arguments, *Health Policy*, 47(1): 1–17.

Brouwer, W. and Schut, F. (1999) Priority care for employees: a blessing in disguise? *Health Economics*, 8(1): 65–73.

Colombo, F. (2001) *Towards More Choice in Social Protection? Individual Choice of Insurer in Basic Mandatory Health Insurance in Switzerland*, Labour Market and Social Policy Occasional Papers No. 53. Paris: OECD.

Comité Européen des Assurances [The European Federation of National Insurance Associations] (2000) Health insurance in Europe – 1998 Data, *CEA eco*, 12.

Couffinhal, A. (2001) *Personal communication*. Paris: Credes.

Europäischer Gerichtshof (1999) *Urteil des Gerichtshofs (Fünfte Kammer) vom 16. Dezember 1999: Vertragsverletzung – Nichtumsetzung der Richtlinien 92/49/EWG und 92/96/EWG – Direktversicherung mit Ausnahme der Lebensversicherung und Direktversicherung (Lebensversicherung), Rechtssache C-239/98*. Strasbourg: Europäischer Gerichtshof.

Greß, S. (2000) *Der Nachbar als Herausforderung? Zur Vorbildfunktion des niederländischen Modells*. Bremen: ZeS-Arbeitspapier 1/2000, Zentrum für Sozialpolitik.

Greß, S. and Wasem, J. (2001) Die Abschaffung der Exit-Option für freiwillig Versicherte in der GKV – Realistische Finanzierungsalternative oder Einschränkung von Wahlmöglichkeiten? *Der Preis der Gesundheit: Wissenschaftliche Analysen, politische Konzepte – Perspektiven zur Gesundheitspolitik*. Landsberg, ecomed: W. Michaelis.

Greß, S., Okma, K.G.H. and Hessel, F. (2001) *Managed Competition in Health Care in the Netherlands and Germany – Theoretical Foundation, Empirical Findings and Policy Conclusions*. Greifswald, Diskussionspapier 04/2001 der Rechts- und Staatswissenschaftlichen Fakultät der Ernst-Moritz-Arndt-Universität Greifswald.

Greß, S., Groenewegen, P., Kerssens, J., Braun, B. and Wasem, J. (2002) Free choice of sickness funds in regulated competition: evidence from Germany and the Netherlands, *Health Policy*, 60(3): 235–54.

Gross, R. (2001) Supplemental health insurance in Israel. Personal communication. Jerusalem: JDC-Brookdale Institute.

Gross, R. and Harrison, M. (2001) Implementing managed competition in Israel, *Social Science and Medicine*, 52: 1219–31.

Gross, R., Rosen, B. and Shirom, A. (2001) Reforming the Israeli health system: findings of a 3-year evaluation, *Health Policy*, 56: 1–20.

Hermesse, J. (2001) *Supplementary Private Health Insurance (PHI) in Belgium*. Brussels: Alliance Nationale des Mutualités Chrétiennes.

Hof, B. (2001) *Auswirkungen und Konsequenzen der demografischen Entwicklung für die gesetzliche Kranken- und Pflegeversicherung*. Köln: Verband der privaten Krankenversicherung e.V.

Hofmarcher, M.M. and Riedel, M. (2001) Health expenditure in EU: no public sector without the private one, focus: the Austrian hospital sector – one system or nine? *Health System Watch, Spring 2001, Institute for Advanced Studies IHS Health Econ*. Vienna: Federation of Austrian Social Security Institutions.

Imai, Y., Jacobzone, S. and Lenain, P. (2000) *The changing Health System in France*, Economics Department Working Papers No. 269. Paris: OECD.

Jost, T.S. (2001) Private or public approaches to insuring the uninsured: lessons from international experience with private insurance, *New York University Law Review*, 76(2): 419–93.

Klingenberger, D. (2001) *Die Friedensgrenze zwischen gesetzlicher und privater Krankenversicherung: Ökonomische und metaökonomische Kriterien einer optimierten Aufgabenabgrenzung zwischen Sozial- und Individualversicherung*. Kölner Schriften zur Sozial- und Wirtschaftspolitik, Bd. 21. Regensburg: Transfer Verlag.

Kocher, R. (2001) *Personal communication*. Bern: Bundesamt für Sozialversicherung.

Mossialos, E. and Thomson, S. (2001) *Voluntary Health Insurance in the European Union*. London: London School of Economics, Discussion Paper No. 19.

OECD (2003) *OECD Health Data 2003: A Comparative Analysis of 30 Countries*, 2nd edn. Paris: OECD.

Okma, K.G.H. (1997) Studies on Dutch health politics, policies and law. Utrecht, Ph.D. thesis.

Schneider, M. (ed.) (1995) *Complementary Health Schemes in the European Union*. Augsburg: BASYS.

Schut, F.T. (1995) *Competition in the Dutch Health Care Sector*. Ridderkerk: Ridderprint.

Schut, F.T. (2001) Prijsconcurrentie ziekenfondsen nog niet effectief, *Economisch Statistische Berichten*, 86: 172–5.

Schut, F.T. and Van Doorslaer, E.K.A. (1999) Towards a reinforced agency role of health insurers in Belgium and the Netherlands, *Health Policy*, 48(1): 47–67.

Shmueli, A. (1998) Supplemental health insurance ownership in Israel: an empirical analysis and some implications, *Social Science and Medicine*, 46(7): 821–9.

Shmueli, A. (2001) The effect of health on acute care supplemental insurance ownership: an empirical analysis, *Health Economics*, 10: 341–50.

Stürmer, W., Wendland, D. and Braun, U. (2000) *Veränderungen im Bereich der Zusatzversicherung aufgrund des KVG*. Bern: Beiträge zur Sozialen Sicherheit 4/00, Bundesamt für Sozialversicherung.

Timmer, H.G. (1990) *Technische Methoden der privaten Krankenversicherung in Europa: Marktverhältnisse und Wesensmerkmale der Versicherungsmathematik*. Karlsruhe: Verlag Versicherungswirtschaft.

Vandevoorde, C. (2001) *Private health insurance in Belgium*. Personal communication, Leuven.

Vektis (2000) *Financiering van de zorg in 1999: jaarboek 2000*. Zeist: Vektis.

Verband der privaten Krankenversicherung e.V. (2000a) *Die Private Krankenversicherung – Zahlenbericht 2000/2001*. Köln, Verband der privaten Krankenversicherung e.V.

Verband der privaten Krankenversicherung e.V. (2000b) *PKV-Info: Der Standardtarif – nach der Rechtslage vom 1. Juli 2000*. Köln: Verband der privaten Krankenversicherung e.V.

Verband der privaten Krankenversicherung e.V. (2000c) *Private Health Insurance – Facts and Figures 1999/2000*. Köln: Verband der privaten Krankenversicherung e.V.

Verband der privaten Krankenversicherung e.V. (2001) *Rechenschaftsbericht 2000: Bestandszuwachs im Trend des Vorjahres, verhaltener Kostenanstieg*. Köln: Pressemitteilung des Verbandes der privaten Krankenversicherung e.V. vom 5.6.2001.

Wasem, J. (1995a) *Regulating Private Health Insurance Markets*. Amsterdam: presentation at the Four-Country-Conference on Health Care Reform and Health Care Policies in the United States, Canada, Germany and the Netherlands, Amsterdam/Rotterdam 23–35 February.

Wasem, J. (1995b) Gesetzliche und private Krankenversicherung – auf dem Weg in die Konvergenz? *Sozialer Fortschritt*, 44 (4): 89–96.

Wasem, J. (2000) *A Framework for Analysis of Opting out Provisions*. Greifswald: unpublished manuscript.

Wasem, J. and Greß, S. (2002) Regulation of private health insurance (PHI) markets, in T. Marmor and K.G.H. Okma (eds) *Comparative Studies and Modern Medical Care: Learning Opportunity Or Global Mythology?* New Haven, CT: Yale University Press.

Yahiel, M. (2001) *Personal communication*. Paris: Inspection generale des affaires sociales (IGAS).

chapter eleven

The changing role of the individual in social health insurance systems

Manfred Wildner, André P. den Exter and Wendy G.M. van der Kraan

Introduction

This chapter focuses on the individual insured and his/her role in social health insurance (SHI) systems. Choice for the insured individual may relate to choice of provider and/or to choice of insurer. This chapter argues that the individual's role in SHI systems is changing, from a passive consumer towards a more active participant attempting to obtain his/her rights ultimately by legal means in the courts. This 'rights approach', combining access to health services (voice) and the emerging notion of free choice of insurer (exit), may encourage health policy-makers to better anticipate consumers' needs. Future policy should support patient and/or citizen empowerment at three levels: *macro* (participation in national policy development, assertion of rights and increased representation); *meso* (participation in and consultation on strategic and management decision-making, increased representation); and *micro* (freedom of choice, changing attitudes of clinicians, involvement in treatment decisions, increased representation and administrative redress).

The individual in SHI systems

The multiple roles of the individual

Members of the public are connected to SHI systems from different perspectives: as a user of health care, as an insured person and as a citizen. Each of these roles involves different relationships with other actors in the SHI system.

The role of the user of health care

A recent tendency towards patient empowerment can be observed within health care services. Increasing numbers of patients are becoming more know-ledgeable, more demanding and are taking more responsibility over their own health (MacStravic 2000). No longer willing to be passive objects of the system, patients are pursuing a more central role at the subject of service delivery (Saltman and Figueras 1997). There has been a shift from the traditional (pater-nalistic) doctor-patient relationship – in which the doctor knows best – towards a partnership between the consumer and physician (a shared decision-making model) (Coulter 1997). This reflects increased interest inpatient autonomy, which means individual freedom of action and choice. In addition to patient choice, 'patient empowerment' has several dimensions. One concern is patients' rights with regard to health care services. Another characteristic is the participation of the patient/consumer in clinical decision-making. The last dimension of patient empowerment may involve increasing use of private sector providers (Saltman and Figueras 1997).

In most SHI countries, patients can select their provider, except in the Netherlands, where the insured is registered with a (freely chosen) general prac-titioner (GP), who in turn acts as a gatekeeper for referrals to specialists and for inpatient care (Paton 2000). Limitations have also been introduced in the 1994 Swiss Health Insurance Act by restricting insurees' freedom to choose providers, tied to efforts to introduce a degree of managed care (Theurl 1999).

The role of the insured

Within traditional SHI systems, the individual has a payment relationship with a sickness fund (Greß *et al.* 2002). Payment of an income-related premium entitles insurees to claim a specific package of health services. In countries like the Netherlands and Germany, SHI systems have introduced reforms focused on limited forms of competition in the insurance market, tied to choice of insurer. In almost all SHI countries, sickness fund members are now allowed to choose and switch between sickness funds. Austria, however, is an exception, member-ship being based on geography and employment criteria. To increase competi-tion between sickness funds, some countries also introduced changes in the financial relationship between the individual and his/her sickness fund. In the Netherlands, for instance, 'market-oriented' reform has introduced an out-of-pocket 'nominal' premium – which differs from fund to fund – in addition to the uniform income-related contribution. The thinking is that this variable payment will create a market based both on quality and price (Paton 2000).

The role of the citizen

Within an SHI system, the individual also participates as a citizen (Sorell 2001). Modern 'citizenship' emphasizes active public responsibilities that extend beyond equal rights to a public interest obligation that focuses on the fair use of public goods and services. An appeal to citizen responsibility can contribute to a fair distribution of care (Struijs 2000). Citizens thus become accountable for both the choices they make in consuming health care and the subsequent financial and health-related consequences of those choices. In the view of some analysts, choice is a *sine qua non* to carry out this public interest responsibility (Struijs 2000).

Conflicting roles

Empowering individuals can be considered from the patient-provider relationship as well as the insurer-insured relationship. However, in each relationship the individual plays a different role with different preferences and interests. As a user of scarce health care resources, an individual has preferences about what diagnostic and therapeutic interventions he/she wants to receive. But an individual is also involved with health care as a sickness-fund member/taxpayer, who contributes to the financial means and who has views about what health care the state/insurer should fund and offer (Lomas 1997).

An individual citizen may express different preferences depending on these different perspectives and his/her expressed preferences may not always be consistent. This means that the same citizen might oppose increased funding as a taxpayer/insured, but demand extra services as a patient (Lomas 1997).

Agents

The conflicting perspectives created by different roles of the individual in a SHI system, and the uncertainties that empowerment of the individual entails, can be related to growing conflict on the macro level, namely solidarity versus individual needs. To guarantee universal access, SHI systems are heavily regulated. Strict regulation, however, impedes incentives for efficiency and innovation. Therefore, limited efforts with competition between sickness funds have been introduced with the objective of enhancing efficiency and innovation, while preserving equity (Schut and Van Doorslaer 1999).

However, recent experiences in Belgium and the Netherlands suggest that national governments remain reluctant to allow insurers a large management role in the provision of services. Thus far, recent developments in SHI systems are characterized by a built-in conflict. On the one hand, there appears to be the desire to maintain a social system that can provide health care to all its members, and which therefore needs to control overall demand. At the same time, however, broader democratic developments in society imply a more empowered health care consumer. Thus the transformation of the patient into an active consumer by enabling choice within a more market-oriented health care system is viewed with both interest and trepidation.

The ethical and legal dimension

Ethical frameworks

The issue of 'choice' in health care is closely related to a fundamental principle of biomedical ethics, *patient autonomy* (Beauchamp and Childress 1994). Different aspects of this principle include patient information on his/her health state and regarding treatment options, the right to adequate access to health care facilities, choice of health care provider, consent to treatment, study participation and participation in teaching of health care professionals. These are all elements of most charters of patients' rights and are important procedural aspects of health care systems.

Patient autonomy incorporates *free action, effective deliberation, authenticity* and *moral reflection* (Beauchamp and Childress 1994). Free action focuses on unimpaired processes and outcomes of choice, such as the right to decide on one's treatment options. Effective deliberation deals with the rationality of the decision-making process in view of information levels and cognitive ability. This means that unimpeded information that can be understood by the patient is provided before and during the decision-making process. It is a necessary precondition for free action. Authenticity requires that choices be consistent with personal preferences and life plans. This involves protecting the individual's personal priorities from alternative or conflicting suggestions by others – individuals or groups. It also requires that the individual's right to health care has priority over the societal perspective. Moral reflection makes reference to consistency with beliefs and values and may be understood as a special extension of authenticity in view of belief systems.

Beyond ethical aspects focusing on the individual, it is also important to be aware of the broader conceptual framework within which health care systems operate. Frequently a *utilitarian framework* is used in the evaluation of health care (e.g. by health technology assessment). It aims at maximizing health gain for a population with respect to spent resources. Consequent applications of the utilitarian framework (e.g. the creation of league tables of preferred health care interventions in the state of Oregon in the USA) have met considerable resistance. *Egalitarian ethics*, in contrast, focuses on the rights of the worst-off in society and regards disproportionate allocation of resources to these individuals as fair. Egalitarian ethics is concerned with health rights, and hence is a 'liberal' approach. While classical libertarian positions are focusing on 'negative' rights, i.e. the freedom from infringement of choice, egalitarian approaches try to ensure adequate services to the worst-off in society as 'positive' rights. The *communitarian perspective*, with its strong emphasis on group identity and the common good, principally accepts diverse ethical frameworks, as long as the community supports the rules and regulations. However, it can lead to the neglect of minority groups, defined by race, age or disease state. Moreover, it may not be suitable as a framework for a common health care market across national borders.

Patients' rights in the purchaser-patient relationship

From a legal perspective, patients' rights as *health rights* are the subject of numerous international and regional declarations and conventions. These standards reflect a trend towards strengthening the rights of patients in health care. Such experiences can be associated with democracy: empowering people is a question of revitalizing representative democracy so as to ensure the smooth functioning of basic social institutions, including health care establishments (WHO 1997; Council of Europe 2000). The increased interest concerns both the classical (individual) rights such as patient autonomy, as well as the social rights, for example the right to health care. Commentators have questioned the emphasis on patients' rights by law (Barolin 1996; Angell 2000). Nonetheless, an explicit consideration of health rights and the patients' perspective fits well with a general democratic evolutionary process in many countries (Reiser 1993; Williamson 1998).

Within the purchaser-patient relationship two seminal values can be discerned: the (social) right to health care, generally interpreted as access to health care services; and patient autonomy, understood in terms of individual choice.[1] At the national level, the right to health care has been formulated in various constitutions.[2] In most SHI models, the constitutional norm has been further elaborated by statutory law (Social Code, General Social Security Act, Sickness Fund Act etc.) and concerns the organization, finance, quality and provision of health care services. These laws affirm or impose on the legislature, *inter alia*, to guarantee equal access to a basic level of health care through establishing a social security programme. In transitional countries, such as the Czech Republic and Poland, recent constitutional reforms have introduced statutory limits to what was – formally – considered as an absolute right. Such developments put pressure on the role of the purchaser of health services, notably in the case of limited resources. Gradually, traditional legal doctrine has undergone a reorientation towards increased interest in the finance, affordability and quality of health care without loosening elementary principles such as equal access. Besides the right to health care, individuals' choice of insurer and provider is inextricably bound up with the principle of patient autonomy. Freedom of choice is a necessary condition for individuals to develop their own aims and interests. The existence of choice mechanisms in domestic law reflects the importance of this value. Developed from a moral concept to an accepted legal right, several legal orders now protect the notion of freedom of choice.[3] The effectiveness of the choice mechanism in enhancing individual liberty remains problematic, however, since it is also related to risk selection and access to information.

The institutionalized role of the individual as insured

In most social insurance models, the role of the individual as insured has been institutionalized by law and/or derived regulatory norms. Formal structures, to a large extent, define the role of insured in health insurance decision-making, notably in terms of supporting participation and (more recently) choice of insurer.

Participation

The examined SHI models present several commonalities in the formal role of the insured in health insurance funds. Since most of the health insurance institutions have the legal status of a public/private (not-for-profit) association or foundation, virtually all funds are familiar with (a kind of) participation by the insured in the fund's day-to-day decision-making or supervision. For instance, the German Social Code Book V (SGB V) regulates the structure of most sickness funds including the executive (day-to-day) management and the assembly of delegates deciding on by-laws and other regulations of the fund, passing the budget, setting the contribution rate and electing the executive board (Busse 2000). Usually, the assembly includes representatives of both insured and employers. The composition in substitute funds, however, differs, the assembly includes only representatives of the insured. Both the representatives of the employees/insured and of the employers are democratically elected every six years. Many representatives are linked to trade unions or employers' associations (Busse 2000: 26). The Austrian governance mechanism of SHI funds corresponds with the described German structure it is closely related to employers and employees in a type of parity (Theurl 1999).

The formal role of insured individuals in the Netherlands is less clear. Although the Sickness Fund Act entitles the Minister of Health to issue rules on participation of the insured in the sickness fund board, up until now, such rules are missing. In 1994, the previous Sickness Fund Council advised that the interests of the insured should be protected by 'a reasonable amount of influence' on the board of sickness funds. This was generally interpreted as meaning that half the number of board members should represent the insured. In practice it appeared that sickness funds are unwilling to let the insured participate on a 50 per cent basis. Instead, most sickness funds established a 'council of insured' (*ledenraad*), reflecting the influence of the insured on the basis of representation, whereas some representatives of insured participate in the supervisory board. The council's competences may include appointment of board members, amendment of statutory laws, approval of the budget and annual accounts. Other issues being discussed include, *inter alia*, the internal organization and the fund's general policy, external policy, collaboration and merger, premiums and service package and complaint procedures (Van der Schee *et al.* 2000).

Major reforms of the Luxembourg sickness insurance system in 1992 transferred the main tasks of existing sickness funds to the Union of Sickness Funds (*Union des caisses de maladie*, UCM). This organization manages and delivers compulsory health insurance. It distributes the health insurance revenues and is responsible for the payment of hospitals, and services delivered on a fee-for-service basis. However, individual sickness funds continue to reimburse the recipient for certified expenditures on goods and services (Mossialos 1999). Patients' participation in the management of health care is rather limited to the UCM, which represents patients in the purchaser-provider relationship.

In Israel, the 1994 National Health Insurance Act empowered the insured with newly defined rights. The law required sickness funds to stipulate the rights of their members in by-laws, for instance safeguarding consumer representation in two statutory decision-making bodies: the directorate councils of the sickness fund, and the National Health Insurance Council known as the 'Health Council' that advises the Minister of Health on changes to the benefit package. In practice, opinions of the elected consumer representatives differ and tend to be dominated by special interests, whereas the Health Council's discussions are still dominated by the agenda of the Ministry of Health. However, on several occasions patients' interest groups were quite effective in influencing policy decisions about the standard basket of health services (Chinitz 2000).

Virtually all SHI countries created a legal basis for citizens' participation in the management of health insurance organizations. Besides formal rules on (indirect) democratic participation, a more direct way of participation of the insured on health insurance issues is issuing complaints, arbitration and court procedures. The issues raised include, *inter alia*, disputes between the insured and the sickness fund on (the refusal of reimbursement of) social insurance entitlements and access to not covered services. Almost all social insurance systems have regulated these types of disputes. For instance, according to Dutch sickness fund and AWBZ legislation, administrative courts deal with health issues.[4] In the Sickness Fund Act (ZFW), similar to the AWBZ, appeals can be made in various ways against decisions made by a sickness fund. Under both acts, the most important type of complaint are disputes concerning entitlement to benefits. Different arrangements apply to disputes relating to entitlement to benefits in kind or to an equivalent payment. The insured must submit a formal objection in writing to the sickness fund (or relevant implementing body in the case of the AWBZ). Before considering the objection, the sickness fund (similar for the AWBZ) must first seek the advice of the Board for Health Care Insurance. After obtaining that advice and sending a copy of it to the insured, the sickness fund issues a decision on the objection. If the insured does not agree with the decision, he/she can bring an appeal to the administrative law section of the district court. As supplementary insurance is private insurance, those insured persons can bring disputes before a civil court.

Disputes on social insurance entitlements in Belgium and France must be presented (to the Labour, or Social law court) within 30 days after the disputed decision is made by the insurer. In Switzerland, any decision by an insurer may be challenged within 30 days by addressing an objection to that insurer. In the second stage, the decision resulting from such objection may then be challenged by an appeal in administrative law (*Kantonale Versicherungsbeschwerde*). Similarly, in Germany, the regional designated insurance court (*Versicherungsgericht*, respectively *Sozialgericht*) hears, *inter alia*, suits brought by an insured person opposing an insurer. The highest appeal body is the Federal Insurance Court (EVG). Disputes between insured persons and contracted providers are resolved by means of arbitration. Finally, in Israel, the National Health Insurance Law 1994 provides several mechanisms for both examining consumers' complaints and dispute settlement between the insured person and insurer. The Ministry of Health operates an Office of the Ombudsman that hears the public's complaints about the health care system. Under the Health Insurance Law, the Ombuds Office competence increased and it now investigates complaints on medical practices, entitlements and patients' rights (Kismodi and Hakimian 2001).

Choice

All studied SHI systems incorporate choice of insurer except Austria, where statutory health insurance is organized on the principle of territoriality: people are assigned to social insurers (*Gebietskrankenkasse*) according to occupation or profession and there is no possibility to opt out of the SHI system (Hofmarcher and Rack 2001). The situation is quite different in other German-speaking countries. In Switzerland, for instance, choice of insurer in basic health insurance was introduced with the 1994 Health Insurance Act (*Krankenversicherungs-gesetz*, KVG). The underlying objective of this law, which came into force in January 1996, was to increase solidarity in basic health insurance while enhancing choice among individuals and competition on quality-price ratios among insurers. Article 4 provides the legal basis of choice of insurer and the right to move among insurers. However, this right is only applicable to basic health insurance (and not to complementary health insurance) within the canton where the individual resides or works. The KVG insurers have to accept all persons within their territory of operation, regardless of individual risk. The insured can switch KVG insurer twice a year. The new law stressed the importance of establishing mechanisms to guarantee that choice of insurer takes place on an equal basis for all individuals. Therefore, a risk equalization system was introduced to compensate insurers for differences in costs arising from differences in risk structures linked to the age and sex structures of insurees (Article 105). In addition, the law imposed requirements for disclosure of information to individual insured (activities, premiums, financial report). These mechanisms have a direct effect on individuals' choice of insurer. Furthermore, the new law introduced the notion of managed care in which the insurees may limit their choice of providers and, therefore, obtain a reduction in premiums. While maintaining the principle of participation on an individual basis, the law mandated a minimum basic level of services, leaving individuals free to express their preferences over insurers and providers (Colombo 2001).

Germany also switched from an obligatory system without choice to a system with the possibility of choice of insurer (with some exceptions). Prior to 1996, the majority of insured people were assigned to the appropriate fund based on geographical and/or job characteristics (Busse 2000). Under the 1993 Health Care Structure Act, however, almost every insured person became entitled to choose and switch SHI from 1996, respectively 1997. By law, the general regional funds and substitute funds were opened to everyone and have to contract with all applicants. Some profession-tied funds retain the system of assigned membership (Busse 2000: 40). Insured persons can also switch their sickness fund when changing employers. Along with choice of insurer, the Health Care Structure Act also established a risk compensation scheme to compensate sickness funds for differences in contribution rates and expenditures.

In 1992 in the Netherlands, health care reforms introduced individual choice of insurer. Sickness funds were permitted to enrol applicants from anywhere in the country, who annually were allowed to switch sickness funds. The Sickness Fund Act by-law stipulates that switching insurer is allowed only once a year and that the insured has to notify his/her sickness fund before a fixed date.[5]

Apart from choice of insurer, individuals and sickness funds were also entitled to select (individual) providers. Evaluation pointed out, however, that sickness funds did not use the option of selective contracting (Ziekenfondsraad 1995). In Belgium, patients' choice of provider as well as insurer is an essential principle (Kerr 2000). Due to the reimbursement system, patients have substantial latitude to select health care providers, and enrollees are also entitled to change insurer annually.

In France, however, choice is limited, since the National Health Insurance Fund (*Caisse Nationale d'Assurance Maladie*) provides almost universal SHI nationwide, which is compulsory for the entire population. Affiliation to the *Assurance Maladie* is through different schemes according to occupation. Those who move from one profession to another automatically change funds, but otherwise there is no choice. Finally, the Israeli National Health Insurance Law introduced 100 per cent enrolment through individual choice of one of four sickness funds, each of which provides a standard package of services against a capitation payment from earmarked revenues raised through a health tax. The sickness funds can no longer be selective in membership by rejecting vulnerable persons, the sick, elderly or the poor (Shalev and Chinitz 1997). Much as in other social insurance models, this rule is supported by a risk compensation mechanism.

Outcomes

Equity

Consumer participation and choice raise concerns regarding equity, responsiveness and patient satisfaction. Equity is inextricably linked to equal access to health care, including an appropriate distribution of resources. Given the scarcity of financial resources, SHI systems face unpleasant dilemmas, for example disputes on the introduction of new, expensive technologies in the benefit package, alleged reimbursement of health insurance entitlements and problems with waiting lists. Occasionally, national and also the European central courts have sought to settle such conflicts.

The Israeli health insurance system, for instance, has on several occasions been sued by individuals seeking reimbursement for certain pharmaceuticals and treatment procedures.[6] One prominent example concerned reimbursement for a drug therapy for multiple sclerosis. Since the disputed drug had not been registered by the Israeli Drug Administration, it appeared that the case would not be successful since the court did not have the power to circumvent the statutory procedure for adding drugs to the coverage. Nonetheless, despite strong treasury objection, the drug was eventually included in the health insurance benefit package. These rulings urged the Ministry of Health to hasten the registration procedure, and eventually paved the way for approval to include the drug in the national health system (Shalev and Chinitz 1997). Other litigation cases challenged administrative and clinical guidelines limiting access to new drugs.[7] Although the validity to issue these ministerial guidelines, and therefore define the health care package, is still under debate, recent cases have made clear that defining the benefit package results in complex interactions among various (political, legal, economic, medical and scientific) factors (Shalev and Chinitz 1997: 576; Chinitz 2000).

Similar examples can be found in other systems, notably Germany, Switzerland, Belgium and the Netherlands.[8] In general, the courts have respected the administrative power to define the benefit package but have imposed more rational decision-making based on objective, evidence-based criteria, excluding discrimination. More problematic is the use of medical guidelines. Court decisions in the Netherlands ruled on the denial of services due to clinical guidelines differently (both accepting and rejecting denial), while Israeli courts have not tested this question yet.[9] As budget restrictions play a more important role, patients are increasingly resorting to the courts to assert their rights to benefits (services) which their health insurers have not contracted for at all, or when the amount contracted for is insufficient, or when the quality of delivered care is poor. In the Netherlands, contractual agreements made between sickness funds and the executive offices of the AWBZ on the one hand, and providers on the other, may contain limitations, but not that frustrate realization of entitlements to the insured. The payer is dismissed from his/her duty to provide benefits and services in cases of *force majeure* (an exception to the legal duty to provide services). In those cases (legal cases involving inadequate resources), the payer has to prove that the cause of unsupplied, not properly or belatedly supplied services and benefits was out of his/her control and power. *Force majeure* is legally accepted where the government itself – in cases of tight planning of health care facilities, for example – is the cause of non-supply. Insurers are not bound to the impossible. The *force majeure* argument has been tested in numerous cases.[10] In those cases, the courts' decisions indicated that government could be held responsible.

The examined cases indicate that the judiciary in various legal systems recognized the patient's right to access to health care, in terms of *enforceable* entitlements, when defined in the benefit package. This can be explained by the legal nature of these statutory entitlements, generally interpreted as contractual obligations within the conditions set by law. Failure to guarantee such contracted services makes insurers, in principle, liable to legal claims. In this respect, the UK's NHS system differs fundamentally since it – generally – does not create legally enforceable entitlements.[11]

The frequency of patients asserting their claims has raised public concern. Since these procedures reflect more structural problems (e.g. restricted resources), depriving patients of the right to file a complaint is not a serious option. An alternative solution (e.g. to have a vaguely-defined benefit package instead of clear entitlements) raises constitutional concerns, notably when excluding services and introducing out-of-pocket payments (Den Exter 2000). Moreover, competitive reforms are often based on contractual relations, which require the explicit definition of entitlements (Chinitz 2000).

Responsiveness

Responsiveness has recently been added to the assessment of health systems (Murray and Frenk 2000). It refers to non-health aspects of the provision of preventive services, care or non-personal services. It includes respect for the dignity of the person, confidentiality, autonomy to decide on treatment options, prompt attention, quality of the amenities (e.g. cleanliness, space, food), access to social support networks and free choice of providers. Hence, rudeness in relation to patients, long waiting times, denial of access to care, unnecessary isolation or insensitivity to cultural values of connectedness, denial of choice and gag clauses all reflect poor responsiveness of health care systems. Poor responsiveness may result in poor take-up of preventive services or treatment options. As responsiveness also reflects *expectations*, its assessment may vary (e.g. with the education level or socioeconomic status of the assessor). Moreover, health systems often consist of compartments (e.g. defined by remuneration for services), and hence perceived responsiveness may be as heterogeneous as the system. Some aspects of responsiveness (e.g. long waiting lists for surgery) are captured by health outcomes like survival or quality of life. Other aspects like respect for the dignity of the person need a special assessment (e.g. by satisfaction questionnaires or expert interviews).

A household survey on the perceived level of patients' rights in Austria, Germany and Switzerland (Wildner *et al.* 2001) suggests that across these countries dignity, humanity, confidentiality, autonomy, free choice and contact with family and friends are fulfilled to a high degree. Deficits were perceived for various information rights, the transition between sectors of care (inpatient, outpatient, acute care, rehabilitation, terminal care) and the possibility to file complaints and protest successfully. Results were superior for the Swiss health care system compared to Austria and Germany, illustrating gradients of responsiveness across SHI systems.

Formal and effective systems to file complaints are of considerable value to enhance responsiveness. Patients may issue a complaint at the health care institution's complaint board or similar institution, or may invoke a disciplinary or civil court action. As an example, the state of Israel has instituted an ombudsman whose task is to protect and restore the balance between health care needs, the aspiration to provide citizens with an adequate health service and inevitable financial limitations (National Health Insurance Act 1994). Complaints filed with the ombudsman are dominated by issues related to sick fund membership, administrative treatment and the service basket. In respect to the service basket, complaints are dominated by reimbursement of outlays, assistance in obtaining treatment and assistance in obtaining medication. In respect to administrative treatment, complaints are dominated by issues regarding the choice of provider, especially for outpatient care and services. In respect to sick fund membership, complaints deal with loss or lack of insurance status. Other SHI systems have developed patient advocates (e.g. Austria) with separate budgets for no-fault compensation payments or professional medical damage conciliation councils outside the formal legal system (e.g. Germany). These provisions do not interfere with the right to seek legal redress.

Patient satisfaction

The legitimacy of *patient satisfaction* as an outcome measure of health care has grown considerably over the past decade. Research has emphasized the influence of the purchaser, notably concerning patient participation and choice. Experiences in the Netherlands, for example, show that involvement of individual insurees in sickness funds has diminished over the last decade. Due to mergers with private insurance companies, most of the sickness funds have now lost their mutual character. Measures to restore insurees' influence in decision-making involved the institutionalization of the 'council of insured'. Experiences with the council revealed both advantages and disadvantages. Advantages include the supervisory role over the board, the council as a platform to assess new ideas from the managerial board, and also good public relations. One disadvantage is potential delay in decision-making (Greß *et al.* 2002). Both the insurees and sickness funds considered the actual influence of the council on the organization to be limited, despite its important formal role. A key reason is the members' lack of professional standing and the complex nature of the issues discussed (Greß *et al.* 2002). In certain cases, however, the council did overrule specific managerial decisions, such as the planned merger between two sickness funds.

Patient satisfaction in terms of ability to choose insurer has increased in most countries. Except for Austria and France, insured persons can select their social insurance funds, and opportunities to switch insurer have been enhanced as well. While the Swiss health insurance reform (1994) introduced important regulatory mechanisms to tackle the risks of adverse selection and risk selection, it is questionable whether some of the initial goals of the reform have been fully attained (Colombo 2001). The majority of the surveyed population has never changed fund since the introduction of the KVG, and annual switching percentages are very low. Switching behaviour seems to be linked with age, health status and canton but not with gender (Colombo 2001: 27). The dominant reason for changing insurer appeared to be price factors but non-price motivations, especially service quality, are also important. The evidence seems to suggest imperfections of the switching mechanism for some people, particularly bad risks.

Although the Swiss system formally prohibits sickness funds from risk adjusting and subsidizes low-income individuals, the funds can risk adjust *indirectly* if they tie the conditions for a complementary insurance cover to the possession of a basic health insurance contract at the same fund (Colombo 2001). Consumers complained about delay in reimbursement after they separated their basic and complementary health insurance between two different insurers, about overlap in insurance coverage and about more expensive complementary health insurance if they were not insured by the same sickness fund for basic insurance (Ombudsman de l'assurance-maladie sociale 1996, 1997). Bad risks may face a substantial premium increase if they change sickness funds for basic or complementary insurance, which may discourage them from switching altogether.

The OECD study suggests strengthening the choice mechanism by improving access to information, eliminating cream-skimming incentives for insurers and introducing a clear separation of KVG coverage from complementary insurance (Colombo 2001). Limited movement among insurers has been confirmed by Israeli experiences, at around 4 per cent of the population annually (Gross *et al.* 1998). A possible explanation of this low figure is a type of *de facto* cartel among the four sickness funds (Chinitz 2000).

Comparative research between Germany and the Netherlands examined the behaviour of consumers after the introduction of choice among sickness funds. Data on contribution rates, member flows and personal motives for changing insurer revealed important differences. In Germany, differences in contribution rates between sickness funds are the main reason for consumers to switch, which occurs on a considerable scale. In the Netherlands, however, premium differences as well as the degree of change are much lower. Survey data show that consumers perceive very small differences between sickness funds and do not see much reason for switching funds. The degree of actual change appears to depend on economic incentives, especially the extent of financial risk that sickness funds have to bear and the extent that premium or contribution rates differ (Greß *et al.* 2002). The introduction of individual choice of insurer in Germany raised the accountability of the funds and stimulated their development from being only payers to more active purchasing (Busse 2001).

Conclusions

This chapter has examined several modes of citizens' participation and choice in western European SHI systems, reflecting the ethical, legal and organizational notion of individual autonomy and of access to health care. Recent reforms in these countries have helped stimulate a conflict of interest between the individual as an insured and the individual as a patient. By appealing to the responsibilities of the individual as a citizen one tries to preserve the balance. In spite of these conflicts, most systems continue to subscribe to the need for strengthening the role of the individual insured in health insurance.

One approach has been to formalize participation and choice in terms of patients' rights. Where these are insufficient, formal legal procedures should allow consumers/patients who are dissatisfied to seek redress in court. Nonetheless, the use of court procedures is controversial and vulnerable to mis-interpretation. Besides individual redress, court procedures concerning the payer's liability can enhance transparency in decision-making, particularly in cases of priority-setting (e.g. Germany, Israel) and waiting lists (e.g. Netherlands). Court decisions require administrators and/or purchasers to justify their decisions to exclude services or contract providers. Although primarily focused on individual cases, such outcomes can have far-reaching consequences at the regional and national levels of decision-making (e.g. regarding benefit packages). Although no one is advocating widespread use of judicial procedures, they can be an additional instrument in protecting the interests of individual patients.

Notes

1 *Cf. e.g.* Article 3 of the Biomedicine Convention requires that countries provide 'equitable access to health care of appropriate quality'. Therefore, accessibility, in particular *timely* access of health care systems, is a common aim to all member states. Patient autonomy has been incorporated in Article 1 of the Convention (protection of human dignity and identity).

2 For instance, the Swiss Constitution incorporated this right in Article 41(1) reading: 'the Confederation and the Cantons shall strive to ensure that, in addition to personal responsibility and private initiative . . . every person shall benefit from necessary health care'.

3 *Cf. e.g.* the new Swiss Health Insurance Act (Art. 4), *mutatis mutandis* the Dutch Sickness Fund Act (art. 34(4)) and the German Social Code Book V (art. 173(2)).

4 Here it is excluded from the third scheme, under the Health Insurance Access Act (WTZ), which is an exception and follows a different approach.

5 Algemene Maatregel van Bestuur 'Inschrijvingsbesluit ziekenfondsverzekering' Stb. 2000, 360 (Implementation regulation enrolment sickness fund insurance), *Official Journal of State* 2000, 360.

6 Case 3-2179/95 *Yehudit Rubin* v. *Leumit Sickness Fund and the State of Israel* (Tel Aviv Labour Court); Case 14-1562/95 *Daniela Eldar* v. *Klalit Sickness Fund and the State of Israel* (Tel Aviv Labour Court) 17 August 1995; and Case 7-2, 7-4,7-5,4-179/96 *Dorit Shirman and others* v. *Kladat Sickness Fund and others* (Tel Aviv Labour Court) (18 January 1996), quoted by Shalev and Chinitz, 1997.

7 HCJ 2570, 2743, 3293, 3179/96 *Medina Bat-Ami and others* v. *Ministry of Health and others* (14 May 1996); C-7-15, 7-16/96 *Yossi Barazani and others* v. *Ministry of Health and others* (Jerusalem Labour Court) (22 May 1996); HCJ 2696/97 *Oliver Riva* v. *Minister of Health and others* (6 May 1997).

8 *Cf. e.g.* German Federal Social Court, Bundessozialgericht (BSG) B 1 KR 2/99 *R-R* v. *Barmer Ersatzkasse* 11 May 2000 (non-recognized treatment methode ATC); B 1 KR 11/98 *R-B* v. *AOK Sachsen-Anhalt* 17 March 2000. *Mutatis mutandis* the Swiss Federal Insurance Court (EVG) KV 90 9 July 1999 (reimbursement of IVF as a non-recognized medical therapy according to the KVG); EVG KV 87 14 June 1999, para 4b (Psychotherapist) discussing the Bundesrat's discretionary competences to issue regulation on the recognition of medical professions. Reimbursement of not covered dental impants. Belgium Labour Court, Brussels 8 January 1997 Rechtskundig Weekblad no. 18, 2 January 1999 pp. 605–8.

9 E.g. Regional Court of Rotterdam. Sentence 31 August 1994 RZA No. 1994/146 (denial of a common heart transplant protocol); Central Appeals Board 17 December 1997. USZ 1997/37 (accepted).

10 Court of Appeal Hertogenbosch, sentence 24 February 1959 RZA 1987; 87/26 (shortage of sickness fund dentists due to the tariff policy). Regional Court of The Hague, sentence 18 June 1987 RZA 87/185 (extension of hospital residence due to lack of beds in recognized nursing homes). Regional Court of Zwolle, sentence 14 February 2000 no. 53325 KG ZA 00–45 (waiting list due to regulatory capacity constraints). Regional Court of Maastricht, sentence 15 September 2000 no. 00/1077.

11 However, this might change since under the current NHS regime the actual delivery of care is secured by a process of contracting. Such contractual relations may – conditionally – impose legally enforceable claims. In the Italian system this is already the case.

References

Angell, M. (2000) Patients' rights bills and other futile gestures, *New England Journal of Medicine*, 342(22): 1663–4.

Barolin, G. (1996) Patient rights alone are not enough, too many rights can also be harmful, *Wiener Medizinische Wochenschrift*, 146(4): 79–84.

Beauchamp, T. and Childress, J. (1994) *Principles of Biomedical Ethics*. New York: Oxford University Press.

Busse, R. (2000) *Health Care Systems in Transition – Germany*. Copenhagen: European Observatory on Health Care Systems.

Busse, R. (2001) Risk structure compensation in Germany's statutory health insurance, *European Journal of Public Health*, 11(2): 174–7.

Chinitz, D. (2000) Regulated competition and citizen participation: lessons from Israel, Health Expectations 3: 90–96.

Colombo, F. (2001) *Labour Market and Social Policy. Towards More Choice in Social Protection? Individual Choice in Insurer in Basic Mandatory Health Insurance in Switzerland*, OECD Occasional Paper no. 53. Paris: OECD.

Coulter, A. (1997) Partnerships with patients: the pros and cons of shared clinical decision-making, *Journal of Health Services Research and Policy*, 2(2): 112–21.

Council of Europe (2000) *Recommendation No. R, 2000*. 5 of the Committee Ministers to Member States on the development of structures for citizen and patient participation in the decision-making process affecting healthcare. Strasbourg: 24 February.

Den Exter, A.P. (2000) Health legal reforms in the Czech Republic and Hungary, in E. Krizova and J. Simec (eds) *Health Care Reforms in Central and Eastern Europe (CEE): Outcomes and Challenges*. Prague: Charles University.

Greß, S., Groenewegen, P., Kerssens, J., Braun, B. and Wasem, J. (2002) Free choice of sickness funds in regulated competition: evidence from Germany and the Netherlands, *Health Policy*, 60(3): 235–54.

Gross, R., Berg, A., Rosen, B. and Chinitz, D. (1998) *The Public's Perception of the Health System after Introduction of the National Health Insurance Law. Principle Findings from a Survey of the General Population*. Jerusalem: JDC Brookdale Institute.

Hofmarcher, M.M. and Rack, H. (2001) *Health Care Systems in Transition – Austria*. Copenhagen: European Observatory on Health Care Systems.

Kerr, E. (2000) *Health Care Systems in Transition – Belgium*. Copenhagen: European Observatory on Health Care Systems.

Kismodi, E. and Hakimian, R. (2001) A survey of patients' rights representatives in Israeli hospitals, *Medicine and Law*, 20: 19.

Lomas, J. (1997) Reluctant rationers: public input to healthcare priorities, *Journal of Health Services Research and Policy*, 2(1): 103–11.

MacStravic, S. (2000) The downside of patient empowerment, *Health Forum Journal*, 43(1): 30–1.

Mossialos, E. (1999) Healthcare and cost containment in Luxembourg, in E. Mossialos and J. Le Grand (eds) *Health Care and Cost Containment in the European Union*. Aldershot: Ashgate.

Murray, C.J. and Frenk, J. (2000) A framework for assessing the performance of health systems, *Bulletin of the World Health Organization*, 78(6): 717–31.

Ombudsman de l'assurance-maladie sociale (1996) *Rapport d'activité 1996* [*Annual report 1996*], pp. 7–8. Lucerne: Ombudsman de l'assurance-maladie sociale.

Ombudsman de l'assurance-maladie sociale (1997) *Rapport d'activité 1997* [*Annual report 1997*], pp. 5–6. Lucerne: Ombudsman de l'assurance-maladie sociale.

Paton, C. (2000) *Scientific Evaluation of the Effects of the Introduction of Market Forces into Health Systems*. Dublin: European Health Management Association.

Reiser, S.J. (1993) The era of the patient: using the experience of illness in shaping the missions of healthcare, *Journal of the American Medical Association*, 269(8): 1012–17.

Saltman, R.B. and Figueras, J. (1997) *European Health Care Reform: Analysis of Current Strategies*. Copenhagen: World Health Organization Regional Office for Europe.

Schut, F.T. and Van Doorslaer, E.K.A. (1999) Towards a reinforced agency role of health insurers in Belgium and the Netherlands, *Health Policy*, 48(1): 47–67.

Shalev, C. and Chinitz, D. (1997) In search of universality, equity, comprehensiveness and competition: healthcare reform and managed competition in Israel, *Dalhousie Law Journal*, 20(2): 553–82.

Sorell, T. (2001) Citizen-patient/citizen-doctor, *Health Care Analysis*, 9: 25–39.

Struijs, A.J. (2000) Burgerschap en eigen verantwoordelijkheid [Citizenship and own responsibility], in Raad voor de Volksgezondheid en Zorg (ed.) *De rollen verdeeld: achtergrondstudies*. Zoetermeer: Raad voor de Volksgezondheid en Zorg.

Theurl, E. (1999) Some aspects of the reform of the healthcare systems in Austria, Germany and Switzerland, *Health Care Analysis*, 7: 331–54.

Van der Schee, E., Delnoij, D.M.J., J Hutten, B.F., Verweij, J.A. and Kerssens, J.J. (2000) *De invloed van verzekerden op het bestuur van ziekenfondsen: verschillende visies belicht* [The influence of the insured on the management of sickness funds: different visions illustrated]. Utrecht: NIVEL.

WHO (Regional Office for Europe) (1997) *Empowering Citizens in the Planning and Management of Health Care*, draft for the consultation on the development of patients' rights in Europe, 18–19 August. Gothenburg: WHO Regional Office for Europe, 4.

Wildner, M., Kerim-Sade, C., Fischer, R., Meyer, N. and Brunner-Wildner, A. (2001) Regionale und geschlechtsspezifische Unterschiede in der Erfüllung von Patientenrechten: Ergebnisse einer repräsentativen Bevölkerungsumfrage in München, Dresden, Wien und Bern [Regional and gender specific differences in the fulfilment of patients' rights: Results from a representative population enquiry in Munich, Dresden, Vienna and Bern], *Sozial Präventivmedizin*, 46: 248–58.

Williamson, C. (1998) The rise of doctor-patient working groups. [Review] [31 refs]. *British Medical Journal*, 317(7169): 1374–7.

Ziekenfondsraad (1995) *Evaluatie overeenkomstenstelsel Ziekenfondswet en Algemene Wet Bijzondere Ziektekosten* [*Evaluation of the Contracting System of the Sickness Fund Act and Exceptional Medical Expences Act*], Report 673. Amstelveen: Ziekenfondsraad (in Dutch).

Beyond acute care

twelve

Prevention and public health in social health insurance systems

Martin McKee, Diana M.J. Delnoij and Helmut Brand

Introduction

If asked to describe social health insurance (SHI), a perfectly reasonable response might be that it provides a mechanism by which an individual who falls ill can receive medical care, secure in the knowledge that the care will be paid for by a sickness fund to which he or she has contributed.

This description has the advantage of brevity while capturing the model's essential elements. But brevity comes at a price. This simplified description is based on a situation in which an individual becomes ill, recognizes the fact, and seeks care. While this is often the case, as in the case of a broken bone or a heart attack, there are also many situations where it does not apply (Stevens and Gillam 1998).

First, an individual with a need for health care may not be aware of it, and thus may not demand it. There are several reasons why this might be so. Symptoms that may be easily treatable may be dismissed as normal or the consequences of ageing (Sarkisian *et al.* 2001), especially among sections in the population that are already disadvantaged, such as the poor, who may have low expectations of the health care system, or people from ethnic minorities, whose cultural characteristics or linguistic ability diminishes their access to mainstream health services (Stronks *et al.* 2001). Second, there are circumstances when the individual has no symptoms but has a condition that, if detected early, could be treated before symptoms appear and the condition has progressed so far that curative treatment is no longer possible. An example is screening for cervical cancer. Third, an individual may fail to seek care, or even actively reject it, even though society has an interest in him or her receiving it. This may be the case with severe mental illness, immunization and some infectious diseases. Finally, whether from altruism or, increasingly, as a means of containing the costs of health care, society may have an interest in the health care sector actively promoting health rather than simply responding to disease.

The traditional model of health-seeking behaviour is also based on the principle that, once a system to pay for care is in place, the various elements in the health care system will respond by configuring themselves in such a way as to provide care in the optimal way possible. Yet this too is problematic, especially where that system is based on a series of relationships between sickness funds and individual health providers. The traditional model is best suited to meet health needs that can be managed by an individual professional during a single course of treatment, as is the case with common infections, but it is less well prepared to address the growing burden of chronic diseases that require the coordinated inputs from different professions and specialties. For example, in addition to their primary care physician, someone with diabetes who has had the misfortune to develop complications may need the skills of an ophthalmologist, a nephrologist and a vascular surgeon. For optimal results, these should be closely coordinated.

Many of these issues come together under the term 'population health', which considers the response of health systems to the needs of *populations*, rather than simply to the needs of groups of *individuals* (McKee and Figueras 2002). It encompasses two broad areas.

The first is where those who pay for health care, whether sickness funds or government, singly or in combination, shift from a reactive system of paying for care demanded by individuals to a more proactive model in which they become active purchasers of care, seeking to determine the health needs of those for whom they are responsible and defining models of care within which these needs can be met. Specifically, this involves addressing explicitly the inequalities in access to care that exist in all societies (Paterson and Judge 2002).

The second area encompasses those health services that are most appropriately provided collectively. In some, collective provision involves the coordinated management of services provided to individuals, such as immunization and screening. If population health outcomes are to be optimized, it is not sufficient simply to make such services available. Even when they are free, some groups, especially those already disadvantaged, will be unlikely to take them up because of the other barriers that they face, such as the non-health sector costs, in money and time, of obtaining care. As a consequence, purchasers in many countries have developed a range of activities to enhance uptake among all those who might benefit (Grilli *et al.* 2003).

Health services also include a range of functions that move back a step, to address the determinants of disease. They include the continuing vigilance necessary to detect the emergence of threats posed by infectious disease (Maclehose *et al.* 2002), as well as timely intervention to protect against health threats posed by the environment. They also include interventions to help individuals make healthy choices, and so reduce their likelihood of seeking health care.

These issues require a new set of roles that depart from the traditional model of social insurance. Some roles have been taken on by sickness funds. Others are the responsibility of the state, through its public health services. There are also increasing numbers of innovative structures in which the state works with sickness funds and other organizations.

Different countries have adopted different solutions, with varying degrees of success. This chapter describes the arrangements they have put in place, what they have achieved so far, and what might be done in the future. It draws on a combination of published literature, in particular the 'Health Care Systems in Transition' series, and a survey of key informants in Austria, Belgium, France, Germany, the Netherlands and Switzerland.

Purchasing health care for populations

Strategic purchasing of health care involves an organization, acting on behalf of the population for which it is responsible, undertaking a series of interlinked steps (Øvretveit 1995). These are assessment of health care needs, specifying models of care to meet those needs, purchasing healthcare that conforms to these models, and monitoring the outcomes achieved. Ideally, these activities would be undertaken within the framework of an explicit strategy to enhance health.

Health reporting

Information on population health is increasingly widely available. Yet while all countries have long produced statistical reports, these have tended to be limited to listing of tables of unprocessed data. In recent years, however, many agencies have developed innovative and user-friendly ways of presenting information that make it easier to assess the health needs of their populations (Evaluation of National and Regional Public Health Reports 2003). For example, the *Rijksinstituut voor Volksgezondheid en Milieuhygiene* (RIVM) has published a series of reports on future public health scenarios in the Netherlands and has made available, on the internet, detailed information on the regional distribution of patterns of health and its determinants in the Netherlands (Rijksinstituut voor Volksgezondheid en Milieu 2003). Many Dutch municipalities also produce local reports.

The French High Committee on Public Health has recently begun publishing annual reports on the health of the French population (Haute Comité de la Santé Publique 2002). In addition, the new regional hospital authorities produce plans for health sector investment that draw on the national reports and on data collected locally.

In Germany, while each *Land* is required to produce an annual report on health statistics, a few, such as Brandenburg, Baden-Württemberg and Hamburg have published more sophisticated health reports that examine trends and patterns of health (see http://www.eva-phr.nrw.de/reports3.html). North Rhine-Westphalia, which now has considerable experience with such reports, has also encouraged local health authorities to work with key stakeholders to produce regular reports (Weihrauch 2002).

However, even where health reports have been produced, with a few exceptions there has generally been little attention to inequalities in either health or access to health care, with the exception of the Netherlands.

The limited extent of health reporting can be attributed to several factors. One is the scarcity of available data. Although data on mortality are universally reported, data protection laws (Lawlor and Stone 2001) and a lack of subsidiary information often preclude analysis of mortality by, for example, socioeconomic status or ethnicity.

The issue of data protection is especially important in Germany, largely because of historic concerns arising from the misuse of linked data in the 1930s, although recently there has been a debate on the concept of a '*Datentransparenz-gesetz*', i.e. a law on data transparency that would permit linkage of data on individuals from a variety of sources, but progress has been slow.

The availability of other sources of data is also often poor in the countries in question. With the exception of the Netherlands, there have been relatively few representative health and lifestyle surveys, such as those conducted regularly in the United Kingdom or the Nordic countries. In Germany, one large survey of more than 7000 adults was undertaken by the Robert-Koch Institute in 1998 and published in a special volume of *Das Gesundheitswesen* in December 1999 (Robert Koch-Institut 1999). It is not, however, utilized to its full potential.

Cancer registries could provide another source of data but again coverage is often quite limited. For example, in the former West Germany such registers only existed in Saarland, Hamburg and the area around the city of Münster, although the University of Mainz also maintains a register of childhood cancer. In 1995, a federal law required each *Land* to establish a registry but by the late 1990s coverage was still extremely low (Schuz *et al.* 2000).

There are, of course, many other sources of health data, from surveys undertaken for specific purposes, such as those within the framework of the WHO MONICA Project (De Henauw *et al.* 2000; Gasse *et al.* 2001), but these are often narrowly focused and designed to answer specific research questions.

Yet lack of data is only one explanation for the relative scarcity of health reports. As the examples described above show, it is possible to make imaginative use of what data do exist. Thus, the second factor is a lack of appropriate public health expertise to undertake the appropriate analyses and to present the results in a meaningful way. This point was made by most of the key informants surveyed for this chapter, who commented on the long-standing weakness of public health in their countries. A notable exception is the Netherlands, which has a strong academic public health community and a large training programme in which several universities collaborate (Netherlands Institute for Health Science 2003). There is, however, evidence that governments are beginning to address this issue, such as in the German federal government's newly created health services research programme.

Identifying effective care

Knowledge of the health needs of the population is only the first step in the process of purchasing care. Strategic purchasing also requires information on the effectiveness of interventions that might be used to meet those needs.

Each country benefits from the international regulatory environment within which safety and efficacy of pharmaceutical products and, to a lesser extent, medical technology is assured. In addition, in recent years, many countries have seen a considerable growth in health technology assessment, which goes beyond the existing regulatory requirements to ask questions such as whether an intervention is cost-effective (Banta 1994). This has yielded many important insights but it has often been focused on individual technologies, such as different types of scanner, rather than looking at the overall framework of care within which the technology is used. Thus, again with the exception of the Netherlands (ZonMw 2003), there are few organizational research programmes such as those within national research programmes in Canada or the United Kingdom.

Purchasing care

The next step is to make the connection with health services. It might be expected that this would be especially problematic in countries with social insurance systems, simply because of the many actors involved. This seems to be the case and there seem to be few examples of structures enabling close links between those producing health reports, typically public health services run by government, and either purchasers (in the form of sickness funds) or providers, such as associations of physicians or hospitals.

The exceptions are where innovative structures have been established, bringing these groups together. For example, a series of new mechanisms to foster coordination has been established in France. Since 1998, the newly-created regional hospital agencies (ARH) have assumed much of the responsibility for purchasing previously undertaken by the sickness funds, combining planning, contracting and, for public hospitals, capital funding. Although experience is still quite limited, they seem to have been able to combine these functions effectively to bring about changes in hospital services that are more closely aligned with population health needs (McKee and Healy 2002).

In North Rhine-Westphalia, a State Health Conference has been established that brings together a wide range of interest groups, both within and outside the health care sector. Since its creation in the early 1990s it has produced a series of health reports that have provided the basis for a regional health strategy, operationalized through a set of targets to which the participants in the Conference have signed up (Weihrauch 2002). In general, however, structures providing effective links between public health services and sickness funds that can inform the process of strategic purchasing of health care remain uncommon.

This analysis suggests that considerations of public health play a relatively small role in strategic purchasing in the countries concerned. The national correspondents who contributed the material on which this chapter is based have identified several reasons why this may be so.

For example, the Dutch health system consists of four discrete silos with limited overlap (Figure 12.1). Overlap between the public health and acute care silos is confined mainly to some screening programmes and immunization against influenza (see below). Overlap between public health and long-term care occurs with mother and child care, childhood screening and immunization.

Figure 12.1 The four silos of the Dutch health care system

Public health	*Acute curative care*	*Long-term care*	*Social services*
Provided by: municipal public health offices, GPs and home care organizations	Provided by: private professionals and institutions	Provided by: private professionals and institutions	Provided by: municipalities
Financed through: municipal budgets and AWBZ	Financed through: ZFW and private health insurance	Financed through: AWBZ	Financed through: municipal budgets

Note:
AWBZ = universal, compulsory fund for 'catastrophic' illness (i.e. most long-term care); ZFW = sickness funds.

Source: Authors research.

The three sources of funding have different geographical boundaries. The AWBZ is organized on a national basis, local government runs public health and the sickness funds no longer have any geographical focus. Consequently, each organizational unit is responsible for a different population, making collaboration difficult.

The scope for strategic purchasing is also constrained by the limited scope for selective contracting. First, sickness funds are obliged to enter into contracts with all accredited hospitals in the Netherlands, and although they are, in theory, able to contract selectively with ambulatory care providers, their scarcity means that this freedom is largely theoretical.

Second, the Dutch tradition of self-regulation means that effectiveness is largely determined by the medical profession. Sickness funds and physicians do negotiate fee schedules, with specialists paid on the basis of fee-for-service. The fee schedules contain a long list of remunerated items and there is currently discussion about moving to a system based on diagnosis groups, but this has not so far included attention to issues of effectiveness. In primary care, as funding is based on capitation, there has again been little attention from purchasers to the care that is provided.

Third, the system of financing creates a disincentive to seek unmet need, with its potential cost implications. Indeed, greater competition has encouraged some funds to concentrate their efforts on employees of large- and medium-sized enterprises, as those in work are more likely to be healthy than the general population. Finally, the ability of any of the sickness funds that function at a national level to influence the configuration of services in a particular area is very limited.

Some of the same issues arise in Switzerland, where insurers must also reimburse all physicians. A law that would give greater freedom to insurers to contract selectively was proposed but faced strong opposition from the Swiss Medical Association, who argued that the insurers have yet to develop a clear concept of purchasing that goes beyond simple cost reduction. The provision of hospital facilities is subject to plans developed by the cantons but, as in the Netherlands, the lack of congruence between populations covered by sickness funds and cantons and the highly decentralized nature of the Swiss health care system has made the coordination of services very difficult (Wyss and Lorenz 2000).

In Germany hospital planning is also the responsibility of regional governments. In addition, German sickness funds are especially constrained by the legal requirement to adhere to decisions on reimbursement by the Federal Committee of Physicians and Sickness Funds, which brings together the SHI-accredited physicians and the sickness funds. This institution produces health technology assessment reports relating to outpatient care and, on this basis, decides whether they can be reimbursed. A similar institution was created in 2002 in relation to hospital care (Busse 2000); it is planned to unify them from 2004.

Furthermore, German sickness funds are precluded from selective contracting. Discussions among the key actors have traditionally focused on financial matters, with issues of effectiveness only now beginning to enter into the decision-making process. The contracting framework, in which separate agreements are reached with hospitals and with physicians working from their own premises, makes it very difficult to develop integrated solutions that cross the interface between the hospital and ambulatory care sectors. Since 2000 some pilot projects have been undertaken that seek to transcend these barriers but they are on a small scale and it is not clear whether they will continue after their initial funding round.

In Belgium, decisions on what to reimburse are made by the sickness funds, but in consultation with physicians and government. The situation is, however, complicated by the incentive, on the one hand, to reduce what is covered by compulsory insurance while increasing the scope of their complementary insurance, in particular by including interventions for which there may be demand but little need.

Unlike its neighbours, Austria has adopted a strongly interventionist approach with the sickness funds. It has a regional hospital planning system, with each *Land* required to draw up a local plan that is in accordance with the *Krankenanstaltenplan* (federal hospital plan) and the *Österreichischer Krankenanstalten- und Großgeräteplan* (Austrian hospital and high technology investment plan) (Theurl 1999). A significant amount of the recurrent costs of Austrian hospitals is paid from taxation, rather than by sickness funds, in part as a means of ensuring geographical coverage. Thus, in some ways, the Austrian structure resembles the French one, with its tight state control over the activities of both sickness funds and hospitals.

Collective health interventions

The second issue to be examined is the provision of collective health interventions. These are characterized both by their collective nature and by the fact that need is often not expressed as demand. As examples, two such services will be examined, namely immunization and cancer screening.

With both immunization and screening, in the absence of effective policies to promote uptake, utilization will generally be lower than desired, especially among disadvantaged populations, even when services are free at the point of use (Gillam 1991; Sutton *et al.* 1994; Bos *et al.* 1998).

There are also certain factors that should be taken into account in the design of screening programmes. Furthermore, outcomes are better where screening is part of an integrated system of early diagnosis and treatment, which includes ensuring the quality of all stages of the screening process as well as mechanisms for referral for further investigation, treatment and follow-up (Hakama *et al.* 1985). With breast screening, radiologists who read large numbers of films have higher detection rates (Esserman *et al.* 2002) and large screening centres obtain better results than smaller ones (Blanks *et al.* 2002). For these reasons, screening programmes are ideally based on population registers, with mechanisms to increase uptake among all sections of the population, with in-built quality assurance systems and integrated pathways for those in whom disease is detected.

Essentially there are three ways of providing collective health services in an SHI-based system:

1 They can be provided outside the relationship between the sickness funds and providers, typically, but not invariably, by public health authorities.
2 They can be undertaken within this relationship, with funding by sickness funds and delivery by private physicians, and public health authorities undertaking an oversight role of some sort.
3 Other organizational structures, bringing together sickness funds, providers, public health authorities and others can provide them.

The *first model* is employed to deliver childhood immunizations in France, Belgium and the Netherlands. In France, childhood immunizations are delivered by school health services managed by the state public health services. In the Netherlands, childhood immunization is provided by organizations that predate the establishment of the social insurance system in the 1940s. These also provide a range of health visiting activities, although they are separate from childhood surveillance, which is undertaken by municipal public health offices. It is intended to merge these two systems in the near future.

In Belgium, the situation is especially complicated because of the different regulations for each vaccine. Immunization against polio is mandatory, with distribution and monitoring of uptake the responsibility of the Federal Health Ministry. The Federal Health Ministry also finances the non-mandatory childhood immunization against hepatitis B. In the late 1990s, in response to an increase in cases, several sickness funds began to offer immunization against meningitis C. Subsequently, the French community obtained funding for 200,000 doses of this vaccine from the federal government. The French

and Flemish communities finance other childhood immunization programmes. The actual delivery is the responsibility of organizations under
the jurisdiction of the Ministries of Culture and Social Affairs of the two
communities, the *Office de la Naissance et de l'Enfance* (ONE) in the French
community and the *Kind en Gezin* in the Flemish community. These organizations administer 50–70 per cent of immunizations, with private physicians
administering the remainder and the vaccines paid for by the communities. The
corresponding ministries in the communities are responsible for monitoring
uptake.

The *second model* can be seen in the delivery of childhood immunization and
cancer screening in Germany, both of which are financed by sickness funds and
delivered by private physicians. This model creates a number of difficulties
(Schmitt 2001). One is simply determining uptake rates. Information on childhood immunization is only collected at school entry, which is at 6 years of age,
so it is long out of date by the time it is obtained, although public health authorities in Saarland and Schleswig-Holstein are trying to develop mechanisms that
would yield more timely data.

In general, responsibility for increasing uptake is unclear, so little is done,
except for some promotional campaigns by pharmaceutical companies or as
part of the general process by which physicians market their services. However,
in North Rhine-Westphalia the State Health Conference (see above) has made
measles eradication a priority and is mobilizing key actors to achieve this goal.

According to a representative survey among 3000 persons above 14 years of
age in 2003, 26 per cent of German SHI-insured persons would like to be
reminded by their sickness fund if an immunization is due (with the younger
agreeing more often with this statement) while 80 per cent would like to see
their GP doing so (and even 87 per cent of those above 60 years). In reality,
however, only 47 per cent say that their GP talks to them about immunizations
(eastern part 62 per cent, western part 44 per cent) (BKK 2003).

Sickness funds measure uptake rates for breast and cervical screening on the
aggregate level, but neither monitor them closely (e.g. in respect to certain
groups) nor approach individuals. Until 2003, there have been no organized
breast screening programmes, but many mammograms have been undertaken,
large numbers of which are by non-specialist radiologists (Perleth *et al.* 2001).
From 2004, a regular mammography screening is included in the SHI benefit
catalogue (Köhler *et al.* 2003).

In Austria, cervical smears are performed routinely at gynaecological attend-
ances but the records are maintained only in the clinic and laboratory involved.
Large numbers of mammograms are performed in a similar ad hoc manner
(Wild 2001). There is also a programme of annual health checks to which all
insured people are invited and where the physician completes a report for the
sickness funds, but these reports so far are not analysed. Uptake of these checks
has increased in recent years but there are large geographical variations, with
the lowest rates in the east of Austria.

In view of the weaknesses of the existing system, the Vienna City Health
Department has established a coordinated programme aimed at women aged
50–70, with targeted invitations supported by an information folder and a
helpline in German, Turkish and Serbo-Croat, quality assurance systems, and

integrated management of women with abnormalities, including counselling and rapid referral to designated surgical clinics.

The *third model* is employed for cancer screening in Belgium, the Netherlands and Luxembourg. In Belgium, the decision to provide cancer screening has been taken at the federal level but with the communities taking operational responsibility (Vermeulen *et al.* 2001). The Flemish government has established five breast screening programmes that provide screening according to agreed standards, using only accredited radiologists. These centres are required to provide data for monitoring and quality control. The breast screening programme in the French community is currently (2002) being established in five provinces, coordinated by a community reference centre, and again using agreed protocols with monitoring.

Cervical screening in Belgium is also funded by the communities but is undertaken by private physicians. Monitoring of uptake and quality assurance systems are both reported to be weak.

In the Netherlands, cancer screening is based on a network of regional cooperatives involving municipal public health offices and cancer centres (Banta and Oortwijn 2001). Luxembourg has also established a separate programme, backed up by the sickness funds' refusal to reimburse screening mammograms outside the screening programme (Autier *et al.* 2002).

Switzerland provides a valuable natural experiment in alternative methods of financing preventive activities within a social insurance system. Since 1996 insurers have been required to pay for a range of preventive activities. One was childhood immunization, which had previously been undertaken by school health services managed by cantonal health authorities. The cantonal health authorities are required to ensure that this provision is equitable and that uptake is high.

The cantons have adopted three types of response. Some have entered into agreements with insurers to provide some funding of existing school health services, while maintaining a monitoring role. Others have gradually reduced support for school health services, on a piecemeal basis, as immunizations by private physicians have increased. Others have explicitly transferred the task to private physicians, while strengthening their monitoring role. Some cantons have also begun to engage in dialogue with non-governmental organizations to explore ways to enhance uptake.

A recent evaluation of this process identified a lack of clear objectives with little attention to implementation. Immunization rates are thought to have declined but this cannot be confirmed as information flows have been disrupted.

Insurers are also required to reimburse breast and cervical cancer screening. This too has been problematic. Programmes have been established in only three cantons, Geneva, Valais and Vaud (Faisst *et al.* 2001). An in-depth study of three cantons without programmes found that, although several organizations, including sickness funds, physicians' associations and cantonal authorities all had a potential role, none had sufficient individual resources to start the process and none was prepared to assume a coordinating role (Gürtner 2002).

A similar situation pertains with cervical screening. Most sickness funds paid for it before reform of the social insurance system, but screening was not provided as part of an integrated programme. This has not changed and there are considerable inequities in provision, which are difficult to address. One specific factor is that, as Swiss social insurance includes an annual deductible amount, many otherwise healthy women who do not use other services have to pay the entire cost of the procedure themselves.

The authors of this evaluation concluded that the changes to preventive services arising from the social insurance reform had not been a success because of a lack of explicit objectives, a failure to consider the process of implementation and the fundamental requirement that such activities should be part of an organized programme, rather than a set of disjointed activities. These conclusions could equally apply elsewhere.

Conclusion

This chapter has examined two areas where the focus of the health care system is on populations rather than on individuals: strategic purchasing and the delivery of collective interventions. In both cases, policy-makers working in systems based on social insurance appear to face considerable challenges.

Effective strategic purchasing requires influence over the scale and nature of facilities to provide care as well as its reimbursement. Yet in many countries examined this is difficult to achieve. One problem is the lack of coherence in the populations covered by each of the relevant organizations. Another is the lack of freedom to contract selectively, either in terms of particular providers or models of care. A third affects only some countries, where contracting systems make it impossible to contract for packages of care that span different sectors or professional groups. Finally, although some purchasing organizations, such as the AOK in Germany and the Federation of Austrian Social Security Institutions, are developing expertise in public health and technology assessment, the level of skills is generally very low.

Yet as France has shown, it is possible to address these problems. Although it is premature to draw firm conclusions, the French regional hospital agencies do seem to have been able to bring about substantial reconfigurations of hospital provision, including the creation of new centres to meet the needs of increasing numbers of people with cancer and AIDS. This has, however, required the state to play a leading role in a range of activities previously undertaken by sickness funds, so creating a model that is quite distinct from that seen in other social insurance systems.

Turning to collective interventions, although the evidence is still limited, and it is likely that outcomes of different policies will be, to some extent, context specific, some tentative conclusions can be drawn. First, simply requiring that sickness funds pay for collective interventions to be undertaken does not mean that they will be done. Second, while public health services have been able to undertake immunization programmes, where the intervention is relatively straightforward, they have not been able to develop their own cancer screening programmes that depend on strong links with mainstream health services. Effective programmes do, however, seem most likely where new structures have been created that provide a means for formal coordination between the actors concerned, including public health authorities, with their population focus and public health skills, sickness funds, with their financial resources, and health care providers.

Although the nature of the tasks involved are quite different, both of these topics raise similar issues. Neither public health systems nor networks of sickness funds and providers are able to implement these activities on their own. Yet when they work closely together, in formal structures with clear lines of responsibility, much can be achieved. The challenge is how to create such structures, especially where change must overcome strongly-held views about what is and is not possible. Perhaps the first step is to undertake a rather more detailed analysis than has been possible in this chapter to identify more explicitly the strengths and weaknesses of different models so that the debate on configuration of health systems can proceed on the basis of evidence rather than anecdote.

Acknowledgement

We are grateful to the following individuals who provided the background material on which this chapter is based: Eleonore Bachinger and Heinrich Tinhofer (Austria); Marina Puddu (Belgium); Marc Brodin and Dominique Polton (France); Niek Klazinga (the Netherlands); as well as Bernard Burnand and Felix Gürtner (Switzerland).

References

Autier, P., Shannoun, F., Scharpantgen, A. *et al.* (2002) A breast cancer screening programme operating in a liberal healthcare system: the Luxembourg Mammography Programme, 1992–1997, *International Journal of Cancer*, 97: 828–32.

Banta, H.D. (1994) Healthcare technology as a policy issue, *Health Policy*, 30: 1–21.

Banta, H.D. and Oortwijn, W. (2001) Health technology assessment and screening in the Netherlands: case studies of mammography in breast cancer, PSA screening in prostate cancer, and ultrasound in normal pregnancy, *International Journal of Technology Assessment in Health Care*, 17: 369–79.

BKK (2003) *Unzureichender Impfschutz laut BKK Umfrage*. Pressemitteilung/Press release 22 April. http://www.bkk.de/bkk/pressemitteilungen/powerslave,id,2,nodeid,15.html (accessed 30 July 2003).

Blanks, R.G., Bennett, R.L., Wallis, M.G. and Moss, S.M. (2002) Does individual programme size affect screening performance? Results from the United Kingdom NHS breast screening programme, *Journal of Medical Screening*, 9: 11–14.

Bos, A.B., Van Ballegooijen, M., Van Gessel-Dabekaussen, A.A. and Habbema, J.D. (1998) Organised cervical screening still leads to higher coverage than spontaneous screening in the Netherlands, *European Journal of Cancer*, 34: 1598–601.

Busse, R. (2000) New German health reform act passes, *Euro Observer*, 2(1): 3.

De Henauw, S., de Bacquer, D., De Smet, P., Kornitzer, M. and De Backer, G. (2000) Trends and regional differences in coronary risk factors in two areas in Belgium: final results from the MONICA Ghent-Charleroi Study, *Journal of Cardiovascular Risk*, 7: 347–57.

Esserman, L., Cowley, H., Eberle, C. *et al.* (2002) Improving the accuracy of mammography: volume and outcome relationships, *Journal of the National Cancer Institute*, 94: 369–75.

Evaluation of National and Regional Public Health Reports (2003) http://www.eva-phr.nrw.de/ (accessed 18 August 2003).

Faisst, K., Schilling, J. and Koch, P. (2001) Health technology assessment of three screening methods in Switzerland, *International Journal of Technology Assessment in Health Care*, 17: 389–99.

Gasse, C., Hense, H.W., Stieber, J. *et al.* (2001) Assessing hypertension management in the community: trends of prevalence, detection, treatment, and control of hypertension in the MONICA Project: Augsburg 1984–1995, *Journal of Human Hypertension*, 15: 27–36.

Gillam, S.J. (1991) Understanding the uptake of cervical cancer screening: the contribution of the health belief model, *British Journal of General Practice*, 41: 510–13.

Grilli, R., Ramsay, C. and Minozzi, S. (2003) Mass, media interventions: effects on health services utilisation (Cochrane Review), *The Cochrane Library*, Issue 2. Oxford: Update Software.

Gürtner, F. (2002) Personal communication.

Hakama, M., Chamberlain, J., Day, N.E., Miller, A.B. and Prorok, P.C. (1985) Evaluation of screening programmes for gynaecological cancer, *British Journal of Cancer*, 52: 669–73.

Haute Comité de la Santé Publique (2002) *La Santé en France*. Paris: Haute Comité de la Santé Publique.

Köhler, A., Gibis, B. and Mühlich, A. (2003) Mammographie-screening: Flächendeckendes Angebot bereits im Jahr 2005, *Deutsches Ärzteblatt*, 100: A1240–3.

Lawlor, D.A. and Stone, T. (2001) Public health and data protection: an inevitable collision or potential for a meeting of minds? *International Journal of Epidemiology*, 30: 1221–5.

Maclehose, L., McKee, M. and Weinberg, J. (2002) Responding to the challenge of communicable disease in Europe, *Science*, 295: 2047–50.

McKee, M. and Figueras, J. (2002) Strategies for health services, in M.J. Detels, R. Beaglehole and H. Tanaka (eds) *Oxford Textbook of Public Health*, pp. 1889–900. Oxford: Oxford University Press.

McKee, M. and Healy, J. (2002) Réorganisation des systèmes hospitaliers : leçons tirées de l'Europe de l'Ouest, *Revue Médicale de l'Assurance Maladie*, 33: 31–6.

Netherlands Institute for Health Science (2003) http://www.nihes.nl/ (accessed 18 August 2003).

Øvretveit, J. (1995) *Purchasing for Health*. Buckingham: Open University Press.

Paterson, I. and Judge, K. (2002) Equality of access to healthcare, in J.P. Mackenbach and M. Bakker (eds) *Reducing Inequalities in Health: A European Perspective*. London: Routledge.

Perleth, M., Busse, R., Gibis, B. and Brand, A. (2001) Evaluation of preventive technologies in Germany: case studies of mammography, prostate cancer screening, and fetal ultrasound, *International Journal of Technology Assessment in Health Care*, 17: 329–37.

Rijksinstituut voor Volksgezondheid en Milieu (2003) http://www.rivm.nl/index_en.html (accessed 18 August 2003).

Robert Koch Institut (1999) *Bundes-Gesundheitssurvey 98*. http://www.rki.de/Gesund/Daten/bgsurvey/bgsurvey.htm (accessed 18 August 2003).

Sarkisian, C.A., Hays, R.D., Berry, S.H. and Mangione, C.M. (2001) Expectations regarding ageing among older adults and physicians who care for older adults, *Med Care*, 39: 1025–36.

Schmitt, H.J. (2001) Factors influencing vaccine uptake in Germany, *Vaccine*, 20 (Suppl. 1): S2–4.

Schuz, J., Schon, D., Batzler, W. *et al.* (2000) Cancer registration in Germany: current status, perspectives and trends in cancer incidence 1973–93, *Journal of Epidemiol Biostat*, 5: 99–107.

Stevens, A. and Gillam, S. (1998) Needs assessment: from theory to practice, *British Medical Journal*, 316: 1448–52.

Stronks, K., Ravelli, A.C. and Reijneveld, S.A. (2001) Immigrants in the Netherlands: equal access for equal needs? *Journal of Epidemiology and Community Health*, 55: 701–7.

Sutton, S., Bickler, G., Sancho-Aldridge, J. and Saidi, G. (1994) Prospective study of predictors of attendance for breast screening in inner London, *Journal of Epidemiology and Community Health*, 48: 65–73.

Theurl, E. (1999) Some aspects of the reform of the healthcare systems in Austria, Germany and Switzerland, *Health Care Analysis*, 7: 331–54.

Vermeulen, V., Coppens, K. and Kesteloot, K. (2001) Impact of health technology assessment on preventive screening in Belgium: case studies of mammography in breast cancer, PSA screening in prostate cancer, and ultrasound in normal pregnancy, *International Journal of Technology Assessment in Health Care*, 17: 316–28.

Weihrauch, B. (2002) North Rhine-Westphalia, in M. Marinker (eds) *Health Targets in Europe: Polity, Progress and Promise*, pp. 103–16. London: British Medical Journal Publications.

Wild, C. (2001) Screening in Austria: the cases of mammography, PSA testing, and routine use of ultrasound in pregnancy, *International Journal of Technology Assessment in Health Care*, 17: 305–15.

Wyss, K. and Lorenz, N. (2000) Decentralization and central and regional coordination of health services: the case of Switzerland, *International Journal of Health Planning and Management*, 15: 103–14.

ZonMw (2003) *Health Care Efficiency Research 2003–2006*. The Hague: ZonMw (The Netherlands Organization for Health Research and Development).

chapter thirteen

Long-term care in social health insurance systems

Aad A. de Roo, Laurent Chambaud and Bernhard J. Güntert

Introduction

Persons with permanent impairment of physical, mental or psychological functions have complex needs, ranging from medical care to adapted environmental conditions. A key need is support for daily life activities and beyond, as loss or absence of functions affects the capacity to perform such activities independently. Dependent persons thus need long-term care (LTC), among other kinds of services, to support the quality of their life.

LTC refers to personal care and practical help for dependent persons. Personal care supports activities of daily life (ADL), like bathing and washing, dressing, feeding, getting in and out of bed, getting to and from the toilet and continence management. Practical help covers support of instrumental activities of daily life (IADL): domestic tasks like cooking, cleaning, laundering and handling personal affairs (Royal Commission on Long Term Care 1999).

LTC can be provided by informal cultural arrangements (involving relatives and neighbours) as well as by formal social ones. Many western European countries face greying populations and eroding cultural arrangements. This generates growing political interest in improving existing social LTC arrangements, to prevent situations in which dependent elderly are left without adequate support (OECD 1997; Jacobzone *et al.* 1998). In this chapter the social logic and dynamics of existing LTC arrangements will be explored, with a special focus on those in western European social health insurance (SHI) countries. The discussion is not restricted to care for the elderly, as LTC covers services needed by everybody with functional disorders. The central focus of analysis is the responsiveness of LTC arrangements to the quality of life (QoL) of such persons. The analytical QoL perspective reflects a growing international consensus that health care is a too narrow perspective to approach LTC issues (WHO QoL Group 1995; De Vries 1996).

Governments use formal social protection arrangements as instruments to support and improve the QoL of their citizens. Arrangements responding to LTC needs of dependent persons vary from country to country, reflecting social, cultural, political and economic differences. There are important variations in services, access procedures, organization of supply, sources of funding, governance structure etc. Most southern European countries offer social protection arrangements to supplement or replace informal care in restricted cases. Scandinavian countries and Great Britain offer tax-based service arrangements for LTC. This chapter discusses both statutory (mandatory) and voluntary LTC arrangements provided by premium-based insurances in western Europe. Such arrangements are present in Austria, Belgium, France, Germany, Luxembourg, the Netherlands and Switzerland, countries with a corporatist tradition towards addressing social security issues.

Premium-based LTC insurance has a complex public-private governance structure. Different layers of government are involved in funding and in defining services and eligibility, while provision of LTC services is in the hands of a mix of public and private (social and for-profit) providers. The public/private characteristics of LTC insurance can be explained in this chapter from a developmental perspective, showing how modern government changed its position from supplementing private social protection arrangements to absorbing them into their own public arrangements – while using in many cases the existing private supplier infrastructure instead of transforming it into a public one. The state's recent interest in LTC arrangements can be explained by showing how traditional cultural mechanisms that deal with the needs of dependent persons are eroding in modern society.

Premium-based LTC insurance is a historically recent phenomenon. The oldest form is the Dutch AWBZ, introduced in 1964. This Dutch arrangement will be taken as the reference point for a comparative discussion of issues and future developments. Preceding this discussion, the notion of premium-based LTC insurance is put in the wider context of a continuum of social QoL service arrangements. Inherent problems of this continuum can explain some major dilemmas concerning effectiveness and efficiency of LTC provision as such. In particular, this continuum is not very user-friendly.

QoL and LTC arrangements

Every country in western Europe has a substantial number of persons with permanent disabilities and chronic diseases (Jacobzone *et al.* 1998). Their (single or multiple) disorders can be physiological, psychological or mental in nature. Etiology is varied. Some people are disabled because of congenital anomalies. Others suffer from loss of function as a lasting result of acute somatic diseases, accidents or chronic diseases like cancer or schizophrenia. Ageing persons acquire somatic handicaps by irreversible functional decline of sensory organs, the musculoskeletal system and the circulatory and respiratory system. The elderly can also become disabled by psychogeriatric diseases like dementia.

Disorders in body or mind impair the personal capacities required for independent management of one's QoL. Mental, physical and psychologically handicapped persons, the frail elderly and the chronically ill are therefore dependent on others for management of that quality, to a degree varying by nature and impact of the functional disorder. They need third-party services to protect or sustain their QoL. The nature of these services can be derived from QoL theory. QoL has objective and subjective dimensions and QoL theory integrates both by explaining subjective experience of life as a function of inter-action between personal characteristics and perceived physical and social environment. Research shows the following seven factors as dominant in determining QoL (Granzin and Haggard 2000):

- emotional support, age and education;
- income;
- physical condition and self-determination;
- home ownership and housing satisfaction;
- community-neighbourhood relationships;
- leisure boredom;
- mental health.

These dimensions can be used to categorize services that elderly, chronically ill and handicapped persons need to sustain their QoL. Depending on the kind and complexity of their disorders, they require services in one or more of the following six categories:

- financial support to cover additional costs of life with a functional disorder and/or to compensate for loss of earning capacity;
- adaptation of the living and working environment (a specially adapted and equipped domestic or institutional setting and transportation facilities);
- health services to sustain the physical and psychological condition;
- support for personal daily life, domestic and household activities;
- support in maintaining community relationships and emotional support;
- specialized training and education.

Developed countries contribute to their citizens' QoL by offering a wide range of social arrangements in areas like income, work, housing, health care, ADL and IADL, education and social support. These combined arrangements can be con-ceived of as a continuum of social QoL support services. Dependent persons can appeal to state agencies for services they need to sustain their QoL. There are no examples, however, of countries offering dependent persons a comprehensive social arrangement for all six support service categories. Some services are pro-vided by specific arrangements, designed for all dependent persons or for sub-categories like the elderly, mentally handicapped or physically disabled persons. Other services, like income support, are available to needy individuals through group-based generic arrangements.

The mix of generic and specific arrangements in the continuum differs from country to country, as there is no international consensus on how to distribute LTC and other services for dependent persons over QoL support arrangements. LTC arrangements in western Europe vary on two dimensions: eligibility and entitlements. Eligible groups range from frail elderly people to all dependent persons, irrespective of age or etiology of their functional disorder. Entitlements range from personal and practical help to a wide range of related services: specialized education and training, adaptation of the living environment, transportation facilities, community relationships, emotional support etc. Traditionally, these entitlements are confined to services in institutional settings, although in advanced arrangements they are offered in independent living situations as well.

Understanding differences between social LTC arrangements

Countries differ in the scope of QoL support services offered by social arrangements to dependent persons. They also differ in the way they distribute those services over generic and specific arrangements in the QoL service continuum. Since January 2002, an LTC arrangement for dependent persons of 60 years and over is operational in France (the APA, *Allocation Personnalisée d'Autonomie*). This arrangement offers benefits in cash to cover expenses for ADL as well as domestic tasks at home. For persons under 60 there is a separate arrangement that offers benefits in kind. Medical care for these groups is offered by sick funds, while other QoL services rely on different arrangements that involve local government and pension funds. In Switzerland, ADL and IADL services for dependent persons are offered as a benefit in kind by SHI. Social insurance for physically handicapped persons here offers benefits in cash to cover costs of practical help in institutions or at home. Other services for dependent persons, like boarding and lodging in institutions, are covered by specific income supplement arrangements set by cantons. Domestic help is covered by arrangements of local authorities or by private payments.

The contrasts between France and Switzerland show how countries differ in the way they distribute services over generic and specific arrangements. Needs not covered by an LTC arrangement may be covered elsewhere in the social care continuum. Thus a comparison of LTC arrangements alone does not allow direct conclusions about how effectively societies in practice meet the needs of dependent persons. It is therefore important to study LTC arrangements by analysing them within the broader context of the national QoL service continuum of which they are each a part.

Differences between LTC arrangements also have to be studied within their cultural context, as countries vary in the way they relate the continuum of social QoL arrangements to cultural and private arrangements. There are important differences between European countries with respect to the social philosophy behind LTC arrangements. In north European countries such arrangements are designed according to social insurance principles. LTC is conceived as a social right at the disposal of any dependent person, like health care. In south European countries, the design of LTC arrangements starts from a somewhat different, social protection philosophy (Assous 2001). Here, dependent persons are expected to be supported in an informal way by their social network. Social services are offered only selectively, in situations where the social network is absent or overloaded and the persons involved do not have adequate financial means to pay for private arrangements. The social arrangement in these countries is designed more to supplement cultural and private arrangements rather than to replace them (Hofmarcher and Riedel 2001). In northern countries, dependency is perceived as a risk that can be covered by social insurance. In southern Europe, dependency is seen as a fact of life and public responsibility is limited to persons in vulnerable socioeconomic situations. In practice, contrasts between the two approaches are not that spectacular, given that co-payments are frequently required in insurance-type arrangements.

These differences in social philosophy are related to cultural differences, as can be illustrated by the role family structures play in care for the elderly. In 1994, 54 per cent of the elderly above 80 years in Spain lived (either alone or together with their partner) in households of their children or others. The corresponding percentages were for Portugal 42 per cent, Greece 35 per cent and Italy 34 per cent, in sharp contrast with 5 per cent in the Netherlands and 2 per cent in Denmark (Assous 2001). In the latter two countries (and in other Scandinavian countries) there is no legal obligation for children to contribute at least some LTC costs for their parents. Such obligations exist in varying forms in southern Europe and also in Belgium, Austria and Germany.

Finally, differences between LTC arrangements also have to be studied in their political context. Great Britain and the Scandinavian countries take a public approach to the QoL service continuum. Their arrangements are tax-based and public organizations are used for administration and provision of services. By contrast, the German speaking countries (Belgium, France, Luxembourg, the Netherlands and Switzerland) use a mix of tax- and premium-financed arrangements and a mix of public and private organizations to administer and provide services. This public-private mix is a deliberate choice, reflecting a deep-rooted corporatist orientation of these countries toward the role of government in social policy-making. In countries with tax-based arrangements, the parliament (and regional representative political bodies like county councils in Sweden) has a constitutional obligation to allocate public funds for services. This constitutional obligation does not apply to premium-financed arrangements in SHI countries. Power over allocation of social insurance premium money in these countries is shared with labour unions, employer organizations, provider organizations and professional groups according to well-institutionalized and highly sophisticated country-specific corporatist patterns. This shared power gives those social groups an institutionalized role in the making and implementation of social policy.

These different cultural, social and political factors interact over time in a way that can help to understand the dynamics of LTC arrangements and clarify the setting for further development. This historical perspective is explored in brief in the next section.

Evolution of the social QoL support services continuum

Societies rely on cultural and structural solutions to help dependent persons to sustain their QoL. The cultural solution is shaped by traditional sets of norms and values aiming at social coherence and integration on the level of family life and the local community. This set also provides for social integration of disabled, chronically ill and ageing persons with family, relatives, neighbours and friends. QoL of dependent persons here is sustained by services provided in an informal way by local social structures. The cultural response is the oldest QoL arrangement and still functions in society at large. Figures presented above about family support of the elderly, however, illustrate that this arrangement plays a greater role in southern than in northern parts of western Europe. It is a solution connected to small local community life. Its role gradually shrinks with structural changes in individual lifestyle and in living, working and social life patterns in modern society. These changes result in an erosion of the potential of family and community relationships to support dependent persons. They also engage a growing number of women in productive economic life, limiting the traditional female role in voluntary care for dependent persons.

During the Middle Ages, clerical and secular initiatives added a structural solution to existing informal cultural approaches. Private social arrangements were developed to contribute to QoL for a wide range of services in areas like care, education, work, welfare, social security and housing. Such arrangements were private social policies that shaped the juridical, financial and organizational dimensions of those services. Social security was offered by benefits in cash or in kind (e.g. free meals). Some arrangements focused on dependent persons, offering them benefits in kind. Several types of specialized care institutions emerged from these initiatives: hospitals (with a predominant nursing home character), institutions for persons with behavioural problems (mentally handicapped persons as well as those with a psychiatric disorder) and institutions for the elderly.

Churches, wealthy citizens, guilds and other corporatist organizations in the emerging medieval cities founded charities or took direct responsibilities in establishing and managing such institutions. They had one thing in common: the transfer of informal family and local community responsibilities to specialized, formally organized living environments removed from normal daily life. As the cultural solution is one of integration in society, the institutional solution brings separation by shaping institutional sub-cultures. The debate on the relative value of both approaches continues, but tends to be outdated now by new notions of consumer choice in social arrangements. These notions explicitly reject the standardized services as offered by most existing arrangements, replacing them by a set of alternatives to meet the needs of different preference groups. Such consumer-oriented approaches offer a choice between integration or living in a sub-culture at a certain distance from modern social life.

From the beginning, political authorities recognized that these private social arrangements had high social value but did not offer final solutions. First, access to institutions was limited to the constituency of the founders: it was a favour, not a right. Second, private social initiatives selectively focused on geographic areas with adequate constituency concentrations, leaving parts of the population without adequate access. Third, access became a problem as clerical and secular organizations fell short in expanding the number and volume of their institutions in pace with population growth. These factors led (local, regional and national) governments to develop their own public social arrangements and to establish public institutions to supplement the private ones. Such political initiatives were also frequently intended to roll back the role of the Church in society, as part of a broader struggle over regulatory powers during the emergence of the modern state. In this way, a situation developed in which public and private arrangements functioned in a supplementary as well as competitive relationship.

This situation principally changed as the modern industrial state gradually pushed clerical and secular arrangements into a subordinate position to the public ones. In building the welfare state, national governments started to make public arrangements available to the whole population, making private ones obsolete. In this way, western European governments established a continuum of social arrangements to support the QoL of their citizens (De Swaan 1988). This continuum is not static. Arrangements continually change over time, as they are upgraded and redefined in response to changing social, economic and political conditions. Such changing conditions have brought intensive attention to the LTC arrangements within the continuum.

The LTC predicament

In building the social QoL services continuum, most western European governments have given priority to the development of health care and income protection arrangements (Okma 2001). The historically developed position of public LTC arrangements as a supplement to private and cultural arrangements was predominant in many countries until recently. It is only in the last decade that revision of public LTC arrangements has become prominent on the political agenda in continental western Europe. This has occurred in reaction to demographic changes, resulting in greying populations, and socioeconomic changes that caused a gradual erosion of the capacity of cultural arrangements to deal with the needs of dependent persons.

Demographic and epidemiological studies predict a disproportional growth of dependent elderly in many countries in the next decades (Jacobzone 1999). Demand for QoL services is increasing in this group as previously fatal illnesses are converted into chronic conditions (OECD 1999). At the same time, studies show a gradual but irreversible change in lifestyle patterns of those who traditionally took responsibility for dependent persons on a voluntary basis (Meyer 2001). Informal care, provided by cultural arrangements, is still the most important source of services offered to the elderly and other dependent persons (OECD 1996), but its potential is eroding due to social changes like divorce rates and consequent changes in family relationships, decreasing fertility rates, growing participation of women in the labour force and urbanization (Randall *et al.* 1998). This has caused a gradual shift in demand for QoL services toward public and private arrangements in recent years.

This shift, in turn, has generated growing political concern about the adequacy of existing public and private arrangements for the elderly and other dependent persons. Six European countries with a corporatist orientation to social policy issues have responded to these concerns by transforming the supplementary nature of their public LTC arrangement into a nationwide premium-based insurance. Austria did so in 1993, followed by Germany in 1995, Luxembourg in 1998 and France in 2002. The oldest premium-based LTC insurance is the Dutch one, established in 1968. In Switzerland LTC insurance was introduced in 1996, not as a separate social arrangement but by broadening the scope of the SHI system.

One major political concern about the introduction of LTC insurance is that it induces an accelerated shift of demand, away from cultural arrangements. Together with a disproportional growth of dependent elderly in the population and expansion of such arrangements to other dependent groups, this can produce a prohibitive increase in collective expenditure. Indeed, the volume and cost of domestic and nursing home care rapidly expanded after the introduction of the German *Pflegegesetz* in 1995. Recent Swiss data confirm this pattern, but also offer additional insights. In 1996 the Swiss government expanded coverage of the *Krankenpflegeversicherung* to ADL and IADL services at home. The number of clients tripled between 1996 and 1999. Home care expenditures increased by 54.5 per cent between 1996 and 2000, from SF 1,100 million to SF 1,700 million. However, the annual growth rate of 18 per cent in 1997 and 1998 fell back to 10 and 12 per cent in 1999 and 2000. In 1996 the share of home care services in overall health insurance expenditure was 1.2 per cent. This grew from 1.4 per cent in 1997, to 1.6 per cent in 1998 and 1999, to 1.7 per cent in 2000 (Mazenauer 2001). Swiss policy-makers believe this increase can be at least partly explained by the replacement of informal family help with formal home care services and by a shift from nursing homes to independent living (Bundesambt für Socialversicherung 2001). This suggests that cost saving in nursing home expenditures has to be taken into account in judging the overall growth of home care expenditure.

The public-private mix in social LTC insurance

The six western European countries that decided to replace existing public and private LTC arrangements with a premium-based social insurance had to decide how to deal with the existing provider structure, established over the years by private organizations as well as local and regional authorities. One option was to change ownership of private organizations, by turning them into public ones. These six countries, however, opted for a solution that better fitted their corporatist culture. They created a public-private mix that allowed existing private (social and for-profit) institutions as well as public ones to continue their activities under the LTC insurance arrangement.

Ownership of provider organizations reflects national differences in the role of churches and other social organizations, public authorities and for-profit entrepreneurs. In Austria, local government owns 4 per cent of the *Pflegeheime* (nursing homes), 8 per cent is owned by churches, 74 per cent by secular non-profit organizations and 14 per cent is owned and run by private persons or companies. In Germany, private entrepreneurship is prominent in LTC institutions, with 36 per cent of the nursing homes run as a private business. Here, 10 per cent of the institutions are owned by local authorities and 54 per cent by not-for-profit organizations (separate figures about Church-owned institutions are not available). French nursing homes can be private as well as owned by local public bodies, mainly municipalities, or by public hospitals. Most institutions for handicapped persons are run by non-profit organizations (College voor Bouw 2001). In the Netherlands, commercial LTC providers are present on a very small scale, as Dutch law excludes them from access to LTC insurance money. Dutch central and lower government withdrew completely from public ownership of health and LTC organizations after 1990. This was based on a general political consensus that public ownership of provider institutions impedes the exercise of political control over the implementation of public arrangements.

In designing their social LTC insurance, the six national governments also had to decide how to deal with lower-level governmental authorities that traditionally administered and funded their own local and regional arrangements. In countries with tax-based arrangements, like Great Britain and Scandinavia, administrative responsibilities are assigned to public authorities. The six SHI governments, in line with their corporatist tradition (and the health care orientation predominant in much LTC policy-making), have devolved these responsibilities to sick funds (or affiliated organizations). In Austria, public expenditure by regional and local authorities of operational LTC costs was taken over by the national government. In the other countries, these expenditures were shifted from local taxes to insurance premiums (with occasional tax-based contributions from the national government).

By this corporatist solution, lower-level authorities lost their traditional role of administering their own local or regional LTC arrangements. However, they continue to be responsible for capacity planning in all countries except the Netherlands, as they still finance capital investment in local facilities. In combination with ownership of local provider organizations, this gives them a negotiating position in the public-private mix. This position is strengthened by the fact that lower authorities control adjoining public arrangements in the QoL continuum, such as welfare services and income supply (to cover costs for boarding and lodging in LTC institutions, for practical help at home etc). In most countries, lower-level authorities have a certain degree of freedom in setting eligibility and entitlements of such arrangements beyond minimal national standards. This creates differences in service level between regions, feeding discussions about equity. In France, for instance, the decision to introduce the APA for elderly people followed a first initiative in 1997 which allowed local bodies to decide the level of funding of QoL support activities. However, an evaluation showed only a low percentage of persons were covered (less than 20 per cent) and that there were large inequalities between the administrative regions, the '*departments*'.

The development and introduction of social LTC insurance has created rather complex structures of LTC governance. National governments share their decision-making authority with lower governmental levels in the area of planning and financial investment, and with insurers in the area of budgeting provider organizations. At the operational level, managers of provider organizations are held responsible by their boards or by lower-level government, depending on the ownership structure. Under such conditions, there is no final political responsibility at the national level, since corporatist governance structures are not hierarchies but networks.

The complex corporatist public-private mix, with governmental involvement on the national and lower level, is not a static one. The demarcation line between the public and private domain is drawn and redrawn as an outcome of changing attitudes and power distribution in political decision-making. In the Netherlands, the Dutch local authorities permanently lobby for the integration of social insurance arrangements for the elderly into the local public arrangements. Their argument is that social insurance arrangements should be under local democratic control.

Dutch LTC insurance in international perspective

The Dutch LTC insurance (AWBZ = Exceptional Medical Expenses Act) was established in 1968. It is a mandatory income-dependent premium-financed social insurance for the entire population. In 2000, the annual premium was over 8 per cent of salary (growing to 10 per cent in 2002 and 12.05 per cent in 2003), with a cap slightly above the level of modal Dutch income. While previously the premium was split equally between employee and employer, now employees pay the full premium themselves.

The AWBZ covers residential and domestic LTC for all dependent persons: frail elderly, chronically ill and persons with a mental, psychological or physical handicap (Schrijvers 1997). Originally the AWBZ focused on institutional LTC only, covering costs of nursing care as well as personal and practical help, boarding and lodging. In 1980, coverage was extended to home nursing as well as personal help. Practical domestic help followed in 1992. Previously those activities had been offered by private arrangements as well as by local public authorities. In 2000, the homes for the elderly arrangement was shifted from regional public authorities to the AWBZ. The AWBZ also covers the cost of medical care provided in institutional LTC settings (by psychiatrists, rehabilitation doctors and nursing home doctors).

The AWBZ's scope of target groups and entitlements is unique for social LTC insurance schemes. Services for handicapped persons are generally provided by other social arrangements. Most social LTC insurances restrict themselves to medical, paramedical and nursing services, as well as personal care in institutions and at home. They do not offer coverage for boarding and lodging in institutions or for IADL activities in institutions and at home. In cases of inadequate personal means, such costs are covered by additional social security income benefits, often provided by local or regional government. In southern European countries, as well as Belgium, Germany and Austria, this coverage is combined with a legal obligation for children to provide financial support for their parents (Hofmarcher and Riedel 2001). This difference in entitlements reflects different sociopolitical ideas about the demarcation of the public and private domain. The Dutch approach in this respect comes closer to public arrangements in Scandinavia and Great Britain. In practice, however, differences are not that spectacular since the AWBZ has an extensive system of co-payments for services offered. For residential care there is an income-dependent co-payment (up to €1750 a month in 2002).

LTC insurance is administered by sick funds, as in Switzerland, or by sick fund related organizations. In the Netherlands, the AWBZ is administered by 32 *zorgkantoren* (care offices), responsible for managing both volume and quality. Their instruments to influence the volume of care are the authority to settle budgets and production levels for provider organizations and to approve capital investment in new residential capacity. Their powers to influence quality are limited, as there is no surplus capacity among providers and they have few instruments for selective contracting. *Zorgkantoren* face no financial risks as an annual adjustment of premiums guarantees that all operating costs are covered. Need assessment is done by RIOs (regional indication organizations) under the organizational responsibility of local government. In other social LTC insurances, need assessment is a responsibility of medical professionals.

Although the AWBZ as an insurance arrangement is separated from health insurance, there are close institutional links between them. Both insurances are regulated by the Ministry of Health and they are supervised and controlled by the same quasi-governmental organizations. All other social arrangements are regulated by the Ministry of Social Affairs and supervised and controlled by another institution. Moreover, the management of the *zorgkantoren* is given to sick funds on five-year contracts issued by the government. This creates an opportunity for the managing sick fund to integrate the formally separated activities of both insurances on a strategic and operational level. In practice, the *zorgkantoren* and sick funds typically share the same buildings.

This close link on the operational level has an unplanned effect on the activities and policies of sick funds. In the Netherlands, sick funds now work within a policy framework that attempts to make them compete on cost leadership. The premium-generated income is deliberately allocated by the national premium pool in such a way that it is not adequate in covering full operating costs. To break even, sick funds therefore need to generate additional income through a nominal premium, paid out-of-pocket by all subscribers (Okma and Poelart 2001). Differences in efficiency between sick funds are presumed to be expressed by different nominal premium levels. Such competitive circumstances are not present in the AWBZ, as operational costs of *zorgkantoren* are fully covered by their premium income. This creates a strong incentive for the sick funds to offload costs from the health insurance to the AWBZ, and the close institutional relations of sick funds and the *zorgkantoren* facilitate this type of cost shifting. At the operational care level, this cost shifting has counterproductive effects on the effectiveness of care. Sick funds will try to keep clients as long as possible in the AWBZ circuit or to transfer them as soon as possible to that circuit, not for medical but for financial reasons.

Political control of premium-based LTC insurance

In most social insurance schemes, money flowing through the system is collected through premiums and not by taxes. The political implication of this is that a parliament has no constitutional right to control directly the money flow through the social insurances. However, unrestricted open-end financing of social insurance can endanger macroeconomic public policies. So national governments develop policy instruments to acquire a degree of control over the expenditures generated by social insurances. In federal or decentralized countries, the national government has to respect the autonomous social protection policy-making rights of lower-level government. In the latter countries, local governments can use their autonomous rights to extend entitlements or eligibility of national arrangements. Their local rights also are used to intervene in national capacity planning activities.

One direct effect of the use of autonomous rights is the existence of differences within countries, between regions, in access, as well as in scope and quality of provided LTC services. In France the social insurance is combined with a centralized political organization. The political goal is to involve local governments in the administration of LTC arrangements, with a role for the central government to maintain equal access. There is a growing interest in developing formal agreements on the basis of partnerships between local bodies, the central government and the insurance organizations. These agreements are seen as an alternative to central budgetary control on the one hand and open-end financing on the other.

The Dutch government does not face such autonomous rights of lower-level governments. All political rights at the provincial and local level are delegated by the central government, so political decision-making at lower governmental levels can be overruled by the central government. In practice, the central government respects the budgetary rights of lower governments. In this way it allows for differences between the public arrangements local authorities are responsible for, i.e. arrangements concerning welfare, income supplement and adaptation of living environment.

The AWBZ is a national arrangement without local variations. The Dutch government uses indirect and direct instruments for a broad control of demand and supply under this insurance. The most important instruments are:

- delineation of entitlements
- control of entry to the suppliers' markets
- regulation of procedures to allocate premium money to insurers and providers
- control of capital investments that influence the production capacity of institutions
- premium level control.

Entitlements are fixed by law. Eligibility is determined by the RIOs, the local need assessment organizations. The income-dependent premium is fixed annually by the central government. Goals for spending new money on an increased volume of services or on improvement of service quality levels are negotiated in national-level annual agreements between the central government and representative supplier and consumer organizations. The central government controls entry to the provider market and institutional capacity via a licensing system. Procedures for allocation of resources are set by guidelines on budgeting providers.

Legislation on entitlements and eligibility is a politically vulnerable process as it touches on the individual interests of every citizen in a very visible way. Governmental efforts to roll back existing entitlements in the Dutch health care and LTC insurances were repeatedly stopped by political resistance fed by strong pressure from public opinion. This suggests that, practically speaking, these instruments can only be used to improve (not to reduce) existing arrangements.

The Dutch government has had a successful record in containing LTC expenditure, largely through two of these instruments: the licensing of (re)building capacity for LTC institutions and the development of a budgeting system for LTC providers. Through the combined use of these instruments, the government has been very successful over the years in controlling the volume of provided LTC services. Currently, however, these instruments have lost much of their effectiveness. Provider organizations escape from building capacity control by switching to the use of buildings owned by parties outside the legal control of the ministry, like social housing organizations. At the same time, the budgeting system has come under attack from clients. Budgeting rules had become so tight during the last ten years that waiting lists started to develop. In 2000 some clients went to court, arguing that the LTC arrangement was an insurance and claiming that they were entitled to instant delivery of insured services after need assessment. The court explicitly confirmed the insurance character of LTC, forcing the government to allow the insurers and providers to expand their volume of services to an adequate level to respond to demand resulting from formal need assessment procedures.

This restoration of the insurance character of the AWBZ has not been helpful in solving a second effect of the Dutch government's cost containment policy. The government never systematically allowed the budgetary rules to accommodate improvement of service quality, despite the reality that the overall standards of living in the society at large improved substantially during the last 20 years. The governmental point of view was and is that such improvements have to be financed from productivity gains by providers. This policy approach has created intense ongoing controversy between the government and health institutions about efficiency and quality of health care. In this controversy, providers argue that their productivity gains have to be used to meet increasing costs for labour safety, institutional hygiene, improvement of salaries and so on. In the meantime, an increasing number of well-off clients have not waited for the end of the debate. As they grew in number, they stimulated existing and new providers to offer privately-paid LTC services, creating a private sector that competes head-on with the social one on quality. This private sector is now well established in home care and is emerging in nursing home care.

Alignment of social arrangements

One major source of public dissatisfaction with the AWBZ does not stem from shortcomings of the insurance itself, but from lack of alignment of the LTC insurance with other components of the QoL service continuum. In an ideal situation, this continuum would constitute a consistent spectrum of social services, offered in a coordinated way. This would require sophisticated coordination between institutionalized social sectors at a structural as well as operational level. However, the continuum is not the result of a deliberate developmental process, but rather a by-product of incremental policy-making that involves varying ministries and changing political coalitions over time. So, while internal coherence of arrangements may not be a problem, consistency of the overall pattern of arrangements is. As a consequence, the continuum is more a collection of loosely coupled service domains, with lacking alignment of:

- scope and taxonomy of entitlements
- the use of public and private sources for financing services
- procedures for need assessment and allocation of services to clients
- public and private responsibilities in governance, supply and control structures.

One important source of incoherence in the QoL service continuum is the absence of a taxonomy that enables standardized specification of entitlements offered in the continuum. Every component uses its own terminology. This results in substantial administrative ambiguity about scope of entitlements and eligibility that can create unintended financial incentives for administrators managing under tight budgetary conditions. Broad interpretation of entitlements opens opportunities to finance a service activity by more than one arrangement at the same time. Although this 'double funding' from a system point of view is inefficient, it can add substantial value to clients if is used to improve service quality. A narrow interpretation of eligibility facilitates denial of entry and referral of (cost-intensive) clients to a neighbouring arrangement. This destroys the added value of multiple arrangements for clients, especially in cases where referral is denied. In practice, this means that clients get no (or inadequate) care.

A second source of incoherence in the system comes from the mix of funding principles in the continuum. LTC insurance is premium-based, while many neighbouring – complementary – arrangements are tax-based. Tax-based arrangements basically have a closed-end financing, as money is made available by annual budgets set by local, regional or national government. These services are provisioned on a rationing basis in case demand exceeds budgetary limits. By contrast, insurance-based arrangements have an inherent open-ended character. Insurance rights imply that services are provided or paid for promptly if the insured risk becomes reality (after a need assessment procedure). One of the recurrent operational consequences is that budgetary limits of tax-funded arrangements prevent coordinated delivery with premium-funded services.

Third, lack of coordinated delivery is aggravated by procedural differences between arrangements in the area of need assessment and allocation of resources. The standard example is a person discharged from hospital after a stroke when adaptations at home are not ready yet. Frequently such persons are transferred to nursing homes – not because they need the care offered there but because such institutions have the required physical living environment. Lack of coordinated provision of services from different parts of the continuum thus creates an important source of inefficient use of resources, in addition to a lack of effectiveness.

The fourth and last source of inconsistency of the QoL service continuum is an institutional one. In the Netherlands, local government is responsible for welfare arrangements, LTC need assessment and adaptation of the domestic living environment of dependent persons. These activities have to be coordinated with the LTC insurance activities of the *zorgkantoren*, that have a monopolistic position in a geographic area that is much larger than the area covered by any single local government. As a result, *zorgkantoren* have to coordinate their administrative activities with more than 18 local governments on average, each one with a specific local policy approach to the arrangements it is responsible for. Home care organizations have comparable problems because of their regional scale. They too have to coordinate with many local governments. It is easy to see that this complexity of coordination is inefficient from an organizational point of view. In practice, it is also ineffective in meeting the needs of dependent persons in a flexible and swift way.

These inefficiencies are highly relevant from a macroeconomic point of view. Even more important is their relevance for the dependent individuals that have to face the incoherence of the continuum the moment they appeal to it. There is an intriguing paradox involved here. Governments in developed countries invest much in arrangements to support the QoL of their dependent citizens. At the same time, the complexity and lack of alignment of the QoL continuum is counterproductive in creating easy access to, and effective provision of, services to those they are created for. As governments fail structurally in adequate alignment of arrangements, the burden of coordination shifts to clients themselves. However, dependent persons have functional problems disqualifying them for performing such tasks.

There are several responses to this paradox. First, there is considerable public administration activity concerning the issue of alignment of arrangements. This activity feeds a continuous, costly and voluminous stream of committee reports, study conferences and research publications. Cost-effectiveness of this is low, as the lack of alignment is rooted in the underdeveloped state-of-the-art of intersectoral coordination within public administration and beyond.

Second, clients (and members of their social system) organize themselves in associations that offer support to their members in handling and coordinating the arrangements. These associations function as resource centres for information, advice and juridical support, and sometimes represent their members at hearings. They also lobby for changes in regulation. Such organizations in fact compensate for shortcomings in the public domain, creating in this way an informal and unplanned public-private hybrid.

Third, provider organizations in the continuum themselves develop resource-centre functions. This is not yet a large-scale phenomenon in the Netherlands as the AWBZ does not cover the cost of such activities. But managers are eager to provide these services, as they see that they have high added value for their clients. At the same time, there is growing support from policy-makers for this development. In recognizing their ineffectiveness in eliminating domain differences on a regulatory level, they have come to embrace the view of client organizations that it is more fruitful to facilitate handling domain differences on an operational level.

Towards a unified taxonomy of entitlements for LTC

At the start of the AWBZ there was a rather clear and unequivocal market segmentation of LTC institutions, reflecting a rough typology of functional disorders causing dependency. This market segmentation was used as a typology for licensing, for describing entitlements and for need assessment. Benefits were exclusively in kind. They were formulated as admission rights to categories of institutions like:

- psychiatric hospitals
- ambulatory psychic centres
- rehabilitation centres
- institutes for mentally handicapped
- institutes for physically disabled persons
- nursing homes.

This description in institutional terms has been effective as long as institutions offered a standard package to all their clients. However, in the 1990s new visions concerning the support of dependent persons developed. Institutions moved away from standardized to tailor-made services and introduced temporary and part-time services. They also opened their facilities to target groups staying at home (e.g. day programmes), started to offer their services in the home situation and developed new services like education tracks for families of handicapped persons.

Such initiatives created financial problems because the methodology of budgeting did not anticipate such new developments. Budgeting of LTC institutions was mainly based on the number of occupied beds as a production parameter. The *zorgkantoren* had no legal means to pay for such new activities, as they were outside the scope of the AWBZ entitlements. The official way out of this was the establishment of temporary 'experimental' arrangements, designed and controlled by the Board for the Health Care Insurances. The unofficial way out was a united effort of provider organizations and *zorgkantoren* to misrepresent the actual situation in administrative procedures.

In 2002 a new taxonomy was introduced in the AWBZ, replacing the institutional description of entitlements by one in terms of seven service domains:

- domestic care
- personal care
- nursing care
- support in social life
- reactivating support and counselling
- residential treatment
- residential stay.

This taxonomy is expected to offer a great contribution to two other issues in LTC: lack of a client-oriented provision of care and lack of competition between providers. The idea is to use the new taxonomy for need assessment purposes and to combine it with the introduction of client-allocated budgets. Currently, institutions are funded by budgets, based on results of negotiations with the local *zorgkantoor*. After need assessment, clients are allocated to providers by a procedure that leaves them little or no choice.

The new situation will offer two alternatives. Clients can get a benefit in cash, based on nationally-fixed prices for services they require. In this case, they contract provider organizations by themselves (or, if unable to do so, representatives will do this for them). Benefits in cash are the rule in LTC insurance in Austria. In Germany, clients have a choice between benefits in cash and in kind, 80 per cent of them choosing the first option (Wasem 1997). The Netherlands follows the German example. In case a client prefers a benefit in kind, the *zorgkantoor* will act as intermediary between clients and provider organizations. Two major changes in the functioning of the AWBZ are expected to emerge from this. First, the role of the *zorgkantoor* will change from budgeting providers to selective contracting for individual clients. Second, provider organizations will face a substantial growth of uncertainty in the continuity of their cashflow as existing procedures, resulting in budgets covering all operational costs and beyond, will disappear. It is expected that this change will improve the client orientation as well as the efficiency of LTC provision.

Concluding remarks

Developed countries face growing numbers of dependent persons in their populations, especially growing numbers of elderly. Existing cultural and social arrangements fall short in meeting the needs of these persons, as general standards of living improve and lifestyles change in the societies they live in. In reaction to these changing socioeconomic conditions, political interest has grown in updating and refining social arrangements. This interest generates fundamental questions about the nature of the needs of dependent persons and the best way to provide services that respond to those needs. It also raises questions about delineation of collective and individual responsibilities for maintaining and protecting the QoL of dependent persons. Most complexly, it raises important questions about how best to finance and arrange the collective responsibilities.

Western European countries with a corporatist tradition towards social protection use a social insurance approach to LTC, building on the institutionalization of health care insurance. To be effective and efficient in answering the needs for QoL services, such insurance has to be coordinated at a legal, administrative and operational level with other welfare state arrangements. The corporatist solution is not based on principles of markets or hierarchies. Rather, it starts from principles of network management (Jarillo 1995). Thus, the clue to successful coherent provision of services in these countries is likely to be the development of core competencies on intersectoral coordination and network management by public authorities, insurers and provider organizations. France has taken an advanced position in this effort by developing over 500 local 'gerontologic' networks all over the country.

Acknowledgements

The authors want to thank Maria Hofmarcher, Ralf Kocher and Manfred Huber for their valuable information and comments.

References

Assous, L. (2001) Soins et aides de longue durée aux personnes âgées [Long term care and aids for elderly], *Revue Française des Affaires Sociales* 2(April–June): 211–31.

Bundesambt für Socialversicherung (2001) *Wirkungsanalyse Krankenversicherungsgesetz* [*Evaluation of the impact of the Federal Sickness Insurance*]. Bern: Bundesambt für Socialversicherung.

College van Bouw (2001) *Signaleringsrapport sturing en financiering van de bouwkundige infrastructuur in andere landen van de EU* [*Report concerning the financing and management of constructional infrastructure in other EU countries*]. Utrecht: CvB.

De Swaan, A. (1988) *In Care of the State*. New York: Oxford University Press.

De Vries, J. (1996) Beyond health status: Construction and validation of the Dutch WHO quality of life asessment instrument. Dissertation, Tilburg University.

Granzin, K.L. and Haggard, L.M. (2000) An integrate explanation for quality of life, in E. Diener and D.R. Rahtz (eds) *Advances in Quality of Life Theory and Research*. Dordrecht: Kluwer.

Hofmarcher, M.M. and Riedel, M. (2001) *Development of Age Structure in the EU: The EU is ageing, even when expanding eastward. Focus: acute care and long term care: an interface to analysis or change? Health system Watch 3/2001*, http://www.his.ac, published in German as supplement to *Soziale Sicherheit* 10/2001, Federation of Austrian Social Security Institutions.

Jacobzone, S. (1999) *Ageing and Care for Frail Elderly Persons*. Paris: OECD.

Jacobzone, S., Cambois, E., Chaplain, E. and Robine, J.M. (1998) *The Health of Older Persons in OECD Countries*. Paris: OECD.

Jarillo, J.C. (1995) *Strategic Networks: Creating the Borderless Organization*. Oxford: Butterworth-Heinemann.

Mazenauer, B. (2001) Spitex [Domiciliary care] in G. Kocher and W. Oggier (eds) *Gesundheitswesen 205–208 Schweiz 2001–2002*. Bern: Verlag KSKrankenversicherer.

Meyer, P.C. (2001) Freiwilligenarbeit und Verwandtenpflege [Voluntary labour and family care] in G. Kocher and W. Oggier (eds) *Gesundheidswesen 49 Schweiz 2001–2002*. Bern: Verlag KSKrankenversicherer.

OECD (1996) *Caring for Frail Elderly People: Policies in Evolution*, OECD Social Policy Studies No. 19. Paris: OECD.

OECD (1997) *Ageing in OECD Countries: A Critical Policy Challenge*, OECD Social Policy Studies No. 20. Paris: OECD.

OECD (1999) *A Caring World: The New Policy Agenda*. Paris: OECD.

Okma, K. (2001) Healthcare and the welfare state, paper for the Belgium presidency conference, '*Toward a new architecture for social protection in Europe?*' Leuven, October.

Okma, K. and Poelart, J.D. (2001) Implementing prospective budgeting for Dutch sickness funds, *European Journal of Public Health*, 11: 178–81.

Randall, C., Fisher, J. and Lennox, I. (1998) *The Long Term Care Opportunity*. London: Swiss Re Life & Health.

Royal Commission on Long Term Care (1999) *With Respect to Old Age*. London: The Stationery Office.

Schrijvers, A.J.P. (ed.) (1997) *Health and Health Care in the Netherlands*. Maarssen: Elsevier.

Wasem, J. (1997) A study on decentralizing from acute care to home care settings in Germany, *Health Policy*, 41(supplement): S109–30.

WHOQoL Group (1995) The World Health Organization quality of life assessment, *Social Science and Medicine*, 41:1403–9.

Index

dental care, 194, 196, 201, 212
dependency, 284–5
  see also long-term care
depoliticization, 165–6
diabetes, Type, 2 131
diagnosis-related groups (DRGs), 194, 218, 224
dignity, 93–6
direct payments, 202–3
disability-adjusted life expectancy (DALE), 84–5, 86
dispute settlement, 42–3, 43–4, 199–200, 254, 260
distribution, 116
distributors, agreements with, 214–15
Dixon, A., 127
doctors *see* physicians/doctors
Dubois, H.F.W., 28
Durand-Zaleski, I., 214

economic sustainability, 10–13, 59, 145
economic volatility, 29–30
Eddy, D.M., 195
effective deliberation, 251
effectiveness
  efficiency and, 180–1
  of interventions and strategic purchasing, 270–1
efficiency, 11, 115–32, 133, 143–4, 167
  administrative costs, 126–7, 128, 129, 130
  costs/expenditure, 116–21
  and effectiveness, 180–1
  relative clinical performance, 127–32
  relative resource levels and utilization rates, 121–5
  technical measures, 145–7
egalitarian ethics, 251
elderly/older people, 183, 184, 287
  long-term care *see* long-term care
  services for, 116
eligibility, 283–4, 292–3
Ellis, R.P., 217
employer/employee contributions ratio, 45
empowerment, patient, 249
Enthoven, A.C., 174–5
entitlements, 283–4, 292–3
  taxonomy of, 294, 295–7
entrepreneurship
  physicians, 211
  regulation to stimulate entrepreneurial opportunities of sickness funds, 59–60
equity, 105–15, 133, 143
  of access, 114–15
  consumer participation, choice and, 256–7
  of funding, 105–14

outcomes of competition, 181–2
PHI and, 235–6
Esserman, L., 274
Estonia, 3
ethical frameworks, 251
Etzioni, A., 146
Eugster, G., 213
EUROASPIRE I and II Group, 132
Eurobarometer surveys, 90, 91–2, 93
European Collaboration on HTA (ECHTA), 198
European Court of Justice (ECJ), 12, 14, 203
European Medicines Evaluation Agency (EMEA), 194, 198
European Union (EU), 10, 12–13, 145
  benefit catalogue, 203
  EU health policy, 14
  national governments and, 166
  regulation of supplementary PHI, 238
EUROPEP general practice study, 96, 98
Evans, R.G., 158
expenditure, 116–21, 143–4, 215
  see also costs
expert advice, 195–8

Faisst, K., 276
family care, 285, 285–6, 287
fee-for-service payment, 215, 216
Ferroussier-Davis, O., 5
Figueras, J., 249, 268
Finland, 3, 113
Fleurette, F., 192
force majeure, 257
France, 3, 29, 159–60, 254
  administrative costs, 126–7
  Agence Centrale des Organismes de Sécurité Sociale, 45
  benefit decisions, 190, 191, 195–200 *passim*
  changes to funding system, 15, 109–10, 148
  class and access, 115
  CMU programme, 240
  CNMATS, 34, 160
  collective health interventions, 274
  competition, 172, 182
  contracting, 209–10, 214, 214–15
  cost containment, 11
  direct payments, 202
  governance, 160–1
  health reporting, 269
  historical and social base, 24, 28
  limited choice, 256
  LTC, 284, 288–9, 292, 297
  organization and financing, 34–58 *passim*
  payment mechanisms, 217, 219, 220–2